Wharton Booth Marriott

**Vestiarium Christianum**

The Origin and Gradual Development of the Dress of Holy Ministry in the Church

Wharton Booth Marriott

**Vestiarium Christianum**
*The Origin and Gradual Development of the Dress of Holy Ministry in the Church*

ISBN/EAN: 9783337201739

Printed in Europe, USA, Canada, Australia, Japan

Cover: Foto ©Lupo / pixelio.de

More available books at **www.hansebooks.com**

# VESTIARIVM CHRISTIANVM

### The Origin and Gradual Development

OF

## THE DRESS OF HOLY MINISTRY

## IN THE CHVRCH

BY THE

REV. WHARTON B. MARRIOTT, M.A., F.S.A.

*(Sometime Fellow of Exeter College, Oxford, and Affiftant Mafter at Eton)*
*Select Preacher in the Univerfity,*
*and Preacher, by licenfe from the Bifhop, in the Diocefe, of Oxford.*

London
RIVINGTONS, WATERLOO PLACE.
HIGH STREET | TRINITY STREET
Oxford | Cambridge
1868

# PREFACE.

Historical or antiquarian investigation is one thing, theological controversy is another. There is time, and there is place, for both; but not for both the same time and the same place, without disadvantage to the former of the two. Under this conviction I have studiously put aside, in the Treatise which follows, all reference to the passing controversies of these days, and have made it my one object to collect every fact of importance bearing upon the subject immediately before me, to set it before my readers in such a way, as shall enable them to form their own estimate of its value, and at the same time to offer, for whatever may be its worth, the interpretation which I myself believe to be the true one.

And even now that my work is complete, a work that originated in the controversies of these days, and that touches, as I believe, upon those controversies in many points of the greatest importance, I still think it better, on many grounds, to adhere to the same course. The objects I have in view will, I believe, be best attained, if I leave the monuments, here reproduced, to tell their own tale, and to produce conviction by their own force, without any attempt on my part to apply their lessons in detail to questions of Ritual, or of Doctrine, now disputed in the Church.

But there is one duty which I must take this opportunity of discharging, though it is beyond my power to do so adequately. I have to express my grateful thanks to all those (they are very many) from whom, in various ways, I have received assistance in my work. Among these I may be allowed to refer more particularly to the Truſtees, and the Officers, of the Britiſh Muſeum. To Mr. Newton as an old friend, to Mr. Bond, and Mr. A. Franks, with no other claim but that of a common intereſt in antiquarian ſtudy, I have often had recourſe, and never without receiving the readieſt and the moſt efficient help.

To Mr. Woodward, Her Majeſty's Librarian at Windſor, I have to acknowledge many ſpecial obligations. And I know that I ſhall do ſo in the manner that will be moſt acceptable to him, if I take this opportunity of ſaying, that in making available for literary ſtudy the reſources of the Library under his charge, he is but carrying out the expreſs commands of H.R.H. the Prince Conſort, under the ſanction of the Queen. It was the Prince's deſire, that as ſoon as the arrangement of the Library, commenced under his direction, ſhould be ſufficiently advanced, it ſhould be made acceſſible for purpoſes of ſtudy as far as might be confiſtent with its ſpecial character. As one of the firſt to have profited, as I have moſt largely, by the permiſſion thus given, I venture to expreſs my grateful acknowledgments, and to make known this additional illuſtration of the generous conſideration for others, and regard for the intereſts of Literature, which were conſpicuous in the lamented Prince.

I have received communications of much intereſt and value in reference to particular queſtions, from Mr. Droop, Mr. Wilſhere, the Rev. J. C. Wynter, Mr. W. Simpſon, and others. I have gladly availed myſelf of the information ſo received.

For the Illuſtrations of this Volume I have been dependent, mainly, upon two very ſkilful Photographers, Mr. Preſton and Mr. Saunders; and on a Copyiſt, all but photographically exact, Mr. A. Reid, of the South Kenſington Muſeum. I am alſo greatly indebted to Signor Scifoni, of Rome, for Drawings made from MSS. in the Vatican Library and elſewhere.

I ought not to conclude without ſaying, how much I owe to more than one foreign writer whoſe books I have laid under contribution. Treating though they do of ſubjects keenly controverted for the laſt three hundred years, they write in a ſpirit of loyal devotion to the Truth, and the Truth alone, ſuch as others, differing widely from them in doctrinal prepoſſeſſions, might well deſire to imitate. In ſaying this, I refer particularly to Dr. Hefele, and the Chevalier De Roſſi, from both of whom I have learnt much, and hope to learn much more.

I have frequently made uſe of the admirable Compendium of Profeſſor Weiſs, and of the ſpecial Treatiſe on Liturgical Veſtments by Dr. Bock. This latter work contains minute information, not to be found elſewhere, as to the material, ſhape, and ornamentation, of Mediæval Veſtments.

Nor muſt I paſs over without mention yet another writer, Dr. Rock, a fellow-countryman of my own. His learned work, "The Church of our Fathers," contains much intereſting information on the early Hiſtory of Veſtments in this country. He writes, as thoſe who know him will not need to be told, with a doctrinal object in view, with which the writer of the preſent Treatiſe cannot ſympathiſe. But I gladly bear teſtimony to the extenſive reſearch, of which his work gives proof; and I regret that my own book was all but completed before I had any opportunity of conſulting his pages.

And now I have only to ſend forth my work to the light, with the expreſſion of my earneſt hope, that it may contribute, in ſome ſmall meaſure at leaſt, to a more accurate knowledge of the Paſt; and, in ſo doing, help in its degree to the guidance of the Church, in our own days, through the difficulties of theſe preſent times, and of the uncertain but not unhopeful Future that awaits Her.

Eton,
*January* 29, 1868.

# ERRATA.

Page xli., note *o*, quoted in App. A. *erase*.
— xxxii., line 13. *For* St. Clement *read* St. James
— xxxviii., note τ. *For* given in the Canons *read* conceded by long custom
— lviii., line 10. *For* fought *read* ought
— lxv., note θ. *For* No. 27 *read* No. 26
— lxxviii., line 14. *For* Vienna *read* Vienne
— lxxxviii., note ψ. *For* 1430 *read* 1438
— 15, line 13. *For* and these of *read* and of these
— 22, line 22. *Remove comma after* pectore
— 42, line 2 of the text. *For* κατηγοράσας *read* κατηγορήσας
— 88, note 157 *in fin. For* Cap. supra *read* Cf. supra
— 106, line 6. *Insert comma (in place of full stop) after* consecrantur
— ,,   note 206. *For* or its place *read* for its place
— 148, line 3. *For* orma *read* forma
— 149, line 3. *For* cum integra fit *read* cum unica fit
— 151, line 3. *For* subjects *read* subject—*for* then *read* them
— ,,   line 12. *For* meniti *read* muniti
— 168, note 144. *For* to homage *read* of homage
— 181, note 374. *For* facco *read* fucco
— 196, line 22. *For* appear *read* wear
— 207, note 427. *For* utuntur *read* utantur
— 209, note 429. *After* Archbishop of Milan *insert* (in the fourth century)
— 222, note 454, line 1. *Omit* which
— 226, note 464. *For* bauiekin *read* baudekin
— 246, plate lxiii. This is so numbered in order to correspond with the number on the plate itself. The number ought to have been lxii. both on the plate and in the description.
— 247, line 19. *For* p. xliii. The Prophet Malachi *read* p. xxxiv. The Prophet Malachi
   [To the List of Woodcuts there given should have been added the following:—
— xliii. A Representation of Our Lord, from the same MS. as that last described.]
— 248. *Erase the words*, the coin just below the roll, the marriage dowry

# CONTENTS.

|   |   | PAGE |
|---|---|---|
| List of Authors and Editions quoted or referred to | . . . . . . | 11 |

## PART I.

Introduction . . . . . . . . . . . i—lxxxiv

## PART II.

Passages from Ancient Authors . . . . . . . . 1—174
    I. The Sacerdotal Vestments of the Levitical Law, as enumerated in Holy Scripture   1
    *II. Josephus on the Levitical Vestments . . . . . . . 2
    *III. Philo Judæus. The White Vestments worn on the Day of Atonement . . 8

### St. Jerome.

    IV. On the Levitical Vestments . . . . . . . . 10
    V. On the Ephod worn by Samuel . . . . . . . . 28
    *VI. On Ezekiel, cap. xliv. The Levitical Vestments . . . . . 29
    VII. On the White Garments of Christian Ministry . . . . . 34

    VIII. Hegesippus. The Linen Vestments of St. James . . . . . 36
    IX. Polycrates of Ephesus. St. John and the Golden Plate of Priesthood . . 38
    *X. Epiphanius. Concerning St. James and the Golden Plate . . . 40
    XI. Theodoret. The Sacred Robe sent by Constantine to Bishop Macarius . 42
    †XII. St. Augustine on the Levitical Vestments . . . . . . 44
    XIII. Pope Celestine on Episcopal Dress . . . . . . . 45
    †XIV. Sirmondus (Jacobus) on the Origin of Ecclesiastical Vestments . . 47
    XV. St. Isidore of Pelusium. Of the Linen Stole and the Woollen Omophorion . 49
    *XVI. St. Chrysostom (so reputed) on the Levitical Vestments . . . 51

### St. Gregory the Great.

    XVII. On the Levitical Vestments and Insignia . . . . . . 56
    XVIII. Of the Breastplate or Rational . . . . . . . 58

---

  \* Of the extracts so marked Translations only are given, particular passages of the Original being added in the Notes.

  † Of the extracts so marked the original only is given in full, translations of particular passages, and illustrative notes, being subjoined.

|    |    | PAGE |
|----|----|------|
| *XIX. | Of the Ephod or Superhumeral . . . . . . . | 59 |
| *XX. | Of the Bells on the Tunic of the Ephod, and of Levitical Vestments in general . | 61 |
| XXI. | The use of the Pallium a matter of Roman Privilege . . . . | 63 |
| *XXII. | The use of the Mappula of Papal Privilege only . . . . | 65 |
| *XXIII. | Use of the Mappula conceded, under restrictions, to the Church of Ravenna . | 66 |
| *XXIV. | The use of the Dalmatic of Papal Privilege only . . . . . | 67 |

### St. Isidore of Seville.

|    |    |    |
|----|----|----|
| XXV. | On the Insignia of Christian Priesthood . . . . . | 68 |
| *XXVI. | On the Vestments of Levitical Priesthood . . . . . | 70 |
| *XXVII. | Enumeration of the Levitical Vestments, [His Notice of the Pallium, the Pænula, the Casula, and the Dalmatic] . . . . . | 72 |

|    |    |    |
|----|----|----|
| XXVIII. | Acts of the Fourth Council of Toledo . . . . . | 75 |
| †XXIX. | Venerable Bede on the Levitical Vestments . . . . . | 78 |
| XXX. | Patriarch Germanus of Constantinople on Christian Vestments, Tonsure, and Monastic Dress . . . . . . . . | 82 |
| *XXXI. | Rabanus Maurus on Sacerdotal Vestments, Jewish and Christian . . | 88 |
| *XXXII. | Amalarius. The same subject . . . . . . | 94 |
| XXXIII. | Walafrid Strabo. Of Holy Vessels and Vestments. [Letter of St. Boniface to Cuthbert Archbishop of Canterbury. Note 209] . . . . | 106 |
| *XXXIV. | Alcuinus (the Pseudo-Alcuin). The Priestly Vestments of the Law and of the Gospel . . . . . . . . . | 110 |
| *XXXV. | St. Ivo of Chartres. The same subject . . . . . | 119 |
| *XXXVI. | Hugo de St. Victor. Christian Vestments . . . . | 131 |
| *XXXVII. | Honorius of Autun. The same subject . . . . . | 134 |
| *XXXVIII. | Pope Innocent III. Vestments of the Law and of the Gospel . . | 143 |
| *XXXIX. | Durandus of Mende. On Sacred Vestments . . . . | 165 |
| XL. | Patriarch Symeon of Thessalonica. On Sacred Vestments . . | 168 |

### APPENDICES.

| A. | Associations of Colour in Primitive Times . . . . . . . | 175 |
|----|----|----|
| B. | Passages of Early Writers supposed to indicate a Levitical Origin for Christian Vestments | 186 |
| C. | Passages from Ancient Authors, illustrating the History of the Pænula, Casula, and Planeta | 192 |
| D. | Vestments worn in the Gallican Church . . . . . . | 204 |
| E. | Passages from Early Writers, illustrating the History of the Orarium (" Stole ") and the Papal Pallium . . . . . . . . . . | 206 |
| F. | The Vestments of the Roman Church . . . . . . | 212 |
| G. | The Vestments prescribed in the First Prayer-Book of Edward VI., and in the later Books . . . . . . . . . . | 223 |

| Description of Plates and Woodcuts | . . | 234 |
|----|----|----|
| Index . . . . . | . . | 249 |

# AUTHORS AND EDITIONS

### QUOTED OR REFERRED TO IN THIS TREATISE.

Acta Sanctorum (AA. SS.) The Bollandift Collection. Fol. Antwerp.
Acta Sanctorum Ordinis Benedicti. 4 voll. Fol. Paris. 1733.
Alcuinus (Albinus Flaccus). Liber de Divinis Officiis. Apud Hittorpium, q. v.
Alemannus (Nicolaus). De Lateranenfibus Parietinis. 4to. Romæ. 1625.
Amalarius Metenfis. De Ecclefiafticis Officiis. Apud Hittorpium, q. v.
Ambrofii D. Opera. Bafle. Fol. 1567.
Ammianus Marcellinus. Rom. Imperatorum Hiftoriæ. 8vo. Paris. 1544.
Anaftafius Bibliothecarius. Apud Muratorium (tom. iii.), q. v.
Antiquités de l'Empire de Ruffie. 6 voll. Fol. St. Peterfburgh.
Aringhi Roma Subterranea. 2 voll. Fol. Romæ. 1651.
Artemidori Daldiani Oneirocritica. 8vo. Lutetiæ. 1603.
Affemani (Steph. Evod.) Bibliotheca Medicea. Florentiæ. Fol. 1742.
Auguftini S. (Hipponenf. Epi.) Opera. Migne's Edition. 12 voll. 4to. Paris. 1841.

Baronii\* Annales Ecclefiaftici. 12 voll. Fol. Antwerp. 1618.
Bartolinus (Bartolus). De Pænula. Apud Grævium, q. v.
Bafilii S. (Seleuciæ Epi.) Opera. 3 voll. 8vo. Paris. 1839.
Bayfius (Lazarus) De Re Veftiaria. Apud Grævium, q. v.
Bedæ Venerabilis Opera. 12 voll. 8vo. London. 1843.
Belethi Rationale Divinorum Officiorum. Apud Durandum, q. v.
Bellarmini (Cardinalis) Opera Omnia. 6 voll. Fol. Coloniæ. 1620.
Bellorius (G. P.). Veteres Arcus Auguftorum. Fol. Romæ. 1690.
Bellorius (G. P.). Colonna Traiana. Fol. 1673.
Bertramni (al Ratramni) Liber de Corpore et Sanguine Domini. London. 12mo. 1688.
Bock (Dr. Fr.). Geſchichte der liturgiſchen Gewänder des Mittelälters. 2 voll. 8vo. Bonn. 1866.
Boiffardus (J. J.). Urbis Romanæ Antiquitates. Fol. Frankfurt. 1597.
Braunius. De Habitu Sacerdotali Hebræorum. 4to. Amft. 1680.
Byzantine Architecture. See "Texier."

Cæleftinus Papa. Apud Labbe Concil. Tom. ii., p. 1618.
Cæfarii Arelatenfis Vita. Apud Baronium (Tom. vi.), q. v.
Capitolinus (Julius). Apud Hiftoriæ Auguftæ Scriptores, q. v.
Chryfoftomi S. Opera. 12 voll. 4to. Paris. 1735.
Ciampini (Joannis) Vetera Monimenta. Romæ. 1699.
†Ciceronis (M. T.) Opera. 2 voll. Fol. Paris. 1539.
Clementis Alexandrini Opera. Potter. 2 voll. Fol. Oxon. 1715.
Codex Theodofianus. Ritter. Lipfiæ. Fol. 1741.
Cotelerius, J. B. Ecclefiæ Græcæ Monumenta. 4 voll. 4to. Paris. 1677.
Councils. See Labbe, Harduin, Raynaldus, Spelman.

---

\* Sometimes quoted from later editions.

† Of the ordinary Claffical Authors, to which every Scholar has ready accefs, I have included in this Lift thofe only which prefent any difficulty in the verification of References.

D'Agincourt (Seroux). Histoire de l'Art par les Monuments. 6 voll. Fol. Paris. 1823.
Damianus (Petrus). Apud Migne, q. v. P. C. C. tom. 144.
De la Bigne (Margarinus). Maxima Bibliotheca Veterum Patrum. 28 voll. Fol. Lugduni. Genuæ. 1677, 1707.
De Rossi. Roma Sotterranea. Fol. Romæ. 1864.
——— Imagines Selectæ Deiparæ Virginis. Fol. Romæ. 1863.
Didron, A. N. Annales Archéologiques. 4to. Paris. 1844, etc.
Donatus. Apud Wetstenium (Nov. Test. Græc. 2 voll. Amsterdam. 1752.)
Ducange. See Dufresne.
*Dufresne, C. (Du Cange) Glossarium Med. et Inf. Latinitatis. 3 voll. Fol. Paris. 1628.
——— Glossarium Med. et Inf. Græcitatis. Lugdun. 1688.
Durandi (R. D. G.) Rationale Divinorum Officiorum. 4to. Lugduni. 1672.
Du Saussay. Panoplia Sacerdotalis. Apud Martigny, q. v.
Duval (Amaury). Monuments des Arts du Dessin. 4 voll. Fol. Paris. 1829.

Ennodii (Magni Felicis) Carmina. Apud Sirmondum (tom. i.), q. v.
Epiphanii (Constantiæ Episc.) Opera. 2 voll. Fol. Paris. 1622.
Eusebii Pamphili Hist. Eccles. Libri x. 4 voll. 8vo. Oxon. 1847.

Ferrandus Diaconus. Apud Thomassinum, q. v.
Ferraria (Octavius) De Re Vestiaria. Apud Grævium, q. v.
Ferrarius, F. B. De Veterum Acclamationibus. Apud Grævium, q. v.
Ffoulkes. Manual of Ecclesiastical History. Oxford. 1851.
——— Christendom's Divisions. Part II. 8vo. London. 1867.
Floravantis (Benedicti) Antiquiores Pontificum Romanorum Denarii. 4to. Romæ. 1734.
Fortunati (Venantii) Carminum, etc. Libri XI. 4to. Mogunt. 1617.

Garrucci (Raffaelle) Vetri Ornati in Oro. Roma. 1864.
Gay (Victor). Apud Didron, q. v.
Gell (Sir W.). Pompeiana. 2 voll. 4to. 1832.
Genebrardi (Gilbert) Chronographia. Fol. Lugduni. 1609. [There are several other Editions of the Chronographia, in which the *Church History* of Genebrard is omitted, and replaced by the shorter compendium of Arnaldus Pontacus. Of four copies in the British Museum, only the one above described contains the passage referred to in p. lxxxiii, note 6, of this Treatise.]
Germanus Patriarcha Constantinop. Rerum Ecclesiasticarum Theoria. Apud De La Bigne (tom. xiii.), q. v.
Gieseler. Ecclesiastical History. Davidson's Translation. Edinburgh. 1848.
Goar. Euchologion Græcorum. Fol. Paris. 1647.
Gorius, A. F. Thesaurus Veterum Diptychorum. 3 voll. Fol. Florentiæ. 1759.
Grævii Thesaurus Romanarum Antiquitatum. 12 voll. Fol. Venet. 1732.
Gregorii D. cogn. Magni Opera. 4 voll. Fol. Paris. 1705. [Sometimes quoted from the Edition of 1586. Fol. Paris.]
Gregorii Papæ I. Sacramentorum Liber. Ed. Hugo Menardus. 4to. Paris. 1642.
Gregorii Nazianzeni Opera. Fol. Paris. 1630.
Gregorii Turonensis Opera. Fol. Paris. 1699.

Harduini Conciliorum Collectio. 12 voll. Fol. Paris. 1715.
Hefele, Dr. C. J. Beiträge zur Kirchengeschichte, u. s. w. 2 voll. 8vo. Tubingen. 1864.
Hefner-Altenek. Trachten des Christlichen Mittelalters. 3 voll. 4to. Frankfurt. 1840—1854.
Hegesippus apud Hieronymum, q. v.
Hemans, C. J. Ancient Christianity and Sacred Art. 12mo. London and Florence. 1866.
Herodiani Historiarum Libri Sex. Aldus. 1523.
Hieronymi, S. Eusebii, Opera. 4 voll. Fol. Paris. 1693.
Histoire Littéraire de la France. 12 voll. 4to. Paris. 1733—52.

Historiæ Augustæ Scriptores. Fol. Hanoviæ. 1611.
Hittorpius de Divinis Catholicæ Ecclesiæ Officiis. Fol. Coloniæ. 1568.
Honorii Augustodunensis Opera. Biblioth. Mag. vet. Patrum. Tom xx.
Hook (Dr. W. F.). Lives of the Archbishops of Canterbury. 8vo. London. 1860.
Hugo de S. Victore. Apud Migne P. C. C. tom. 175—177.

Innocentii III. Pont. Max. Opera. Fol. Coloniæ. 1552.
Joannis Damasceni Liber De Hæresibus, apud Cotelerium, q. v.
Joannes Diaconus. [D. Gregorii Vita, etc.] Apud Gregorii Magni Opp., q. v.
Joannes Ravennas apud Gregorii Magni Opera, q. v.
Josephi (Flavii) Opera. 2 voll. Fol. Oxon. 1720.
Ivo, St. De Rebus Ecclesiasticis Sermones. Apud Hittorpium, q. v.

King, Dr. J. G. Rites and Ceremonies of the Greek Church in Russia. 4to. London. 1772.
Kirchen Ordnung zu Brandenburg, u. s. w. See Note 458.
Knight (Gally). Ecclesiastical Architecture of Italy. Fol. London. 1842.
Knox (Alex.), Remains of. 4 voll. 8vo. London. 1837.
Kreutz (Johann). La Basilica di San Marco. Fol. Venice. 1843.

Labbe. Concilia Sacrosancta. 16 voll. Fol. Paris. 1671.
Lampridius (Ælius) apud Historiæ Augustæ Scriptores, q. v.
Louandre et Maugé. Les Arts Somptueux. 4to. Paris. 1852—58.
Lucilii Satirarum quæ supersunt. Ed. F. J. Douša. Lugduni. 1597.
Luitprandi Epi. Historia. Muratori. R. S. S. Tom. ii.
——————— Legatio. Apud Pertz Mon. Germ. Hist.

Mabillon. Museum Italicum. 2 voll. 4to. Paris. 1689.
Mansi. Sacrosancta Concilia. 29 voll. Fol. Venet. et Lucæ. 1728—1752.
Marriott, W. B. Eirenica. 8vo. London. 1865.
Martene (Edmund). De Antiquis Ecclesiæ Ritibus. 4 voll. Fol. Venet. 1788.
——————— Thesaurus Novus Anecdotorum. 5 voll. Fol. Paris. 1727.
Martigny. Dictionnaire des Antiquités Chrétiennes. 8vo. Paris. 1865.
Martini (Epi. Bracarens.) Capitula. Apud Labbe (q. v.) Tom. v. p. 912.
Menardus (Hugo). D. Gregorii Papæ Sacramentorum Liber. 4to. Paris. 1642.
Menologium Græcorum. Urbini. 1727. 3 voll. Fol. 1727.
Migne. Patrologiæ Cursus Completus. Series Latina. 221 voll. 4to. Paris. 1844—64.
Millin. Voyage en Italie. Apud Martigny, q. v.
Mömmsen (Theodor). The History of Rome. London. 1864.
Monete dei Romani Pontefici, ecc. Domenico Promis. Torino. 1858.
Montfaucon. L'Antiquité Expliquée. 15 voll. Fol. Paris. 1719—1724.
Muratorius, L. A. Rerum Italicarum Scriptores. 28 voll. Fol. Mediolani. 1723—51.

Nicephori Callisti Historia Ecclesiastica. 2 voll. Fol. Paris. 1630.
Nicolai, PP. I. Responsa ad Bulgaros. Apud Labbe. Tom. viii.

Ordines Romani. Apud Mabillon (Museum Italicum), q. v.

Paley (F. A.). Fasti of Ovid. 8vo. London. 1854.
Palmer (Rev. W.). Dissertation on Primitive Liturgies, prefixed to Antiquities of the English Ritual. 2 voll. 8vo. Oxford. 1832.
Perret. Catacombes de Rome. 6 voll. Fol. Paris. 1851, etc.
Pertz (G. H.). Monumenta Germaniæ Historica. 18 voll. Fol. Hanoviæ. 1826—1863.
Philonis Judæi Opera. Fol. Paris. 1640.
Photii Bibliotheca. Fol. Rothomag. 1653.
Pistolese (Erasmo). Il Vaticano Illustrato. 6 voll. Fol. Roma. 1829.
Plutarchi Chæronensis Opuscula. H. Stephanus. 1572.

Pollux (Julius). Onomasticon. 2 voll. Fol. Amsterd. 1706.
Polycrates, Bp. of Ephesus. Apud Eusebium, q. v.
Procopii Historiarum Libri viii. 2 voll. Fol. Paris, 1662.
Promis Domenico (Memoria di). See "Monete."
Prudenti Clementis Opera. Paris. MDCLXXXVII.
Pugin. Glossary of Ecclesiastical Ornament. Fol. London. 1846.

Rabanus Maurus. De Instit. Clericorum. Apud Hittorpium, q. v.
Radberti (Paschasii) Opera. Fol. Paris. 1618.
Ramboux (J. A.). Beiträge zur Kunstgeschichte des Mittelalters. Fol. Köln. 1860.
Raynaldi Annales Ecclesiastici (Continuatio Baronii). 8 voll. Fol. Colon. Agrip. 1693.
Raynaudus (Theophilus). De Pileo. Apud Grævium, q. v.
Regino (Abbas Prumiensis). De Disciplina Ecclesiastica. Migne P. C. C. Tom. 132.
Renaudot. Liturgiarum Orientalium Collectio. 2 voll. 4to. Paris. 1716.
Riculfus Eps. Apud Migne P. C. C. Tom. 132.
Rock, Dr. Church of our Fathers. 3 vols. 8vo. London. 1849.
Rubenius (Albertus). De Re Vestiaria. Apud Grævium, q. v.

Salviani et Vincentii Lirinensis Opera. Ed. Baluzius. Paris. 8vo. 1669.
Salzenberg. Altchristliche Baudenkmale von Constantinopel. Fol. Berlin. 1854.
Senecæ (L. Annæi) Opera. Coloniæ. 1614.
Sirmondi (Jacobi) Opera Varia. Tom. v. Fol. Paris. 1696.
Spartianus. Apud Historiæ Augustæ Scriptores, q. v.
Spelman. Concilia, Decreta, etc. Fol. London. 1639.
Stephani Tornacensis Epistolæ. Apud Migne P. C. L. Tom. 212.
Strutt. Manners and Customs, etc. 2 vols. 4to. London. 1775.
Suetonii. De XII Cæsaribus Libri VIII. J. Casaubon. Fol. Paris. 1610.
Symeon (Archbishop of Thessalonica). Fol. Jassii. 1683.

Tertulliani (Q. S. F.) Opera. Semler. 5 voll. 8vo. Magdeburg. 1773.
Texier and Pullan. Byzantine Architecture. Fol. London. 1864.
Theodoreti Epi. Cyri Opera. 5 voll. 8vo. Halæ. 1771.
Theodulfi Epi. Apud Sirmondum (Tom. ii.), q. v.
Thomassini Vetus et Nova Ecclesiæ Disciplina. Mogont. 4to. 1787.
Trebellius Pollio. Apud Historiæ Augustæ Scriptores, q. v.

Valentini (Agostino). Basilica Vaticana Illustrata. 6 voll. Fol. Roma. 1845.
Vopiscus (Flavius). Apud Historiæ Augustæ Scriptores, q. v.

Walafrid Strabo De Rebus Ecclesiasticis. Apud Hittorpium, q. v.
Weiss, H. Kostümkunde. Tracht und Geräth in Mittelalter. Stuttgart. 1864.
——— Tracht u. s. w. des Alterthums II. Abtheil. Stuttgart. 1860.
Westwood, J. O. Miniatures and Ornaments of Anglo-Saxon and Irish Manuscripts. Fol. London (Quaritch). 1868.
Wyatt, M. D. Notices of Sculptures in Ivory. London. 1856.

# THE ORIGIN AND GRADUAL DEVELOPMENT OF ECCLESIASTICAL DRESS.

## INTRODUCTION.

### Chapter I.

The queſtion, what veſtments are to be regarded as proper to offices of holy miniſtry in Chriſt's Church, is one that of late has been keenly debated, and is ſtill for various reaſons exciting confiderable intereſt.

There are thoſe who believe that the dreſs of Chriſtian miniſtry was from the firſt, under Divine guidance, and, by Apoſtolic authority, modelled, in detail, upon the dreſs of the Aaronic prieſthood. But, after all that has been written in diſproof of this opinion of late years, eſpecially by learned Roman Catholic writers, whoſe bias would naturally incline them to its ſupport, this belief muſt be regarded as an opinion due to doctrinal prepoſſeſſions on the part of the few who ſtill maintain it, rather than as one which admits of ſerious ſupport upon hiſtorical grounds.

On the other hand, it may be ſaid with truth, that there were features of analogy between the two types of dreſs, although the points of difference were in primitive times far more ſtrongly marked than the points of reſemblance.

Among thoſe[a] who have examined the queſtion upon

---

[a] See, for example, the conciſe ſtatement of Jacobus Sirmondus quoted in the ſecond part of this volume (p. 47). | Nearly the ſame concluſions are maintained by Dr. Hefele in his eſſay on the "Liturgical Veſtments" [Beiträge

purely antiquarian or historical evidence, the more general opinion is such as this:—That in the Apostolic age there was no essential difference between the dress worn by Christians in ordinary life, and that worn by bishops, priests, or other clerics, when engaged in offices of holy ministration. But that after the lapse of three or four centuries the dress of ordinary life became changed, while that worn in ecclesiastical offices remained in form unchanged, though ever more and more richly decorated. That from these causes a marked distinction was gradually brought about between the dress of the clergy and that of the laity (to say nothing of the monastic orders who were distinguished from them both); that, as time went on, the ordinary dress of the clergy themselves came to be distinguished, in form, in colour, and in name, from that in which they ministered; while at length yet a further distinction was introduced as between the dress of the more ordinary ministrations, and the more splendid Vestments reserved for the highest Offices of all, and for occasions of special solemnity.

There is much in this second statement which is undoubtedly true. But the evidence to be alleged in the following treatise will show, that important modifications of that statement, and additions to it, must be made, if we wish to convey an exact idea of what was the Primitive and Apostolic type of ministering dress, and what the successive stages of its gradual development. The most important of these modifications and additions of which I speak, it may be well, before proceeding further, briefly here to indicate.

---

zur Kirchengeschichte &c., von Dr. C. J. Hefele, Tubingen, 1864.] Even Dr. Bock, who with great erudition and much ingenuity, traces out resemblances between the Roman vestments *now in use* and those of the Levitical priesthood, is constrained by the force of facts to admit that this resemblance was brought about by changes first made after the close of the eighth century. [Geschichte der liturgischen Gewänder des Mittelalters, Band i. cap. vi. p. 413.] Compare Thomassinus, *Vetus et nova Ecclesiæ Disciplina.* Part i. Lib. ii. cap. xliii. 299.

Dividing the hiſtory of the Church, for the purpoſes of this inquiry, into three periods, we may regard the firſt, or Primitive Period, as extending to the cloſe of the four firſt centuries. The ſecond, or Tranſition Period, as of four hundred years more, to the cloſe of the eighth century. The third period may be conſidered as extending to the preſent time, but as ſubdivided, in reſpect of the churches of the Weſt, by the age of the Reformation.

## The First, or Primitive Period.

In the Primitive Period, of about 400 years, the dreſs of Chriſtian miniſtry was in form, in ſhape, in diſtinctive name, identical with the dreſs worn by perſons of condition, on occaſions of joyous feſtival, or ſolemn ceremonial. And this was a dreſs which in ſuch wiſe differed from the Habit of every-day life, and of ordinary wear, that it was marked out plainly in the eyes of all as a garb proper to occaſions of religious worſhip, and of ſolemn aſſembly in the Preſence of God.

In the centuries that have elapſed ſince the cloſe of that firſt Period, modifications of the Primitive type, and additions to it, have been made from time to time. Theſe modifications and additions have varied in degree, and in kind, in various branches of the Church. And when traced (as they admit of being traced) to their cauſes, they are found to reflect faithfully important changes through which ſuch churches have paſſed, either inwardly, by reaſon of innovations upon Primitive Doctrine, or outwardly through viciſſitudes of political poſition. For a ſtriking example of what is here aſſerted, we may do well to confine our attention for the preſent to the Churches of the Weſt, as being thoſe in which we ourſelves have chief concern, and as affording ampler materials for investigation than do the Eastern Churches.

## THE SECOND, OR PRIMITIVE PERIOD.

Passing on then to the Second Period (from *circ.* 400 to 800 A.D.) the facts which come before us are these. When in the fifth century overwhelming tides of invasion from the North swept in succession over the face of Southern Europe, the purity of the old Latin speech, and the dignity of the old Roman garb, became, for the first time, distinctive marks to which the inheritors of the older civilisation of Rome clung with affection, as separating them, even in outward semblance, from the revolutionary barbarism about them. And, accordingly, after this older costume had disappeared from common use, it was still preserved in the state dresses of Roman official dignitaries, and in the vestments which alone were considered seemly for such as ministered in the various offices of the Church. During this period of transition, the slight but significant distinctions, both of dress and Insignia, which from very early times had been employed in the Church, were not unfrequently the subjects of special regulation, and were modified and added to by degrees.

## THE THIRD PERIOD.

Passing now to the Third Period, we shall find that in the sudden but very brief revival of learning and of art which marks the age of Charlemagne, the peculiarities of ecclesiastical dress began to attract the special attention of the more learned ecclesiastics of the time. Certain points of analogy between the older vestments of the Levitical priesthood and the ministering dress of the Church, had been made the subject of occasional allusion even in earlier writers. But now for the first time was the attempt made to trace out in detail a correspondence between the 'eight vestments' of the Jewish high-priest, and those of Christian ministry. The idea once embraced took strong hold upon the mind of churchmen. And as, in the ninth century, the points of difference between the two types of dress were, to say the least, quite as evident, as the marks of resemblance, changes and additions were rapidly made with a view to assimilating, as far as might be, the Christian to the older Levitical type. So that, if we take the eleventh or twelfth century as the period for comparison, instead of the age of the Apostles, the theory of an analogy in detail between the Levitical and the Christian vestments admits of being maintained with great plausibility.

The type of dress which was thus at length established has been maintained in the Roman Church, with very slight modifications only, to the present time. But when, after the revival of ancient learning, the Church of England reformed her faith and her discipline, upon the authority of Holy Scripture and the model of the Primitive Church, considerable changes were made among ourselves in that Mediæval and Roman type of dress. And the result has been that the customary ministering dress of the English clergy during the last three hundred years, has been in colour and general appearance, though not in name, all but exactly identical with that which we find assigned to the Apostles in the earliest monuments of Christendom, and which, upon similar evidence, we shall find reason to conclude was, in point of fact, the dress of Christian ministry in the primitive ages of the Church.

Such is, in general terms, the result to which the monuments of successive centuries, and the testimony of successive writers, seem to point. And now, as a first step towards establishing by direct evidence the various statements above made,

vi     *Opinions as to Primitive Veſtments.*

it will be well to remind ourſelves what was the prevailing type of dreſs, and what the nature of official Inſignia, in that firſt age of Chriſtianity with which our inquiry begins.

But this opens up a ſomewhat wide ſubject, to which it will be well to devote a ſeparate chapter.

## CHAPTER II.

### Civil Dress in the First Century.

With a view to the question now before us, it is important to observe that the dress of ordinary life, in the first[β] century of our era, was in all essential respects the same[γ] in Syria, in Asia Minor, in Greece, and in Rome.

Nor have we far to seek in order to determine what this was. In the various monuments of ancient art in which representations of civil dress have been preserved to us, we find

---

[β] I speak here of the *first* century, because it is then that *in some way or other* the question of a dress proper to offices of Christian ministry must first have been practically determined. But what is stated above of the first century will apply to the first four hundred years of the Christian era. Throughout that time there were changes of fashion at Rome as between Toga and Pallium, and Pænula and Caracalla, and the like, but the general characteristics of the dress above described remained but little changed.

[γ] The following passage will serve to suggest the true cause of the general resemblance here noticed. "Greece and Rome may be regarded as the medium through which, in the designs of Providence, a flood of *Eastern civilisation* was destined to overspread the otherwise barbarous West . . . The influence of Rome . . . has never yet ceased, though the *essentially Eastern characteristics* of Pelasgic Rome have long since passed away. In truth, it is not easy to contemplate, even in imagination, a people walking about in sandals and white blankets, living in houses which retained, amidst all their incomparable splendour and luxury, the primitive Eastern arrangement of a central fireplace and a hole in the roof above it; reclining, like Turks or Arabs, on cushions at their meals; burning their dead like Hindus, and with all the idol accessories both in their homes and their temples (to say nothing of the impure rites), which still mark the pantheism of the unchanging East."—*Preface to Paley's Fasti*, p. xiv.

on examination two prevailing types, the characteristics of which can be recognised at a glance. They may be described respectively as the dress of active exertion, and the dress of dignified leisure, of festivity, or of solemn state. And of these two leading types two articles of dress are respectively characteristic. The χίτων, or *tunica*, the *chetoneth* of Holy Scripture, is the dress of activity. That same χίτων, or tunic, *with the addition of some full and flowing supervesture*, is the dress of dignity or of solemn state.

Of these two main constituents of ancient dress, common to both men and women, the Tunic was fitted somewhat closely to the body, and, when need required, was girt up so as to leave the lower limbs more or less free. It admitted, accordingly, of but little variety in shape, though it did admit, of course, of variety in material and in texture. And because of this simplicity the names by which it was known vary comparatively little. But there was a longer form of the tunic suited for occasions of state, known as the χίτων ποδήρης, *tunica talaris*, that is, " reaching to the feet," or " to the ankles," as well as the shorter tunic commonly worn.

The supervesture, on the other hand, the prevailing form of which was that of a large blanket, or of a Highland plaid, admitted, as does such a plaid now, of the greatest variety in arrangement,—admitted too of every degree of splendour in respect of material, texture, and ornamentation. And to this portion of ancient dress we find, accordingly, a great variety of names assigned, indicative, many of them, of special modifications of the general type. Now a supervesture of this kind, full and flowing, was in the nature of things unsuited to energetic action, and even incompatible[3] with it. It was,

---

[3] Hence the frequent allusions in ancient authors to the throwing off of the outer garment (ἱμάτιον) when active exertion was required. Hom. Il. B. 183, is the earliest instance. Compare note 128, p. 73. (Part ii.)

therefore, associated in men's minds either with the peaceful
occupations of rulers, statesmen, and councillors, or with those
more solemn occasions of festivity or of worship, when, in the
presence of the father of their house or of the chief of their
tribe, or of God, at once their Father and their King, men
gathered together in solemn assembly, and with a natural in-
stinct of propriety put on their more beautiful apparel.
Better illustrations of these two types of dress cannot be found
than in two representations of our Lord which are of frequent
occurrence in the early Catacombs. When He is represented
(see Plate XIII.) as "The Good Shepherd," the figure (of
classical origin, and nearly resembling the Ἑρμῆς κριόφορος of
Calamis) is that of an actual shepherd, clad in the χίτων only,
and that girt up, and reaching barely to the knee. But when
He is represented, not allegorically but directly, as sitting in
the midst of His disciples or of the Jewish doctors, as giving
food, which He Himself had blessed, to the feeding of great
multitudes, as blessing young children, or raising dead Lazarus to life; in all these cases alike both our Lord Himself
and the Twelve (when they, too, are represented) are clad in
what men then deemed a dress appropriate to all such occasions,

---

 This accounts for the idiomatic
use of the word *toga*; as in the *cedant
arma togæ* of Cicero, or in the words
preserved by S. Isidore of Seville
(*Etym.* lib. xix.) as addressed to
Roman citizens by the Senate, "*De-
positis togis, Quirites, ite ad saga.*"
[The *sagum* being a short *military*
cloak.] Herein, too, note the preg-
nant implication of the closing epithet
in the well-known line,—

"Romanos rerum dominos gentemque togatam;"

"Lords of the world, a nation clad in
garb of peaceful rule."

 See Plates XIV. and XV. The
first of the two has by some antiquaries
been interpreted as representing our
Lord among the Jewish doctors. Compare Plate XII.

 This subject, suggestive of the
deeper truths which underlie the mi-
racle of the loaves, and which are dwelt
upon by our Lord Himself in His subsequent discourse (John, chap. vi.), is
one of very frequent occurrence in the
earlier frescoes of the Roman Catacombs. See Aringhi, R. S. tom. ii. pp.
59, 91, 95, 101, 249, 269, 333, &c.

 See Plate XI.

 Aringhi, R. S. tom. ii. pp. 87,
123, 183, 205, 269, &c.

viz. in a full and flowing super-vestment worn over the χιτων, or tunic already spoken of.

## Long Garments when Worn.

This distinction between the long, full, and stately robes of which I have last spoken, and the shorter, closer, and more convenient dress of active life, is one which meets us again and again both in the literature of antiquity, and in early monuments of art. It is one, too, which it is specially necessary to bear in mind in reference to the questions on which we are now engaged. And with a view to these the following points should specially be noticed.

The wearing of long garments by *men*, except for special reasons and on exceptional occasions, was, as is well known, regarded as a proof of effeminacy.[a]

But, on the other hand, on occasions of stately ceremony, —especially of religious ceremony,—this wearing of long garments (τὸ ποδηροφορεῖν in Greek phrase) was regarded[b] as a natural and appropriate mode of marking the cessation from laborious exertion proper to occasions of solemnity. Hence

---

[a] In the *East*, the tunic was as a rule worn longer than by the Romans. But even there the same feeling may be traced. Thus Clement of Alexandria, referring to Homer's well-known epithet for the Ionian people, says, οὓς Ὅμηρος ἑλκεχίτωνας ἑλκεσιπέπλους καλεῖ (*Pædag.* ii. p. 233). Compare p. 238: τὸ σύρειν τὰς ἐσθῆτας ἐπ᾽ ἄκρους καλεῖς τοὺς πόδας κομιδῇ ἀλαζονικὸν, ἐμποδὼν τῇ ἐνεργείᾳ τοῦ περιπατεῖν γινόμενον. For the West, St. Augustine's authority may suffice (*De Doct. Christ.* lib. iii.). He says, *Talares ac manicatas tunicas habere olim apud Romanos opprobrium.* Compare Cicero's reproach against the companions of Catiline as being conspicuous *manicatis ac talaribus tunicis, velis amictos non togis.*

[b] As to the length of the *tunic*, the following is the *locus classicus* commonly referred to. Quintilian, *De Or.* lib. xi., *Cui lati clavi jus non erit, ita cingatur, ut tunicæ prioribus oris infra genua paulum, posterioribus ad medios poplites usque proveniant. Nam infra mulierum est, supra centurionum.* In other words, women wear a tunic reaching to the feet (*talaris*); soldiers, a short tunic, girt up above the knee; the orator, in his forensic habit, is to observe a medium between the two.

their use in representations alike of the last farewell spoken by a father over his daughter's grave (Pl. I.), by an emperor presiding at a sacrifice (Plate III.), by a bridegroom (Plate V. *bis*), pledging troth to his bride.

And in all the monuments of art bearing upon this matter it will be found that a long tunic is almost invariably worn whenever any supervestment of state,<sup>n</sup> or official dignity,<sup>o</sup> is worn above it.

### Change in the Use of the Toga.

A further point of importance to the understanding of our present subject is this, that the older usage of the *toga* had ceased, and a new etiquette with regard to it had become

---

<sup>n</sup> Hence explain Artemidorus, *Oneirocritica*, ii. 3 (p. 886), ἐν μὲν ταῖς ἑορταῖς καὶ πανηγύρεσιν οὔτε ποικίλη οὔτε γυναικεία βλάπτει τινὰ ἐσθής. Artemidorus, who will be often quoted upon the subject now before us, was a native of Asia Minor, a Greek by birth and education, a Roman by domicile, and a witness therefore who combines the traditions both of Greece and Rome. He practised as a physician at Rome early in the second century. The *Oneirocritica* is a treatise (as the title implies) on the interpretation of dreams, and abounds with curious details as to the dress and costume of that age.

<sup>o</sup> The only exception is in military dress, and that for obvious reasons. And because in military dress, therefore also in the dress of *emperors*: the original idea of the *imperator* being that of the first citizen of the republic in his character of commander of the Roman armies. When appearing in that character he wears a short military cloak so arranged, generally, as to leave the *right*, or *sword* arm, wholly free from wrist to shoulder. But when he appears as *Pontifex Maximus* (as often on coins), and engaged in sacrifice, or as *Princeps Senatus*, he wears the full and flowing vestments, *Toga* and *Tunica talaris*, which were regarded as proper to religious ceremonial and to the stately dignity of a citizen prince — *rerum dominus, gentisque togatæ*, to paraphrase Augustus' own quotation. Hence explain Lampridius in *Alex. Severo: Accepit prætextam* (h. e. togam prætextam) *etiam tum cum sacra faceret, sed loco Pontificis Maximi, non Imperatoris*. For the two types of imperial dress compare the two principal figures in Plates III. and IV., and see the same distinctions illustrated in the various figures on the diptych of St. Paul forming the frontispiece to this volume.

established, before the introduction of Christianity into Rome. Under the republican *régime*, the free citizen, who as such had a right to share, and commonly did share, in the most exalted functions of government in a municipality which gave law to the "world," would never appear in Forum, in Senate (if such his rank), or in assembly of the people, without the characteristic dress (note ε, p. ix), which marked him out as one of the "masters of the world." But when, after the establishment of the empire, the whole powers of government at home and abroad came to be concentrated in the hands of one man, and of his nominees, the general use of the *toga* was at once abandoned; and the far more convenient super-vestments, the *lacerna*,ʋ or the *pallium*,ϖ substituted for it. Augustus attempted, but in vain, to resist an innovation

---

ξ Tertullian (*De Pallio*, p. 214) alludes to the many inconveniences involved in the use of the Toga. "Quid te prius in toga fentias, indutum anne onuftum? Habere veftem, an bajulare? Si negabis, domum confequar; videbo quid ftatim a limine properes. Nullius profecto alterius indumenti depofitio quam [*i.e.* magis quam] togæ gratulatur."

ʋ The *Lacerna* (χλαμυς, μανδυης, or ἱματεις) was originally regarded as a garment proper to foldiers, and was confidered therefore wholly unfeemly in republican times within the walls of Rome. But under the empire it came into general use even in the city. Martial alludes to it as worn by fpectators at the games. Epig. iv. 2, quoted in Appendix A.

ϖ The word *Pallium* has a great variety of meanings (note 125) both in claffical and in ecclefiaftical Latin (notes 127, 129, 157, 195, 227) At Rome in the first century the word when specifically used served to defig- nate the characteristic *Greek* dress (the ἱματιον) in contradiftinction from the *toga*, the national drefs of Latium. The *pallium* varied in fize (as did the *toga*) according to the wealth and dignity of the wearer, and the occasion of greater or lefs ceremony on which it was worn. But there was one marked diftinction between it and the *toga*, that the former was (when opened out) either fquare or oblong; the latter either circular or oval. [This muft be faid with fome referve, *ut in re adhuc fub judice*.] The following paffages will illuftrate what has been faid. Suetonius *in Augufto*, cap. 98: "Ceteros continuos dies, inter varia munufcula, togas infuper ac pallia diftribuit, lege propofita (*i.e.* making it a condition), ut Romani Græco, Græci Romano habitu uterentur." Valerius Maximus, lib. ii. cap. 2, fpeaking of the Romans when in Greece perfifting in ufing Latin in the law courts: "Nulla non in re pallium togæ fubjici debere arbitrabantur." See Plate V. *bis*.

which was due not to any mere caprice of fashion, but to the complete change in the status of Roman citizens brought about by Augustus himself. But what was in his own power he did, aided as he was by those traditional associations which connected the *toga* in Roman minds with the whole course of their history even from earliest times. It was still thought of as the distinctively Roman dress,*e* in contrast with the Greek *pallium* (ἱμάτιον); it was still regarded as the proper dress for ceremonial use on all occasions of state, of social or religious celebration. Thus it was contrary to etiquette to dine with the emperor, except in a *toga*. Advocates* were still required to wear it; and Clients,* at least on important occasions, in attendance upon their Patrons.

---

*e* Suetonius, speaking of Augustus: *Visa quondam pullatorum* (the ordinary *lacerna* was of a dark colour) *turba, dedit negotium Ædilibus ne quem paterentur in Foro aut in Curia nisi positis lacernis togatum consistere.* It was on the like occasion that he is represented as quoting, with indignation, the well-known line of Virgil, commented on in note *e*, p. ix.

*e* Spartianus *in Severo.* "Habuit etiam aliud omen imperii, cum rogatus ad coenam Imperatoriam palliatus venisset, *qui togatus venire debuisset*, togam praesidiariam ipsius Imperatoris accepit."

*r* To this probably refers Juvenal, Sat. viii.

"Veniet de plebe togata
Qui juris nodos et legum aenigmata solvat."

And so Ovid, *Remed. Amor.* 150.

"Da vacuae menti, quo teneatur, opus.
   Sunt fora, sunt leges, sunt, quos tuearis, amici.

Vade per urbanae splendida [al. candida] castra togae."

On this passage I may note in passing that *splendida*, which is probably the true reading, would convey to a Roman ear nearly the same meaning as *candida*, which, as a various reading, is probably a gloss upon the former word. Compare Seneca, Epist. v. "Non *splendeat* toga; ne sordeat quidem." And for *candidus*, equivalent to λαμπρὸς, see note 19.

*v* Hence the phrase, *opera togata*, used of "full-dress" ceremonial in general, and more particularly of the ceremonious attendance upon persons high in office or in station. Hence explain Martial, Lib. iii. Ep. 46.

"Exigis a nobis operam sine fine togatam;
   Non eo, libertum sed tibi mitto meum."

And, again, Lib. ix. Ep. 101:

"Denariis tribus invitas, et mane togatum
   Observare jubes atria, Basse, tua;
Deinde haerere tuo lateri, praecedere sellam,
   Ad vetulas tecum plus minus ire decem."

## The Toga as a Garment of Religion.

But for our present purpose it is of special importance to note the use of the *toga* on occasions which were more particularly of a religious character. It was worn (but then black, or at least of dark colour) at funerals by mourners; while in a *white* toga were the dead themselves carried out to burial. It was worn by those who took part in public sacrifices,[*] as in the earlier times it had ever been. To this use of the *toga* Martial alludes when in writing to a friend (iv. Ep. lxv.) he congratulates him on the easy life he leads; and on this among other things, that living away from Rome, as he does, in a country town, he has not to take his *toga* out more than once or twice a month on " temple days," so to say.

> " Egisti vitam semper, Line, municipalem,
>  Qua nihil in vita dulcius esse potest.
>  Idibus, et raris togula est excussa Kalendis."

And a similar usage of the *toga* is alluded to by Tertullian (*De Cor. Mil.* p. 358). He is speaking of a particular kind of *Corona* (or chaplet, note 54, p. 32) known as *Corona Hetrusca*. *Hoc vocabulum*, he writes, *est coronarum, quas gemmis, et foliis ex auro quercinis, ob Jovem insignes, ad deducendas thensas cum palmatis togis sumunt.*

## Summary.

Passages to a similar effect might be multiplied if need were. But enough has been said to determine the two points which it is of chief importance to my present purpose to make clear. First, that the use of long, full, and flowing gar-

---

[*] See, for example, the figure of the Emperor presiding at a sacrifice in Plate III. And see note * above.

ments, was regarded in the Roman world generally, in the firſt century, as ſpecially appropriate to all ceremonial occaſions, whether civil or religious. And, ſecondly, that at Rome the *toga* had ceaſed to be worn as a garb of ordinary life, but was retained as the habit of ceremony, both civil and religious.

I need only add that where Greek dreſs prevailed, the *pallium* (ἱμάτιον), in its fuller and more dignified form, occupied the ſame place relatively, as a dreſs of ceremonial, as did the *toga* in Rome itſelf, and in thoſe parts of the Roman world which adhered to Roman uſage.

## CHAPTER III.

### § 1. Associations of Colour in the First Four Centuries.

Enough has been said in the laſt chapter on the ſubject of Dreſs in general to allow of our proceeding now to a further queſtion, that of the Colour, which, in the primitive age, was thought appropriate to the Dreſs of Chriſtian Miniſtry.

The earlieſt monuments bearing upon this queſtion, whether in literature, or in early Chriſtian art, point to the conclusion that that Dreſs was white.

And before we proceed to any more detailed examination of thoſe monuments, it will be well to take note of the ideas which prevailed in the ancient world upon this ſubject of Colour, and of the cauſes to which that feeling may be traced.

In this place I ſhall do little more than ſtate the general reſults to which the language of antiquity points; reſerving to an Appendix[χ] the more detailed ſtatement of the evidence bearing upon this queſtion.

### § 2. Associations of Colour in Classical Writers.

And, firſt, a few words as to the feeling of the ancient world generally upon this matter of Colour, apart from, and antecedent to, any excluſively Chriſtian influences.

---

[χ] See Appendix A.

## Associations of Colour in Classical Writers.

Black and sombre ψ colours, bright and gaudy colours, and lastly, white, these are the three main divisions with which we have to deal. And each of these had, in the minds of men generally, a certain accepted significance in the times of which we now are speaking, and that both in the East and in the West.

Black or dark garments, by a natural association, have ever been regarded as the expression of mourning.α They were also worn for obvious reasons of economy and of convenience by the poor, and by labouring men in general.

White, on the other hand, was the colour thought appropriate to joyous festivity of all kinds. Donatus (commenting on Terence) speaks for the general feeling upon this subject when he says, that " Bright white garments are for them that rejoice, and sombre clothing to them that grieve." *Læto vestitus candidus: ærumnoso obsoletus.*

A further point should here be noticed, that not among the Jews α only, but in the ancient world generally, white was regarded as the colour especially appropriate to things divine, and to religious worship. Thus Plato, β when speaking of the kind of offerings which may with most fitness be made to the gods, says, that *" White colours will be most seemly for gods, as in other things, so also in this of woven garments offered*

---

ψ μέλαινα or φαιὰ ἐσθὴς, in Greek writers: *atræ, nigræ, fuscæ, pullæ, vestes,* in the West; or to express a meaning nearly, though not exactly the same, *sordidæ* and *obsoletæ.*

α It may be well, however, to note that in some exceptional cases white was for women a colour of mourning; as to a certain extent it still is among ourselves. This, however, was only the case where, as an ordinary rule, bright and gay colours were worn. In all ages, and in all countries, the conventional signs of mourning are to be explained by remembering that they consist in a reversing (more or less complete) of the habit of ordinary life. Thus where the hair is ordinarily worn short it is a sign of mourning to let it grow long; where the hair is generally long, as with women, it is a sign of mourning to cut it off.

α See Appendix A, Part II.

β Περὶ νόμων, xii. p. 956. Appendix A, No. 1.

to them. Dyed garments," he adds, "*should not be offered, save only as ornaments of war.*"γ

Brilliant and gaudy colours, lastly, had some more special associations of which a few words may be said before proceeding further.

And first, these more brilliant colours which could only be added to wool by art, and were very costly, were naturally associated in men's minds with ideas either of the splendour and luxury of the more wealthy, or of the ornate costume appropriated to designation of royal or official dignity. More especially was this the case with regard to purple, which from its exceeding costliness was reserved, commonly, for designation of imperial rank, or to be worn by those, who from delegated office, or special privilege of favour, were allowed to wear imperial colours. Thus the Emperor Commodus, near the close of the second century, writes to Albinus, then high in

---

γ He refers of course to red, or colours approaching to red (*blood-red*), which have ever had a special association with the idea of war. The red shirt of Garibaldi's troops, of which we heard so much not long since, was the signal for battle with the Legions of the Republic two thousand years ago.

δ Ποικίλαι, ἄνθιναι, δεδυσμένα with the Greeks, answering to the *pictæ vestes* of Roman writers. With these are contrasted in ancient writers βάμματα τίμια, or *nativi colores*, the natural colours belonging to various kinds of wool. Some curious information as to the varieties of *natural colour* in wools, will be found in the Treatise of Lazarus Bayfius, *De Re Vest.* p. 563. Apulia was famous for its white wools; Spain for black; Liguria (the city Pollentia is specially named) for red; and Tarentum for the various shades of tawny yellow designated by the epithet *fulvus*.

ε The *purpura* itself varied in price according to the varieties of quality and of manufacture [See Ferrarius *De Re Vest.* lib. ii. cap. 7.]. The Tyrian διάφος was the most costly; next to it the Tarentine dye; and, lastly, a much cheaper dye of home manufacture, such as was used at Rome in the earlier and simpler days of the Republic, and was retained (owing to the consecration imparted by long custom) in the dresses of some of the Roman magistracies to a much later time.

ζ Capitolinus *in Albino, Hist. Aug. Sane ut tibi aliquod Imperialis majestatis accedat, habebis utendi coccinei pallii facultatem, habiturus et purpuram, sed fine auro.*

his favour, and in command of the Roman forces in Britain, and tells him that in order to confer upon him something of imperial greatness, he gives him license to wear a scarlet mantle (*pallium coccineum*) *even in the presence of the emperor*, and to wear the purple, but without decorations of gold.

The higher magistrates, too, under the empire, as previously under the republic, wore, on state occasions, a *toga* bordered (*prætexta*) with purple. This was always the case when they presided at the public games;[a] occasionally also, when taking part, officially, in public sacrifice.[b]

It is worth noting that at Rome the *toga prætexta* (or *toga picta*), which, with the embroidered tunic (*tunica palmata*) worn beneath it, was reserved for these state occasions, was not the private property of the various magistrates on whom it devolved to wear it, but belonged to the State, and was laid up in the Temple of Jupiter Capitolinus, or in the Palatium. The Emperor Gordian[c] was the first to make a change in this respect, and to provide himself, while yet a private citizen, with a *tunica palmata* and *toga picta* of his own.

Not to dwell further upon particulars of this kind, let us now further take note that as bright and brilliant colours[a]

---

[a] See the Consular Diptychs photographed among the Illustrations of this volume. Plates XXII., XXIII.

[b] Thus, for instance, Appian ('Ἐμφύλια, iii. *apud Ferrarium*) speaks of Asellius wearing, as prætor, ἱερὰν καὶ ἐπίχρυσον ἐσθῆτα, ὡς θυσίᾳ περικείμενος, a sacred vestment, adorned with gold, as being occupied in sacrifice. Compare the mention of that ἱερὰ στολὴ which was sent by Constantine to Bishop Macarius of Jerusalem, *infra*, p. 42.

[c] Capitolinus *in Gordiano*, *Hist. Aug.* p. 370. *Palmatam tunicam et togam pictam primus Romanorum privatus suam propriam habuit: cum ante Im-* *peratores etiam de Capitolio acciperent, vel de Palatio.* The dresses kept in the Palatium would be those of the Pontifex Maximus, whose official residence was part of the "Palace of Augustus."

[a] I may notice here one exceptional association of idea with purple, that of having "*a certain affinity with death*," as Artemidorus (quoted in Appendix A) has noted. We may trace the same feeling in the use of purple (violet) as a colour of mourning in the Greek Church (See p. 174), and in court etiquette.

are such as naturally attract the eye and draw attention to those who wear them, garments of brilliant colour, *if not worn in official costume*, were regarded, not by Christians only, but in the ancient[λ] world generally, as immodest and meretricious.

### DRESS OF HEATHEN PRIESTHOOD.

Before we pass on further, it may be well to state, that while white garments were, as we have seen, regarded as specially appropriate to religious solemnity of all kinds, they were not in heathen notion regarded as the insignia *of the higher official priesthoods*.[μ] Two reasons there were why this should not be. One, that where white dress was worn, or at least might be worn, *by all*, some distinctive dress was required, when the object was to mark out one or another as the possessor of any special hierarchical dignity. The other reason was this, that there were special consecrations of colour, so to speak, to particular divinities, either from natural or conventional associations, which made of these colours a kind of livery appropriate to such gods. When we find purple spoken of as specially characteristic of Priests of Dionysus[ν] (or Bacchus), or of Mars, we can hardly doubt that in this there was thought had of the purple vine, or of the juice of the grape, in the one case, of the blood of the battle-field in the other. And so, too, in those many other instances in which purple is found associated with the dress of those honorary priesthoods, whether in Asia Minor, in Greece, or in Italy,

---

[λ] One passage may suffice in confirmation. Pliny, alluding to the dyes produced in Gaul [then as now proverbial for love of gay dress: cf. Martial, Epig. xiv. 129], speaks of them as furnishing *per quod facilius matrona adultero placeat, corruptor insidietur nuptae* (*Hist. Nat.* xxii. cap. 11).

[μ] Evidence for the statements here following, concerning the costume of heathen priesthood, will be found in Appendix A. See No. 12, to 18.

[ν] See Appendix A, No. 15.

of which we find such frequent mention in antiquity.§ In almost all of them the tunic of official costume had its stripes of purple; in almost all, the super-vestment, whatever its shape might be, was either bordered (*prætexta*) with rich ornament, or wholly made of purple, of scarlet, or of both combined. And here again the reason may probably be traced to the idea of setting forth authority,* as of a royal priesthood, by the royal purple of official dress. The actual sacrificers, on the other hand, wore not those flowing vestments. Amid those fouler forms of heathenism which prevailed in many parts of the East, the nakedness of the priests was a natural accompaniment to rites of revolting grossness. But even in Italy and Greece the dress of the actual sacrificers was for obvious reasons a very scanty one. They were *nudi* (or γυμνοί) in the conventional⸰ sense of the word; at times, too, if we may judge by monuments, not in a conventional sense only. [See the figures of the sacrificing priests in Pl. III., and the central figure in Pl. VI.; and contrast with these the figure of the Greek ἀρχιερεὺς in Pl. VII.]

§ 3. ASSOCIATONS OF COLOUR TO THE MIND OF CHRISTIANS OF THE PRIMITIVE TIME.

The various ideas above spoken of as associated generally

---

§ See Appendix A, No. 12 to 18.

* The Priests of whom I here speak were regarded in the later Republican Constitutions, both of Greece and Rome, as inheritors of that "royal Priesthood" which had formerly been vested in their kings. Hence the retention of the royal title, Ἄρχων Βασιλεύς, *Rex Sacrificulus*, for religious ceremony, in cities where in any other connection the title of king would not have been endured.

⸰ A man clad in a tunic only, without super-vestment of any kind, was a sight common enough in the country; but in capital cities, and in important towns, for a man of position so to appear would have been thought as strange as it would be for one in like position now to walk down Regent Street in his shirt-sleeves. Hence the various meanings of the words *nudus* and γυμνός. It *may* mean (often does mean) "clad in tunic only;" it *may* mean (sometimes does mean) actually naked.

in men's minds with particular colours, or claſſes of colours, had come to be ſo aſſociated, not from any ſingularity of faſhion peculiar to any one age or country, but as the reſult of natural cauſes, and of the ordinary conditions of civiliſed ſociety.

The uſe of thoſe gay and brilliant colours, for example, of which we laſt ſpoke, is to be explained preciſely in the ſame way, whether they were worn as decorations of official coſtume, for the greater dignity of a court, or to miniſter to vanity; or worſe than vanity, by thoſe who aſſumed them only for the ſake of perſonal decoration. In all caſes the effect at leaſt was the ſame, that of attracting the eyes of men to him or to her who wore them, and of marking them out from others among whom they moved. And this effect was the more eaſily ſecured becauſe the great coſtlineſs of thoſe more brilliant colours was ſuch, as to prevent their being adopted by any but a very few.

In going on now to conſider the language of early Chriſtian writers upon this ſubject of colour, we muſt bear in mind that they were influenced not only by thoſe traditionary feelings which were common to the ancient world, but alſo by the language of Holy Scripture, by the uſages of the Church of which they formed a part, and laſtly by a natural repugnance to all that favoured of heathen forms of worſhip.

The witneſſes of chief importance for this firſt period of four hundred years, are St. Clement of Alexandria,[e] Tertullian, and St. Jerome.

The firſt of theſe, a native,[e] there is a reaſon to think, of Athens, but reſident during the greater part of his life at Alexandria, had "viſited the cities, and learnt to know the mind of many men." He had travelled in Magna Græcia,

---

[e] Quoted in Appendix A, No. 36 to 43; Tertullian, *ibid.* No. 44 to 46; St. Jerome, *infra*, p. 34.

[e] The date of his birth is uncertain, but he died A.D. 220.

in Palestine, in Syria, in Egypt; and everywhere he had sought to the most learned of every land, that he might add to the stores of varied knowledge which he had acquired. And as a witness, therefore, for the feeling of primitive Christendom in a matter such as this, it would be difficult, nay, not possible, to find one better qualified than is he.

The book from which I quote is the Παιδαγωγός, "The Divine Guide in the path of Christian Life." In the second and third books of that treatise he has frequently occasion to speak on the subject of dress, of personal ornament, and the like. And we find him giving expression again and again, and in the strongest manner, to precisely the same feelings in respect both of bright and brilliant colours, and of white, which we have already traced elsewhere, and adding thereto much that reminds at once of the new atmosphere of religious thought, which now at length we breathe.

For to St. Clement too, as to others to whom we have been listening, these dyed garments, coloured like unto flowers, form a fitting ʳ garb only for women that are without modesty, and men that are without manhood. In his eyes they savour of falsehood, and of treachery; they are proofs of a corrupted taste, they are signs of an evil disposition. But, on the other hand, white to him is the appropriate garb "for men of peaceful heart and inwardly illuminate." White he deems the colour befitting all solemnity and reverence; and he quotes with delight the "*excellent Plato*," "*herein as in other things a follower of Moses*," as one in opinion with himself upon this matter.

But it may be objected to the relevancy of all this, and of much else to the same effect which might be quoted, that he is speaking of these brilliant colours as worn in ordinary life, not of any such when consecrated to the service of the Christian sanctuary.

---

ʳ For the expressions which follow, see Appendix A, Nos. 36 to 43.

Most true. It would not become me to say in reply that the reason of this silence is that he had never heard or dreamt of any such consecration. For this would be assuming the very point in dispute. But I will appeal to all my readers, let their prepossessions on this question be what they may, and I will ask whether on any other supposition it is possible to account for his using language such as this which follows. Had he known of vestments "coloured like unto flowers" being used in highest offices of Christian ministration, could he possibly have said, as now we may hear him say, that together with the dealers in costly ointments and the preparers of incense, *the dyers of various wools should be banished one and all from the Commonwealth of Truth?* Could he in that case have said, as in fact he does, that "*these colours bright like flowers are fit only for the worshippers of Bacchus, for the mummeries of heathen mysticism, for the vanities of the stage?*" One only answer can be given to such a question, by any save those (to use St. Clement's own words) to whose imagination, as unto men mad, white and black are both alike.

I will not now detain my reader by further quotations, in proof of the feeling of the primitive age in respect of those varieties of colour of which alone we have spoken hitherto. Those who would pursue the subject further will find the means of doing so in the passages collected in the Appendix. At present I have only to point out, that in the moral scale of colours, as recognised at the time of which we speak, there was a middle point between the solemnity of a pure or brilliant white, and the luxurious extragavance of the more costly dyes. Sober colours there were, or, as commonly they were called, natural or native colours,[u] which were recognised as fitted for the every-day garb of the sober-minded Christian

---

[u] *Nativi colores*, βάϊχρα ἵματα, are terms of frequent occurrence. Compare note ᵈ, p. xviii.

man or woman.φ Such sober colours we may see depicted in the series of plates (XVIII. to XXI.) from the Church of St. George at Thessalonica, among the illustrations of this volume. And with this hint to guide us, in addition to what has already been said in earlier pages of this Introduction, we shall have no difficulty, I think, in apprehending the general nature, at least, of the dress, which in the passage now following is described.

### § 4. The Dress of Christian Men and Women worshipping in the Assemblies of the Church.

It is St. Clement that speaks:—

"The wife and the husband should take their way unto the church, in seemly apparel, with unaffected gait, and speech restrained; having love unfeigned; pure in body and pure in heart; fitly decked for prayer to God. And this further let the woman have: let her wholly cover her head, (unless perchance she be at home), for so dressed she will have respect, and be withdrawn from gazing eyes. And if thus with modesty, and with a veil, she covereth her own eyes, she shall neither be misled herself, nor shall she draw others, by the exposure of her face, into the dangerous path of sin. For this willeth the Word; seeing that it is meet for the woman that she pray with covered head. . . . But then so as they, who are joined to Christ, adorn themselves, in a more solemn fashion, for assemblies of the church, even such should they ever be, even so be fashioned, all the days of their life. 'To be, not seem to be,' let that be their watchword; gentle, reverend, full of holy love, at one time not less than at another.

---

φ "As there is a dress," says St. Clement, "proper to soldiers, to sailors, to magistrates, so is there a garb befitting the sobriety of the Christian."

xxvi  *Dress of Primitive Christians.*

"But it is not so indeed. Somehow doth it come about, that, with change of place, they change both their habit and their manners; even as the polypus is said to change each one his colour, to the semblance of the rock whereby he dwells." [*Pædag.* lib. iii. p. 300.]

From a Syriac MS. of the year 586 A.D.

## CHAPTER IV.

### Direct Evidence as to the Dress of Christian Ministry during the Four First Centuries.

In the two laſt Chapters ſufficient has been ſaid to enable the reader to appreciate, at their true value, the facts which will preſent themſelves, now that we enter upon the conſideration of the direct evidence applicable to the queſtion before us.

That evidence naturally divides itſelf under two heads; and of theſe we may firſt conſider that afforded by the earlieſt monuments of Chriſtian art.

I will aſk the reader to refer to the ſeries of Plates numbered XIV., XV., and XVII., among the illuſtrations of this volume, and to bring to bear upon their interpretation thoſe general diſtinctions, as to form and colour, with which we have been hitherto occupied. He will ſee, I think, at once, that the dreſs there portrayed is one, which, in thoſe earlieſt ages now in queſtion, would be ſuggeſtive to the mind by its form of occaſions of eſpecial ſolemnity, and by its colour of a garb ſuited, as none elſe could be, to ſuch as ſhould miniſter before God in the courts of His houſe.

Of thoſe Plates, the two firſt are repreſentative (the firſt, probably, and without doubt the ſecond) of our Lord ſeated on a central Throne, with His Apoſtles on either hand, ſeated, or ſtanding, about Him. In another very ſimilar freſco[x] to theſe, the twelve Apoſtles, ſeated on ſecondary θρόνοι, or apoſtolic

---

[x] Given by Perret in his great work on the *Catacombs*, vol. iii. Pl. xxxv.

thrones, on either side of our Lord (nearly as in Pl. XIV.), realise exactly one of the pictures of the heavenly kingdom set forth to us by our Lord Himself; a kingdom which is upon earth, though not "of" ↓ the earth, wherein He, our Lord, sitteth upon His "throne of glory," while to the twelve, by delegation from their Lord, it is given to sit upon twelve thrones, judging (*i.e.* ruling) ⁂ the twelve tribes of the spiritual Israel.

And this type of Apostolic dress, I may observe in passing, is preserved by the traditions of the Church, and especially appropriated to the Twelve, throughout almost all the later centuries of Christian art.⁂

For our present purpose, however, it is yet more important to note, that in the earliest Christian representation of any of the more solemn acts of religion by bishops, priests, or deacons (I refer to Pl. XVII.), the dress attributed to them is, as might have been expected on *à priori* grounds, almost an exact counterpart of that which we have already seen attributed to the Apostles.

In few words, one who examined those early monuments of the primitive age, with a competent knowledge of the habits, and the associations of colour, characteristic of that time, would come to the conclusion that the dress he there saw was exactly such as we have pointed to in the three preceding Chapters. He would see there a garb which thus far differed from the dress ordinarily worn, that by its form and colour it would at once suggest the solemn office of them who wore it, whether as drawing near on behalf of God's people unto God, or as His servants and messengers delivering to His people the messages of the Divine word, and the sacraments of His Divine grace.

---

↓ In expressing origin. See *Eirenica*, p. 75, note 14.

⁂ Matt. xix. 28, commented on in *Eirenica*, pp. 186, 187.

⁂ See Plates XIX., XLV.

And now we have only to turn, in the second place, to the second source of available evidence which is open to us, and we shall find the strongest confirmation of the conclusions just stated. The contemporary references to any dress of actual ministry in the Church, are, in the first four centuries, very few. But what there are, point all (or almost all\*) to the same conclusion. In the second part of this treatise will be found all the chief passages from early writers that can be brought to bear upon this question. And among these there are some to which, as containing a direct reference to the subject now before us, I will now ask more particular attention.

The first occurs in the Commentary β of St. Jerome on Ezekiel, cap. xliv. His subject there had led him to speak of the dress worn by "Egyptian priests, not only within their temples, but without also." He then adds (see note 53, p. 31), *Porro religio divina alterum habitum habet in ministerio, alterum in usu vitaque communi.* "Moreover that worship which is of God has one habit. in (holy) ministry, another for the usage of common life." In a note on that passage (note 53) I have pointed out, that the primary reference at least of these words is (as context shows) to Jewish rather than to Christian observances. But a comparison with other passages of the same author will justify the belief expressed in the note to which I allude, viz. that St. Jerome has purposely here chosen a very inclusive term, "*religio divina,*" as having in his mind the usages of the Church in his own time, as well as those of the Jewish priesthood in times past. I should not myself rest any weight upon a passage of such doubtful reference. But as writers on ritual habitually quote this passage (and generally without any reference to its context), it may be well to point out that *the utmost* the passage will prove is this, that there was a difference of some kind between the habit worn in ordinary life, and that which was recognised as proper

---

\* See Appendix B.     β See Part II., p. 28, *sqq.*

to services of holy ministry. And this I for one should regard as so self-evident (I might almost say) as to require no proof from isolated passages such as this.

A difference there was beyond all doubt, but in what did that difference consist?

Another passage in the same commentary will advance us yet one further step, and a somewhat more secure one, in replying to this question. At p. 30 (see also note 51) will be found a somewhat clearer intimation of what St. Jerome thought to be the "*habitus religionis.*" Having to speak of the holy vestments worn by the Levitical priests, and which they were required to put off before leaving the sanctuary, he adds, "*By all which we learn, that we too ought not to enter into the most holy place in our everyday garments, just such as we will, when they have been defiled from the usage of ordinary life; but with a clean conscience, and in clean garments* (mundis vestibus) *hold in our hands the sacraments of the Lord.*"

The word *mundus*,[γ] which he here employs as the characteristic epithet for the dress of Christian ministry, is one which to no dress could more fitly be applied, than to one white, bright, and of stately solemnity, such as that which is presented to us in the Plates to which I have referred. And if any doubt still remain as to what was the colour, which in St. Jerome's time (the close of the fourth century) was thought proper to the highest offices of Christian ministry, that doubt will be removed by yet a third passage (see p. 57, Part II.), in which, when defending the usages of the Church against the strictures of Pelagius, he asks, what offence there would be against God if "*in the administration of the holy things* (sacrificiorum) *bishop, presbyter, and deacons, and other officers of the Church* (reliquus ecclesiasticus ordo) *should come forward dressed in white garments.*"

---

[γ] On the meaning of *mundus* see note 57, p. 34.

Before we quit this subject of colour it may be proper to notice an argument by which some among ourselves have sought to found a claim to antiquity for the " splendid " vestments now worn in the Roman Church. Unable to resist the force of evidence which they found absolutely inconsistent with the idea of the primitive dress of Christian ministry having been modelled upon that of the Levitical priesthood, they yet contend for " splendid " dresses, brilliant in colour, having been worn as Eucharistic vestments even in primitive times. The two passages to which they refer are a "rubric," (so to call it) in the Liturgy appended to the " Apostolical Constitutions," and one which speaks of Constantine the Great having sent a " sacred vestment " (ἱερὰν στολὴν) made of gold tissue, to Macarius, Bishop of Jerusalem. As for this last piece of evidence the reader has only to refer to the original passage (p. 42) in which this story is first told, to see that it proves nothing about Eucharistic vestments at all, for Constantine sent it to be worn in the administering of holy baptism. He will find too that the successor of Macarius, Cyril Bishop of Jerusalem, sold[3] this vestment not very long after, and that it passed into the hands of a stage-dancer. The truth is, that this custom of emperors distributing splendid garments, as marks of honour, had now become common in the West, as it long continued to be; and Constantine, with his half-heathen, half-Christian notions about religion, may not improbably have sent to Macarius one of the ἱεραὶ στολαὶ which had been laid up (as was the custom of the times) in some Roman temple, for the use on festal days, of Flamen, of Pontiff, or of Augur. If so, I may add, it was probably taken from his own *Vestiarium Pontificium*, from the store

---

[3] Nicephorus, the Byzantine historian, alluding to this story many centuries later, says that some supposed that Bishop Cyril sold it in time of famine in order to feed the poor. But he adds, that it is difficult to suppose this could have been, else why was not this defence offered at the time in excuse to the emperor?

of splendid vestments reserved for the emperor's use in his character of *Pontifex Maximus*.

The other passage referred to deserves particular notice, were it only as affording a notable proof of the little weight to be attached to isolated phrases of ancient authors, quoted, as they often are, in English, without reference to the original language, or to the context in which they occur; or, as in this case, of passages from Liturgies, the framework of which may be very ancient, but which have been largely interpolated from time to time, as, on the most conclusive evidence it is evident that they have been.

In the instance before us, a rubrical direction is quoted from the Liturgy of St. Clement, prescribing that the priest should commence his office λαμπρὰν ἐσθῆτα μετενδύς. This expression proves, as it is argued, that *splendid* garments were in use for Christian ministry from an early period of the third century, to which this Liturgy may not improbably be assigned.

The simple answer is this. First as regards the authority quoted, it is for the most part impossible to determine whether any particular passage in any of the Liturgies, *as they now come into our hands*, is a portion of the original Liturgy or not. We know, both by direct testimony,⸹ and by internal evidence, that even those Liturgies whose framework is really ancient, have been largely added to from time to time; and that the rubrical directions more particularly are in almost all cases

---

⸹ There is a remarkable passage in Walafrid Strabo bearing upon this point and worthy of especial attention (*De Rebus Eccl.*). After describing the great simplicity with which in primitive times mass was celebrated, he goes on to say that as time went on, *multi apud Græcos et Latinos missæ ordinem, ut sibi visum est, statuerunt.* The Romans, he says, having received their "Use" from St. Peter, *suis quique temporibus, quæ congrua judicata sunt addiderunt.* On the endless variation in the various MSS. of the Greek Liturgies, and the uncertainties of the Rubrics, see the Introduction to Goar's *Euchologium Græcorum*.

### Dress of the First Four Centuries.

of comparatively recent date. Therefore, even if the meaning of the Rubric here quoted really were what those who quote it suppose, nothing would really be proved as to the usage of the Church at the time (possibly the third century) in which, *in its earliest form*, the Liturgy was originally composed.

But, secondly, in point of fact, the meaning of the passage (whether genuine or not) is *exactly the reverse* of what an uncritical reader might suppose. For the word λαμπρός, which means literally "shining" (λάμπειν), is the word habitually used[a] in the later Greek writers in speaking of a "shining" or glistening white; corresponding to the Latin *candidus*. And this disposes of the only plausible objection which, as far as I know, has been made to the conclusion already stated.

On a review, then, of the whole evidence from early literature bearing upon this question, we should conclude, without doubt, that the dress appropriate to the most solemn offices of holy ministry, during the primitive age, was white.

And if we turn next to the monumental evidence, whether in the frescoes of the Roman Catacombs,[f] or in the mosaics of early churches at Rome,[j] Ravenna,[k] Constantinople,[λ] we shall find that it confirms in the strongest manner the conclusion, which by a separate path we shall have already reached.

And lastly, I may add, that the traditions of the Church, both in literature and in art, for nearly a thousand years after the primitive period with which we are now occupied, bear witness incidentally to the same conclusion. Again and again,[μ] even in mediæval writers, do we find recognition of

---

[a] See note 19, p. 9. And to the passages there referred to, add No. 3, p. 176 in Appendix A, and note τ, p. xiii.

[f] See Plates XI., XII., XIV., XV., XVII.

[j] See Plate XXIX.

[k] See Plate XXVIII.

[λ] See Weiss, fig. 65 (Tracht und Geräth u. s. w.), p. 125. And with this compare the figure of St. James given in Pl. LXIII.

[μ] See, for example, Hugo à S. Victore, quoted p. 131; and Symeon of Thessalonica, quoted p. 171, l. 8.

white vestments as being the *proper* garb of Christian ministry. And in the later[1] art monuments exhibited in this volume, it will be seen, that the dress attributed to the Apostles in the frescoes of the Roman Catacombs, and in early monuments of the East, is reproduced century after century as their special characteristic, long after the general type of ministering dress had been altogether changed.

On every ground, then, we may accept without hesitation a conclusion, in which all the best authorities on the subject are agreed; and hold that white was the colour appropriated in primitive times to the dress of Christian ministry.

---

[1] See, for example, Pl. XXXVIII., XLV.

From a Syriac MS. of the year 586 A.D.

## CHAPTER V.

### Ornament of the Primitive Dress of Christian Ministry.
### Of Official Insignia generally.

THE points of chief importance concerning the primitive dress of holy ministration have been examined in the preceding chapters. But there are still some minor particulars which it seems desirable here to notice, with a view to the fuller understanding of the art monuments of antiquity, and of allusions which frequently are made in the pages of old writers.

### § 1. Ornament of Primitive Vestments.

And, first, a few words must be said concerning the peculiar ornament which may be seen in almost all the more ancient representations of dress figured in this volume.

A special interest attaches to this ornament, owing to the fact that in appearance and in colour (though not in name), it presents an almost exact resemblance to the scarf or stole now customarily worn in the English Church.

On the walls[ξ] of Roman Catacombs, and in the mosaics of early churches at Rome,[a] Ravenna, and elsewhere, the long[π]

---

[ξ] See Plates XI., XII., XIV., XV., XVI., XVII.

[a] See Plates XXVIII., and for Ravenna, see Plate XXIX.

[π] Occasionally also the short tunic, when for special reasons this is assigned, exceptionally, to dignified persons.

See, for example, the figures of the Magi in the woodcut at p. vi. Regarded as just arriving from *a journey*, they have a short tunic (*itineri babilis*, see note 203, p. 105) assigned to them. But this ornament is added as an indication of dignity.

tunic of more solemn dress is almost invariably represented with the addition of an ornamental stripe, extending from between the neck and shoulders, on either side, to the lower edge of the tunic. In some cases similar stripes are represented running round the lower extremity of the sleeve. [Pl. V. and XXVIII.]

Similar ornaments are to be seen in other representations of Roman dress, as, for example, in some of the illustrations of the Vatican Virgil, dating from the fourth century.

But this ornament is by no means peculiar to the costume of Rome. We find on the walls of the Catacombs, not only our Lord and His Apostles, but Abraham, Moses, the " Three Children," and other Easterns, wearing a tunic so ornamented. But from this, if this were all, we could not infer more with certainty, than that the Christian painters of the second, third, or fourth centuries, to whom those frescoes are to be traced, believed this ornament to be common in the East as it was among themselves. But, in point of fact, we have abundant evidence, both in literature and in art, which proves that they were right in so thinking. The ornamental tunics of heathen priesthood, for example, in the Tyrian colonies, and in Tyre itself, were distinguished, as we have seen, by stripes of purple. And the seventy translators in their rendering of Isaiah, iii. 21, speak of garments which are striped (μεσοπόρφυρα) and bordered (περιπόρφυρα) with purple. And the stripes of purple there spoken of differed only in colour and material, but not in form, from the simple ornament commonly worn on the full-dress tunic of ordinary[e] people.

So common, indeed, is this particular kind of ornament

---

[e] Compare the comment of St. Basil, tom. i. p. 661, D. Τὸν ἐν τῇ ἐσθῆτι κόσμον τῶν καλλωπιζομένων γυναι- | κῶν ὡς περίεργον διαβάλλει, πορφύρας ποτὲ μὲν κατὰ τὰ ἄκρα παρυφαινόντων, ποτὲ δὲ κατὰ τὸ μέσον αὐτῆς ἐντιθέντων.

in early monuments, both in the East[e] and in the West, that I cannot but suppose it to have originated in some simple cause, incident to the prevailing form of the garment now in question. It may be conjectured that in joining together the various "breadths," of linen or woollen stuff, out of which the tunic was to be made, a seam was made from between the neck and shoulders on either side down to the lower edge; and that these ornamental stripes were so sewn on as to hide (compare p. 3, l. 27) what would otherwise have been unsightly, and yet admit of being easily removed when the tunic itself needed washing.

What has been said hitherto points onward to a further point of interest concerning the ecclesiastical dress of the primitive age. We know that various grades of rank were distinguished at Rome, from very early times, by the colour and by the relative width of the ornamental stripes worn upon the tunic by senators, and by knights. Whether two such were worn, stole-wise, or one only, is uncertain. But, however, this may be, the broad *clavus* was the distinctive mark of a senator; the narrow *clavus* of a knight. And it is wholly in accordance with this, that in one of the monuments figured in this volume (see Plate XIV), the black *lora* (or "*clavi*") on the *tunica talaris*, worn by our Lord, are considerably larger than those worn by the six persons (probably Apostles) in the midst of whom He is seated.

Facts such as these would lead us antecedently to expect, that distinctions between the higher and the lower offices of

---

[e] A remarkable example may be seen in a very ancient fresco in a rock-church at Urgub, in Mesopotamia. See Texier, B.A., Pl. V. One of the principal figures (representing, probably, one of the Old Testament prophets) seen approaching with reverence to the Holy Child before him, is dressed in a white tunic under an outer garment of reddish brown. And this white tunic (στιχάριον, it would probably be called by those who originally drew it) has narrow black stripes by way of ornament, which exactly correspond with the *lora*, or ornamental stripes, of the Roman Dalmatic.

the Christian ministry might probably be indicated, in early times, by means of these ornamental stripes.[r] The history of the "dalmatic," which was just such an ornamented tunic as that now described, strongly confirms the probability that this was really the case; and of this we shall shortly have occasion to speak more at length.

For the present it is only necessary to add, that these ornamental stripes vary in colour, according to the colour of the dress upon which they are worn. But in all the examples of *white* dress, worn by Apostles or by ecclesiastics, belonging to the first 600 years of Christian history, these stripes, as far as I have observed, are invariably black.

But it was not only by these ornaments on the tunic that difference of official rank could be indicated. We have abundant evidence to show, that, at Rome, almost every modification of the ordinary dress had a certain well-understood significance in the eyes of men. The unusual fulness, or the scant dimensions, of *toga* or of *pallium*, were as significant then, as is the long graceful train that sweeps the ground now worn by ladies of fashion, when contrasted with the shorter, simpler dress of those who, from motives of economy, or for any other reason, study convenience and comfort rather than stately beauty and grace. And as with the outer garment (whether *toga* or *pallium*), so with the tunic also. Nay, so minute and rigorous was the etiquette of dress at Rome under the Empire, that people of any position varied the kind of shoes which they wore, according to the nature of the upper garment in which they might be clad. And we shall find, when we come to examine the later monuments bearing upon the subject here under discussion, that distinctions such as these, familiar to Romans and to Greeks under the imperial

---

[r] As among ourselves, for example, the right of wearing a "scarf" is given, in the Canons, to such as are members of Cathedral bodies, and to the chaplains of noblemen.

system, were reproduced from time to time in the regulations made for the miniftering drefs of the Church.

### § 2. Official Insignia.

But diftinctions of drefs, minute and varied though they may be, are, for the moft part, not fufficient of themfelves to ferve as expreffions for all thofe diverfities of rank and office, which are characteriftic of highly civilifed ftates. Therefore is it that in fuch ftates the cuftom has at all times obtained, of marking out, by conventional fymbols, both grades of relative dignity, and varieties of official occupation. Of thefe conventional fymbols, two claffes may be particularly noticed : thofe which are worn upon the head, fymbols moftly of *authority;* and thofe borne in the hand, fymbols, for the moft part, of fpecial departments of activity.

Ornaments, firft, of the head. To the head, the crown and apex of the human form, itfelf the nobleft and moft godlike of all created things,—to the head, which with a nod, or with a glance, or with an uttered word, can give expreffion to the Sovereign Will which therein fits enthroned,—to this, by a natural inftinct, men have ever affigned the fymbols of power to rule, whether with a fupreme and all-embracing rule, as did great kings, or in fpecial departments of delegated authority, as did others in their name.

But the hand, alfo, the organ and inftrument of that fovereign will, furnifhes fignificant expreffion, by appropriate fymbols, of the various fields of fpecial activity in which the powers of man find exercife. The fceptre\* of the king, the lituus of the augur, the written fcroll of philofopher or man

---

\* It is not an eafy matter to determine what was the *original* affociation of idea in confequence of which the word σκῆπτρον, for example, fuperadded to its primitive meaning of a "ftaff," or ftout ftick, that of "fceptre" or fymbol of royalty, actual or delegated. In what we read in the Iliad of fuch a

of law, the instruments of sacrifice of the heathen priest, the pastoral staff of Christian bishop, or the book of the Gospels held in his hand, these, and other such, are significant, each of some special department of official ministration, to which prominence is given by the mere fact of such symbolic representation.

We may apply these general principles to the subject immediately before us. In Egyptian monuments we find the symbols of priesthood to be either such as could be worn upon the head, a high cap or mitre, indicative of authority; or such as could be carried in the hand. And these last, again, are of two kinds: instruments of sacrifice, marking them out as sacrificers; or *a roll of papyrus inscribed with hieroglyphics*, indicative of their office as keepers and expounders of divine knowledge. And at an interval of some two thousand years, we find the same symbolic language employed in Christian art. On the walls of the Catacombs the Divine power of our Lord is symbolised by "the rod of power" which He holds, when working miracles; His office as "The Word," the revealer of Divine truth to man, by the inscribed scroll which He holds, or by the two open *capsæ* on His right hand and on His left, filled each with written scrolls, and representative, we cannot doubt, of the Old and New Testament [Pl. XII.]. And, lastly, His own revelation of Himself as the true Manna, as the Bread of Life, as one whose Body offered on the Cross, and whose Blood thereon outpoured, are the food of them that hunger, and the refreshment of them that thirst: this, too, is set forth again and again in the seven baskets filled with

---

σκῆπτρον being laid, and that with a heavy hand, upon the shoulders of Thersites, we have, if I mistake not, an indication of the original use from which this "staff" was derived. In the rude assemblies wherein a warrior chief gathered about him his armed followers for council of battle or, in time of peace for judgment of wrong done, the "right of the staff" would be frequently exercised, both for the maintenance of order, and for the punishment of offenders.

bread which He hath blessed and broken; in loaves, marked with a cross, which He bears in His own bosom.

But that which now more specially concerns us is the question of the Insignia, with which, in early Christian monuments, either the Apostles themselves, or their successors in offices of Christian ministry, were invested. One φ such monument there is, and one only I believe, in which the Apostles are represented as wearing a peaked cap, such as in ancient times was known as a τιάρα (see note 84, p. 52). This representation would serve to indicate the "*royal* priesthood" with which the Lord had invested them. And thus the monument, of which I now speak, offers an exact parallel to one or two exceptional passages in ancient authors, in which this same idea is either alluded χ to, or (as by Epiphanius) ψ expressly stated.

A similar suggestion of power *to rule*, committed to the Twelve, under Christ, and by delegation from Him, is set forth by the apostolic thrones on which they are sometimes represented as seated. [See Frontispiece, and compare note χ, p. xxviii.]

With these exceptions (the first of which appears to have been unobserved hitherto by writers on ritual), the insignia of Apostles, in the early monuments of Christian art, are such, as mark them out as the deliverers of a Divine message, of the "Word of God," to man. This their office is indicated by the "scroll" † held in their hand, a "*volumen*" (note 79, p. 50) in the original sense of the word. At times, however, we find in place of this scroll a "martyr's crown," or chaplet, held in the hand. Thus, in a remarkable monument, of which

---

φ Ciampini, *Vet. Mon.* tom. i. Pl. LXX.

χ See the letter of Bishop Polycrates, quoted at p. 38, and compare note 62. And see further, on this side of the question, the passage referred to in Appendix B.

ψ See the passage quoted at p. 40, and refer to note 65.

† See Pl. XII., XIII., XXIX., and the figure of St. Peter, Pl. XLV.

*f*

there is a drawing in the collection at Windsor, our Lord is represented between St. Paul (at His right hand) and St. Peter (on the left); and while St. Paul holds the scroll of an apostle, St. Peter holds in his hands the chaplet (*corona*) which designates his martyrdom.

The special designations by which particular Apostles were indicated (as still they are) in the later and more developed symbolism of Christian art, are not met with in the primitive period with which we are now concerned.

Passing on now from the Apostles themselves to the various orders of the Christian ministry, we find that a chair † of state (*sedes* or καθέδρα), or "episcopal throne," serves to mark the authority to rule committed to a bishop; while his office as a teacher of Divine truth is indicated by the Book of the Gospels, which he holds in his left hand. From a passage of great interest in a sermon attributed to St. Chrysostom (see note 89, p. 53), we learn that at the consecration of bishops,* the book of the Gospels was laid upon their heads, as being "the true evangelical tiara," and as a sign to the bishop himself, that "*though he be head of all, yet doth he act in subjection to God's laws; though he be ruler of all, yet is he too under rule to the law; though in all things a setter forth of the Word, yet is he himself, to that Word, in subjection.*"

The pastoral staff is first mentioned as one of the distinctive insignia* of a bishop, in the acts of the Fourth

---

† See Pl. XVII., and for full details see Martigny D. A. C. *in voc.* Chaire.

* τῶν ἱερέων is the expression used. But context shows that by ἱερεὺς here, as after in early writers, is meant a bishop. Compare note 90, p. 54, and see Index *in voc.*

* The various insignia above mentioned (the "staff" only excepted) may be seen in the Frontispiece to this volume (a diptych of St. Paul), and in Pl. XI. (the "virga" or rod of power), XV., XVII. (the "throne" there represented, as in Aringhi, is, I should think, incorrectly drawn), XXIX. (the earliest example, as far as I know, of a "crozier," is there seen), XXX., XXXI. Later examples of such insignia may be seen in almost all later Plates published in this volume.

Council of Toledo (see *infra*, p. 75). But it does not appear to have been found in monuments of Chriſtian art till the tenth century. Its ſymboliſm is well ſet forth in a paſſage of Honorius, quoted later in this volume (p. 140). And whatever be the date of its firſt uſe as one of the diſtinctive inſignia of a biſhop, it ſerves, more fully and expreſſively perhaps than any other ſuch ſymbol, to ſet forth that paſtoral aſpect of the miniſterial office, which at all times, and in all places, has conſtituted its ſureſt paſſport to the hearts and affections of God's people.

From a Syriac MS. of the year 586 A.D.

## CHAPTER VI.

### The Transition Period from 400 to 800 a.d.

We enter now upon the second of the three periods, into which, for the purposes of this inquiry, the history of the Christian Church has been divided. This, and the succeeding period, may be treated much more briefly than the first, in which I have been obliged to occupy what is in some measure new ground,—new, at least, in connexion with the question, with which, in these pages, we are occupied.

At the very outset of this second period two facts arrest our attention, as having had a momentous influence on the history of the Church generally. And this influence may be traced, as in other particulars of far more intrinsic importance, so also in this of ecclesiastical dress with which here we are more especially concerned.

The two facts of which I speak are, the dualization of the Roman empire, somewhat earlier in date, but to be traced in its effects throughout this period; and the first outburst, in the year 408, of that great flood of barbarian invasion, whose successive waves spread, with overwhelming force, over the face of Southern Europe. Goths, Vandals, Lombards, a "triple wave of woe," poured down in succession, from the North, upon the rich land which lay open, and almost undefended, to their attacks; and the older Roman civilisation was all but destroyed,—would have been destroyed altogether, had not the fpiritual force, that was in the Church, proved a more effectual fafeguard, than the degenerate valour of the imperial armies.

The firft of the two events above mentioned requires fpecial notice in this place, becaufe the eftablifhment of the imperial fyftem in the "new Rome" of the Bofphorus, ferves to account for the development of both civil and ecclefiaftical drefs, in nearly parallel lines, at Conftantinople and at Rome, during the period of 400 years with which we now are occupied. Let the reader examine the two monuments of confular coftume, one of the Eaft, the other of the Weft, among the illuftrations of this volume (Plates XXII. and XXIII.), and he will fee at a glance, that not the official titles only, but the coftume and infignia of the older Rome of the Seven Hills, had been transferred, before the date of thofe monuments, to the New Rome of the Bofphorus. And at Conftantinople, not lefs than at Rome, modifications were brought about, during this tranfition period, in the drefs of Chriftian miniftry, owing to the application to ecclefiaftical ufe of peculiarities of coftume and of infignia, which were of the Empire, before they were of the Church.

And now, for reafons already indicated, we will confine our attention, for the prefent at leaft, to the churches of the Weft. And we fhall have no difficulty in feeing how the political circumftances of thofe times were outwardly reflected, on the one hand, in the revolution effected in the general coftume of civil life, and, on the other, in the fpirit of confervatifm, which maintained, in official coftume at Rome, and in the miniftering habits of the Church generally, that type of drefs, characteriftic of the older Roman civilifation, of which we have already treated at length in the earlier chapters of this Introduction.

A complete change was brought about, this firft we have to note, in the ordinary coftume of civil life. The type of dress by which the invaders from the north were distinguished, differed widely from that older Roman habit (Eastern in its character), of which we spoke in the earlier chapters of this Introduction. The new dress was a dress for soldiers (a *sagum*, or short mantle, its prevailing form, worn over a short tunic like a Highland kilt); the old dress, as we have seen (note ε, p. ix.) a dress of citizens. The contrast between the new and the old type of dress may be seen at a glance, on comparing the dress of the Emperor Charlemagne in Pl. XXXIII. with that of the Emperor Justinian (which is of the older type with Byzantine additions) in Pl. XXVIII. And in a less exalted rank, we may compare the figure of the layman, in Pl. XXXVII., and that of Beno de Rapiza (somewhat later in date), in Pl. XLIII., with those of the courtiers in attendance on Justinian in the S. Vitale mosaic already referred to; with that of Gordianus (a senator), in Pl. XXV., or with those of the several laymen represented in the mosaics of the Church of St. George in Thessalonica (Pl. XVIII. to XXI.).

The contrast between these two types of dress was matter of observation at the time; and adhering to the "old ways" was regarded as a mark of orthodoxy. That this was the case as late as the close of the sixth century, we have the evidence of the biographer (a very well-informed one) of St. Gregory the Great. Speaking of the household of the good bishop, whose life he writes, he says, "That not one among them, from the least to the greatest, had any taint of 'barbarism' (using the word in its Latin sense) either in speech or in dress; but the *toga* or the *trabea*, of old Latin usage, maintained distinctly the old Latin spirit, in that palace to which Latium had given a name."[β]

---

[β] Joan. Diac. Vita S. Gregorii, lib. ii. cap. 13. "Nullus Pontifici famulantium a minimo usque ad maximum barbarum quodlibet in sermone vel habitu præferebat; sed togata Quiritium more vel trabeata Latinitas suum Latinum (Latium ?) in ipso Latiali palatio singulariter obtinebat."

A passage such as this, even if it stood alone, would prepare us, after the facts that have already been considered, to find that even as late as St. Gregory's time the old types of dress were still maintained, with little change, at Rome itself, however much they might be modified where the new influences were predominant. And in distinctly ecclesiastical dress, we find, accordingly, that, in some of the Roman monuments of that period, scarcely any difference is to be detected between the representations dating from that time, and those which we meet with in the "Ciclo Biblico" of the earlier Roman Catacombs. In the mosaic of the Church of St. Lorenzo (Pl. XXIX.), dating from just before the pontificate of St. Gregory, not only the Apostles, but the then Bishop of Rome, Pelagius, have the same white vestments, with black *lora*, which we have already seen in earlier monuments (Pl. XIV. and XV.). And if Anastasius is to be understood literally when he says, that Pelagius II. "made" (*fecit*) the Cemetery of St. Hermes, it must follow that the remarkable fresco represented in Pl. XVII. cannot be of earlier date than about the close of the sixth century.

I speak advisedly of "distinctly ecclesiastical dress," because we have to remember that the Bishops of Rome, from the close of the fourth century, occupied a great civil position also in the state. Their civil power was indeed wholly anomalous and undefined, and in theory subordinate to that of the *Præfectus Urbis*, Representative of the Emperor; but it was often very real, at a time when the titular magistracies were for the most part names and nothing more. And this will account for a phenomenon, so strange at first thought, as that of Christian bishops assuming, as insignia of their office, decorations derived from the civil magistracies of the old Roman republic. These magistracies were preserved first, under the Imperial system, as honorary distinctions, conferred by the emperor; and their insignia, at a later period still, were imitated in ecclefiaftical ufe at Rome and Conftantinople, and thence [y] fpread to other churches.

A moft remarkable evidence of the clofe connection, to Roman ideas, between the drefs of high civil magiftracy and that of their own chief bifhop, is to be found in the monument reprefented in Pl. XXIV., in which St. Gregory the Great is reprefented with nearly the fame drefs and infignia as would have been his had he been " Conful" under the empire, inftead of " Præful,"[z] in the Church. And the clofe refemblance between the dignified drefs of a fenator, and that of a bifhop of the Church, is well indicated in the plate [a] immediately following (Pl. XXV.), in which, but for the Papal *pallium*, and the Book of the Gofpels, carried (as one of the *infignia* of a bifhop) in the left hand, it would be impoffible (as Cardinal Baronius remarked long ago) to diftinguifh which were the fenator, and which the bifhop.

### LITERARY MONUMENTS.

Turning now from thefe art-monuments to the contemporary notices of ecclefiaftical drefs, to be met with in ancient literature, it may be well here to point out one or two

---

[y] To this, as regards Rome, Thomaffinus bears teftimony. *De Ben.* tom. ii. p. 327. " Conftat ab ecclefia maxime Romana cæteras identidem varia extorfiffe privilegia, ut cum ipfis magnificentiora quædam divini cultus indumenta communicarentur. Antiquiffimas enim et pretiofiffimas has veftes et frequentius ufurpaverat, et retinuerat conftantius, urbs Imperii totius regina. Imperatoriæ etiam in vefte et ornatu magnificentiæ copia major facta fuerat Ecclefiæ Romanæ.

Ab ea ergo effundebantur hi veluti pompæ gloriæque facerdotalis rivuli in reliquum Chriftianum orbem."

[z] This is a title frequently given to the Bifhops of Rome in the earlier Roman documents.

[a] The paffages of chief importance are given in the later part of this work, pp. 42 to 87. Others will be found quoted in the chapter next following, in which the veftments in ufe at this period are feparately noticed.

features which are common to all, and which it is important to note for the better underſtanding of the preſent queſtion.

It will be found that paſſages quoted from writers of this period have reference, either to the veſtments of Levitical ¿ prieſthood, or to the dreſs and inſignia which were regarded as proper to biſhops, prieſts, deacons, or others holding offices of miniſtry in the Church. And as regards the firſt of theſe two claſſes, thoſe in which the Levitical veſtments are deſcribed or referred to, a marked diſtinction will be obſerved between the writers of this period and thoſe of the ſucceeding centuries. If St. Jerome, St. Auguſtine, St. Chryſoſtom (or the writer * who bears his name), if St. Gregory, or Venerable Bede, deſcribe in detail the Levitical veſtments, they do ſo without giving the ſlighteſt intimation that the veſtments of Chriſtian miniſtry correſponded in number, in form, and colour, or in name, with thoſe of the older prieſthood. Oftentimes, on the contrary, the language they employ ſhows, that they recogniſed the marked contraſt between the two [Notes 94, 96, 101, 139]. But in the later writers, from the beginning of the ninth century [Notes 169, 170], we find, on the contrary, that the Levitical veſtments are ever mentioned as the prototypes, to which thoſe of Chriſtian prieſthood may be referred, and the names proper to the one are transferred, often upon the moſt imaginary grounds, to thoſe which were then in uſe for offices of Chriſtian miniſtry [Note 253].

But the claſs of paſſages, of which I have now been ſpeaking, affords only negative and indirect evidence upon the

---

¿ See Nos. XII., XVI., XVII., XVIII., XIX., XX., XXVI., XXVII., XXIX. With theſe ſhould be included the paſſages from St. Jerome (pp. 10 to 35). For theſe, though they precede by a few years the cloſe of the fourth century, are the ſources to which, directly or indirectly, all the writers in the Weſtern Church are mainly indebted for their knowledge on the ſubject of the Levitical veſtments. For apparent exceptions to the general ſtatements of the text, ſee Appendix B.

* See note 80, p. 51.

history of the vestments of the Church. Of more direct interest are the passages, in which these last are enumerated and described. And among these, in regard of the West, I may here mention, as of chief interest and importance, the extracts (No. XXV., p. 68, *sqq.*) from St. Isidore of Seville, and from the Acts (No. XXVIII., p. 75) of the Fourth Council of Toledo held under his presidency. For Eastern usage, some seventy years later, we have as a guide the description, given by St. Germanus of Constantinople (No. XXX., p. 82, *sqq.*), of the vestments recognised in the East at the time he wrote. Of these we shall have to speak in detail, in the following chapter.

But before proceeding further, I may mention two passages as having a special interest for English readers. I refer to the extracts from the *De Tabernaculo* of Venerable Bede (p. 78, *sqq.*), and to the nearly contemporary letter of St. Boniface (Winifrid of Crediton) to Cuthbert, Archbishop of Canterbury, quoted in note 209, p. 106.

Both of these passages date from an early period of the eighth century. And both show, though in different ways, what was the feeling of those times in respect of the questions now under discussion. We see, on the one hand, a man wise and learned, and of the greatest piety, such as Bede, still regarding the Levitical vestments in the same light precisely as had all the earlier Fathers. "The outward splendour," so he writes,[1] "which, in the former times, shone brightly in ornamented vestments, is now to be spiritually understood; inwardly conspicuous in the hearts of Christian priests, and outwardly so also in their activity in all good works." And it is matter of interest to observe from what source he derived his thought, viz. *from the service then in use for the consecration of bishops.* In a very ancient MS. of the *Liber Sacramentorum* of St. Gregory the Great, edited by the

---

[1] See note 135, p. 78, and Appendix B.

learned Benedictine Hugo Menardus, the same thought is expressed nearly in the same words.¹ And with this again agrees the description given of St. Germanus of Paris by Fortunatus (writing in the sixth century):—

> Senſim incedit velut alter Aaron,
> Non de veſte nitens, ſed pietate placens.
> Non lapides, coccus, clarum aurum, purpura, byſſus,
> Exornant humeros, ſed micat alma Fides.

The other paſſage, that from St. Boniface, "the apoſtle of Germany," preſents great difficulties, the ſolution of which, I own, I cannot as yet ſee. For the expreſſions that he uſes indicate, on the one hand, that the "veſtimenta" which he ſo ſtrongly condemns were in ſome way connected with *superſtitious*[x] uſe (ſo at leaſt he deemed it); that they were of recent introduction (ſo the general tone of his letter ſeems to imply); and apparently alſo that they were brought into England through ſome foreign[λ] influence. On the other hand, he ſpeaks of theſe as tending to luxury and unclean living, and to evil companionſhips, among the younger members of the monaſtic houſes; to the neglect of reading and of prayer, and to the ruin of ſouls. Whatever may have been the exact ſtate of circumſtances which called out this his ſtrong denunciation, this much at leaſt is clear, that in the Engliſh monaſtic houſes, early in the eighth century, there

---

¹ Illius namque Sacerdotii anterioris habitus, noſtræ mentis ornatus eſt; et Pontificalem gloriam non jam honor commendat veſtium, ſed ſplendor animarum. . . . Et idcirco huic famulo tuo quem ad ſummi ſacerdotii miniſterium elegiſti, hanc, quæſumus, Domine, gratiam largiaris, ut *quicquid illa velamina in fulgore auri, in nitore gemmarum, in multimodi operis varietate ſignabant, hoc in ejus moribus actibuſque clareſcat.* D. Greg. Papæ *Sacram. Liber*, p. 239. [The MS. is *not earlier* than the eighth century, and probably not much later. See Menardus' Preface.] Other paſſages to the ſame effect are quoted in Appendix B.

x *Veſtimentorum ſuperſtitionem, Deo odibilem.* Cf. *infra*, note 299, p. 106.

λ He ſpeaks of them as *tranſmiſſa*, "ſent acroſs," by Antichriſt, and as precurſors of his advent.

had been a great development of external fplendour in drefs, either fecular *μ* or minifterial, or both; and that this had been defended upon fome grounds of religion, which were regarded as fuperftitious and anti-Chriftian by St. Boniface.

---

*μ* Of the fplendid fecular drefs affected by ecclefiaftics in the eighth century, we have many notices in early writers. Compare note 336, p. 165.

From a Drawing in Her Majefty's Collection. [See Defcription of Pl. XXXIII.]

## CHAPTER VII.

### Special Vestments and Insignia of Christian Ministry between 400 and 800 a.d.

We have already mentioned the two principal authorities for the Christian vestments of this period,—St. Isidore,[1] and the Fourth Council of Toledo, for the West; St. Germanus[1] of Constantinople, for the East. We may take the enumerations, there given, as a basis, in proceeding now to consider these vestments more in detail.

#### Ministering Vestments in the West.

The vestments and insignia mentioned in the Acts of the Council of Toledo, a.d. 633, are the Alb, the Planeta, the Orarium; and, in addition to these, the Episcopal Ring, and Pastoral Staff, as the distinctive insignia of a bishop. These Acts, however, determine, with certainty, only the vestments recognised at that period in Spain. From other sources we learn the names of additional vestments, such as the Dalmatic, and the Pallium, connected more particularly with Rome; and of these also we will take the present opportunity of speaking.

---

[1] See *infra* pp. 68 and 75; and for S. Germanus, p. 82.

### 1. THE ALB.

The "tunica alba," or, as it is more briefly called,[g] the *alba*, is the term used of the long white tunic worn, as we have seen, from Apostolic times, by those who ministered in the Church. Even as early as the Fourth Council of Carthage,[e] we find a canon regulating its use as a garb to be worn, by deacons,[v] only at specified times. And by this name, probably for more than four centuries, rather than by *dalmatica*, was the tunic of holy ministration known in all the Latin churches, Rome only excepted.

Later notices of the "alb" occur in the Council of Narbonne[ε] (A.D. 589), indicative of the growth of great irreverence in the celebration of the "mass," an irreverence which required to be checked by special enactment. And if we find in the Acts of the Council of Toledo, already alluded to, that the "alb" is there spoken of as the characteristic vestment of a *deacon*, it is not that bishops and presbyters did not wear a white tunic under the "planeta," but that the

---

[g] *Alba* is first used virtually as a substantive, in a passage from Vopiscus (*in Claudio*, 14 and 17), in which we read of an *alba subserica, i.e.* made of linen interwoven with silk, sent as a present by Trebellius Pollio to Claudius (*circ.* A.D. 265).

[e] Concil. Carthag. iv. Can. 41 (Labbe, vol. ii. p. 1203). *Ut diaconus tempore oblationis tantum vel lectionis alba utatur.* It is very doubtful whether there was ever such a Fourth Council of Carthage actually held. The Canons, however, which are attributed to this Council, are of about the date assigned, viz. towards the close of the fourth century.

[v] It is to this white vestment of Deacons that John the Deacon alludes (Vita S. Gregorii, lib. i. 25), saying, that on being ordained deacon, St. Gregory appeared *non solum nitore habitus, verum etiam claritate morum probabilium, divinis angelis adæquari.*

[ε] See Labbe, tom. v. p. 1020. *Nec diaconus, aut subdiaconus certe, vel Lector, antequam missa consummetur, alba se præsumat exuere.*

deacon, having no super-vestment,' was specially designated by the white alb in which he ministered.

Before proceeding further it may be well to notice a special form of the ministering tunic, connected more especially with Roman use.

## The Dalmatic.

The Dalmatic⸱ (see Pl. VI. and XXVIII.) was a tunic with long and full sleeves, differing therein from the *colobium*, which had a very short and close sleeve, reaching a few inches only below the shoulder.⸱

Like other garments appropriated at a comparative early time, to ecclesiastical use at Rome, the Dalmatic had been in use by persons high in secular position, before it was adopted by the Church. In the West,ᵠ the earliest secular traditions connected with it are peculiarly unfortunate. For the first persons recorded to have worn it are the Emperors Commodus († A.D. 190) and Heliogabalus († 223). Their biographer Lampridius ˣ records, as an outrage upon all pro-

---

ᵉ Compare Pl. XXVIII. where Archbishop Maximian wears a planeta over a dalmatic, whereas the two clerics in attendance on him are in dalmatics only. See also Pl. XVII.

ᵗ The full expression was *tunica dalmatica*, but this very rarely occurs, the word *dalmatica* being used as a substantive, as was " alba." The name was derived from the province of Dalmatia. See note 131.

ᵘ See, for example, the woodcut in p. xxxiv.

φ Of a different kind are the first traditions in the East, if the word διλματίκιον, used by John Damascene, be not an anachronism. Speaking of the pretences to special sanctity made by the Pharisees, he mentions, *inter alia*, σχήματα ἰδιλοχυσκευτικὰ τῆς ἐνδυσίας, διὰ τὶ τῆς ἀμπιχόνης, καὶ τῶν διλματικίων, ἤτουν κολοβίων, καὶ τοῦ πλατυσμοῦ τῶν φυλακτηρίων, τουτέστι σημάτων τῆς περφύρας, καὶ κρασπίδων, καὶ ροίσκων ἐπὶ τὰ πτερύγια τῆς ἀμπιχόνης. [Cotelerii *Eccl. Græc. Monumenta Inedita*, vol. i. p. 284.]

ˣ Lampridius *in Heliogabalo*, cap. 26. *Dalmaticatus in publico post cenam sæpe visus est; Gurgitem Fabium et Scipionem se appellans, quod cum ea veste esset cum qua Fabius et Cornelius a parentibus, ad corrigendos mores, adolescentes in publicum essent producti.*

priety,✟ the fact of their being seen in public wearing this particular kind of tunic. Of the latter he writes, that he would often appear in public, after dinner, clad in a Dalmatic; and calling himself a second Fabius or Scipio, "because he wore a garment such as that in which Fabius and Cornelius, before they attained to manhood, were made by their own parents to appear in public, as a punishment for some offence committed." It may seem strange, at first thought, to hear of precisely the same garment being worn, "in public," only some thirty years later, by a Christian bishop. St. Cyprian of Carthage († 258), when led out to death, was wearing (if the "Acts" of his martyrdom may herein be trusted), first a byrrhus,* then, under that, a Dalmatic; and again, under the Dalmatic, a "*linea*," or shirt. That dress was, of course, not that which he would use in offices of holy ministry, but the seemly attire which he would wear on other occasions. And it is probable, for reasons already fully set out in earlier chapters* of this Introduction,

---

✟ The impropriety may have consisted either in coming out into the streets, *sicut erat*, in the dalmatic, in which he had reclined at table, without toga or pallium; or possibly in his wearing a *tunica manicata*. This last would have been thought effeminate in the days of those older Fabii and Scipios. And hence the *punishment* involved in making two high-spirited boys appear in a tunic fit only for women. But I can hardly think, with Dr. Hefele, that a dalmatic worn by an emperor *under a super-vestment* (*toga, pallium,* or *lacerna*), would have been thought an outrage upon propriety in the third century of our era.

* We hear elsewhere of a "byrrhus" as the secular dress of bishops, and others of the clergy. St. Augustine (*Serm. de Diversis*, ccclvi., tom.

v. p. 1579, *sqq.*), for example, says, that he could not wear a *byrrhus pretiosus*, even if it were given him. A byrrhus of costly material *might perchance be fitting for a bishop*, but not fitting for Augustine, "*hominem pauperem de pauperibus natum.*" If good folk wished to give him what he should actually wear, it must be such as he could wear "without blushing." If it were more than this, he should sell it, and put the money into the common stock. For other references, see Raynaudus, *De Pilis*, &c., p. 1285. The *word* byrrhus, in older Latin *burrus*, is probably the Greek πυρρός. So St. Isidore, Orig. lib. xix. cap. 24. *Birrus a Graeco vocabulum trabit: illi enim birrum bibrum* [*leg.* πυρρὸν] *dicunt*.

* See Chapter II., p. vii., *sqq.*

that a bishop, in so important a place as Carthage, would habitually wear a long and stately tunic, like the Dalmatic, which even ordinary persons would at times assume, on occasions of unusual solemnity. And when worn, as by St. Cyprian, with a super-vestment over it, it would at once become appropriate to a solemn occasion, and to a person of dignified rank.

That the use of the Dalmatic, as a tunic of ceremony for state officials, and other such, continued at Rome itself side by side with its ecclesiastical use, we have proof afforded in the description [β] given by John the deacon, of the dress worn by Gordianus, a senator, father of St. Gregory the Great [see Pl. XXV]. That double usage, secular and ecclesiastical, has continued ever since. A Dalmatic is still worn as one of the imperial and royal coronation robes, both on the Continent and in England. Of its use as an ecclesiastical vestment, in ancient and in modern times, we proceed now to speak.

The earliest traditions [γ] on the subject go back to the time of Constantine. Sylvester, then Bishop of Rome, is said to have ordered that the deacons should wear Dalmatics in place of the *colobia*, which had previously been in use in offices of holy ministry. The fullest account of the subject is that of Rabanus Maurus (*infra*, p. 106, *sqq.*), written about the middle of the ninth century. He says, that "In the earliest times mass was performed in the dress of ordinary life, as some Easterns are said to do even to this day. But

---

β Joan Diac. Vita S. Gregor. lib. iv. cap. 84. *Gordiano . . . castanei coloris Planeta, sub Planeta Dalmatica, in pedibus caligæ.*

γ See Rabanus Maurus (*infra*, p. 88), *De Inst. Cler.* lib i., 7 and 20; Amalarius *De Eccl. Off.* lib. ii. cap. 21 (*infra*, p. 99), and note 103, p. 105); Alcuinus *De Div. Off.* (*infra*,

p. 116); Honorius of Autun (*infra*, p. 137.) With these agrees Anastasius, drawing as he did from the same sources as the early writers above quoted. *De Vit. Pontif.* p. 105. In S. Sylvestro. "*Hic constituit ut diaconi Dalmatica uterentur in ecclesia, et pallio linostimo læva eorum tegeretur.*"

Stephanus,² twenty-fourth Pope, directed that priests and Levites should not employ their sacred vestments in the ordinary usage of daily life, but reserve²¹³ them exclusively for the Church. And Sylvester ordained, that deacons should wear Dalmatics in Church, and cover their left hands with a pallium²¹⁴ of mixed linen and wool. And at first (*primo*), before Chasubles came into use, those of the priestly order wore Dalmatics. But afterwards, when they had begun to wear Chasubles, they conceded the use of Dalmatics to deacons. And yet, that pontiffs themselves sought to wear Dalmatics, is clear from this, that Gregory ᵉ and other Roman primates ᶜ allowed the use of them to some bishops, forbade it in the case of others. And from this we may gather that in those days that was not matter of general privilege, which now almost all bishops, and some presbyters, regard as their right, to wit, the wearing of a Dalmatic under the Chasuble."

This account, compared with the original passage quoted by Anastasius from the *Gesta Pontificum* (note γ, p. lvii), leaves some questions still open to doubt. Both writers agree in stating that St. Sylvester's ordinance had special reference to *deacons*. And it is *possible*, therefore, that the Dalmatic, or full-sleeved tunic, may have been worn by bishops and priests in the Roman Church, at an earlier period. And so some writers ᵃ have maintained. But it appears more probable that the fuller tunic was assigned to the deacons,ᶠ because they

---

δ *Sed.* 253-257.

ε See, for example, the letter quoted *infra*, p. 67.

ζ So Pope Zachary (*sed.* 741-752), writing to Austrobert, Bishop of Vienne: *Dalmaticam usibus vestris misimus, ut, quia ecclesia vestra ab hac sede doctrinam Fidei percepit, et morem habitus sacerdotalis, ab illa etiam accipiat decorem honoris.* For Pope Symmachus, at a much earlier date, see below note *i*.

ε Visconti *De Apparatu Missæ*, lib. iii. cap. 25. Du Saussay, *Panoplia Episc.* lib. vi. cap. 3 and 4. *Apud* Martigny, D. A. C. *in voc.* Dalmatique.

ϝ With this would agree again the concession of the Dalmatic to the *deacons* of the Church of Arles, by Pope Symmachus (*sed.* 498-514). [*Vita Cæsarii Arelat. apud* Baron. Annal. tom. vi. p. 601, *ad ann.* 508]. " Ipse Pontifex præclara ejus (*sc.* S.

wore no fuper-veftment, fo that the fcantinefs of the older *colobium* was in their cafe fpecially confpicuous.

However this may be, it is clear that, as late as the eighth century, the Dalmatic, as a veftment of Chriftian miniftry, was regarded as fpecially belonging to the Roman Church; and that it was only by fpecial privilege from Rome (or by invafion of that privilege) that it was worn in any of the diocefes fubject to the Roman See.

With this accords the fact, noticed by foreign ritualifts,[1] that, with fpecial exceptions only, the Dalmatic was not worn in the Gallican Church till, in the time of Hadrian I., her own Liturgy was difplaced (under preffure from the Crown) by that which was in ufe at Rome.

One word muft be faid, in conclufion, as to the ornaments of the Dalmatic at this period. From a paffage of St. Ifidore (quoted below at p. 74), it has been inferred by fome, that that all Dalmatics had *clavi* or ornamental ftripes, of *purple*.[a] But this is evidently a miftake. Of the very few ecclefiaftical Dalmatics, earlier than the year 600, whofe date[λ] and whofe colour I have been able to determine, none have any other than black ftripes. And even if exceptions fhould be found, no more would be proved than that the *clavi* of fuch dalmatics *might* be purple. The fhort notices of words like "*dalmatica*," which have been preferved to us by S. Ifidore, are often copied ftraight down from Scholiafts on Plautus,

---

Cæfarii) meritorum dignitate permotus, non folum eum veriffime Metropolitani honore præditum voluit, fed etiam fpeciali quodam privilegio pallii ufum ei permifit, et *diaconos ejus perinde ac Romanæ Ecclefiæ diaconos Dalmaticis uti voluit.*"

[1] Martigny D. A. C. *in voc.* Dalmatique.

[a] Dr. Hefele, who is generally very exact, has been led into error as to the colour of the *clavi* on the Dalmatics in the Ravenna mofaic (Pl. XXVIII). They are black, not purple, as he fuppofes. See p. 206 of his treatife.

[λ] A mofaic, of which there is a coloured drawing in the Windfor collection, reprefents the Apoftles with red *clavi* upon their tunics. This mofaic dates from the year 640, and is the earlieft which I have found fo ornamented.

Terence, and other old writers, and are not in all cafes to be regarded as the refults of careful refearch of his own. This being fo, I think it not impoffible, [μ] that his account (p. 74, note 131) of the Dalmatic (a veftment which does not appear to have been ufed in Spain) may be derived from fome fuch older fource; and that the word *facerdotalis* may have referred (when originally penned by its actual author) to a tunic of heathen priefthood, fuch as we have feen to have been in not unfrequent ufe.

## 2. THE PÆNULA, CASULA, AND PLANETA.

Moft writers on ritual affume that the three words, with which this fection is headed, are but different names for one and the fame garment. There are many queftions of intereft involved in the inquiry whether this affumption is well grounded, or no. And I propofe therefore to ftate here the general refults of a careful inveftigation of the hiftory of thefe three words; and to fet out in full, in an Appendix,[,] the evidence upon which thofe refults have been reached.

### THE PÆNULA.

I give precedence to the Pænula, as being, in all probability, far the oldeft word of the three. We have *direct* evidence that garments, called by this name, were in ufe in Italy from the third[ξ] century before Chrift, to the fifth[•] century of our era. In the Eaft the φαινόλης (the fame word

---

[μ] A contrary opinion to this is expreffed in note 131, p. 74. But that note was written a year ago, when the writer knew lefs of St. Ifidore's mode of working than he does now. See

Appendix A, Nos. 12, 13, 14.
[,] See Appendix C.
[ξ] Appendix C, No. 1.
[•] Appendix C, No. 22. Compare what is faid under No. 23 and 25.

under another form) has had a still wider range. We hear of it first in a writer[r] of the fourth century B.C., but then in a context which implies a belief, that such a garment was in use "*ante Agamemnona.*" And the same word, in its Byzantine form (note 153) having been adopted in the East, at an early period,[s] as the designation for the super-vestment worn in offices of Christian ministry, survives even to this day, both in the Greek Church itself, and, with slight modifications, in other Churches of the East.[t]

Deferring, for the present, any further reference to its use in the East, we shall do well to note here those points only in the history of the Pænula, which will illustrate its relation to the Planeta or Casula, the "Chasuble" of Western usage.

And, first, for its form. Whether, in the later times of the Roman empire, the primitive form of this garment was always exactly adhered to, may reasonably be doubted. But this at least is certain, that the prevailing idea, connected with this word, was that of a garment which so completely enveloped the whole person, as to interfere entirely with active exertion of the arms. It was probably much such a cloak as the "poncho," which was in fashion in England not many years ago; with this addition, however, that it was furnished with a hood (as such outdoor garments for common use generally were) for protection of the head, if need were, from cold or wet. This primitive shape of the garment is probably that which was long retained in the East (as it still is, I believe, in many parts of it), and which may be seen represented

---

[r] Rhinthon, quoted by Julius Pollux. See Appendix C, No. 16.

[s] The earliest *direct* evidence of such adoption, as far as I know, is the passage of Patriarch Germanus, referred to in Appendix C, No. 24.

[t] In the Syriac Liturgies φαινόλιον appears as Fainó, Filono, or Phaino. [Isá-Bar-Hali, quoted by Renaudot, *Lit. Orient.* Coll. ii. p. 55.] In the Arabic version of the Coptic Liturgies it is generally *Albornos*, "The Burnous," with which we are more or less familiar. But in Sclavonic the Greek word reappears as *Pheloni.*

[r] See Appendix C, No. 3; and compare No. 16, and note 396.

in Pl. LVIII., No. 1 (St. Sampson). But in the West it is very possible that the older form may have been so far modified, that a garment such as that shown in Pl. V. *bis* (No. 5), may really be intended for a Pænula, as most antiquaries believe.

We have abundant evidence in Roman literature of the uses to which the Pænula served, and of its gradual exaltation in dignity from a garb of slaves or of peasants[φ] to one which even emperors[χ] might wear in travelling, and which was expressly prescribed, in the fifth century of our era, as the dress of senators.[ψ]

A Pænula, of some kind, was from very early times recognised as the proper dress for travellers.[ω] But to wear a Pænula *as an ordinary dress*, in the city, would, in republican times, have been regarded as a grave breach of etiquette on the part of any one who pretended to the character of a gentleman. But the use of the Pænula in rainy or very cold weather, as an outer cloak to be worn over the ordinary dress, had in the first century of our era become well established even in Rome.[α] Yet even in the second century of our era the older plebeian associations still clung about it, so that an emperor[β] could not appear in such a dress in the city, be the weather what it would. In the third century[γ] a special permission was given by the Emperor Alexander Severus, by which senators were allowed to wear the Pænula in cold weather, even *intra Urbem*. But the same decree forbade its use by ladies, except when on a journey. It is not till yet two hundred years later[δ] (A.D. 438) that we find

---

v See Octavius Ferrarius, p. 831; Bartolus Bartolinus, *De Pænula*, cap. iv.; Weiss, Kostümkunde im Mittelalter, p. 14, fig. 8.

φ Of slaves, Appendix C, No. 1; of peasants, Appendix C, No. 4 (compare No. 9).

χ See Ferrarius D. R. V. pars ii. lib. ii. cap. 5.

ψ Appendix C, No. 22.
ω Appendix C, Nos. 3, 5, 15.
α Appendix C, Nos. 7, 12, 13.
β Appendix C. No. 13.
γ Appendix C, No. 15.
δ Appendix C, No. 22.

the Pænula formally inftalled, in the place of the older toga, as the diftinctive garment of peaceful dignity, and as fuch to be worn by fenators, to the exclufion of the warlike "terrors" affociated with the *chlamys*.[142]

An important queftion now arifes, Was this Pænula the fuper-veftment adopted by the Weftern Church as the diftinctive garb of bifhops and priefts in the higheft offices of Chriftian miniftry? By the Weftern Church *in Apoftolic times*, or in the centuries immediately fucceeding, moft undoubtedly it was not. The proof of this may be feen in the Appendix.[1] And to what is there ftated I may add here, that I have neither feen alleged by others, nor have I myfelf found, one paffage of any Latin writer from the firft century to the fourteenth, in which mention is made of the Pænula as the proper name of a veftment of Chriftian miniftry. But, on the other hand, the ufage of the *phænolion* by the Greek Church, and early monuments of ecclefiaftical drefs in the Weft, fuch as thofe in Pl. XXVIII., XXX., and XXXI., lead to the conclufion, that the fuper-veftment worn in the fixth century, though called Planeta, was not unlike *in form* to the Pænula of which we have been fpeaking. And it is of courfe *poffible* that, in fome local churches, the name Pænula may really have been employed rather than Planeta, as a defignation for this veftment. All that can be faid is that no evidence has ever yet been alleged to prove that fuch was the cafe.

## The Casula.

There is no certain evidence of the word *cafula* ever being employed in fpeaking of a veftment of Chriftian miniftry before the ninth century of our era. If, therefore, the arrangement adopted in this treatife were ftrictly adhered to, this word would firft come under difcuffion at a later period

---

[1] See Appendix C, under No. 17.

than the present. But it will be convenient to give the earlier history of the word in this place, in order to make it clear how the Casula stands related to the Planeta and the Pænula.

And, first, for the origin of the word. There is no doubt that the derivation given by St. Isidore is the true one.[ζ] He regards it (see p. 74, note 130) as a diminutive of "*casa*," "a little house," or "hut." And we find, in point of fact, that the word had in his time the meaning of a "hut," or "booth,"[130] side by side with that of a garment, which is its more common meaning.

As regards its primitive shape we have no certain evidence to guide us, in respect of the first eight centuries, because, as far as we can now judge, the super-vestments in the monuments of ecclesiastical dress, dating from the sixth and seventh centuries, would have been originally called *Planetæ*, and not Chasubles. But there is a strong probability that *in form* the Casula of earlier times differed but little,* if at all, from the Planeta and the Pænula. What difference there was consisted chiefly in material, and possibly in ornament; the Casula being in those older days a garb chiefly worn by the poor, and, because worn by the poor, therefore also by monks. [Appendix C, No. 26, 28, 32, 33.]

---

[ζ] A passage of Philo Judæus, *De Victimis* (quoted by Alb. Rubenius D. R. V. lib. i. cap. 6) contains a curious anticipation of this application of the term *casula*, to a cloak. αὐγὰς δὲ αἱ τρίχες αἱ (leg. καὶ) δοραὶ συνυφαινόμεναι τε καὶ συββαπτόμεναι, φορηταὶ γεγόνασιν ἰδιαιτέραις οἰκίαι, καὶ μάλιστα τοῖς ἐν στρατιαῖς, οὓς ἔξω πόλεως ἐν ὑπαίθρῳ διατρίβειν ἀναγκάζουσιν αἱ χρείαι τὰ πολλά. He is evidently describing the φαινόλης, which in his time was in use in the East as well as in Greece and Italy. And by speaking of it as "*a portable house*" for travellers, he makes it very probable that he was acquainted with the term *casula*, as employed in the *lingua vulgaris* for the same garment, by the Latin-speaking peoples.

* Among other points of resemblance the older Casula was, like the Pænula, a *vestis cucullata*, provided with a cowl or hood for the protection of the head. See the quotation from St. Isidore, p. 74. *Casula est vestis cucullata, &c.* And see, further, Appendix C, No. 38.

## The Casula.

In the Appendix will be found all the earliest notices that have been preserved to us, having reference to the Casula. And their general result, it will be seen, is this. The word was originally used of a garment worn, in outdoor use, by men of the lower class,[1] as a protection against cold and wet. The same word was occasionally employed (in the African provinces at least) in speaking of the cloak worn for similar purposes by persons in somewhat higher station. Thus St. Augustine employs the word, in one place, in speaking of the outdoor garment worn by a journeyman tailor at Hippo (before his own time). At another time, speaking to an ordinary congregation (Sermo CVII.), he expresses his wonder that when men are careful that every thing about them should be good of its kind, they care not that their own souls should be so also. "Thou choosest not a bad house, but a good one,— nor a bad wife, but a good one,— nor a bad Casula, or a bad shoe,— and why then art thou content that thine own soul be bad?" (See Appendix C, Nos. 26 and 27).

The *Casula* was also, from the sixth to the eighth century, recognised as the characteristic dress of monks; and was worn, in outdoor dress, by many bishops, and by the clergy generally. St. Boniface (Appendix C, No. 36) in Council prescribed it as the proper out-door dress of the clergy (note 416), forbidding the use of the Sagum, or short cloak worn by the laity. (Appendix C, Nos. 27, 28, 29, 31.)

Lastly, at the beginning of the ninth century,[2] we find the word Casula used for the first time, as a designation for the vestment previously known as *Planeta*; and from that time, down to the present, the word Casula has in common usage almost superseded the older term.

---

[1] See Appendix C, Nos. 27 and 32.  [2] See p. 203, note 420.

## The Planeta.

This last-named vestment is that with which we are more properly concerned in reference to the transition period, between the fourth and the ninth centuries.

We hear of the Planeta first in the fifth century, and again in the seventh (see Appendix C, Nos. 38 and 42), as a dress too costly to be worn by monks. And with this agree later notices, from which (Appendix C, Nos. 39 and 41) we find that it was worn by laymen of rank, both in Rome itself and in the African Provinces, in the course of the sixth century of our era.[*]

The first mention of it as worn in offices of Christian ministry is found in the Acts of the Council of Toledo, early in the seventh century (see p. 75). But we find it there spoken of not as any new thing, but as the recognised habit of bishops and presbyters, distinguishing them from the deacons, who wore an alb only.

St. Isidore, who presided at that Council, and whose pen may be clearly traced (note 133) in the record of its acts, has given elsewhere a derivation of the word Planeta. In an enumeration of a great variety of garments worn in ordinary life, he comes to the mention of "*Casula*" already noticed. And he proceeds in the same sentence (see p. 74) as follows. "The Casula is a garment provided with a cowl, the name being a diminutive from '*casa*,' a house, because, like a little house, it covers the whole man. . . . . In like manner, people say that in Greek *Planetæ* are so called, because the border of the Planeta 'wanders' in vague lines about the body. For which cause some stars are called 'Planetæ,' as implying that their movements are erratic and divergent." Rabanus Maurus, in the ninth century, while adopting verbatim (see p. 91) St. Isidore's derivation of the

---

[*] See, further, Appendix C, Nos. 40, 42, 44, 45.

word *Casula*, says, expressly, "*hanc (sc.* Casulam) *Græci Planetam vocant*," identifying, distinctly, the *Casula* and the *Planeta*. In so identifying them he was so far right, that *in his own time* the distinction between the two was no longer recognised. But in the sixth and seventh centuries it is evident that they were distinguished, the *Casula* as the *humbler* and *simpler* dress, proper to poor men and to monks (Appendix C, No. 26); the Planeta as the handsomer and more costly habit, worn in ordinary life at Rome, alike by senators and by popes (Appendix C, No. 41); and in Spain certainly, if not elsewhere, the distinctive vestment of bishops and presbyters.

The form of the Planeta (as an episcopal vestment), at that time, may be seen in Pl. XXVIII., compared with Pl. XXX. and XXXI., and to these we may add Pl. XXV., in which St. Gregory and his father Gordianus, a Roman senator, are both represented as wearing a Planeta.

SUMMARY OF EVIDENCE RELATING TO PÆNULA, CASULA, AND PLANETA, IN THE TRANSITION PERIOD.

On a review of the whole evidence as to these three garments, we arrive at the following conclusions.

First, that in general form the three differed little, if at all, the one from the other. But there is no evidence to show that a vestment of Christian ministry was ever called Pænula in the Latin Churches; nor *Casula* before the ninth century. That till about the close of the eighth century, "Planeta" was the name given to the super-vestment of Christian ministry, which in form and in use corresponded to what at a later time was known as the Chasuble (*Casula*).

That all these garments were worn, in ordinary life, by laymen as well as by ecclesiastics; the Planeta, however, as worn by laymen, being regarded, in all probability, as a mark of official dignity.

### 3. The Orarium (the later "Stole.")

1. In the Acts of the Council of Toledo, which we have taken as our starting-point for the present period, we find the Orarium recognised as a distinctly ministerial vestment, worn by bishops, presbyters, and deacons; the Orarium of the deacon, however, being worn upon one (the left) shoulder only.

Whence this word Orarium, and what the origin of the vestment so called? To these questions such reply as *can* be given will appear upon consideration of the following facts.

For the origin and derivation of the word itself, we must look not to the technical connotations of the word, whether secular or ecclesiastical, but to what is older than these technicalities, the common usage of the word as a term of ordinary speech. So guided, we shall probably be right in thinking, that the word is connected with *os*, the mouth (of which *or* is the real root-form), or, in its plural form, *ora*, the face; and regard the term as originally equivalent to our own "handkerchief." (See Appendix E, No. 1).

But of the passages, *now extant*, in which the word occurs, those of earliest date (Appendix E, No. 1 *b*) employ it in a somewhat technical sense. We first hear of it in the pages of Trebellius Pollio, a writer of the fourth century, and a contemporary of Constantine. According to him the Emperor Gallienus (Imp. 260–268) sent to Claudius (his successor in the empire) as an imperial present, four *oraria sarabdena*. Not very many years later we hear of Aurelian (Imp. 270–275) being "the first who distributed *oraria* as presents to the people, to be used by them '*ad favorem*,'" *i.e.*, probably as colours to be worn and waved at the circus, on occasion of public games, much in the same way as ribands of various colours are worn now, '*ad favorem*,' among ourselves, whether as emblems of political party, or (in contexts of another kind) of rival univerſities, or of rival ſchools.

Once more. At a period not very long ſubſequent to that laſt named, we find, upon the Arch of Conſtantine (ſee Pl. IV.), a repreſentation of the Emperor and his attendant courtiers; and of theſe latter many are diſtinguiſhed by a broad riband, or ſcarf, worn over their other dreſs, preſenting nearly the appearance of the "riband" of the Order of Knighthood, ſtill worn as an honorary diſtinction in our own times. And the ſcarf, or broad riband, ſo worn, *correſponds, in general appearance, to the Orarium of the earlieſt eccleſiaſtical monuments* in which this veſtment is repreſented (ſee Pl. XXVIII., XXX., XXXI.), though in point of arrangement ſome difference is obſervable.

In another Roman monument (not eccleſiaſtical), of which an engraving is given by Boiſſardus, a ſimilar "ſcarf" is ſeen worn over the reſt of the dreſs by two of the principal perſonages repreſented. But here the arrangement differs conſiderably from that ſeen in the plates, reproduced in this Work, to which reference has juſt been made; and approaches very cloſely to the form of the later archiepiſcopal pallium, as it may be ſeen in Pl. XXV., XLII., &c.

To theſe facts ſhould be added that to which I here allude by anticipation, viz. the uſe of *pallia linoſtima*,^ or cloths partly of linen and partly of wool, employed at Rome from the time of S. Sylveſter, as diſtinctive inſignia of deacons; and the carrying of an ἐγχείριον, a napkin, or towel, to ſimilar purpoſe, by deacons in the Eaſt.

And with all theſe facts before us we ſhall probably not

---

^ See note 214, p. 108. The ſame words are employed (being taken from the ſame ſource) by Anaſtaſius, De V. R. P. p. 105. But this writer records a preciſely ſimilar order made by Zoſimus (*ſed.* 417 A.D.): *Hic multas conſtituit eccleſias, et fecit conſtitutum ut diaconi lævas tectas haberent* [*hora ſacrificii*, ſo one MS.] *de pallis* (ſic) *linoſtimis, et per parochias conceſſa licentia cereos benedici.*

do wrong in concluding, that the use of "*oraria*," of "*pallia linostima*" (mappulæ or *manipuli*), of the *pallium pontificium*, in the West—of ὠράριον, ἐγχείριον, ὠμοφόριον, in the East—are all instances of the adaptation, with certain modifications, to Christian use, as distinctive insignia in the church, of what had been previously used in secular life as marks of special privilege, or of official dignity.

The fact that the date of these adaptations, both in East and West, is not earlier than that of the "peace of the church," so called, in the time of Constantine, adds considerably to the probability of this conjecture, because of the more fully developed organisation which then first became possible.

We need only add that the vestment now known in the Western Church as a "Stole," was called "Orarium" (not Stole) till the close of the Transition Period. It is in accordance with this fact that the Greek word στολή is never used in the Latin sense of a "Stole," but retains, in ecclesiastical and Byzantine Greek, its older classical meaning. [Note 141, p 83.]

#### 4. THE MAPPULA AND PAPAL PALLIUM.

The three vestments already described, the Alb (or the Dalmatic, as the case might be), the Planeta, and the Orarium, these alone can be described as vestments of Christian ministry, properly so called, recognised in the West during the Transition Period. But a few words must here be said of two vestments, connected more especially with the Roman Church, viz. the *Mappula* and the Papal Pallium.

From two letters on the subject of the Mappula, which are quoted in the Second Part of this work (pp. 65 and 66), we learn that, even before St. Gregory's time, a custom had obtained, that the clergy of the Metropolitan City should carry *Mappulæ*. The Roman clergy considered this a distinctive privilege, to which no other church could lay claim;

and resented extremely the pretension to a similar right put forward by the clergy of Ravenna. St. Gregory, by way of appeasing the strife, gave his consent at last that the principal deacons of the Church of Ravenna should wear them, but only when in attendance, on ceremonial occasions, upon the archbishop. Compare Appendix C, No. 40, and note 418.

The matter is only so far of importance, that it illustrates a tendency of which we find many instances at a later time. At Rome, the centre of the wealth, the luxury, the power, of the older empire, special developments of outward dress and insignia were brought about from time to time; and for the very reason that these were connected, at first, with the seat of government, and of the "Apostolic see," the clergy of other churches became desirous of the like distinctions, and so the example set at Rome was sooner or later followed in the West generally. This we shall find to have been the case with the Mappula of which now we are speaking. The Maniple, which, to the eyes of Latin writers of the ninth century, was one of the "sacred vestments" of Christian ministry, was but a development of this earlier *Mappula*.

A far greater historical importance attaches to the "Pallium," in that new, and exclusively ecclesiastical sense, in which we find it employed from the fifth century downward. Of the ordinary meaning of the word we have already had occasion to speak. (Note π, p. xii).

But the "Pallium" now in question is that known as the Papal or archiepiscopal Pallium, the earliest form of which may be seen in Pl. XXVIII, the latest* in Pl. LXI. (No.

---

\* The successive variations in the form of the Papal Pallium may be traced in the following among the illustrations of this volume. For the beginning of the ninth century, see above, p. lii, compared with Pl. XXXIII. and XL.; for the tenth century, Pl. XLII. (probably, also, XXXIX.) and XLIII.; for the eleventh, Pl. XLIV.; for the twelfth, the figures of popes in Pl. XLV. and XLVI. From the representation of the modern Pallium, given in Pl. LXI., and of the "Orfrey" of the

16). The monuments lately difcovered by De Roffi in the Roman Catacombs (fee Pl. XXX., XXXI.), and which date, probably, from the eighth century, will fhow what, during this tranfition period, was reputed to have been the primitive form of this veftment. As there fhown, it is fimply *a white orarium worn outfide the planeta*, and croffed over the left hand, fo as to keep it from actual contact with the Book of the Gofpels, then the traditional infignia of a bifhop. It is very poffible that in the frefcoes in queftion it is an Orarium (and not a Pallium) which the painter defigned to reprefent. If he were accurately acquainted with the epifcopal drefs of the third century which he had to reprefent, he would no doubt have faid (and faid with truth) that it would have been an anachronifm for him to reprefent, in a drefs of *that time*, a veftment fuch as the Papal Pallium, which was then unknown to the Church.

We have only to confider for a moment the contraſt between the pofition of the Church in the firft three centuries, and that to which fhe attained after the age of Conftantine, in order to fee why the Papal Pallium, as a diftinctive veftment, fhould not have been known in that earlier period. While the empire was in antagonifm to the Church, as it was till the time of Conftantine, it was not in the nature of things that a completely organifed hierarchical fyftem fhould be developed, by the formal aggregation of diocefes into metropolitan provinces, the fubordination of metropolitans to patriarchs, of patriarchs to an œcumenical patriarch, or to the " Apoftolic fee." We find, accordingly, that the veftments worn in that earlier period were veftments for bifhops, prefbyters, deacons, the three orders of the Chriftian miniftry which had exifted from the very firft. But

---

prieſt's Chafuble fhown in the fame plate, it will be feen that the latter far more nearly refembles in fize and general appearance the Pallium of the eleventh century, than does the Pallium itfelf as now worn by an archbifhop.

from the period of the "peace of the church" under Conſtantine, the Chriſtian hierarchy was developed in two directions—downwards in reſpect of the minor orders, ſubdeacons, acolytes, readers, and the like,—upwards, in a graduated aſcent, which, by ſlow degrees, and with much, at times, of even bitter conteſt, culminated at length in the recognition of the Biſhop of Conſtantinople in "New Rome," as ecumenical Patriarch in the Eaſt, and of the Biſhop of Rome as having firſt place in precedence among all the patriarchal ſees throughout the world. And it is in accordance with theſe facts that we find ſo many of the early councils, in the latter part of the fourth century, occupying themſelves with the regulation of diſtinctive veſtments, or inſignia, ſuch as marked off, on the one hand, the poſition of the deacon, as one to be diſtinguiſhed even in outward ſemblance (by the wearing of an orarium) from that of the minor orders; and, on the other hand, ſerved to diſtinguiſh Metropolitans and Patriarchs from the ſuffragan biſhops of their reſpective provinces.

## Ministering Vestments in the East.

What has been already ſaid of the various veſtments recogniſed in the Weſt during the Period of Tranſition (400 to 800 A.D.), will apply, with ſlight modifications only, to thoſe of the Eaſt.

The veſtments recogniſed at this time were the Sticharion, correſponding to the Alb, or rather to the Dalmatic

---

[1] For the *word* ſee note 346, p. 169. I may add, however, that as one meaning of στοῖχος is a "line," it is not improbable that this veſtment may have been ſo called from the λῶριa (note 146), or coloured ſtripes, by which it was decorated. We hear of the Sticharion as a veſtment of holy miniſtry as early as the time of S. Athanaſius.

of the West; the Phænolion,[f] answering to the Planeta (the later "Chasuble"); and the Orarium,[e] a term common to both East and West in respect of the deacon's Scarf (or "Stole"), Pl. LIX., but which was known as Peritrachelion, or Epitrachelion, when worn pendent round the neck by bishops or priests. See Pl. LVI., No. 1, and the description.

And as we hear of Mappula and Pallium (see above, p. lxx) in the West, so also of ἐγχείριον (Napkin or Towel), and Omophorion in the East. This last vestment, from the fifth century, if not from an earlier time, down to the present, has been worn by Patriarchs and Metropolitans, and by almost all bishops in the East. And if the reader will compare the consular dress, represented in Pl. XXIII., with that attributed to Patriarchs in Pl. XLI., LVIII., and to St. James in Pl. LXIII., he will see how close is the resemblance between the distinctive ornament of the two costumes. On the dress, too, of Emperors of the East, a similar ornament is conspicuous. And there can be little doubt that the imperial (or consular) Omophorion was the type upon which the patriarchal Omophorion was formed.

The passages from early writers, of chief importance, bearing upon the ecclesiastical dress of the East at this period, will be found in the later pages [r] of this volume.

The art-monuments dating from before 800 A.D. are but few. Those from the Church of St. George at Thessalonica,

---

[f] Called φιλόνιον by St. Germanus. See p. 84, note 143. For various forms of the Eastern φιλόνιον, at various times, see Plates XVIII., XIX., XX., XXVII., XLI., and the figure of St. Sampson in Pl. LVIII. Several Phænolia, attributed by tradition to bishops or patriarchs of the twelfth and following centuries, are accurately depicted in the first volume of the *Antiquités de l'Empire Russe*.

[e] See note 144.

[r] See St. Isidore of Pelusium, p. 94; St. Chrysostom, or the author who bears his name (see note 94), p. 51; St. Germanus, p. 82; and with these compare St. Symeon of Thessalonica, p. 168.

some of which are figured in this volume (Pl. XVIII., XIX., XX., XXI.), do not represent a dress of holy ministry, but of dignity, common, with very slight modifications only, to priests and people alike. These mosaics date, probably, from the fourth century. Two centuries later in date are the mosaics of the great Church (St. Sophia) at Constantinople. And among those which, from their position, have escaped destruction at the hands of the Turks, are some *e* of bishops of the fourth century, dressed in white *f* vestments (Sticharion and Phænolion), and with an Omophorion, resembling in form that attributed to St. James, in the fresco reproduced in Pl. LXIII.

Upon a review of the whole evidence, literary *g* and monumental, bearing upon the question, we should conclude that the sacred vestments, recognised in the Greek Church in the eighth century, were the Sticharion, Girdle, Orarium,*h*

---

*e* See Salzenberg's *Alt-Christliche Baudenkmale*. Pl. XXVIII. and XXIX. The bishops represented are Anthenios, Bishop of Nicomedia, † 311; Basileios (St. Basil the Great), † 379; Dionysius the Areopagite, † 96; Nicolaus, Bishop of Myra (one of the 318 at Micæa), † 330; and Gregorius of Armenia, † 325.

The Church of St. Sophia was built 532–538 A.D., and the mosaics are of the same date.

*f* The dress closely resembles that attributed to St. James in Pl. LXIII., with this difference only, that in every case the Sticharion, or long tunic, has double stripes on either side, and running round the sleeve, this latter fitting closely round the wrist, instead of being full and loose as is the sleeve of the Roman dalmatic. In five out of the six figures, the *lora*, or stripes, are two lines of purple and red; in one (that of Gregory of Armenia) of red only. The crosses on the Omophorion correspond in colour, in every case, to those of the *lora*.

*g* The passage of St. Germanus, quoted at p. 82, *sqq.* presents some difficulty owing to his mixing up the mention of garments worn in holy ministry with those of ordinary usage, such as the Mandyas,[152] and the Cowl.[151]

*h* The ἰθὼν mentioned by St. Germanus (p. 86, note 154) as a part of the deacon's dress, is probably only another name for the Orarion, having reference to the material (linen) of which it was formed. The word is evidently so used in the passage, attributed to St. Chrysostom, quoted at p. 49, note 78.

and (ἐγχείριον*) Napkin, for deacons; the Sticharion, Girdle, Phænolion, and Peritrachelion, for priests; while the bishop, over and above these, wore an Omophorion as his distinguishing badge.

---

* The ἐγχείριον, mentioned by St. Germanus, as carried by the deacon, suspended from his Girdle, may have been of local use only, as was, at one time, the Mappula at Rome. But the use of the ἐγχείριον died out (or at least the mention of it as thus carried by the deacon); but that of the Mappula spread by degrees throughout the Western Churches.

From the Roma Subterranea of Aringhi.

## CHAPTER VIII.

### THE THIRD PERIOD, FROM THE YEAR 800 A.D. TO THE PRESENT TIME.

We attain now to well-trodden ground, and have for the first time ample materials for our guidance, in contemporary monuments, both of literature and of art, such as those published in the later pages of this volume.

These have been so arranged in chronological order as to tell, in great measure, their own tale. A few words only are needed by way of preliminary remark.

One who takes a review of the literature of the eighth and the ninth centuries can scarcely fail to remark, how rapid, in the later period of the two, was the succession of writers upon subjects mainly relating to ritual. It is not difficult, on reflection, to account for this being so. The restoration of peace to Europe, consequent upon the victories of Charlemagne, gave men leisure for a devotion to study, which had been all but impossible amid the wars and rumours of wars, by which for nearly four hundred years the minds of men had been distracted. The example, too, and the liberal patronage of that monarch, favoured the interests of letters; and new schools of learning were founded both in France and Germany, under the auspices of our countryman Alcuin, or of such worthy inheritors of his learning as Rabanus Maurus[153] and Walafrid Strabo[154].

The circumstances of the time account for the direction then given to literary activity. It was not unnatural that in the Carlovingian age the minds of earnest men, shocked by the contemplation of the awful corruption, both in Church and State, which everywhere met their gaze, should turn back with fond and reverential affection to the earlier and purer ages of the Church; and in the writings of those whom they, like ourselves, spoke of as "the Fathers," seek for guidance in building up anew the ruined fabric of the Church.

To causes such as these may probably be traced the sudden outburst, early in the ninth century, of a new spirit of inquiry into all that concerned the discipline and the ritual of the Church. And the question of vestments was one which naturally, at that time, assumed a special prominence. Churchmen, who had travelled widely, as then some did, in East as well as West, could hardly fail to notice the remarkable fact, that at Constantinople as at Rome, at Canterbury as at Arles, Vienna or Lyons, one general type of ministering dress was maintained, varying only in some minor details; and that this dress everywhere presented a most marked contrast[x] to what was *in their time* the prevailing dress of the laity. And as all knowledge[↓] of classical antiquity had for three centuries or more been well-nigh extinct in the Church, it was not less

---

[x] See this illustrated in pictures dating from the ninth or tenth century, such as those in Pl. XXXVII. and XLIII.

[↓] At the close of the sixth century St. Gregory writes to a bishop in Gaul, saying that he cannot send him the Pallium till he gives up studying Grammar and teaching it to others (Ep. xi. 54). He himself, as he tells us, *knew nothing of Greek;* and at Constantinople in his time there was no one who knew enough of Latin to translate one of his letters intelligibly (Ep. vii. xxx). With a few rare exceptions this ignorance of Greek continued in the West, till the fall of Constantinople, in the fifteenth century, sent learned Greeks for a refuge into Italy, and so contributed powerfully to the restoration of learning, and the reformation of Western Christendom. When a Roman Cardinal spoke in Greek (or in what passed for Greek) at the Council of Florence, A.D. 1430, it was held to be (so Raynaldus gravely tells us) clear proof of miraculous agency. I state these facts not for the purpose of casting a reproach upon the Church of past ages; but because this fact of prevailing ignorance of the ancient languages serves to explain many of the phenomena (among them some that are very painful) of the history of the Church in mediæval times.

natural that they should have sought a solution of the phenomenon thus presented to them, in a theory of Levitical origin, which, from that time forward, was generally accepted. It was not till the revival of classical learning, many centuries later, that men were led to form a truer estimate of this and of other kindred questions. The successive documents, dating from the ninth and the two following centuries, contained in the later part of this volume, show very plainly the progressive development of this theory. Thus Rabanus Maurus, perhaps the earliest of these writers, when speaking of the older Levitical vestments, and of their spiritual meaning, does but follow, as he says, in the steps of the older writers. But in what he says of the *habitus sacerdotalis* of his own day, he makes a kind of apology for speaking *secundum modulum ingenioli sui* (see note 169), as one who felt that he had entered upon new and somewhat doubtful ground. And we have only to compare the dress of a bishop of the ninth century (as in Pl. XXXVII.) with that of the Jewish high-priest (Pl. IX.), in order to see what difficulties had to be got over in identifying the one with the other. Some accordingly (as Walafrid Strabo) contented themselves with saying (p. 108) that *in number* the Christian vestments corresponded to those of the law; and with such vague resemblances as that of the "plate of gold" being worn only by the High-priest, as the pallium was worn only by chief pastors. But others, while recognising points of strong contrast[α] between the two types of dress, too obvious to be overlooked, sought, by the most far-fetched comparisons[α] to find features of likeness between them. And where this was not possible, additions[β] were made from time to time to the

---

[α] Such as the absence of *tiara* or *lamina aurea* (p. 112 and Appendix E, No. 12).

[α] As of the Amice to the Ephod (see p. 111,††4); of the Jewish Rational [a jewel of twelve precious stones worn on the breast] to the Pallium of an Archbishop (Note ††7).

[β] As of an actual jewel to represent the Rational (Note 936, p. 124, and more certainly at p. 138, Note ††3), and of a mitre with its *circulus aureus*,

"*Sacræ Veſtes*" of the Church, in order to create a ſimilarity where none had exiſted hitherto.

We find, accordingly, both in the literature and in the monuments of art, dating from the period now under conſideration, diſtinct evidence of the rapid development of the miniſtering dreſs of the Weſtern Church, from the beginning of the ninth to the end of the twelfth century.

Rabanus Maurus (p. 88), and Amalarius (p. 94), early in the ninth century, and the reputed Alcuin, probably in the tenth (p. 110, note 218), all ſpeak of eight γ veſtments as worn by biſhops, beſide the Pallium proper to archbiſhops. St. Ivo (p. 128), writing at the cloſe of the eleventh century, adds but one to the older enumeration, he being the firſt to ſpeak of the "*caligæ byſſinæ*," "leggings," or ſtockings, made of linen, as among the ſacred veſtments. But within a period of about fifty years, at the moſt, from the time of St. Ivo's writing, we find in Honorius of Autun (note 296\*, p. 142), the number of the ſacred veſtments exactly doubled. He reckons ſeven veſtments as proper to prieſts; ſeven more (fourteen in all) as belonging to biſhops; while two others, the Pallium and the Crozier, are appropriated to archbiſhops. Innocent III., by the further mention (p. 153) of a veſtment (the "*orale*" [314]), and an ornament (the pectoral croſs [315]), which he regarded as belonging excluſively to the Roman Pontiff, added yet more to the whole enumeration. And by him, accordingly, ſix veſtments are aſſigned to preſbyters, fifteen in all to biſhops, one, the Pallium, ſpecially to archbiſhops; making, with the two which he regarded as proper to the Biſhop of Rome, no leſs than eighteen in all.

With this rapid development of the veſtments in the

---

to repreſent the Tiara of the Highprieſt, Appendix G.

γ Walafrid Strabo (p. 106) mentions but ſeven, omitting, as he does, all mention of the Amice.

Roman Church, may be contrasted the fixity which, in this as in other matters, is characteristic of "the unchanging East."[3] Patriarch Simeon, writing in the fifteenth century, knows of but five vestments proper to a priest, and of two more, making seven in all, as belonging to a bishop.[337] And though he mentions the Pectoral Cross,[342] and the Staff,[345] as insignia of a bishop, he classes them with the Mandyas, or Mantle, as part of the non-liturgical costume, as in point of fact they are still regarded.

But to return to our more immediate subject,—the history of the vestments in the West,— it will be found that the multiplication of the "sacred vestments," above spoken of, was effected, partly by actual additions to the less elaborate dress of earlier centuries, partly by the promotion, so to speak, to sacred rank, of articles of dress, or of ornament, which had long been in use, but without being consecrated to symbolical significance, or to any specially sacerdotal usage.

As the most convenient way of bringing before my readers the general results of the documents printed in full in the later pages of this volume, I have drawn out in an Appendix (see Appendix F), an enumeration of the sacerdotal vestments, at the time of their fullest development in the Roman Church; with such brief notices to each as will indicate their origin, and the successive modifications which they underwent.

For the present it will be sufficient to point out some of the more general conclusions which result from the whole inquiry.

---

[3] Yet there are not wanting indications that in the East also, in particular instances at least, and in the later mediæval times, the idea of directly imitating Levitical vestments was entertained. See, for example, the curious monument reproduced in Pl. LVII., and the Description at p. 245.

And, first, it will be seen, that of all the various types of ministering dress, now retained in different branches of the Church, there is one, and one only, which approaches closely both in form and distinctive ornament to that of primitive Christendom, that dress being the Surplice (Appendix G, 5), with Scarf or Stole (see note on Pl. LXIII), now worn in the English Church.¹ The reader has only to refer to Pl. XV. and XVII., in which monuments of that ancient dress have been preserved, in order to see that this is the case.⁵

It appears further, that the original elements out of which the present ministering dress was developed, are common to the Greek, the Roman, and the Anglican Churches. But in the ministering dress of the Roman Church that primitive dress *has been overlaid by successive additions*, till the older type can scarcely be recognised under the changed forms in which it now appears. See Pl. LXI. We, ourselves, at the Reformation, had no sooner thrown aside those mediæval additions, merely Roman in their character, than we placed ourselves at one again with the Primitive Church, in this, as in other matters of far higher importance, in which a similar course was pursued.

Of the additions which at various times have been made to the really primitive dress, some few, as the Orarium and Planeta, date from the fourth century. And these are common to both East and West. But by far the greater number date from the ninth, to the middle of the twelfth, century;

---

¹ See particularly the central figure of the right-hand group (*spectator's right*) in Pl. XV. The dress of an English clergyman of the present day is there exactly delineated.

⁵ The only difference is that the black stripes represented on those primitive vestments were *attached to the tunic* instead of being separate, as was the later Orarium, and the modern "Stole."

a period of darkness, both intellectual* and moral, (especially so at Rome itself), such as the Christian world has never known either before or since.

It is not within the scope of the present work to enter upon matter of theological controversy. And I therefore only state here, as matter of history, that this development of the sacerdotal dress was exactly coincident in time with the development of innovations in eucharistic doctrine, which were distinctly mentioned for the first¹ time early in the ninth century, and which culminated in the decree of the Eleventh Lateran Council,*⁷ concerning transubstantiation, *anno* 1215. It was but natural that this should be. The formation of

---

* Baronius (Cardinal) ad ann. 900. "Incipit annus Redemptoris nongentesimus . . . . quo et novum inchoatur Sæculum, quod sui asperitate ac boni sterilitate, ferreum, malique exundantis deformitate plumbeum, atque inopia scriptorum appellari consuevit obscurum." [*Ann. Ecc.* tom. x. p. 629].

† *Id. ad ann.* 912, No. 14, p. 663. "Quæ tunc facies sanctæ Ecclesiæ Romanæ, quam fœdissima, cum Romæ dominarentur potentissimæ æque ac sordidissimæ meretrices, quarum arbitrio mutarentur Sedes, darentur Episcopi, et quod auditu horrendum et infandum est intruderentur in Sedem Petri earum Amasii Pseudopontifices, qui non sint nisi ad consignanda tantum tempora in catalogo Romanorum Pontificum scripti. Quis enim a scortis hujusmodi intrusos sine lege, legitimos dicere posset Romanos fuisse Pontifices?" For a *contemporary* picture of what Rome then was—a picture which more than justifies such language as the above—see the sixth book of the *Historia Luitprandi Episcopi*.

Genebrardus, Archbishop of Aix (Chronographia, lib. iv. p. 553), speaks of this period of awful corruption in the Papal See itself as lasting for 150 years, and through a succession of fifty pontiffs.

₁ In the treatise of Paschasius Rubertus, of whom Cardinal Bellarmine (Opp. tom. vii. p. 121) writes, "*Hic auctor primus fuit qui serio ac copiose disseruit de veritate Corporis ac Sanguinis Domini in Eucharistia.*" By this, of course, he means that he is the earliest writer who distinctly maintains *the Roman doctrine* on this subject. So understood, his assertion is perfectly exact. The doctrine of Paschasius was thought so strange, that Charles the Bald *called upon Ratramnus (al.* Bertramnus) *of Corbey to answer it,* which he did in a treatise which is of special interest to ourselves, as having formed the mind of Ridley and Cranmer upon this particular question. For further particulars of interest concerning it, see *Knox's Remains,* vol. ii. p. 157, and *Christian Remembrancer,* July, 1867.

what was deemed a diſtinctly ſacerdotal dreſs, modelled in detail upon the veſtments of Levitical prieſthood, both promoted, and in its turn was promoted by, ſuch developments of doctrine as thoſe to which I refer.

With this much of Preface, I may aſk my readers to proceed to the ſtudy of the many monuments, both of primitive and of mediæval times, which are ſet out in the later pages of this volume.

Ancient Glaſs from the Roman Catacombs. See deſcription at p. 247.

# PASSAGES FROM ANCIENT AUTHORS.

## I.

### NAMES OF THE SACERDOTAL VESTMENTS AS ENUMERATED IN HOLY SCRIPTURE.

THE various passages[1] in Holy Scripture in which the vestments of the Levitical priesthood are described or referred to, need not be quoted at length, as they are easily accessible to all. But it will be convenient for purposes of reference to specify the various names by which those vestments were known in the Apostolic age, and in those which followed, whether in Greek, through the LXX., or in Latin, through the early Italic Versions, and that of S. Jerome.

| | LXX. | S. JEROME. | ENGLISH A. V. |
|---|---|---|---|
| 1. The Linen Drawers. | περισκελῆ λινᾶ. | Feminalia linea. | Linen Breeches. |
| 2. The White Tunic (of linen). | χιτὼν ποδήρης, or χιτὼν βύσσινος. | Tunica talaris, or linea stricta. | Coat, long robe. |
| 3. The Girdle. | ζώνη. | Balteus, cingulum, or zona. | Girdle. |
| 4. The Priest's Cap. | κίδαρις, or μίτρα. | Cidaris, or mitra. | Bonnet. |
| 5. The Tunic of Blue worn under the Ephod. | χιτὼν ὑακύνθινος, or ὑποδύτης ὑπὸ τὴν ἐπωμίδα. | Tunica superhumeralis. | Broidered coat, or Robe of the Ephod. |
| 6. The Ephod, with the bands thereof. | ἐπωμίς. (The Girdle of the Ephod is not mentioned by LXX.) | Superhumerale and Balteus (Exod. xxxix. 5). | Ephod, and 'curious Girdle' of the Ephod. |
| 7. The Breastplate, or Jewel of the Ephod. | λόγιον, or περιστήθιον. | Rationale. | Breastplate. |
| 8. The Tiara, or High-Priest's Mitre, with the Plate of Gold. | κίδαρις, or μίτρα, with πέταλον. | Cidaris, or Tiara, with Lamna. | Mitre, with the Plate of Gold, or Holy Crown. |

[1] The passages of chief importance are Exod. xxviii. xxix. and xxxix.; Lev. viii. and xvi. (compare below, note 17); Num. x 26-28; Ezek. xliv. 17, sqq. In the Apocryphal Books, Ecclus. xlv., and 1 Macc. x. 21, where by ἡ ἱερὰ στολή is meant not one single robe only (as in A. V. "put on him the holy robe"), but the entire investiture of the high-priest.

## II.

## JOSEPHUS.

### ON THE SACERDOTAL VESTMENTS OF THE LEVITICAL PRIESTHOOD.

1. Antiq. Jud. III. 7.

[He begins by saying that there are vestments proper both to the ordinary priests known as Χαναίαι,[2] and to the 'Αναραβάχης,[3]—*i.e.* chief of priests or high-priest. These he proceeds to describe in detail.]

*Dress of the Priests* (of the second order).—1. *The Linen Drawers.* The dress of the priests is such as I shall now describe. When any one of them is about to engage in offices of priesthood he performs the ablutions required by the law, and then puts on, first, the garment called Μαναχασής,[4] equivalent in meaning to the Greek συνακτήρ. These are drawers made of linen, fastened about the middle, into which the feet are passed, as would be the case with Persian trousers. They do not reach higher than the waist, where they are securely fastened.

2. *The long white Tunic*, and (3) *the Girdle thereof*. Over these drawers he wears an under-garment of linen, made of byssus.[5] It is called Χιθομένη,—that is, "made of linen;" for χεθὸν with us means flax. This garment is a full-length tunic (χιτὼν ποδήρης), fitted exactly[6] to the body, and with its sleeves fastened closely about the

---

[2] Χαναίαι is, probably, the Hellenic representative of כהן.

[3] The reading here (as often is the case with foreign words in old MSS.) is probably corrupt. Various emendations have been proposed, as Ραβαχαάνης, or Ραβαχανης,—*i.e.* chief of the priests. But these are in the highest degree uncertain.
Heb. כהן.

[4] The Greek βύσσος = Heb. בד; which means sometimes (*a*) fine flax, sometimes (*β*)

the fine linen thence prepared. It would seem to be used occasionally (γ) with a primary reference to its *bright white* colour (*candor*). Compare Note 19.

[5] τὰς χειρῖδας περὶ τοῖς βραχίοσιν συνεσφιγμένας. This closeness of fit, and the absence, generally, of all loosely-flowing garments, in the dress of the Levitical priesthood, is a characteristic necessarily entailed (for cleanliness sake) by the nature of their ministrations in respect of animal sacrifice.

arms. This they gird in to the breast, not far from the armpit, passing the girdle round the body, very high up.† This girdle is four fingers broad, and woven in open pattern, like the scales of a serpent. Upon it flowers are worked in divers colours of purple, blue, and white; but the woof is made of byssus only. When worn, the priest begins by placing one end upon his chest, and then passes it twice round him, and fastens it: after which, if he is not engaged in the active duties of his ministry, he lets it flow down full as far as the ankles. The beauty of the girdle is thus fully displayed. But whenever he is required to busy himself about the sacrifices, or in other acts of ministry, he throws it over his left shoulder, and so wears it that its movements may not interfere with the work in which he may be engaged. This girdle was named by Moses 'Αβανήθ, but by us of these days it is called 'Εμίαν, a name which we learnt from the Babylonians, by whom it is still employed. The tunic above spoken of has no loose folds in any part of it; but the opening for the neck is left of full size, and is fastened up, upon the chest and back, just above either collar-bone, by strings attached to the border. Μασσαβαζάνης is the name by which it is known.

4. *The Priest's Cap.* On the head he wears a cap without any peak,[7] extending, not over the whole head, but over a little more than half of it. It is called μασναιμφθής. Its construction is such as to present the appearance of a turban,[8] being a band of linen weft, and of considerable thickness, folded upon itself several times, and so stitched together. At top of this band there is a covering of fine linen (σινδών) which overlaps it and reaches to the forehead, and is so arranged as to hide the stitching of the thick band below, which would have been unseemly if left exposed, and to lie flat upon the skull. It is made to fit with great exactness, so as not to fall off while the priest is engaged in sacrifice. Thus much as to the dress of the priests generally, as distinct from that of the high-priest.

---

† ἐλίγει τῆς μασχάλης ἐπεράνω τὴν ζώνην περιάγοντες. The translation above given is suggested for want of a better. To render the words with former translations, *paulo supra axillas*, gives a meaning which is unintelligible as applied to *a girdle*.

[7] σίλον ἄκωνον. He mentions thus particularly the *absence* of any "cone" or peak, because among the priestly insignia of many heathen rites such a peak was conspicuous. See Pl. V. Or the contrast intended may be that of the high-priest's tiara.

[8] τῇ κατασκευῇ τοιοῦτός ἐστιν ὡς στεφάνη δοκεῖν. The exact meaning of στεφάνη is doubtful.

## VESTMENTS WORN BY THE HIGH PRIEST ONLY.

5. *The Tunic of blue with its Girdle.* The high-priest wears the vestments already described, without omitting any; but over them he wears further a tunic of blue,⁹ reaching to the feet, like that first described, and known in our tongue as the μσιρ. This is fastened about him with a girdle of the same colours as that already described, but with gold thread also introduced. Along the lower border is a fringe attached, coloured and fashioned so as to resemble pomegranates; and with them golden bells devised with great beauty of appearance, and so arranged that, between each two bells a pomegranate is set, and between each two pomegranates a bell. This tunic is not formed in two separate parts, fastened together by a seam upon the shoulders and at the side, but consists of one long piece, woven throughout, and has an opening slit for the neck, not horizontally, but lengthwise (vertically) towards the chest and the middle of the back. Upon the opening thus made, an edging, or border, is sewn, so as to conceal anything unseemly in the opening thus made. A similar slit is made at the wrists.

6 and 7. *The Ephod and the Breastplate.* Over and above these he puts on, thirdly,¹⁰ the ephod, as it is called, resembling the ἐπωμίς of the Greeks. The fashion of it is as follows:—It is woven for the space of a cubit in depth of various colours, with wrought work of gold, and leaves the middle of the breast uncovered. It is furnished with sleeves, and in its whole fashion is constructed as a tunic. In the space left void by the ephod itself, a piece of cut (squared) cloth is fastened, wrought in divers colours like those of the ephod. It is called 'Εσσήνης, and means in the Greek tongue "Oracle." This exactly fills up that space which in the weaving of the ephod was left as an opening on the breast. It is united by golden rings at each corner to the ephod, which is itself provided with corresponding rings for the purpose, and the one set of rings is attached to the other by a band of blue cloth. And that the parts intervening between these rings might not hang loose and out of shape, a plan was devised for

---

⁹ χιτῶνα ἐξ ὑακίνθου πεποιημένον.
¹⁰ He speaks of the ephod as *third* among the distinctive vestments of the high-priest, reckoning the tunic of blue as the first, and the girdle, or bands, belonging to this outer tunic (by which it was attached to the ephod) as the second.

keeping all in place by (ῑμάτα ὑακίνθινα) a stitched edging of blue. The ephod has a clasp of sardonyx on either shoulder, each of the two projecting ends being wrought in gold, so as to fit in with the clasps. Upon these stones are inscribed the names of the twelve sons of Jacob in the letters proper to our native language, six on either stone. The elder sons' names are on the right shoulder, those of the younger on the left. So likewise on the breastplate (or "Oracle") there are set twelve stones of unusual size and beauty, forming an ornament such as men generally could not possibly obtain because of its exceeding costliness. These stones are arranged in lines, there being four rows, and each of these containing three stones. They are worked into the stuff on which they are fixed with a setting of gold, whose ornamental work is so inserted into the stuff as to hold together without giving way. Of the four rows the first contains a sardonyx, a topaz, and an emerald; the second a carbuncle, a jasper, and a sapphire. In the third are, first, a lyncurius, then an amethyst, and an agate; making up nine in all, thus far. In the lowest row a chrysolite stands first; afterwards an onyx, and, lastly, a beryl. On all these stones letters were engraved, which served to designate Jacob's sons, whom we regard as the heads of our twelve tribes. Each stone bears a name of some one patriarch, according to the order of birth. The rings already mentioned are too weak of themselves to bear the weight of the stones. Accordingly, the border of the breastplate, where it reaches upwards towards the neck, is furnished with two larger rings, inserted into the principal texture. These rings are to receive certain chains of wrought work, which, on the top of either shoulder, met and were attached to cords of gold. The end of these cords was turned up, and reached [11] as far as a ring projecting from the hinder border of the ephod. Thus was the breastplate secured from all danger of giving way.

The ephod was also furnished with a girdle, wrought in divers colours and in gold, as already described; and this encircled the ephod, and was then brought back and fastened at the seam, and then hung down. The fringes of the ephod were bordered on either side, and kept in place, by cylinders of gold.

8. *The High-priest's Cap, or Mitre.* A cap,[12] such as that already

---

[11] ἀνίμαντι ἀρίων τρείχοντι. I suspect that the true reading is ἰνίμαντι, with the meaning "was inserted into."

[12] πίλος = Latin *pileus*, or *pileum*.

described as worn by the priests generally, was assigned to the high-priest also. But above this, and sewn on to it, he had another, made of blue, and richly ornamented. Round this cap ran a circlet of gold, wrought in three tiers,[13] and upon this circlet is a cup-shaped flower, exactly resembling what our own people call Saccharus, but is known to the Greek herbalists as Hyoscyamus. [Here follows in the original text a long description of the plant in question, which I have omitted as being very obscure, and not of importance to the questions now before us.] The golden circlet thus formed extends from the back of the head to either temple. But to the forehead itself the flower-shaped ornament, just described, does not extend. But there is here a plate [14] of gold, on which is engraved, in sacred letters,[15] the holy name of God. Thus have I described the adornment of the high-priest.

2. DE BELLO JUDAICO. (LIB. V. CAP. V. § 7.)

Those of the priests who, by reason of any bodily defect, did not engage in holy ministrations, were wont to appear, together with those who had no such defect, inside the enclosure, and received the portions due to them by right of birth, but wore the garments of ordinary life. For the sacred dress was worn only by one who ministered (at the altar). But those of the priests who were without

---

[13] στεφέχεται στέφανος χρύσεος ἐπὶ τρισυχίαις σιχαλλιωμένος. No mention of this triple crown is made in H. S. But Josephus tells us (Antiq. Jud. xx. cap. 9), that Judas son of Hyrcanus, being at once high-priest and king, διάδημα στιμἰστο πρῶτος, was the first to assume a royal crown (in addition, i.e. to the sacerdotal tiara). And then we read at a later period that when Pompey restored another Hyrcanus to the high-priesthood of which, and of the royalty then attaching thereto, he had been deprived by his brother Aristobulus, τὴν μὲν τοῦ Ἰησοῦ ἀρχιερασίαν ἐπέτρεψε, διάδημα δὲ φορεῖν ἐκώλυσε, he made over to him the government of his own people, but prevented his wearing a (royal) crown. It is probable, therefore, that the tiara with triple crown described by Josephus, was a combination of the symbols of spiritual and temporal power, as is the triple crown (see Pl. 33) of the later Roman popes. The triple crown of the Jewish priest-king may have had reference to the three governments (1 Macc. x. 30) of Judea, Samaria, and Galilee.

[14] ετέλαμὼν χρύσεω. "Band" is the more literal rendering. But St. Jerome was no doubt right in considering the word as being here equivalent to the Latin *lamna*, *a thin plate* of metal.

[15] ἱεροῖς γράμμασι τοῦ θεοῦ τὴν προσηγορίαν ἐνετετυπωμένος. The expression is not inconsistent with that which is recorded in Holy Scripture, viz., that the words upon the plate were, "Holiness unto the Lord." (Exod. xxviii. 36.) By ἱερὰ γράμματα are probably meant the older "Samaritan" letters, so called.

disqualifying defect went up to the altar and the Holy Place, having about them a vesture of fine linen,[16] and abstained carefully from strong wine, out of reverence for the duty they had to perform, that in nothing they might transgress while engaged in their holy ministration. And the high-priest went up with them, yet not always so, but on the seventh days, and on the new moons, and at any national festival, or general assembly of the people, of annual observance. And he performed his ministry, covered from the thighs to the groin with a girding band; and wearing an inner garment of linen, and over this a long vesture of blue, circular in form, and furnished with a fringe. To these fringes were fastened golden bells, and pomegranates alternating therewith; the bells significant of thunder, the pomegranates of lightning. [Then follows a description of the ephod, the breastplate, and the tiara, much such as that already quoted; and he then adds] :—This dress he (the high-priest) was not in the habit of wearing at other times, but put on one of simpler character; but he did wear it on occasions of his entering (ὁπότε εἰσίοι) the most Holy Place, which he did once only in each year, and alone, on the day (of Atonement) when it is customary for all to keep fast unto God.[17]

---

[16] Ἐπὶ τὰ θυσιαστήρια καὶ τὸν ναὸν ἀνιβαίνον οἱ σὺν ἱερέων ἄμωμοι βύσσον μὲν ἀμπεχόμενοι. . . . This dress being of linen would, in the nature of things, be white. Compare the passage of Philo commented on in note 17.

[17] The statement here made, that the high-priest wore his "golden vestments" on the Day of Atonement, is not really inconsistent (as has been supposed by some) with the distinct assertion made by Philo (see below, p. 8), and confirmed by Lev. xvi. 4, 23. From both these last we gather that the high-priest, before actually entering within the vail on the Day of Atonement, *laid aside* his garments of glory, and entered the Most Holy Place clad in white only. What Josephus here states is perfectly consistent with this; though all that he speaks of is the fact of these garments of glory being worn on occasion of this particular day. The fact being, no doubt, that the high-priest went into the Holy Place, in his robes "of glory," and laid them aside, in the Temple, before entering within the vail.

# III.

# PHILO JUDÆUS.

## OF THE WHITE VESTMENTS WORN ON THE DAY OF ATONEMENT.

### 1. Liber de Somniis, p. 597.

τὸν μὲν ἀρχιερέα ὁπότε μέλλοι τὰς νόμῳ προστεταγμένας ἐπιτελεῖν λειτουργίας ὁ ἱερὸς ἰδικαίωσι λόγος ὕδατι καὶ τέφρᾳ περιρραίνεσθαι τὸ πρῶτον εἰς ὑπόμνησιν ἑαυτοῦ, καὶ γὰρ ὁ σόφος Ἀβραάμ ὅτι ἐντευξόμενος ᾔει γῆν καὶ σποδὸν εἶπεν ἑαυτὸν, ἔπειτ' ἐνδύεσθαι τὸν ποδήρη χιτῶνα καὶ τὸ ποικίλον ὃ κέκληκεν ἐπ' αὐτῷ περιστήθιον, τῶν κατ' οὐρανὸν φωσφόρων ἄστρων ἀπεικόνισμα καὶ μίμημα. Δύο γὰρ ὡς ἔοικεν ἱερά θεοῦ· ἓν μὲν ὅδε ὁ κόσμος ἐν ᾧ καὶ ἀρχιερεὺς ὁ πρωτόγονος αὐτοῦ θεῖος λόγος· ἕτερον δὲ λογικὴ ψυχὴ ἧς ἱερεὺς ὁ πρὸς ἀλήθειαν ἄνθρωπος, οὗ μίμημα αἰσθητὸν ὁ τὰς πατρίους εὐχάς τε καὶ θυσίας ἐπιτελῶν ἐστιν, ᾧ τὸ εἰρημένον ἐπιγέγραπται χιτῶνα ἐνδύεσθαι τοῦ παντὸς ἀντιμίμημα ὄντα οὐρανοῦ, ἵνα συνιερουργῇ καὶ ὁ κόσμος ἀνθρώπῳ, καὶ τῷ παντὶ ἄνθρωπος. Δύο μὲν οὖν εἴδη τό τε ῥαντὸν καὶ τὸ ποικίλον τύπων ἔχων ἐπιδέδεικται· τὸ δὲ τρίτον καὶ τελειότατον ὃς ὀνομάζεται διάλευκος αὐτίκα σημανοῦμεν ὅταν εἰς τὰ ἐσώτατα τῶν ἁγίων ὁ αὐτὸς οὗτος ἀρχιερεὺς εἰσίῃ τὴν μὲν ποικίλην ἐσθῆτα ἀπαμφίσκεται λιπὴν δὲ ἑτέραν βύσσου τῆς καθαρωτάτης πεποιημένην ἀναλαμβάνει· ἡ δ' ἐστι σύμβολον εὐτονίας αὐγοειδεστάτου φέγγους. Ἀρραγεστέρα γὰρ ἡ ὀθόνη καὶ ἐξ οὐδενὸς τῶν ἀποθνησκόντων γίνεται, καὶ ἔτι λαμπρότατον καὶ φωτοειδέστατον ἔχει μὴ ἀμελῶς καθαρθεῖσα χρῶμα.

The high-prieſt, when about to perform the holy offices by law aſſigned to him, was required by the ſacred word (of God) to ſprinkle himſelf, in the firſt place, with water and aſhes, as a remembrance to him of his own ſelf (for even Abraham, the wiſe, when he was going to make interceſſion, ſpake of himſelf as being duſt and aſhes) and then to put on the long ("tunic") robe, and the ornament of curious work called the breaſtplate, being a copy and image of the light-giving conſtellations that are in heaven. For the Temples of God are, as it ſeemeth, two. One is this, our own world, wherein also the Divine Word, God's first-begotten, is High-priest; but the other temple is the reasonable soul, whose Priest is the true Man, whose embodied representation is he who duly offers the prayers and sacrifices after the manner of our fathers, to whom is given that precept of which I spake, that he should put upon him the robe which is the image of the whole heaven, in order that, in one act of sacrifice, the world may join with man, and man with all creation.

We have seen now that two kinds of the types spoken of above are to be found in the person of the high-priest. We will now signify the same truth in respect of the third and most perfect (colour) that which is called "throughly white."[18] Whenever that same high-priest, of whom we spake, entereth into the innermost sanctuary of the Most Holy Place, he putteth off his variegated garments, and assumeth another vesture of linen, made of byssus, and this serveth to indicate the intensity of most brilliant light. For the cloth thus formed is very hard to rend, neither is the material thereof furnished by any creature subject unto death, and if it be carefully cleansed, it hath a most bright and luminous colour.[19]

---

[18] He had been speaking of the mystical meaning of the three colours mentioned in Gen. xxx. and xxxi., λιάλιυκα, i.e. partly white, but capable of meaning ("throughly" or "thoroughly," and so) "very white;" ποικίλα, variegated; and ῥαντιδῶ ῥαντά, "of the colour of ashes (and) sprinkled," or "speckled." The play on words to which Philo has recourse can scarcely be reproduced in English.

[19] Note here the brilliancy (λαμπρότης, or candor) which ancient writers, both in East and West, attribute to vestments of white linen. Those who have observed the effect produced by white linen, as seen in the bright light of a southern climate, will not wonder at such expressions as that of Philo above quoted. With it compare λίνον καθαρὸν καὶ λαμπρὸν (Apoc. xv. 6), and again (xix. 8), in speaking of the marriage garment worn by the Bride of the Lamb, ἰδόθη αὐτῇ ἵνα περιβάληται βύσσινον καθαρὸν καὶ λαμπρόν. Elsewhere white garments are said ἀστράπτων, to gleam as does lightning (Luke, xxiv. 4); or στίλβων (Mar. ix. 3), to shine as do the stars.

## IV.

## HIERONYMUS.

### EPISTOLA AD FABIOLAM DE VESTE SACERDOTALI.[*]

[Vol. ii. p. 574.]

Usque hodie in lectione veteris Testamenti super faciem Moysi velamen positum est. Loquitur glorificato vultu, et populus loquentis gloriam ferre non sustinet. Quum autem conversi fuerimus ad Dominum, auferetur velamen: occidens littera moritur, vivificans spiritus suscitatur. Dominus enim spiritus est, et lex spiritalis. Unde et David orabat in Psalmo: *Revela oculos meos : et considerabo mirabilia de lege tua.* ....

Et ne longum faciam (neque enim propositum mihi est nunc de tabernaculo scribere) veniam ad sacerdotalia vestimenta : et antequam mysticam scruter intelligentiam, more Judaico, quæ scripta sunt, simpliciter exponam : ut postquam vestitum videris sacerdotem, et oculis tuis omne ejus patuerit ornamentum, tunc singulorum caussas pariter exquiramus.

Discamus primum communes sacerdotum vestes atque pontificum. Lineis feminalibus, quæ usque ad genua et poplites veniunt, verenda cælantur, et superior pars sub umbilico vehementer astringitur: ut si quando expediti mactant victimas, tauros et arietes trahunt, portantque onera, et in officio ministrandi sunt, etiam si lapsi fuerint, et femora revelaverint, non pateat quod opertum est. Inde et gradus altaris prohibentur fieri: ne inferior populus ascendentium verenda conspiciat : vocaturque lingua Hebræa hoc genus vestimenti MACHNASE (מכנסי) Græcè περισκελῆ, à nostris feminalia, vel bracæ[†] usque ad genua pertinentes. Refert Josephus (nam ætate ejus adhuc templum stabat : et necdum Vespasianus et Titus Jerosolymam subverterant, et erat

---

[*] Written at Bethlehem in the year 396 or 397.
[†] *A nostris feminalia vel bracæ ad genua pertingentes.*" This last is exactly our own "knee-breeches."

## IV.

## ST. JEROME

### ON THE SACERDOTAL VESTMENTS.[20]

#### LETTER TO FABIOLA.

IN the reading of the Old Testament, even to this day, there is a veil upon the face of Moses. There is a glory upon his face as he speaks, and the people cannot bear to look thereon. But when we have turned unto the Lord the veil shall be taken away. Then doth the letter which killeth die, and the spirit, which giveth life, is stirred up. For the Lord is a Spirit, and spiritual, too, is the Law. For which cause David prayed in the Psalm (cxix. 18) " Take thou the veil from mine eyes, and I will consider the wondrous things of thy law."

[Then after a digression concerning the parts of the various victims reserved for the use of the priests under the Levitical law, and a statement of their mystical signification, he proceeds as follows:]

I come now to the sacerdotal robes (of the Levitical priest), and before inquiring into their mystical meaning, I will set down literally, after the manner of the Jews, what is written, that so, when you have seen the priest clad in his robes, and all his adornment has been set out before your eyes, we may then inquire likewise into the reasons of each particular.

Let us observe, first, what were the vestments common to priests and to high-priest alike. They have a covering for the thighs made of linen, and reaching down to the knees and the back of the leg, the upper part thereof being tied tightly about the middle of the body, so that when lightly clad for the flaying of victims, dragging forwards bulls or rams, carrying burdens, or engaged in other office of ministration, there may be no unseemly exposure. . . . This kind of vestment is called in Hebrew, MACHNASE [מכנסי], in Greek περισκελῆ, and in Latin *feminalia* (thigh-pieces) or *bracæ*.[21] It is said by Josephus (and in his day the Temple was yet standing, and Jerusalem not yet

ipse de genere sacerdotali, multoque plus intelligitur quod oculis videtur, quàm quod aure percipitur) hæc seminalia de bysso retorta ob fortitudinem solere contexi, et post quàm incisa fuerint, acu consui. Non enim posse in tela hujuscemodi fieri.

Secunda ex lino tunica est ποδήρης, id est, talaris, duplici sindone, quam et ipsam Josephus byssinam vocat, appellaturque CHOTONATH (כתנת) id est, χιτών, quod Hebræo sermone in *lineam* vertitur. Hæc adhæret corpori, et tam arcta est et strictis manicis, ut nulla omninò in veste sit ruga: et usque ad crura [a] descendat. Volo pro legentis facilitate abuti sermone vulgato. Solent militantes habere lineas, quas camisias [b] vocant, sic aptas membris et astrictas corporibus, ut expediti sint vel ad cursum, vel ad prælia, dirigendo jaculo, tenendo clypeo, ense vibrando, et quoquumque necessitas traxerit. Ergo et sacerdotes parati in ministerium Dei, utuntur hac tunica, ut habentes pulchritudinem vestimentorum, nudorum celeritate discurrant. [Note 6, p. 2.]

Tertium genus est vestimenti, quod illi appellant ABANET (אבנט), nos cingulum, vel baltheum, vel zonam possumus dicere. Babylonii novo vocabulo HEMIAN (המין) vocant. Diversa vocabula ponimus, ne quis erret in nomine. Hoc cingulum in similitudinem pellis colubri, qua exuit senectutem, sic in rotundum textum est, ut marsupium longius putes. Textum est autem subtemine cocci, purpuræ, hiacynthi, et stamine byssino, ob decorem et fortitudinem: atque ita polymita arte distinctum, ut diversos flores ac gemmas artificis manu non textas, sed additas arbitreris. Lineam tunicam, de qua supra diximus, inter umbilicum et pectus hoc stringunt baltheo, qui quattuor digitorum habens latitudinem, et ex una parte ad crura dependens, cum ad sacrificia cursu et expeditione opus est, in lævum humerum retorquetur.

Quartum genus est vestimenti, rotundum pileolum, quale pictum

---

[a] S. Jerome here distinctly states (what is contrary to general impression) that the χιτὼν ποδήρης of the Jewish priests extended only *ad crura*, i.e. about half-way between the knee and the ankle. He is probably right. Though ποδήρης means literally (like *talaris*) *reaching to the feet*; it was probably a conventional term for any of the *longer* tunics worn on occasions of state, whether it actually reached to the feet or no. And it is difficult to understand how a close fitting tunic that really reached to the feet, and was not open at the sides, could have allowed of the active (even violent) exertions that would sometimes be required of the Levitical priests.

[b] *Camisia*. S. Isidore (Orig. xix. 22, 29) derives the word *a camis*, "*quod in his dormimus in camis, id est in stratis nostris.*" With him it is a night-shirt. In S. Jerome's time it was evidently a term of the *lingua vulgaris*, for which he offers a sort of apology. From it are descended It. Camicia (and Camice "an alb," to which *camisia* is compared above); Fr. and Eng. Chemise.

overthrown, and he was himself of the priestly order, and the eye in such matters as this is more to be trusted than the ear) that these *feminalia* were woven of byssus, doubled upon itself for greater strength, and sewn together with a needle when properly cut out; it being impossible to make a garment of this kind in the ordinary way upon a loom.

Next comes a linen tunic, of the kind called ποδήρης, that is, reaching to the feet, made double of the fine linen called *sindon*, or, according to Josephus, of *byssus*, like the last. The name of this is CHOTONATH (*i.e.* χιτών), a word equivalent in Hebrew to the Latin *linea*. This is closely fitted to the body, and is so scanty, and with sleeves so narrow, that there is no fold in this garment. It reaches a little below the knee.[82] For better understanding of what I say I may employ a somewhat common word of our own. Our soldiers, when on service, wear linen garments, which they call "shirts,"[83] fitting so closely, and so fastened about the body, as to leave them free for action, whether in running or in fighting, hurling the javelin, holding the shield, wielding the sword, or whatever else, as need may require. And so the priests, standing prepared for the service of God, wear a tunic such as this, so that while they have their robes of beauty, they may hasten to and fro like men that stand stripped for speed.

The third of the priestly vestments is what the Jews call ABANET, a word which may be rendered girdle, belt, or zone. In Chaldaic it has a different name, HEMIAN. I mention these different names to prevent mistake. This belt is made like the skin of a serpent, wherewith it puts off the decay of old age. And it is woven round so as to resemble a long purse. The warp thereof is of scarlet, purple, and blue; the web of fine flax for beauty and strength. The ornaments thereon are so wrought by the skill of the embroiderer, that the various flowers and gems might well be deemed to have been set there in reality, rather than woven by the hand of the artificer. The linen tunic, already spoken of, is girt into the waist by this belt, which is four fingers broad, and with one part of it pendent below the knee, but is thrown back on to the left shoulder when the more active duties of actual sacrifice so require.

The fourth of the vestments is a small round cap, such as we see on the head of Ulysses, much as though a sphere were to be divided

in Ulyſſe conſpicimus, quaſi ſphæra media ſit diviſa, et pars una ponatur in capite: hoc Græci et noſtri τιάραν, nonnulli galerum vocant, Hebræi MISNEPHETH (מצנפת): non habet acumen in ſummo, nec totum uſque ad comam caput tegit: ſed tertiam partem à fronte inopertam relinquit: atque ita in occipitio vitta conſtrictum eſt, ut non facilè labatur ex capite. Eſt autem byſſinum, et ſic fabrè opertum linteolo, ut nulla acûs veſtigia forinſecus appareant.

His quattuor veſtimentis, id eſt, feminalibus, tunica linea, cingulo quod purpura, cocco, byſſo, hiacynthoque contexitur, et pileo, de quo nunc diximus, tam ſacerdotes quàm Pontifices utuntur. Reliqua quattuor propriè Pontificum ſunt, quorum primum eſt MAIL (מעיל), id eſt, tunica talaris, tota hiacynthina, ex lateribus ejuſdem coloris aſſutas habens manicas, et in ſuperiori parte qua collo induitur aperta, quòd vulgò capitium[u] vocant, oris firmiſſimis ex ſe textis, ne facilè rumpantur. In extrema parte, id eſt, ad pedes, ſeptuaginta duo ſunt tintinnabula, et totidem mala punica, iiſdem contexta coloribus, ut ſuprà cingulum. Inter duo tintinnabula unum malum eſt: inter duo mala unum tintinnabulum, ut alterutrum ſibi media ſint: cauſſaque redditur. Idcirco tintinnabula veſti appoſita ſunt, ut quum ingreditur Pontifex in Sancta Sanctorum, totus vocalis incedat, ſtatim moriturus ſi hoc non fecerit.

Sextum eſt veſtimentum quod Hebraica lingua dicitur EPHOD (אפד). Septuaginta ἐπωμίδα, id eſt, ſuperhumerale appellant. Aquila ἐπένδυμα, nos EPHOD ſuo ponimus nomine. Et ubiquumque in Exodo, ſive in Levitico ſuperhumerale legitur, ſciamus apud Hebræos EPHOD appellari. Hoc autem eſſe Pontificis veſtimentum, et in quadam Epiſtola ſcripſiſſe me memini: et omnis Scriptura teſtatur ſacrum quiddam eſſe, et ſolis conveniens Pontificibus. Nec ſtatim illud occurrat, quòd Samuel qui Levita fuit, ſcribitur in regnorum primo libro, habuiſſe ætatis adhuc parvulæ *ephod bad*, id eſt, *ſuperhumerale lineum*: quum David quoque ante arcam Domini idem portaſſe referatur. Aliud eſt enim ex quattuor ſupradictis coloribus, id eſt, hiacyntho, byſſo, cocco, purpura, et ex auro habere contextum: aliud in ſimilitudinem ſacerdotum ſimplex et lineum. Auri laminæ, id eſt, bracteæ, mira tenuitate tenduntur, ex quibus ſecta fila torquentur, cum ſubtegmine trium colorum, hiacyntho, cocci, purpuræ, et cum ſtamine byſſino: et efficitur

---

[u] *Capitium*, here the opening of the tunic, its "head-piece" ſo to ſay. Compare Papias (apud Ducange), "Capitium, ſummitas tunicæ, capitis foramen in veſte."

through the centre, and one-half thereof to be put upon the head. This is what in Greek and in Latin is called a tiara, but sometimes also *galerus*; in Hebrew, MISNEPHETH. It has no peak at top, nor does it cover the whole head as far as the hair extends, but leaves about a third of the front part of the head uncovered. It is attached by a band (*vitta*) on to the back of the head, so as not to be liable to fall off. It is made of byssus, and is so skilfully finished with an outer linen cover that no marks of the needle are to be seen without.

These four vestments, viz. the drawers, the linen tunic, the girdle woven with purple, scarlet, fine linen, and blue, and the cap just described, are in use by priests and high-priests alike. The remaining four belong exclusively to the high-priests. And these of the first is the MAIL, a full-length tunic, entirely of blue, with sleeves on either side of the same colour; and made open at top, where the opening is made for the head,[24] a strong edging being attached to the selvage to prevent its tearing. On its lower edge, at the feet, there are seventy-two bells, and as many pomegranates, made in the same colours as the girdle above described. The bells and the pomegranates alternate one with the other. And a reason is assigned for the addition of these bells, namely, that when the high-priest enters into the Holy of Holies, there may be a sound heard all about him as he goes, seeing that he would incur instant death were this not done.

The sixth of the vestments is called in Hebrew EPHOD, by the LXX, ἐπωμίς, i.e. *superhumerale*. In the version of Aquila it is ἐπένδυμα [or "superveftment"], with our own writers the original word, ephod, is often retained. And wherever in Exodus or in Leviticus the word *superhumerale* is read, this is to be understood as representing the Hebrew EPHOD. That this vestment belongs exclusively to the high-priest, I remember to have said in one of my letters, and all Scripture proves the same, that this vestment is of a sacred nature and suited for the high-priests alone. Let it not be objected that, in the first Book of Kings, we read of Samuel, who was a Levite, having, when yet quite a child, a "linen ephod," EPHOD BAD, for David also is said to have worn a similar dress before the ark. But it is one thing to have an ephod woven in the colours already described (blue, fine linen, scarlet, purple and gold); another thing to have a simple linen ephod resembling (in shape) that

palliolum miræ pulchritudinis, præstringens fulgore oculos in modum Caracallarum,[25] sed absque cucullis. Contra pectus nihil contextum est, et locus futuro Rationali derelictus. In utroque humero habet singulos lapides clausos et astrictos auro, qui Hebraicè dicuntur SOOM (שהם): ab Aquila et Symmacho et Theodotione onychini: à Septuaginta smaragdi transferuntur: Josephus, sardonychas vocat, cum Hebræo Aquilaque consentiens: ut vel colorem lapidum, vel patriam demonstraret. Et in singulis lapidibus tena Patriarcharum nomina sunt, quibus Israeliticus populus dividitur. In dextro humero majores filii Jacob, in lævo minores scripti sunt: ut Pontifex ingrediens Sancta Sanctorum, nomina populi pro quo rogaturus est Dominum, portet in humeris.

Septimum vestimentum est mensura parvulum, sed cunctis supradictis sacratius. Intende quæso animum, ut quæ dicuntur, intelligas. Hebraicè vocatur HOSEN (חשן), Græcè autem λόγιον, nos *Rationale* possumus appellare, ut ex ipso statim nomine scias mysticum esse quod dicitur. Pannus est brevis ex auro et quattuor textus coloribus, hoc est, iisdem quibus et Superhumerale, habens magnitudinem palmi per quadrum, et duplex, ne facile rumpatur. Intexti sunt enim ei duodecim lapides miræ magnitudinis atque precii per quattuor ordines: ita ut in singulis versiculis terni lapides collocentur. In primo ordine sardius, topazius, smaragdus ponitur. Symmachus dissentit in smaragdo, ceraunium pro eo transferens. In secundo carbunculus, sapphirus, jaspis. In tertio lyncurius, achates, amethystus. In quarto chrysolithus, onychinus, berillus. Satisque miror cur hiacynthus prætiosissimus lapis in horum numero non ponatur: nisi fortè ipse est alio nomine lyncurius. Scrutans eos qui de lapidum atque gemmarum scripsere naturis, lyncurium invenire non potui.[26] In singulis lapidibus secundum ætates duodecim tribuum sculpta sunt nomina. Hos lapides in diademate

---

[25] The *caracalla*, originally a Gaulish dress, was introduced among the Romans by M. Aurelius Antoninus [Emperor A.D. 210 to 217], surnamed "Caracalla" from his habitual wearing of it. It was furnished with a hood (*cuculla*), and this is the reason why S. Jerome adds here "*sed absque cucullis.*" An Emperor having set the fashion, it speedily passed into general use. And we find it mentioned from time to time either as a splendid dress (such as the context here shows to be meant) or as worn in ordinary life, by persons high and low, the name being retained in reference to its shape, though in material and in colour it might vary infinitely. In the story of the martyrdom of St. Alban given by Bede [Hist. Eccl. lib. i. cap. 6], we find it worn by a clergyman (*clericus*) in Britain, and the context there implies that at that time it was a somewhat unusual dress. This was during the persecution of Diocletian at the close of the third century.

[26] See Theophrastus περὶ τῶν λίθων, 28, 31, and Plin. Hist. Nat. lib. xxxvii. c. 4.

of the priests. The gold-leaf used in making this robe is drawn out to a marvellous thinness, and then twisted into separate threads. The woof is of three colours,—blue, scarlet, and purple, and the web of byssus; and so a vestment is formed of wondrous beauty, dazzling the eyes as does our own caracalla,[25] but not furnished with a hood. Upon the breast there is an open space left, affording room for the " Rational," which is there to be. On either shoulder there is a single stone, enclosed and set in gold. These stones are in Hebrew called SOOM, explained as meaning *onyx* by Aquila, Symmachus, and Theodotion, but by the LXX as *emeralds*. Josephus, following the Hebrew and Aquila, calls them *sardonyx*, to indicate either the colour of the stones, or, it may be, the place where they are found. On each of these stones are the names of six of the twelve patriarchs, who give their names to the twelve Tribes of Israel. On the right shoulder are inscribed the elder sons of Jacob, the younger on the left; in order that the high-priest, as he enters the Holy of Holies, may bear upon his shoulders the names of the people for the which he is about to entreat the Lord.

The seventh vestment is small in size, but more holy than all those above mentioned. Give me your especial attention now, for the better understanding of what I say. It is called in Hebrew HOSEN, in Greek λόγιον. We ourselves may call it the " Rational," that the very name may at once point to a mystical meaning. It is a small piece of cloth, woven in gold and four colours, the same as the ephod. It is square, and of a palm's breadth each way, and made double for greater strength. Into it were fastened twelve precious stones of great size, and very costly, in four rows, three stones to each line. On the top line were a sardine stone, a topaz, and an emerald. Symmachus differs as regards the " emerald," which he renders " *ceraunius*." On the second line, a carbuncle, sapphire, and jasper. On the third, lyncurius, agate, and amethyst. On the fourth, a chrysolite, an onyx, and a beryl. I greatly wonder that so precious a stone as the jacynth has here no place. But perhaps the lyncurius is but another name for it. I have examined treatises on precious stones and gems, but have found no mention [26] of the lyncurius. On these several stones are engraved the names of the tribes according to the ages of the patriarchs. We read (Ezek. xxviii.) of these stones on the diadem of the Prince of Tyre, and in the Revelation of John (Rev. xxi.), where they form the walls of

D

principis Tyri, et in Apocalypsi Joannis legimus, de quibus ex
struitur cœlestis Jerusalem: et sub horum nominibus et specie, virtutum vel ordo, vel diversitas indicatur. Per quattuor Rationalis
angulos, quattuor annuli sunt aurei, habentes contra se in Superhumerali alios quattuor: ut quum appositum fuerit λόγιον in loco,
quem in Ephod diximus derelictum, anulus veniat contra anulum, et
mutuo sibi vittis copulentur hiacynthinis. Porrò ne magnitudo et
pondus lapidum contexta stamina rumperet, auro ligati sunt atque
conclusi: nec suffecit hoc ad firmitatem, nisi et catenæ ex auro
fierent, quæ ob pulchritudinem fistulis aureis tegerentur,[17] haberentque
et in Rationali suprà duos majores anulos, qui uncinis Superhumeralis
aureis necterentur, et deorsum alios duos: nam post tergum in
Superhumerali contra pectus et stomachum, ex utroque latere erant
anuli aurei, qui catenis cum Rationalis inferioribus anulis junge-
bantur: atque ita fiebat, ut astringeretur et Rationale Superhumerali,
et Superhumerale Rationali, ut una textura contra videntibus puta-
retur.

Octava est lumina aurea, id est, SIS ZAAB (ציץ זהב), in qua scriptum est nomen Dei Hebraicis quattuor litteris JOD, HE, VAV, HE
(יהוה), quod apud illos ineffabile nuncupatur. Hæc super pileolum
lineum commune omnium Sacerdotum, in Pontifice plus additur,
ut in fronte vitta hiacynthina constringatur, totamque Pontificis pulchritudinem Dei vocabulum coronet et protegat.

Didicimus quæ vel communia cum Sacerdotibus, vel quæ specialia
Pontificis vestimenta sint: et si tanta difficultas fuit in vasis fictilibus,[20]
quanta majestas erit in thesauro, qui intrinsecus latet! Dicamus igitur
prius quod ab Hebræis accepimus: et juxta morem nostrum, spiritualis postea intelligentiæ vela pandamus. . . . .

---

[17] In Josephus σύριγγες. But his description here differs somewhat from that of S.
Jerome. See above, p. 5.

[20] In vasis fictilibus. He alludes, of course, to 2 Cor. iv. 7, where the Vulgate is, "Habemus autem thesaurum istum in vasis fictilibus
ut sublimitas sit virtutis Dei et non ex nobis."

the heavenly Jerusalem; and under their names and species are suggested the order and diverse nature of the several virtues. Through the four corners of the Rational are inserted four golden rings, having four others on the ephod just opposite to them; so that when the λόγιον is fitted to the place which I have described as left open in the ephod, ring may be over against ring, and be fastened together with bands of blue. Moreover, the stones were fastened together with a setting of gold, for fear that from their size and weight the web to which they are attached should give way. Nor would this have been sufficient security, had not chains of gold been made (covered, for greater beauty, with small cylinders[17] of gold), having two larger rings on the upper part of the Rational (to be attached to the golden hooks of the ephod), and two others on the lower part. For, on the back of the ephod, at a height to correspond with the breast and lower part of the throat, there were golden rings on either side, joined by chains to the lower rings of the Rational; and so it was that the Rational was closely fastened to the ephod, the ephod to the Rational, in such manner as to appear to the spectator as if they were all of one piece.

Eighth in order was the plate of gold, SIS ZAAB, on which was inscribed the name of God in the four Hebrew letters Yod, He, Vav, He, "The unutterable Name," as they declare it. This is added in the case of the high-priest over and above the linen cap common to all the priests. It is attached to his forehead with a fastening band of blue. And so the Divine Name is as a crown and protection to the whole of that "fair beauty" with which the high-priest is clad.

We have now learnt what robes the high-priest has in common with the priests, and what specially appropriated to himself. And if we had so much of difficulty in speaking of "earthen vessels"[28] what majesty shall there be in the treasure that lies concealed within! First, then, let me say what I have learnt on this matter from Hebrew authors, and after that, as our wont is, we may spread open the sails of spiritual interpretation.

[Here follows, at some length, the mystical meaning attributed by the Jews to all the details already given. The four colours represent the four elements—earth, air, fire and water; the pomegranates and bells mean the thunder and lightning, or else the harmony of all the elements. The ephod, and its two precious

Tetigimus expofitionem Hebraicam, et infinitam fenfuum fylvam alteri tempori refervantes, quædam futuræ domus ftravimus fundamenta.[29] . . . . Legimus in Levitico, juxta præceptum Dei, Moyfen laviffe Aaron et filios ejus: jam tunc purgationem mundi, et rerum omnium, fanctitatem Baptifmi, facramenta fignabant. Non accipiunt veftes, nifi lotis prius fordibus, nec ornantur ad facra, nifi in Chrifto novi homines renafcantur. Vinum enim novum in novis utribus mittitur. Quòd autem Moyfes lavat, legis indicium eft. Habent Moyfen et Prophetas, ipfos audiant. Et ab Adam ufque ad Moyfen omnes peccaverunt. Præceptis Dei lavandi fumus, et quum parati ad indumentum Chrifti tunicas pelliceas depofuerimus,[30] tunc induemur vefte linea, nihil in fefe mortis habente, fed tota candida:[31] ut de baptifmo confurgentes, cingamus lumbos in veritate, et tota priftinorum peccatorum turpitudo celetur. Unde et David: *Beati quorum remiffæ funt iniquitates, et quorum tecta funt peccata.* Poft feminalia et lineam tunicam induimur hiacynthino veftimento,[32] et incipimus de terrenis ad alta confcendere. Hæc ipfa hiacynthina tunica, à Septuaginta ὑποδύτης, id eft, fubucula nominatur, et propriè Pontificis eft, fignificatque rationem fublimium non patere omnibus, fed majoribus

---

[29] *Quædam futuræ domus ftravimus fundamenta;* i.e. he had prepared the way for his own myftical application.

[30] He takes up here the thought, alluded to as we have feen, by Philo (p. 8), that garments of *animal* origin (whether of fur or of wool) favour of mortality and corruption. Hence the expreffion of the text is equivalent to the ἀπεκδυσάμενοι τὸν παλαιὸν ἄνθρωπον, "ftripping off the old humanity" of St. Paul (Col. iii. 9).

[31] *Sed tota candida.* On the meaning of *candidus,* fee above note 19. The allufion is here to the white garments worn by the newly baptized.

[32] *Veftimento hiacynthino.* In fpeaking of the Jewifh myftical interpretation of this colour, "*the foundation for his own building,*" he had noticed that to them this "jacynth blue," was fignificant of the fky. Hence what he here fays. So again below, *cidaris et vitta hyacinthina cælum monftrant.*

stones, are the two hemispheres, whereof one is above and the other below the earth. The girdle is the ocean. The rational (or breast-plate) the earth. The general result is described by S. Jerome as being this, that God's high-priest bearing upon his vestments the typical representation of all created things, should show how all creatures stand in need of the mercy of God, and that, in sacrificing unto Him, expiation might be for the state of the entire universe, and that he might pray, both by voice and by the dress he bare, not for children, and parents, and kinsmen only, but for all creation.[33] He then proceeds as follows] :—

I have now touched upon the exposition of these things given by the Jews, and while reserving for another opportunity an infinite number of mystical meanings, have laid something of a foundation for the building that is to be.[29] . . . We read in Leviticus that, according to God's commandment, Moses washed Aaron and his sons. So even at that early time there were sacramental acts signifying the purifying of the world and of all created things, and the sanctity of baptism. They receive not their robes till they have washed off the filth of the flesh, nor are they adorned for holy rites, except they be born again as new men in Christ. For new wine is put in new bottles (*utribus — ἀσκοις*). And in that it is Moses who washeth them, this pointeth to the law, "*They have Moses and the prophets, let them hear them,*" and, "*From Adam even unto Moses all sinned.*" It is by God's commandments that we are to be washed clean, and when, being made ready for the garment of Christ, we shall have laid aside our garments made of skins,[30] then shall we be clad in the linen robe which hath in it nothing which is of death, but is wholly bright and pure,[31] that so rising up from our baptism we may gird up our loins with truth and all the deformity of former sins be put out of sight. Whence also David saith, "*Blessed are they whose iniquities are forgiven, and whose sins are covered.*" After the drawers and the linen tunic, we put upon us a vestment of blue,[32] and begin to mount up from things on earth to things above. This very tunic of blue is called by the Seventy ὑποδύτης, that is, "under-garment," and belongs properly to the high-priest; and it signifieth that the meaning of the higher things of God lies not open to all, but only to those somewhat advanced in the Christian life, or who

---

[33] Compare the passage of Philo to the same effect, given above, p. 8.

atque perfectis.³⁴ Hanc habuerunt Moyses et Aaron et Prophetæ, et omnes quibus dicitur: *In montem excelsum ascende tu, qui evangelizas Sion.* Nec sufficit nobis priorum ablutio peccatorum, baptismi gratia, doctrina secretior, nisi habuerimus et opera. Unde jungitur et Ephod, id est, Superhumerale,³⁵ quod Rationali copulatur: ut non sit laxum, neque dissolutum, sed hæreant sibi invicem et auxilio sint. Ratio ³⁶ enim operibus, et opera ratione indigent: ut quod mente percipimus, opere perpetremus. Duoque lapides in Superhumerali, vel Christum significant et Ecclesiam, duodecim Apostolorum, qui ad prædicationem missi sunt, nomina continentes: vel litteram et spiritum, in quibus continentur legis universa mysteria. In dextra spiritus, in læva littera est. Per litteras ad verba descendimus, per verba venimus ad sensum. Quàm pulcher ordo, et ex ipso habitu sacramenta demonstrans. In humeris opera sunt, in pectore ratio.³⁶ Unde et pectusculum comedunt sacerdotes. Hoc autem Rationale duplex est,³⁷ apertum et absconditum, simplex et mysticum, duodecim in se lapides habens, et quattuor ordines, quos quattuor puto esse virtutes, prudentiam, fortitudinem, justitiam et temperantiam, quæ sibi hærent invicem: et dum mutuo miscentur, duodenarium efficiunt numerum: vel quattuor Evangelia, quæ in Apocalypsi describuntur plena oculis, et Domini luce radiantia mundum illuminant. In uno quattuor, et in quattuor singula. Unde δήλωσις et ἀλήθεια, id est, doctrina et veritas in pectore,³⁸ Sacerdotis est. Quum enim indutus quis fuerit veste multiplici, consequens est, veritatem quam corde retinet, sermone proferre: et ob id in rationali veritas est, id est, scientia, ut noverit quæ docenda sint: et manifestatio atque doctrina, ut possit instruere alios, quod mente concepit. Ubi sunt qui innocentiam Sacerdoti dicunt posse sufficere?³⁹ Vetus lex novæ congruit: idipsum Moyses quod Apostolus. Ille sacerdotis scientiam ornat in vestibus: iste Timotheum et Titum instruit disciplinis. Sed et ipse vestimentorum ordo præcipuus. Legamus Levi-

---

[34] *Majoribus atque perfectis*. *Majoribus* has reference (as elsewhere to growth in years, so here) to growth in grace. For *perfectus* = τέλειος, 'full-grown,' see "Eirenika," note 68, p. 120.

[35] The shoulder and arm, he means, are naturally associated with ideas of *activity*, and so of good works.

[36] *Ratio* (Reason and Understanding) used in reference to "*Rationale*," the word used throughout for the λόγιον, the "breastplate" of our English Version.

[37] It was made *duplex* ne facile rumperetur, as he had said above.

[38] To the Romans not the head but the breast (or the *heart*) was the seat of the understanding. "*Non tu corpus eras sine pectore.*" "*Rudis et sine pectore miles.*"

[39] *i.e.* that it mattereth not greatly that he have *knowledge*. As to the meaning of *sacerdos* (bishop, as well as priest), see Index *in voc.*

have attained unto fulness of growth. With this garment were clad Moses, and Aaron, and the prophets, and all they to whom that word is spoken, "*Ascend up unto the lofty mountain, thou that bringest glad tidings to Sion.*" (Isa. xl. 9.) But the washing away of sins, the grace of baptism, the more hidden knowledge, these are not sufficient for us, unless we have also (good) works, and therefore there is joined to those other vestments the ephod, that is, the "Superhumeral,"[35] which again is so coupled to the ("Rational") breastplate, that it may not be loose nor unattached, but that both may be closely joined and be a mutual help each to other. For reason[36] needeth works, and works need reason; that so what we mentally perceive we may by works carry out in act. And the two stones upon the ephod signify, either Christ and the Church (as containing the names of the twelve apostles who were sent to the preaching of the Gospel), or the letter and the spirit, wherein are contained all the mysteries of the law. On the right is the spirit; on the left is the letter. Through letters we reach unto words: through words we come to meaning. How beauteous is the order, showing forth sacramental truths even by the very dress of which we speak. On the shoulders are (good) works: on the breast reason. For which cause the priests have the breast (of the sacrifice) to eat. But this Rational is two-fold,[37] open and yet hidden; simple, and yet mystical; having upon it twelve stones, and four rows, which I hold to be four virtues, viz. wisdom, courage, justice, temperance, which are closely united one unto the other, and by their mutual conjunction produce a duodecimal number. Or else they may be the four Gospels, which in the Apocalypse are described as full of eyes, and which, beaming with the light of the Lord, enlighten the whole world. In one, the four; and in the four each and all the separate parts. And, therefore, δήλωσις and ἀλήθεια, "manifestation" and "truth," are on the breast[38] of the priest. For when a man hath been clad in the manifold vesture, it followeth that he express in word the truth which he holdeth in his heart. And therefore in the Rational there is "truth," that is "knowledge," that he may know what is to be taught, and "manifestation" and "doctrine" that he may be able to instruct others of that which his own reason hath comprehended. Where are they that say that it sufficeth for a priest[39] that he be of innocent life? The old law agreeth with the new; Moses was in the one, what the Apostle was in the other.

ticum. Non prius Rationale, et sic Superhumerale, sed ante Superhumerale, et deinceps Rationale. *A mandatis tuis*, inquit, *intellexi*: prius faciamus, et sic doceamus: ne doctrinæ auctoritas cassis operibus destruatur. Hoc est quod in Propheta legimus: *Seminate vobis in justitia, et metite fructum vitæ: illuminate vobis lumen scientiæ*. Primùm seminate in justitia, et fructum vitæ æternæ metite: postea vobis scientiam vindicate. Nec statim absoluta perfectio est, si quis Superhumerale et Rationale habeat:[40] nisi hæc ipsa inter se forti compagine solidentur, et sibi invicem connexa sint: ut et operatio rationi et ratio operibus hæreat: et his præcedentibus, doctrina sequatur et veritas.

Lamina aurea rutilat in fronte: nihil enim nobis prodest omnium rerum eruditio, nisi Dei scientia coronemur. Lineis induimur, ornamur hiacynthinis, sacro baltheo cingimur, dantur nobis opera, Rationale in pectore ponitur: accipimus veritatem, profert sermo doctrinam: imperfecta sunt universa, nisi tam decoro currui dignus quæratur auriga, et super creaturas creator insistens, regat ipse quæ condidit. Quod olim in lamina monstrabatur,[41] nunc in signo ostenditur crucis.[42] Auro legis sanguis Evangelii pretiosior est.[43] Tunc signum juxta Ezechielis vocem gementibus figebatur in fronte: nunc portantes crucem dicimus: *Signatum est super nos lumen vultus tui Domine*. . . .[44]

Jam sermo finitur, et ad superiora retrahor. Tanta debet esse

---

[40] "Both ephod and breastplate," i.e. both good works and knowledge.

[41] i.e. "Holiness unto the Lord." See above, Note 15.

[42] i.e. the sign of the cross traced *upon the forehead* in baptism, putting, as it were, Christ's mark thereon, and declaring the newly-baptized to be "Holy unto the Lord."

[43] The sign of *the cross* carries out thoughts to the precious blood thereon shed, called by St. Paul, τὸ αἷμα τοῦ σταυροῦ.

[44] *Quæ sequuntur de feminalibus apud ipsum requirant eruditi lectores. Virgineis Fabiolæ oculis parum apta videntur.*

For Moses deviseth " knowledge " among the vestments of the priests; Paul furnisheth Titus and Timothy with "Doctrine." But the very order of the vestments is noteworthy. Let us read Leviticus. It is not, first, the rational, and after that the ephod; but, first, the ephod, and afterward the rational. "*From thy commandments,*" saith one, "*have I got understanding.*" (Ps. cxix. 104.) Let *doing* be first in order with us, and so let us go on to teaching, lest the authority of our teaching be done away by the worthlessness of that we work. This is that we read in the Prophet (Hos. x. 12), "*Sow your seed in righteousness, and reap the fruit of life; Kindle ye for you the light of knowledge.*" First sow in righteousness, and reap the fruit of life; afterward claim knowledge as your own. Yet fulness of Christian growth is not then at once completely attained when one hath both ephod and breastplate; unless these two be firmly compacted one unto the other, and in such wise mutually connected, that both our working of that which is good be close joined to reason, and reason close joined to works; and that, while these lead the way, doctrine and truth follow.

[He then defers further explanation concerning the twelve stones of the breastplate, saying that his letter is already too long, and adding a few further particulars, he says:]

A plate of gold glitters on the forehead, for learning the most universal is nothing worth unto us, unless we be crowned with the knowledge of God. We are clothed in linen, we are adorned with the vestments of celestial blue, we are girt about with the sacred belt, works are given unto us, the rational is put upon our breast, we accept the truth, our words bring forth doctrine—all these together are imperfect, unless for so fair an equipage a fitting guide be found, and the Creator, set on high above His creatures, Himself direct that which He hath made. What in old times was shown upon the golden plate is now set forth in the sign of the Cross. The gold of the law is less precious than the Blood of the Gospel. In those former times, according to that word of Ezekiel (Ezek. ix. 4), a mark was put upon the brow of them that mourned; but now we that bear the cross (upon our foreheads) say, "The light of thy countenance, O Lord, is signed upon us."

And now my discourse is drawing to a close, and I return to that of which I was speaking above. Such should be the knowledge

scientia et eruditio Pontificis⁴⁵ Dei, ut et greſſus ejus, et motus, et univerſa vocalia ſint. Veritatem mente concipiat, et toto eam habitu reſonet et ornatu: ut quidquid agit, quidquid loquitur, ſit doctrina populorum. Abſque tintinnabulis enim et diverſis coloribus et gemmis floribuſque virtutum, nec Sancta ingredi poteſt, nec nomen Antiſtitis⁴⁶ poſſidere.

---

⁴⁵ *Pontificis*. *Pontifex* is literally a "*bridgemaker*," γεφυροποιός, as the Greek writers sometimes translate it. And the following quotation will suggest the origin of the term: "The Tiber was the natural highway for the traffic of Latium; and . . . formed from very ancient times the frontier defence of the Latin stock against their northern neighbours. . . . Rome combined the advantages of a strong position, and of immediate vicinity to the river; *it commanded both banks of the stream* down to the mouth. . . . That Rome was indebted accordingly, if not for its origin, at any rate for its importance, to these commercial and strategical advantages of its position, there are many indications to show. . . . *Thence arose the unusual importance of the bridges over the Tiber, and of bridge-building generally*, in the Roman commonwealth. Thence came the galley in the city arms." MOMMSEN, *History of Rome*, book i. cap. iv. Bearing in mind how in ancient times all matters of grave import to the state were invested with the sanctions of religion, we shall not wonder to find the construction and care of these *bridges* placed under the superintendence of that College of Magistrates (not *priests* in our sense of the word) which from the very beginning of Roman history was supreme in all matters pertaining to religion. With this body of sacerdotal "Bridgemakers," with the first citizen of the Republic, or, as in later times, an emperor, at their head (as *Pontifex Maximus*), we may compare our own "*Trinity Board*," with a prince of the blood as "Master." [The parallel might be extended, *in-experto si fas ita dicere*, in respect of the *Pontificum cœnæ* and the Greenwich banquets.]

The Christian use of the term is owing mainly to St. Jerome's version of the Bible. From the 5th century onwards, the use of *Pontifex* as = *sacerdos* (Note 61), or bishop, and of *Pontifex summus* as = *archbishop*, or metropolitan, became very common. In earlier writers it is very rare; and in the older Italic version we find *sacerdos* or *summus sacerdos* where St. Jerome (*writing at Rome*) speaks of *Pontifex*, or *Pontifex summus*. [For the term *Pontifex Maximus*, which has a special meaning of its own, see Index of Notes.]

and the learning of one chief[45] in holy miniſtry to God, as that his walk and movement, and everything about him ſhall be vocal to the ears of men. With his mind let him embrace the truth, and in all his habit and adornment cauſe it to ſound forth to others; that whatſoever he doeth, whatſoever he ſpeaketh, may be for inſtruction unto all men. For without the bells, and the divers colours, and the gems, and the flowers of divers virtues, he can neither enter the Holy of Holies, nor make his own the name of one chief[46] among God's ſervants.

---

[45] *Antiſtes* (*ante-ſtes* — compare the Greek προ-στάτης), properly one *in foremoſt place*, and hence occaſionally uſed by claſſical writers of heathen prieſts (*ſacrorum antiſtes*, Cic. and Juv. *antiſtes Jovis* Nep. and the fem. *antiſtita Phœbi*, Ov.) and frequently in Chriſtian literature of biſhops. Hence, in later Latin, the forms *antiſtitium* = *ſacerdotium*, and *antiſtitari* = *epiſcopum agere*.

## V.

## S. JEROME.

### EPISTLE TO MARCELLA CONCERNING THE EPHOD WORN BY SAMUEL.

[Written at Rome, a.d. 384.]

[Wishing to explain how it was that, while the "ephod" or *superhumerale* is properly a garment of the high-prieft alone, we yet read of Samuel, and of the priefts at Nob, wearing an ephod, and of David, in one place, doing likewife, he fays that thefe ephods were of *linen* only, and *white*.]

"*Propterea autem Samuel et octoginta quinque viri sacerdotes ephod lineum portasse referuntur, quoniam sacerdos magnus solus habebat licentiam ephod non-lineo vestiendi, verum, ut Scriptura commemorat, auro, hyacintho, purpura, cocco, byssoque, contexto. Cæteri habebant ephod non illa varietate distinctum et duodecim lapidibus ornatum, qui in humero utroque residebant: sed lineum et simplex et toto candore purissimum.*"

"The reafon why Samuel, and the eighty-five priefts are faid to have worn an ephod *of linen*, is this, that the high-prieft alone had the right to wear an ephod made, not of linen, but, as the Scripture records, made of gold, and blue, and purple, and fcarlet, and fine linen. All the reft had an ephod,[47] not varied in colour like to this, nor ornamented with the twelve ftones of the breaftplate, but of linen and unadorned, and moft pure in the perfection of i brilliant whitenefs."

---

[47] This difficulty about the ephod of David and of Samuel has often been noticed by modern writers. The folution of the difficulty is, no doubt, that which S. Jerome (as, nearer our own times, Lightfoot) suggefts, viz. that the term ephod was originally a *general* term for an upper garment of a peculiar fhape: *the* ephod, peculiar to the high-prieft, being diftinguifhed from other ephods by its material, colour, and infignia.

## VI.

## S. JEROME.

### ON EZEKIEL XLIV.

[Vol. III. 1028, sqq.]

[He is commenting on the words that occur ver. 17, sqq.: which are as follows:

"*When they enter the gates of the inner court, they shall be clothed with garments of linen: and nothing that is of wool shall come upon them when they minister at the gates of the inner court, and further within. Bands of linen shall be upon their heads,*[48] *and they shall have linen drawers upon their loins; they shall not gird themselves with that which causeth sweat.*[49] *And when they go forth out of the outer court unto the people they shall put off the garments*[50] *wherein they had ministered, and shall replace them in the treasuries of the sanctuary, and shall put on other garments, and they shall not sanctify the people with their ministering garments. But their heads they shall not shave, nor yet let their hair grow long; but they shall poll their heads; neither shall any priest drink wine when he is about to enter into the inner court.*"

Upon this he comments as follows:]

In the first place, I must explain the words here recorded. Among other precepts given by the Word of the Lord to the priests this is one, that at the very gates of the inner court they shall put

---

[48] S. Jerome here gives as an alternative rendering, "*They shall have linen caps* (cidares) *upon their heads.*"

[49] Here, too, as an alternative rendering (for *in sudore*) *violenter*.

[50] *Stolas* in the text. In the LXX. στολή is used either (α) as a generic term for the entire vesture of the priest, considered as a whole, or (β) (generally in the plural στολαί) of particular vestments spoken of as portions of that whole. And this double use of στολή is reproduced, in the use of *stola*, first in the Latin versions, and secondly in the early Christian writers. From the usage here noticed, two others require to be distinguished: (γ) the *classical* use, according to which *stola* was particularly used of the long robe, edged with the *instita*, characteristic of the Roman matron; and (δ) the *later Christian usage*, discussed in the Introduction, according to which *stola*, like our own "stole," is the equivalent of *orarium*.

on garments, that is, sacred robes, of linen, and use no under garments of wool, either in the gates of the inner court, or yet farther within, that is in the Holy and the Most Holy Place; and, again, that bands, or caps of linen, be on their heads, and linen drawers upon their loins. . . . And as he had once already prescribed what vestments were to be worn by the priests when engaged in their ministries within, he now again enjoins that when they go forth they shall put off their former vestments in the treasuries or side-chambers of the Holy Place, and put on others; lest by retaining the holy garments they should sanctify the people who stand without, who have not as yet been sanctified, nor made themselves ready for the sanctification of the Temple, so as to be Nazarites unto the Lord. [51] By all this we learn that we, too, ought not to enter into the Holy of Holies in our every-day garments, just such as we please, when they have become defiled from the use of ordinary life, but with a clean conscience, and in clean garments, hold in our hands the Sacraments of the Lord.[51] As for what follows, "*Their heads they shall not shave, nor suffer their locks to grow long, but polling they shall poll their heads,*" by this it is clearly shown that *we* ought not to have shaven heads like the priests and worshippers of Isis and Serapis, nor yet, on the other hand, to wear long, flowing hair, which is for the luxurious only, for barbarians or men of the sword; but in such wise that the seemly habit of priests may be set forth in our very outward features. But in place of what I have quoted, the LXX. say, "*Their heads they shall not shave, and their hair they shall not closely poll, but a covering shall they have upon their heads.*" And according to this we learn that we are not to make a baldness upon our heads with a razor, nor to cut the hair of the head so closely[52] that we shall look as though we were shaved, but to let the hair grow long enough to cover the skin. Or it may be simply that priests ought always to put a covering on their heads, according to that line of Virgil, "*With purple amice covered o'er, veil thou thy locks.*" But this is a forced interpretation. But wine is not to be drunk by priests and Levites, and this not only in the time of their

---

[51] The original is as follows: *Per quæ discimus non quotidianis et quibuslibet pro usu vitæ communis pollutis vestibus, nos ingredi debere in Sancta Sanctorum, sed munda conscientia et mundis vestibus tenere Domini sacramenta.*

[52] Note this passage as proving clearly that in St. Jerome's time, "the tonsure" was, at Rome, at any rate, unknown as a mark of the Christian priest.

ministration, but even (beforehand) when they are about to enter into the Holy of Holies, lest the mind become oppressed, and the senses dulled. Hence that of the Apostle,—"*It is good*," saith he, "*not to drink wine nor to eat flesh*." And in another place: "*And wine, wherein is excess.*" "*For the people did eat, and drink, and rose up to play.*" (1 Cor. x. 7.) And for that of his allowing Timothy to drink a little wine, he showed plainly why he allowed this. "*For thy stomach's sake*," he says, "*and for thine often infirmities.*" Garments of linen are used by the Egyptian priests, not only inside their temples, but without also. [53]Moreover, the religion that is of God has one dress for holy ministry, another for the usage of common life.[53] Drawers (of linen) are rightly put on, that seemliness and propriety may be maintained, lest when they ascend the steps of the altar (Exod. xx. 26), and hasten to and fro in the work of their ministry there be any unseemly exposure. Heathen superstition has its shaven heads. But as far as my knowledge goes, I do not think that any heathen abstains from wine.

The spiritual meaning of all this will be seen by what follows. That there are garments holy and spiritual the Apostle himself teaches us, saying, "*Put ye on*" ("clothe yourselves with") "*the Lord Jesus Christ.*" And elsewhere, "*Put ye on bowels of mercy, of goodness, of humility, of gentleness, of patience.*" And again, "*Having stripped off the old man, together with his deeds, and having put on the new man which is renewed unto (fulness of) knowledge after the likeness of the Creator.*" [He then quotes 1 Cor. xv. 54, saying that this, too, appears to him to have a similar reference.] As to the priestly vestments there is a full account in Exodus, and I myself once wrote a book on the subject, to which and the interpretation there given the enquiring reader may be referred. For the subject is too wide a one to be embraced within the compass of a short discourse. These vestments we make for ourselves by our own exertion, even such a garment (*tunicam*) as the Lord had, and which could not be rent.

---

[53] The original is as follows: *Porro religio divina alteram habitum habet in ministerio, alteram in usu vitaque communi.* It is doubtful whether, by *religio divina*, St. Jerome refers to Jewish or to Christian observances. The reference to the *feminalia linea* that immediately follows seems to show that *Sirmondus* (quoted later in this work) was right in supposing him to speak here of *Jewish* observances. Most writers on ritual, *quoting the passage without its context*, have assumed the exact contrary, as though there were no doubt at all about the matter. [As a matter of controversy it matters little which of the two be really referred to, or whether both, as I believe.]

And thefe veftments we put on when we come to the knowledge of the fecret and hidden things of God, and have that fpirit that fearcheth even the deep and profound things of God, things not to be fet forth before the people, nor brought before the eyes of them that are not fanctified, nor made ready for the holinefs of the Lord; left haply if they hear things beyond their capacity, they be unable to endure the greatnefs of fuch knowledge, and be choked, as it were, with this "ftrong meat," whereas they had need ftill to be fed with milk. . . . As for that which follows, "*Bands (vittæ) or caps (cidares) of linen fhall be on their heads*," this, I think, points to the feftive crown of grace, of which it is written (Prov. iv. 9), "A crown[34] of grace fhall be fet on thine head." Nor need we find difficulty in thofe words of the Apoftle concerning the covering, or the leaving bare, the head. "*A woman*," he faith, "*ought to have a covering upon her head becaufe of the angels. For if a woman will not be thus covered, then let her cut clofe her hair. But if it be a fhame unto a woman that her hair be clofe cut or fhorn, then let her cover (her head). For the man ought not to cover his head, feeing he is the image and glory of God. But the woman is the glory of the man* (or "*of her hufband.*") For if it be not proper for men to cover the head, it might be thought inconfiftent with this that the priefts are here bidden to cover their heads with caps or bonnets. But if we read fomewhat more carefully, the words that preceded will folve the difficulty of thofe now before us. For it is faid above, "*When they minifter in the gates of the inner court and yet farther within*" (*i.e.* in the Holy Place.) For if we enter in to the Holy Place and ftand before the face of the Lord, we ought to cover our heads:[35] "*For in the fight of the Lord fhall no flefh living be juftified.*" (Ps. cxlii. 2.) And, "*Even from a child man's heart is fet upon*

---

[34] *Coronam enim gratiarum fufcipiet tuus vertex.* It is hardly neceffary, probably, to point out that our modern word "crown," is generally fuggeftive (in the Englifh verfion of the Bible, for example) of an entirely different idea to that fuggefted to claffical readers by *corona*, or by the correfponding Greek word στέφανος. In claffical, and in *early* Chriftian ufage, thefe words are expreffive of the *chaplet* (of whatever materials) worn by perfons of all claffes on feftive occafions, worn by priefts (and prieftefles) in honour of particular deities, by victors in the circus or the like, or by triumphant foldiers. The diftinctive word for the crown of royalty is διάδημα (*diadema*). But it may be well to mention that in *later* Chriftian writers, as we fhall fee as we proceed, the word *corona* is occafionally ufed, as our own "crown," with reference to infignia of royalty.

[35] "We ought to cover our heads," *i.e.* in felf-abafement, as confcious of our own unworthinefs, of which he proceeds to fpeak.

*wickedness.*" (Gen. viii. 21.) Then, laſtly, we wear inwardly a veſture about our loins, leſt, in the preſence of God, aught of unſeemlineſs appear, belonging to a polluted conſcience, or to that which pertaineth unto married life. With ſuch under-garments the Saviour would have His Apoſtles girt when He ſaith, "*Let your loins be girded, and burning lights be in your hands.*" (Luke, xii. 35.) And the Apoſtle ſaith unto the faithful, "*Stand, therefore, having your loins girt about in truth.*" (Eph. vi. 14.) And to the followers of Chriſt doth that apply which is written concerning Chriſt Himſelf, "*Righteouſneſs ſhall be the girdle of his loins, and with the truth ſhall his ſides be clothed.*" (Iſa. xi. 5.) And with this girdle that is here ſpoken of, he that is holy, and hath attained unto the height (*culmen*) of all virtue, doth not bind himſelf " violently."[86]

---

[86] See above, note 49.

## VII.

## S. JEROME.

## WHITE GARMENTS WORN IN OFFICES OF CHRISTIAN MINISTRATION.

Adversus Pelagianos, Lib. i. Vol. iv. p. 502.

[After speaking of the pretences made by the Pelagians to something approaching to a direct revelation of Divine Truth, he adds]:—

"*Nec hoc sufficit, sed repente mutaris in Stoicum, et de Zenonis nobis tonas supercilio, Christianum illius debere esse patientiæ ut si quis sua auferre voluerit gratanter amittat. Nonne nobis satis est patienter perdere quod habemus, nisi violento atque raptori agamus gratias, et cum cunctis benedictionibus prosequamur? Docet Evangelium ei qui nobiscum velit iudicio contendere, et per lites ac jurgia auferre tunicam, etiam pallium esse concedendum: non præcipit ut agamus gratias, et læti nostra perdamus. Hoc dico, non quod aliquid sceleris in hac sententia sit, sed quod ubique ὑπερβολικῶς; mediocria transeas et magna sceleris. Unde adjungis gloriam vestium et ornamentorum Deo esse contrariam. Quæ sunt, rogo, inimicitiæ contra Deum si tunicam habuero mundiorem:[57] si Episcopus, Presbyter, et Diaconus, et reliquus ordo Ecclesiasticus, in administratione sacrificiorum candida veste processerint? Cavete Clerici, cavete Monachi: viduæ et virgines periclitamini, nisi sordidas vos atque pannosas vulgus aspexerit. Taceo de hominibus sæculi quibus aperte bellum indicitur, et inimicitiæ contra Deum si preciosis atque nitentibus utantur exuviis.*"

"Even this does not content you. You turn stoic of a sudden, and thunder against us with all the sternness of a Zeno, and declare that a Christian should be so patient as to rejoice in losing whatsoever any man may choose to take from him. Is it not enough, then, for us to submi

---

[57] *Mundiorem. Mundus* as applied to clothing has a primary reference to cleanliness, but is often used with a secondary implication of the seemly beauty that belongs to garments bright and pure. So Livy speaks of a *cultus justo mundior*—an over-elegance of personal attire.

patiently to loss of what is ours, unless we thank him who with violence has robbed us, and follow him with every expression of blessing? The Gospel teaches, it is true, that to one who would contend with us at law, and rob us of our under garment we should give up our outer garment also, but it bids us not express gratitude to the wrongdoer, and show gladness at the loss of our goods. I mention this, not as though there were anything criminal in your holding such an opinion, but because in everything alike you are actuated by the same spirit of exaggeration, and without thought or regard for any moderate course, are ever aiming at great things. Hence you go on to say that all splendour of dress or ornament is offensive unto God. But I would fain know what offence there would be against God in my wearing a somewhat handsome[n] tunic; *or if, in the administration of the Holy Things, Bishop, Priest, and Deacon, and the other officers of the Church, come forward dressed in white garments.* Beware ye that are of the Clergy, beware ye Monks: and you too, widows and virgins, are in peril, unless you appear in public in squalid habit and in rags. I say nothing of men of the world, against whom war is thus openly proclaimed, and who are accused as enemies of God if they wear costly or splendid garments."

## VIII.

## HEGESIPPVS.[a]

### LINEN VESTMENTS SAID TO HAVE BEEN WORN BY JAMES THE BROTHER OF THE LORD.

APUD S. HIERONYMUM, IN CATALOGO SCRIPT. ECCLES.

JACOBUS qui appellatur frater Domini, cognomento Juftus, ut nonnulli exiftimant Jofeph ex alia uxore, ut autem mihi videtur Mariæ fororis matris Domini, cujus Johannes in libro fuo meminit, filius, poft paffionem Domini ftatim ab Apoftolis Ierofolymorum Epifcopus ordinatus, unam tantum fcripfit epiftolam, quæ de feptem Catholicis eft, quæ et ipfa ab alio quodam fub nomine ejus edita afferitur: licet paullatim tempore præcedente obtinuerit auctoritatem. Hegefippus, vicinus Apoftolicorum temporum, in quinto commentariorum libro de Jacobo narrans ait: *Sufcepit ecclefiam Ierofolymorum poft Apoftolos frater Domini Jacobus, cognomento Juftus. Multi fiquidem Jacobi vocabantur. Hic de utero matris fanctus fuit, vinum et ficeram non bibit, carnem nullam comedit, nunquam attonfus eft nec unctus unguento, nec ufus balneo. Huic foli licitum erat ingredi Sancta Sanctorum. Siquidem veftibus lineis non utebatur fed lineis, folufque ingrediebatur Templum, et flexis genibus pro populo deprecabatur: intantum ut camelorum duritiem traxiffe ejus genua crederentur.*

"The government of the Church of Jerufalem was committed, after the Apoftles, to James, the brother of the Lord, furnamed ' *The Juft*,' there being many then who bore the name of James. He was holy from his mother's womb: he drank neither wine nor ftrong drink, ate no flefh-meat, never cut clofe the hair of his head, nor anointed himfelf with unguents, nor ufed the bath. To him alone was it allowable to enter the Holy of Holies, feeing that he wore garments made, not of wool, but of linen; and he was wont to enter

---

[a] Hegefippus, a Jew converted to Chriftianity, died *circa* A.D. 180. Only fragments of his works have been preferved.

the Temple alone, and on bended knees to entreat God on behalf of His people; insomuch that men believed that his knees had grown hard, even as are the knees of a camel."[59]

---

[59] In judging of the historical references to be drawn from this statement we must remember, first, that we have not the *ipsissima verba* of Hegesippus, but a Latin translation of his words by S. Jerome. We cannot, therefore, now tell whether the *Sancta Sanctorum* of S. Jerome represents τὰ ἅγια simply (which might mean only "the Sanctuary," as a somewhat vague designation), or ἅγια ἁγίων, which could only mean "The Most Holy Place," entered once in the year by the high-priest alone.

And so again of that "*Templum ingrediebatur*," we cannot now say whether the original spoke of τὸν ναόν, or of τὸ ἱερόν. The former would imply the actual building (made up of "the Holy" and "the Most Holy" Place). The latter term includes the whole sacred enclosure, with its many subordinate buildings.

However this be, it would be contrary to all historical probability that St. James, the head of the Christian Church at Jerusalem, and not of Levitical descent, should have been allowed, as a literal matter of fact, to enter the "Holy of Holies" of the Jewish temple. The real explanation of this, as of some other similar passages which will be quoted, I believe to be this,—that some early writers, who were themselves thoroughly conversant with the significance of the insignia of priesthood and of royalty among the Jews, used, occasionally, expressions in speaking of Apostles and others, which would be φαντάσια συνεσέως, suggestive of important truths to men as well informed as themselves, but which could only lead to error if taken as literal statements of historical fact. Compare the passage from Epiphanius, quoted below, p. 40, and Note 62 upon that passage.

## IX.

## POLYCRATES,[60] OF EPHESVS.

### OF THE GOLDEN PLATE WORN BY ST. JOHN.

#### Apud Eusebium. Hist. Eccl. v. 24.

Eusebius is speaking of the dispute between Victor, Bishop of Rome, and certain Eastern Bishops, concerning the proper time of the Easter Festival. As to this the traditionary usage of the Churches in Asia Minor differed from that of other Churches. And Polycrates of Ephesus, who held first place among the Bishops of Asia Minor, wrote as follows " to Bishop Victor and the Roman Church ":—

. . . Ἡμεῖς οὖν ἀραδιούργητον ἄγομεν τὴν ἡμέραν, μήτε προστιθέντες μήτε ἀφαιρούμενοι. Καὶ γὰρ κατὰ τὴν Ἀσίαν μεγάλα στοιχεῖα κεκοίμηται ἅτινα ἀναστήσεται τῇ ἡμέρᾳ τῆς παρουσίας τοῦ Κυρίου ἐν ᾗ ἔρχεται μετὰ δόξης ἐξ οὐρανῶν, καὶ ἀναστήσει πάντας τοὺς ἁγίους, Φίλιππον τῶν δώδεκα ἀποστόλων ὃς κεκοίμηται ἐν Ἱεραπόλει, καὶ δύο θυγάτερες αὐτοῦ γεγηρακυῖαι παρθένοι. Καὶ ἡ ἑτέρα αὐτοῦ θυγάτηρ ἐν Ἁγίῳ Πνεύματι πολιτευσαμένη ἐν Ἐφέσῳ ἀναπαύεται, ἔτι δὲ καὶ ὁ Ἰωάννης ὁ ἐπὶ τὸ στῆθος τοῦ Κυρίου ἀναπεσὼν ὃς ἐγενήθη ἱερεὺς τὸ πέταλον πεφορεκὼς καὶ μάρτυς καὶ διδάσκαλος, οὗτος ἐν Ἐφέσῳ κεκοίμηται.

[Then follows an enumeration of other bishops of renown and martyrs whom Polycrates alleges as having all adhered to the same tradition in this matter.]

" For our own part we observe the day with scrupulous exactness, neither adding nor taking away. In Asia great luminaries of the Church have been gathered to their rest, who shall rise again in the day of the Lord's coming, when He cometh with glory from heaven, and shall raise up all the saints, such as were Philip, one of the twelve, who now is at rest in Hierapolis; and his two daughters

---

[60] As Polycrates was contemporary with Irenæus of Gaul and Victor of Rome (sed. A.D. 192 to A.D. 202), the date of this letter is determined to the close of the second century.

who waxed old in virgin estate, while his other daughter, after a Christian life in the Holy Spirit, resteth now in Ephesus. Yea moreover, John also, he that reclined on the Lord's breast, *and became a priest*[61] *wearing the golden plate,*[62] and a Witness, and a Teacher, he, I say, now sleepeth in Ephesus."

---

[61] As the terms ἱερεύς and *Sacerdos* are used in a great variety of meanings in ecclesiastical writers, and as the ambiguity thence arising will frequently come under notice in the course of these extracts, it may be well here briefly to enumerate those meanings, and to designate each by a separate (Greek) letter for facility of reference. The two words then (which may be regarded as equivalent) are used,—

α. Of the Jewish high-priest. [So ὁ ἱερεύς not unfrequently in LXX.]

β. Of Levitical priests of the second order.

γ. Of the Levitical priests generally, so as to include both the high-priest and the priests of the second order.

δ. Of our Lord Jesus Christ. [So in Heb. v. 6; vii. 21; x. 21.]

ε. Of Christian bishops.

ς. Of Christian presbyters, or priests.

ζ. Of those who in Christ's Church minister in holy things unto God, whether bishops or presbyters.

What is here briefly stated will be shown more at length with regard to *Sacerdos* in a subsequent note (See Index *in voc.*), in the extract from Pope Celestine's Letter to the Bishops of Gaul. [I shall refer, whenever necessary, to the various modifications of meaning above enumerated, by the number of the Note prefixed to the various letters. Thus 62 α will indicate a reference to the Jewish high-priest, 62 ε to Christian bishops, and so for the rest. But it must be understood that it is *only by context* that we can determine which of the above meanings was present to the mind of the writer in any given passage. And my references therefore are only to be regarded as expressions of *opinion* founded upon study of such context.]

[62] I quote both the context and the words of the original text, that the reader may judge for himself what is their true meaning. The word ἱερεύς by itself is ambiguous, and may mean either a high-priest or a priest of the second order, as context may suggest. But, as the distinctive mark of a high-priest was the πέταλον, or plate of gold, marking his supreme authority, or "royal priesthood," Polycrates uses here the descriptive expression, "a priest that had worn the πέταλον" (much as ecclesiastical historians speak of a "mitred abbot"), in order to bring out the fact on which he was then concerned to insist, viz., *the supreme Apostolic authority* of St. John, whose office in the Christian Church was to bear rule in spiritual things over the spiritual Israel, even as the high-priest of old over Israel after the flesh. For this last compare the passage from Epiphanius that follows (p. 40.) I may observe that the explanation above given will at once account for the very peculiar use of the participle of the *præsens perfectum*, πεφορεκώς. The proper connotation of that participle is (see *Eirenica*, Notes 49, 52, and 61) that of a *state* or *condition* resulting from a past act. And this idea (slightly modified by the peculiarities of this exceptional context) is exactly coincident with the explanation above suggested.

## X.

## EPIPHANIVS.[63]

### BISHOP OF SALAMIS, A.D. 367 TO A.D. 403.

#### ADV. HÆS. LIB. I. CAP. 29.

[THE writer has been speaking of the prophecies concerning One who should "*fit on the throne of David.*" These prophecies, he adds, must needs have their fulfilment, seeing that no declaration of Holy Scripture faileth of accomplishment. He proceeds as follows] :—

By the "throne of David," and by the "fitting as a king," is meant the office of priesthood in God's Holy Church, which is a rank at once of royalty and of supreme priesthood, together conjoined of Christ, which He hath bestowed upon His holy Church, removing and placing in that His Church the throne of David, which abideth for ever. . . . . Now, when the seat of kingly power had thus been transferred in Christ to the Church, the royal dignity was likewise transferred from the family of that Judah that was after the flesh, and from the Jerusalem that once was. And now the throne is set in God's Holy Church, and that for ever, having two titles to this dignity, in respect of kingship the one, in respect of supreme priesthood the other. It is a throne of royalty first, by inheritance from Christ Jesus our Lord: and this after two manners, because of His being of the seed of David the king, by natural descent, and as being what indeed He is, a greater King, from all eternity, in respect of His Godhead. It is a throne, too, of priesthood, because he is himself a high-priest, and first in rank in a line of high-priests, seeing that James (called the brother of the Lord, and apostle) was straight-

---

[63] Epiphanius, surnamed ὁ πεντάγλωσσος, as being acquainted with five languages, was born in Palestine *of Jewish parents.* He was chosen bishop of the Metropolitan See of Constantia (formerly *Salamis*) in Crete, A.D. 367. The passage here given is quoted, or rather referred to, by St. Jerome in his "Catalogus Illustrium Virorum."

way established as bishop, and he again was, by birth, the eldest son of Joseph, but, in regard of rank, was called brother of the Lord, because of their association one with the other.

For this James was a son of Joseph, begotten of Joseph's (first) wife, not of Mary (the mother of the Lord), as I have already often said, and clearly proved. Moreover, we find that he was of the seed of David, as being Joseph's son, and became a Nazarene. For he was Joseph's first-born and consecrated unto God. Beside this, I find that he exercised priestly office,[64] after the manner of the ancient priesthood, and for this reason was allowed to enter the Holy of Holies once in every year, as the law according to Scripture bade the high-priests do. For so many before me have recorded of him, such as were Eusebius, Clement, and others. Moreover, it was allowable for him to wear the golden plate upon his head, as is testified by the afore-mentioned trustworthy writers.[65]

---

[64] The original is as follows: 'Ἔτι δὲ καὶ ἱεράτευντα αὐτὸν κατὰ τὴν παλαιὰν ἱερωσύνην εὕρομεν, διὸ καὶ ἀφεῖτο αὐτῷ ἅπαξ τοῦ ἐνιαυτοῦ εἰς τὰ ἅγια τῶν ἁγίων εἰσιέναι, ὡς τοῖς ἀρχιερεῦσιν ἐπέλευσεν ὁ νόμος κατὰ τὸ γεγραμμένον. οὕτω γὰρ ἱστόρησαν πολλοὶ πρὸ ἡμῶν περὶ αὐτοῦ Εὐσέβιος τε καὶ Κλήμης καὶ ἄλλοι. Ἀλλὰ καὶ τὸ πέταλον ἐπὶ τῆς κεφαλῆς ἐξὸν αὐτῷ φορεῖν καθὼς οἱ προειρημένοι ἀξιόπιστοι ἄνδρες ἐν τοῖς ὑπ' αὐτῶν ὑπομνηματισμοῖς ἐμαρτύρησαν. In referring to "Eusebius," he no doubt has in view the letter of Bishop Polycrates preserved by Eusebius, and quoted above, p. 38.

[65] It will be seen that the general scope of this passage is to prove the applicability to our Lord of the prophecies concerning One who should *sit on the throne of David for ever.* This was so, he argues, in respect both of the Kingship of Christ, and in respect of His Priesthood. And all that he says of James is brought in by way of showing how the fact of *his relationship*, as half-brother in the eye of the law, *to our Lord*, pointed him out as having a claim, as nearest of kin, to preside (*reign*, as it were) over the Church at Jerusalem immediately after our Lord Himself had ascended into heaven. His argument is based upon the fact (familiar to him as originally a Jew) that the offices both of the highpriest and of the *Rosh Abbeth*, or head of the Sanhedrim ( = the Greek πανριάρχης), were regarded by the Jews as hereditary, and passing, therefore, in default of direct heirs *to the nearest of kin.*

## XI.

## THEODORET.[60]

### THE SACRED ROBE SENT BY CONSTANTINE TO MACARIUS OF JERUSALEM.

[Eccles. Hist. Lib. ii. Cap. xxiii.]

Κωνστάντιος γὰρ ἀπὸ τῆς ἑσπέρας ἐπανελθὼν ἐν ταύτῃ διέτριβε. Πολλὰ δὲ τῶν συνεληλυθότων ἐπὶ τοῦ βασιλέως (ὁ Ἀκάκιος) κατηγορήσας καὶ σύστημα πονηρῶν ἀνθρώπων ἀποκαλέσας ἐπ' ὀλέθρῳ καὶ λύμῃ τῶν ἐκκλησιῶν συγκροτούμενον, τὸν βασιλέως ἄνηψε θυμόν. Οὐχ ἥκιστα δὲ αὐτὸν χαλεπῆναι πεποίηκεν ἃ κατὰ τοῦ Κυρίλλου συντέθεικε. Τὴν γὰρ ἱερὰν στολὴν ἣν ὁ πανεύφημος Κωνσταντῖνος ὁ βασιλεὺς τῶν Ἱεροσολύμων ἐκκλησίαν γεραίρων δεδώκει τῷ Μακαρίῳ τῷ τῆς πόλεως ἐκείνης ἀρχιερεῖ, ἵνα ταύτην περιβαλλόμενος τὴν τοῦ θείου βαπτίσματος ἐπιτελῇ λειτουργίαν, ἐκ χρυσῶν δὲ αὕτη κατεσκεύαστο νημάτων, πεπρακέναι τὸν Κύριλλον ἔφη, καὶ ταύτην τινὰ τῶν ἐπὶ τῆς θυμέλης λυγιζομένων πριάμενον περιβαλέσθαι μέν, ὀρχούμενον δὲ πεσεῖν καὶ συνθλιβῆναι καὶ θανάτῳ παραδοθῆναι.

"Conſtantius, after his return from the Weſt, continued for ſome time in this city (Conſtantinople). Acacius brought many accuſations to the Emperor againſt the biſhops who had aſſembled at Seleucia, abuſing them as a pack of miſchievous men got together for the ruin and deſtruction of the Churches, and ſo excited him to anger againſt them. What more than all excited his indignation was the charge which Acacius deviſed againſt Cyril (Biſhop of Jeruſalem). The Emperor Conſtantine, of famous memory, as a mark of honour to the Church at Jeruſalem, had ſent to Macarius, then biſhop of that city, a ſacred robe, made of threads of gold, which he ſhould put upon him when performing the office of holy baptiſm. This robe Acacius

---

[60] Theodoret, born at Antioch, *circa* A.D. 393, ſtudied under Theodore of Mopſueſtia and S. Chryſoſtom; became Biſhop of Cyrus in Syria, A.D. 420; died A.D. 457.

declared had been sold by Cyril, and that a stage-dancer had bought it and put it on, but that, in dancing, he fell and received injuries which proved fatal."[67]

[67] I have quoted the above passage, because the fact of a "sacred vestment" being given to Macarius of Jerusalem is one which is often referred to by writers on ecclesiastical vestments. What really follows from the above passage is that Constantine thought that a splendid robe of some kind might properly be worn by a patriarch at the Office of Holy Baptism. What was the nature of the robe does not appear. But it is evident that whether the story of Cyril's having sold it be true or no, it was one of which, with at least a show of probability, it could be said that it had been purchased by a stage-dancer, and by him worn in public exhibitions. As to the *apostolic* origin of the so-called "sacerdotal vestments," the story proves nothing at all, but if anything, goes to prove their imperial and secular origin.

## XII.

# ST. AUGUSTINE[a] OF HIPPO.

## ON THE LEVITICAL VESTMENTS.

QUÆSTIONES IN HEPTATEUCHUM, LIB. II. CAP. CXXIX.

IN this chapter he has occasion to notice the dress of the high-priest as a whole, and also special portions of it, as the λόγιον, or *rationale*, and the *lamina aurea*. In all these he sees a mystical reference to Christ or to sacraments of the Church, but does not even in the slightest way allude to any corresponding vestments worn in offices of Christian ministry. The concluding words of the chapter are the following:—

Quod autem præfiguratum est in sancto sanctorum, ut super arcam quæ Legem habebat esset propitiatorium, ubi Dei misericordia significari intelligenda est, qua propitius fit eorum peccatis qui Legem non implent; hoc mihi videtur etiam in ipsa veste sacerdotis[b] significari: nam et ipsa quid aliud quam Ecclesiæ sacramenta significat? Quod in λογίῳ, id est Rationali, in pectore sacerdotis[b] posito, judicia constituit, in lamina vero sanctificationem et ablationem peccatorum: tanquam Rationale sit in pectore simile arcæ in qua Lex erat, et lamina illa in fronte similis propitiatorio quod super arcam erat, et ut utrobique servaretur quod scriptum est, *Superexultat misericordia judicio.* (Jac. ii. 13.)

---

[a] Bishop of Hippo, 365; died A.D. 450.
[b] *Sacerdos* throughout this passage is used, as the previous context shows, of the Jewish high-priest. See above Note 61 a.

XIII.

## POPE CELESTINE.[70]

### ON EPISCOPAL DRESS.

[THE letter from which extracts are here given, will be found in Labbé's "Concilia," vol. ii. p. 1618. It is addressed "To all the Bishops of the Provinces of Vienna and Narbonne."]

"We have been informed that certain priests[71] of the Lord are devoting themselves rather to superstitious observances in dress than to purity of thought and of faith. But it is not to be wondered at that the customs of the Church should be broken by men who have not grown up in the Church, but coming in by another way, have introduced with them into the Church what had been theirs in another[72] mode of life. By dressing in a *pallium*[73] and wearing a girdle[74] round their loins, they think to fulfil the truth of Scripture, not in the spirit but in the letter. But if the precepts to which they refer were for this end given, that after this strange fashion they should be observed, why are not the precepts which follow observed in like manner, and so 'burning lights' held in the hands as well as 'a staff?' The words they quote have a mystical meaning of their own, and to men of understanding are so clear as to be observed according to a more fitting interpretation. For by the girding up of the loins is signified Chastity, and by the staff Pastoral Rule, and by 'burning lights' the brightness of good works, concerning which it is said (Matt. v. 16), 'Let your works shine.' But supposing it so to be, that men dwelling in remote districts, and far from others, wear this dress, out of custom rather than of reason, yet whence such a dress in the Churches of Gaul? And why is the custom, observed for so many years, and by such great bishops, to be discarded for another garb? We should be distinguished from the common folk, and from the rest, by our learning, not by our gar-

---

[70] Bishop of Rome from November, 423, to April, 432.

ments; by our mode of life, not by what we wear; by purity of thought, not by peculiarities of dress. For if we begin to affect innovations, we shall tread under foot the traditions of our fathers, only to make room for worthless superstitions. We ought not, therefore, to attract to objects such as these the untrained minds of the faithful. It is teaching they require, not mockeries like these. Nor is it an imposing appearance to the eye that is needed, but precepts to be instilled into the mind."

The original is as follows:—

*Didicimus quosdam Domini sacerdotes*[71] *superstitioso potius cultui inservire quam mentis vel fidei puritati. Sed non mirum si contra ecclesiasticum morem faciunt qui in ecclesia non creverunt, sed alio venientes itinere secum hæc in ecclesiam quæ in alia conversatione*[72] *habuerant, intulerunt. Amicti pallio,*[73] *et lumbos præcincti,*[74] *credunt se scripturæ fidem non per*

---

[71] *Sacerdotes Domini.* I have translated the word *Sacerdos* by priest for want of a better word. In point of fact, however, this term, when employed in a Christian sense, is in early writers used far more frequently of bishops than of priests,—not unfrequently of bishops and priests inclusively—and is seldom if ever used as the distinctive appellation of the second order of the Christian ministry.

St. Gregory *always* (as far as I have observed) uses *Sacerdos* as the equivalent of *episcopus, sacerdotium* of *Episcopatus*. So St. Gregory of Tours (De Gloria Episc. cap. cx. p. 989), Venerable Bede, and others, Honorius of Autun (apud Ducange *in voc.*), lib. i. cap. 182; and Rhabanus Maurus de Instit. Cleric. cap. 5, p. 314; recognise the properly inclusive use of the term. *Sacerdos autem vocari potest sive episcopus sit sive presbyter.* In a letter of John of Ravenna to St. Gregory the Great, and in passages of Innocent III., quoted below, we shall come upon one or two instances in which it is clear from the context that *Sacerdos* is used as a designation of a presbyter. Compare Note 61.

[72] *In alia conversatione.* He means, probably, "while living under *monastic* rule," (see the next Note). Several instances are alluded to in early writers of monks who retained their monastic habit after promotion to episcopal dignity. A well-known instance is that of Fulgentius, Bishop of Ruspa. *Ororio quidem sicut omnes episcopi nullatenus utebatur.*

*Pelliceo cingulo tanquam monachus utebatur. . . . Casulam pretiosam vel superbi coloris nec monachos suos habere permisit, nec ipse habuit. Subtus casulam nigello vel lacteineo pallio circumdatus incessit. Quando temperies aeris invitabat solo pallio intra monasterium est coopertus. Nec deposito saltem cingulo somnum potivit. In qua tunica dormiebat in eadem sacrificabat.* [Ferrandus Diaconus apud Thomassinum.]

[73] *Amicti pallio.* By *pallium* is here meant the coarse outer garment traditionally associated in idea with the prophets of the old covenant, and adopted in early Christian times by hermits and monks (see next Note), and by others living a life of similar austerity. The word *pallium* occurs in a great variety of meanings in early writers. Several of these will come before us in the course of this work, and will be noticed in the order of their occurrence.

[74] With this mention of *pallium* and *cingulum* as characteristic of a monastic dress, compare Salvianus (apud Thomassinum) ad Eccles.Cathol. lib. iv. Addressing a monk of unworthy character, he says: *Licet religionem* (i.e. monastic life) *vestibus simules, licet fidem cingulo afferas, licet sanctitatem pallio mentiaris,* etc. The mention of a *pelliceum cingulum* (ζώνη δερματίνη) in the passage quoted in Note 72 is an indication that the dress of John the Baptist was taken as a type by the earlier monks. So S. Germanus (quoted later in this volume) more distinctly implies.

*spiritum sed per literam completuros. Nam si ad hoc ista præcepta sunt ut taliter servarentur, cur non fiunt pariter quæ sequuntur, ut* lucernæ ardentes in manibus una cum baculo teneantur? *Habent suum ista mysterium, et intelligentibus ita clara sunt ut ea magis qua decet significatione serventur. Nam in lumborum præcinctione castitas, in baculo regimen pastorale, in lucernis ardentibus boni fulgor operis, de quo dicitur,* Opera vestra luceant, indicantur. *Habeant tamen istum forsitan cultum, morem potius quam rationem sequentes, qui in remotioribus habitant locis, et procul a ceteris degunt. Unde hic habitus in ecclesiis Gallicanis, ut tot annorum tantorumque pontificum in alterum habitum consuetudo vertatur? Discernendi a plebe vel ceteris sumus doctrina non veste, conversatione non habitu, mentis puritate non cultu. Nam si studere incipiamus novitati, traditum nobis a patribus ordinem calcabimus ut locum supervacuis superstitionibus faciamus. Rudes ergo fidelium mentes ad talia non debemus inducere. Docendi enim potius sunt quam illudendi. Nec imponendum est eorum oculis, sed mentibus infundenda præcepta sunt.*

---

## XIV.

## JACOBUS SIRMONDUS.[75]

### ON THE ORIGIN OF ECCLESIASTICAL VESTMENTS.

(From his Annotations on the Letter above quoted.)

[Having quoted a bishop of Rome I may be allowed here to add the comment of a learned Jesuit, Jacobus Sirmondus. He writes as follows:—]

Taxat Cælestinus episcopos quosdam qui novo et insueto habitus genere uterentur: docetque discerni ab aliis debere clericos non veste sed vita et moribus. Sunt qui habitum interpretentur quo incedebant:

---

[75] He was born a.d. 1559; was made Confessor to Louis XIII. in 1637; and died, at a great age, 1651.

alii ut Dionyſius Exiguus, quo miniſtrabant. *Quod non debeant*, inquit, *ſacerdotes aut clerici amicti pallio et præcincti lumbos in ecclefia miniſtrare.* Sed res eodem relabitur. Nam primis ecclefiæ ſæculis clerici quas in vita communi veſtes uſurpabant, iiſdem etiam in ſacris utebantur, ſed mundioribus et optimis, id eſt, ut Hieronymus exponit in caput xliv. Ezechielis, *non quotidianis et quibuslibet pro uſu vitæ communi pollutis, ſed mundis.* Quod idem aliis verbis ſignificat lib. i. contra Pelagianos, Pelagium exagitans. [*Here he quotes the paſſage already given,* p. 34]. Candidam enim veſtem dicit Albam, quæ in uſu tum erat more Romano, eamque nitidam et lautiorem, qualis prenſantium magiſ-tratum, qui candidati propterea vocabantur. Et color igitur et forma veſtium eadem principio fuit eccleſiaſticis et reliquis. Sed cum formam alii poſtea mutaſſent, eccleſia prudenti conſilio priſtinam in ſacris re-tinuit: et ornatum licet preciumque ad venerationem veſtibus ſacris adjecerit, formam tamen non mutavit; ita ut Romanas veſtes nunc etiam referant, Alba tunicam, caſula togam, niſi quod caſula ſeu planeta anciſis proavorum noſtrorum memoria lateribus a togæ amplitudine abire cæpit. Et quia vetus hæc forma non perinde in quotidianis clericorum veſtibus, ut in ſacris, retenta eſt, ex eo factum ut nunc in Eccleſia quod de veteri lege ad Ezechielem obſervarat S. Hieronymus, *religio divina alterum habitum habeat in miniſterio, alterum in uſu vitaque communi.* Quod ipſum quoque accidit in lingua Latina, qua Divina officia celebramus. Nam cum ea quondam in uſu publico paſſim eſſet ſub imperio Romano, eademque ſacrorum in eccleſia vox eſſet, quæ populi; populus linguam, ut ſolet, poſtea mutavit, eccleſia Latinam merito retinuit.

## XV.

### ISIDORE OF PELUSIUM.[76]

#### OF THE LINEN STOLE AND THE WOOLLEN OMOPHORION.

Epist. Lib. i. Cap. 136.

Ἑρμίνῳ Κόμητι.[77]

Ὅσον αὐτὸς ἄπληστος εἶ πρὸς τὴν μάθησιν τοσοῦτον ἐγὼ πρόθυμος πρὸς τὴν δήλωσιν, μόνον εἰ θεὸς δῷ ταῖς εὐχαῖς σου τὴν εὕρεσιν ἄνωθεν.

Ἡ ὀθόνη[78] μίαϛ ἧς λειτουργοῦσιν ἐν τοῖς ἁγίοις οἱ διάκονοι τῆς τοῦ Κυρίου ἀναμιμνήσκει ταπεινώσιν, νίψαντος τοὺς πόδας τῶν μαθητῶν καὶ ἐκμάξαντος. Τὸ δὲ τοῦ ἐπισκόπου ὠμοφόριον ἐξ ἐρέας ὂν ἀλλ᾽ οὐ λίνου τὴν τοῦ προβάτου δορὰν σημαίνει ὅπερ πλανηθὲν ζητήσας ὁ Κύριος ἐπὶ τῶν οἰκείων ὤμων ἀνέλαβεν. Ὁ γὰρ ἐπίσκοπος εἰς τύπον ὢν τοῦ Χριστοῦ τὸ ἔργον ἐκείνου πληροῖ, καὶ δείκνυσι πᾶσι διὰ τοῦ σχήματος ὅτι μιμητής ἐστι τοῦ ἀγαθοῦ καὶ μεγάλου ποιμένος ὁ τὰς ἀσθενείας φέρειν τοῦ ποιμνίου προβεβλημένος. Καὶ προσχὲς ἀκριβῶς. Ἡνίκα γὰρ αὐτὸς ὁ ἀληθινὸς ποιμὴν παραγένηται διὰ τῆς τῶν εὐαγγελίων τῶν προσκυνητῶν ἀναπτύξεως,[79] καὶ ὑπανίσταται καὶ ἀποτίθεται τὸ σχῆμα τῆς μιμήσεως ὁ ἐπίσκοπος, αὐτὸν δηλῶν παρεῖναι τὸν Κύριον, τὸν τῆς ποιμαντικῆς ἡγεμόνα, καὶ θεόν, καὶ δεσπότην.

#### To Count Herminus.

"As thou art ever unwearied in learning, so am I ever ready to teach, if only God, in answer to thy prayers, grant me from above the finding of that thou seekest.

---

[76] *Isidorus, gente Ægyptius, ortu forsan Alexandrinus, et Chrysostomi discipulus, claruit circ. ann.* 412. *Vitam egit monasticam circa Pelusium, ex septem Nili ostiis maximum.* Cave, Hist. Lit. vol. i. p. 390.

[77] Κόμης. One of the many Latin words (*comes*) which under the Empire were adopted into Greek, and thence again, in many cases, into the Eastern languages, with which that Greek was brought in contact. It is here used probably of the governor of a province, in which sense *comes* is often used by the later Latin writers.

[78] ἡ ὀθόνη. Taken by itself this word might imply a linen vestment of any kind, whether shaped like a maniple, or like a stole. But there is no trace of the maniple in the Eastern Church, and there is little doubt but that the vestment here spoken of resembled the Latin *orarium*,—our own "stole." So St.

"The linen vestment [78] with which the deacons minister in the Holy Place, is a memorial of the humility of our Lord, in washing, and wiping dry, the feet of the disciples. But that which the bishop weareth on his shoulders, made not of linen but of wool, signifieth the fleece of the sheep, for which, when it had wandered away, the Lord sought, and took it up on his own shoulders. For the bishop, being a type of Christ, fulfilleth Christ's work, and by the habit he wears setteth forth unto all that he who is set to bear the infirmities of the flock is a follower of the good and great Shepherd. And this do thou note carefully. For when, by the unrolling [79] of the adorable Gospels, the true Shepherd Himself cometh nigh, the bishop riseth up to do Him honour, and layeth aside the habit of His semblance, showing that the Lord Himself is present, who is the chief Shepherd, and God, and Ruler over all."

---

[78] Chrysostom (or rather a sermon that bears his name), in the sermon on the Prodigal Son, speaks of the deacons as μιμούμενοι τὰς τῶν ἀγγέλων πτέρυγας ταῖς λεπταῖς ὀθόναις ταῖς ἐπὶ τῶν ἀριστερῶν ὤμων κειμέναις, "presenting the semblance of angels' wings in the light vestments of linen which rested on their left shoulders." And with this agrees the reference made to the same *item* by S. Germanus of Constantinople (quoted later in this volume).

[79] ἀναπτύξεως—unrolling, and so opening. To St. Isidore, writing early in the 5th century, the Gospels were probably still actually *columina*, "rolls," as we see them represented in the picture which forms the frontispiece to the present work. Comp. Luke, iv. 17, ἀναπτύξας τὸ βιβλίον.

## XVI.

## INCERTI AUCTORIS HOMILIA DE UNO LEGISLATORE S. CHRYSOSTOMI NOMINE INSCRIPTA.[80]

### THE LEVITICAL VESTMENTS.

[THE writer is enlarging on thofe words of David, ὁ Κύριος ἐβασίλευσεν (Ps. xcvi. 1), and on the parallel expreſſion (Ps. xcii. 1), ὁ Κύριος ἐβασίλευσεν· εὐπρέπειαν ἐνεδύσατο. Commenting on thefe laſt words, "He clothed Himſelf with beauty," he proceeds as follows]:—

We men clothe ourſelves outwardly with raiment, in order that we may hide whatever is unſeemly in our nature. But for what end ſhould God cover over His incorporeal nature, replete as it is with light, or rather itſelf the radiant ſource of light? But in truth He ſpeaketh here of the body of Chriſt as itſelf the garment wherewith He is clothed. "*The Lord is King: He hath put on beauteous apparel.*" By this beauty of which David ſpeaks he meaneth the body of Chriſt's fleſh. For beauteous this was, having nothing of the uglineſs of ſin. *For He did no ſin, neither was guile found in His mouth.* "The Lord hath clothed Himſelf with power: yea, He hath girded Himſelf about." Seeing that a girdle is the ornament of kings,[81] and ſerveth as an indication of a king and of a judge, therefore doth he here ſet

---

[80] Photius, writing in the 9th century, and at Conſtantinople, ſpeaks of this ſermon as one of the genuine works of S. Chryſoſtom. Moſt modern critics, however (Biſhop Pearſon is the only notable exception), regard it as the work of another and later author. The Benedictine editors follow Uſher in aſcribing it to the age of Juſtinian, or about the middle of the 6th century. See Montfaucon's Preface, Chryſoſtomi Opera, tom. vi. p. 469.

[81] Ἰδοὺ τὸν βασιλέα ζώνη κοσμεῖ. In the Byzantine repreſentations of royal perſonages, the embroidered girdle, of conſiderable width, and ſtudded with jewels, forms one of the moſt conſpicuous ornaments. See, for example, the figures of the Emperor Michael, and of the Empreſs Theodora, given by Dufreſne in his *Diſſertatio de Imperatorum Conſtantinopolitanorum Nummis* (appended to the Gloſſary), pl. vi. This reference by S. Germanus of the *girdle* of our Lord to royal, rather than to prieſtly, inſignia, is to be accounted for by the fact that the girdle was not, till after the 8th century (at the earlieſt) recogniſed as part of the *ornament* of the dreſs of Chriſtian miniſtry, ſeeing that if anything of the kind was worn, it was for convenience not for ſhow, and did not appear. In the Levitical dreſs, on the other hand, it was the moſt marked ornament of the ordinary ſacerdotal coſtume.

Him forth as both reigning and judging. For Esaias saith: "*There shall come forth a rod*[82] *out of the root of Jesse, and a flower shall spring therefrom, and the Spirit of God shall rest upon Him; and with righteousness shall His loins be girded, and with truth His sides be clothed.*" (Isa. xi. 1, 2, 5.)

This vesture of Christ, I mean His flesh, was worn after a hidden manner, and in image, by the high-priest under the law. And mark now with attention how the shadows served as interpreters of the Truth, how the types gave their light before the fuller light of the Gospel. I speak now with reserve, and accommodate my words as far as may be, to simple and unlearned hearers, that they be not carried to and fro with uncertainties of doctrine.

The high-priest, then, when he entered into the Holy of Holies, put upon him a ποδήρης (a garment, that is, that hung down from the head to the feet) together with ephod,[83] girdle, drawers, golden plate, tiara,[84] or priestly cap,[85] the Rational upon his breast, and all that the

---

[82] ῥάβδος. In this word which according to context may mean either (a) the young shoot of a tree, or (β) among many other secondary meanings, *a sceptre*, the writer sees a prophecy of Christ's royalty, as in the words βασιλεύσω and ἀλήθεια which follow, he finds symbolised His office as a Judge.

[83] ἐπωμίδα. Following the LXX.

[84] Τιάρα [also τιάρας, τιήρης, τιήρης], a Persian word, and Persian head-dress. So S. Chrysostom speaks of it, Homil. 17, in Acta: καθάπερ οἱ Πέρσαι τὰς τιάρας περιελόντες, καὶ τὰς ἀναξυρίδας καὶ τὰ ὑποδήματα τὰ βαρβαρικά, τὴν ἄλλην στολὴν τὴν ἡμῖν ἐπιχώριον ὑπελθόντες, καὶ κειράμενοι χρῶ μεύσονται τῷ σχήματι τῶν πολίτων. "As the Persians, by taking off their tiara, their trousers and foreign shoes, and assuming the dress commonly worn by ourselves, and shaving the skin, conceal under this outward semblance the war they bear in their hearts." But a tiara of a peculiar shape, *with an upright peak*, was the distinctive mark of Persian kings. So Æschylus speaks of it, *Pers.* 662, where the Chorus implore Darius to reappear on earth, βασίλειον τιάρας φάλαρον εἰφαίνων. Comp. Aristoph. *Aves.* 487. And of ecclesiastical writers, St. Jerome uses the word of the high cap (shaped like a "Cap of Liberty") which was then regarded as the characteristic mark of "men of the East."

[On Ezech. cap. xxiii. and on Dan. cap. iii.] *Tiara genus pilcoli quo Persarum Chaldæorumque genus utitur.* So again St. Isidore, Hisp. Orig. lib. xix. cap. xxx. *Imperatores Romani, et reges quidam gentium, aureis coronis utuntur. Persæ tiaras gerunt, sed reges rectos, satrapæ incurvas. Reperta autem tiara a Semiramide Assyriorum regina. Quod genus ornamenti exinde usque hodie gens ipsa retinet.* And Photius (9th century), κυρβασία, τιάρα· ἡ οἱ μὲν βασιλεῖς ὀρθῇ ἐχρῶντο, οἱ δὲ στρατηγοὶ ἐπικαλιμένην. As for this contrast of form compare Xen. *Anab.* ii. 5, 23, where Tissaphernes is represented as saying, τὴν ἐπὶ τῇ κεφαλῇ τιάραν βασιλεῖ μόνῳ ἔξεστιν ὀρθὴν ἔχειν. The use of the term as a designation for the *regnum*, or crown of royalty, worn by the later popes, is, as may be supposed, of very late date indeed.

[85] τιάρας, τουτέστι κιδαρίδιον. Two things are here to be remarked. First the mere fact that the preacher should find it necessary to explain the LXX. word τιάρα by κιδαρίδιον, affords of itself a strong presumption that no tiara, nor anything corresponding thereto in shape, could, in his time, have been generally known as the characteristic decoration of Christian bishops (compare below, Note 89). And secondly as to the word κιδαρίδιον itself. [The *var. lect.* κιδαρίας must be regarded as an explanatory gloss, substituting a comparatively common word for one which in literary Greek

Scripture there setteth forth, and which yourselves may see. In [86] all this that which outwardly is fashioned is one—other is that which thereby is to be understood. For God delighteth not in blue, and purple, and scarlet, and fine linen. That for which God looketh is purity of heart. But in the embodiment of these colours He setteth before us, as in a picture, the semblance of the divers virtues. For if God did indeed find pleasure in those vestments of glory, why did He not clothe Moses therewith before that he clothed Aaron? But Moses was himself without that vesture, and yet clothed therewith the priests. Moses was not washed with water, and yet did he wash *them*. He was not anointed with oil, yet did he anoint them. He wore not a priestly vestment, yet he put that vestment on the priests; that thou thereby mightest learn that to him that is perfect [87] virtue sufficeth for all adornment.

But let us set the priest before us, from the head downwards. For the very name of what he putteth upon him is matter of doubt and question, and has been rendered by another word in Greek. To begin then with the head. What was first? "Tiara," or what, is the name it bears? And why [88] is that which he weareth fashioned as a tiara? Because the high-priest was head of the people, and there was need that one who was made head of all, should himself have power set upon his head. For absolute and arbitrary power is not to be endured, but if it have the symbol of supreme power set upon it, then is it made subject unto law. Therefore it is commanded that the head of the priest be not bare but covered, in order that he who is head of the people may learn that he too hath a Head (in heaven). For [89] this cause in the church also, in the ordaining of priests (61 s), the

---

is very rare, and confined to very late writers.] It is properly an adjective, with the meaning "pertaining to the Corybantes," or priests of Cybele, and hence used of a cap, or bonnet of peculiar shape, such as they wore. *In Græcitate, quæ dicitur, vulgari, κιςυβάριον nihil aliud significat quam κυρβασία* (a Persian cap, or tiara). Lobeck on Soph. *Ajax.* p. 374, Note.

[86] Ἀλλὰ μὲν τὰ σχήματα, ἄλλα δὲ τὰ νοήματα. Οὐ γὰρ πάντως Θεὸς ἀναπαύεται ὑακίνθῳ καὶ πορφύρᾳ καὶ κόκκῳ καὶ βύσσῳ· Θεὸς γὰρ ψυχῶν ἀνακτῶν καθαρότητα· ἀλλ' ἐν ταῖς σωματικαῖς ἐσθῆσι διαγράφει τῶν ἀρετῶν τὰς εἰκόνας. Εἰ γὰρ ἀληθῶς ταῖς στολαῖς ἐπι-

ταῖς ταῖς ἐνδόξοις ἀπεπαύετο διὰ τί περὶ τοῦ Ἀαρὼν τὸν Μωυσῆν οὐκ ἐνέδυσεν.

[87] ἵνα μάθῃς ὅτι τῷ τελείῳ ἀρκεῖ ἡ ἀρετὴ πρὸς κόσμον. For the meaning of τέλειος compare Note 34. The word seems here to be used of the perfection of the Gospel as compared with the imperfect and typical character of the law.

[88] The original text seems to be corrupt. As no question of importance is involved, I need not enter into the history of the conjecturally amended text translated as above.

[89] διὰ τοῦτο καὶ ἐν τῇ ἐκκλησίᾳ ἐν ταῖς χειροτονίαις τῶν ἱερέων τὸ εὐαγγέλιον τοῦ Χριστοῦ ἐπὶ κεφαλῆς τίθεται, ἵνα μάθῃ ὁ χειροτ-

gospel of Christ is laid upon their heads, that he who is ordained may learn that he then receiveth the true tiara of the Gospel; and may learn this also, that though he be head of all, yet doth he act in subjection to God's laws; though he be ruler of all, yet is he too under rule to the law; though in all things a setter forth of the Word, yet himself to that Word in subjection. Therefore said one, a worthy man of the former times, Ignatius by name, of high renown as bishop and as martyr, when writing to a certain priest,[90] "*Without thy will let nought be done: but thyself do nought without the will of God.*" We see then that to one who is chief in priestly ministry to God the Gospels (laid upon his head) are a sign that he is under authority. For this cause Paul speaketh concerning a woman having her head covered, "*The woman ought to have wherewith to cover her head,*" this covering being the symbol of authority. The tiara then was the sign of authority; and so, too, was the golden plate, whereon was inscribed that which is written in God's Word, the Name of God being thereon engraved, and showing this first, that the Name of God is none other than the power of God.

After the priestly cap and the golden plate, there are two emeralds on the shoulders of the high-priest, having upon them the names of six tribes on the one side, and of the other six on the other side. Herein is a sign of what, in the priest, should be set forth to view. And the emerald is assigned unto him, as having a twofold beauty; in respect of its colour, pale, yet lovely to look upon, and in respect of its purity, like in power to a mirror. And as a priest should exercise himself in all holy abstinence, and in his life be as a mirror unto men, therefore doth God will that the high-priest should bear the symbol of virtue upon his shoulders. Yet why upon the shoulders? As the name of God is set upon his head, so is joint[91] set upon

---

τιθέμενοι ὅτι τὴν ἀλήθειαν τοῦ εὐαγγελίου τιάραν λαμβάνει· καὶ ἴνα μάθῃ ὅτι εἰ καὶ πάντων ἰστι κεφαλή ἀλλ' ὑπὸ τούτους πράττει τοὺς νόμους, κ. τ. λ. Thomassinus, referring to this passage, says, and with good reason: *Inde non inepte colligeret quis simplicissima tunc fuisse pontificum capitis indumenta.* He might have said yet more, that from this passage compared with that of S. Germanus, (quoted later in this volume) to which also he refers, it scarcely admits of doubt, that no episcopal insignia corresponding to the tiara of the high-priest were known at Constantinople in the 6th century, or even at the beginning of the 8th.

[90] ἱερεὺς is here used in reference to a Christian bishop (it is the letter to Polycrates that is here quoted). Compare Note 61.

[91] The two precious stones here spoken of served the purpose of a *clasp*. Hence apparently the allusion in the text: ἴσχυε εἰ τοῦ ταῦ ὄνομα ἐπὶ τῆς κεφαλῆς, οἱ ἄρμοι ἐπὶ τοῦ ἄρμου. The explanation is unsatisfactory, but I have no better to suggest.

joint. And once more, why upon the shoulders? Because the shoulders are significant of activity,[92] seeing that to them doth active power belong. . . . Upon the breast of the priest was worn the oracle, or breastplate, containing the twelve graven stones,—sardius, topaz, emerald, carbuncle, sapphire, jasper, jacynth, agate, amethyst, chrysolith, beryl, onyx. Among these twelve stones were distributed the names of the twelve tribes. And here, too, is a saying hard to be understood. Above, upon the shoulders, the stones were of one kind, and bearing but one name, as emeralds. But lower down upon the breast the stones are thus diverse. What doth this mean? Seeing that human nature, of which we had our birth, is one, but that by diversities of will we are divided, therefore is one of these symbols assigned unto the will, the other to that nature which is common to man. By the Name of God, then, was signified active virtue, the elements whereof are reason and truth.

On the lower border of the priest's (61 α) robe, is the fringe[93] thereof, whereon are flowers and pomegranates, with golden fruits and bells. And what meant these in the vesture of the priest (61 α)? Shall we deem that God found pleasure in these flowers? Was it of His desire that the priest should be clothed round about with flowers that are of earth (61 α)? Not so. But in this outward habit of the priest (61 α) He setteth forth the image of all virtues. Above, upon the head, the Name of God; upon the breast, the Oracle; below, flowers and fruits, even the righteous habits of Christian virtues, such as are merciful kindness, justice, brotherly love.[94]

---

[92] Ἰωσῆθε πρᾶξίς ἐστι σημεῖον. Ἡ γὰρ πρακτικὴ δύναμις ἐν τοῖς ὤμοις ἔχεται. Compare Note 35.

[93] λῶμα, as in the LXX.

[94] It will be seen on perusal of the passage above given that its language throughout is such as none could with any probability be supposed to use, who deemed that the dress worn in offices of holy ministry by himself and by other Christian bishops or priests, had been modelled of set purpose, by apostolic, or by later ecclesiastical, authority, upon the type of the Levitical vestments. See more particularly the passages quoted in Notes 86, 87, and 89.

## XVII.

## DIVUS GREGORIUS PAPA.[95]

### ON THE LEVITICAL VESTMENTS AND INSIGNIA.

EXPOSITIO MORALIS IN BEATUM JOB, LIB. XXVIII. CAP. VI.

[COMMENTING on the words, *Ubi eras quando ponebam fundamenta terræ* (Job, xxxviii. 4), he writes as follows:]—

"*In Scriptura sacra quid aliud fundamenta quam prædicatores accipimus? Quos dum primos Dominus in sancta Ecclesia posuit, tota in eis sequentis fabricæ structura surrexit. Unde et Sacerdos cum tabernaculum ingreditur duodecim lapides portare in pectore jubetur: quia videlicet semetipsum pro nobis sacrificium offerens Pontifex noster, dum fortes in ipso exordio prædicatores exhibuit, duodecim lapides sub capite in prima sui corporis parte portavit. Sancti itaque Apostoli et pro prima ostensione ornamenti lapides sunt in pectore, et pro prima soliditate ædificii in solo fundamenta. Unde David Propheta cum sanctam Ecclesiam in sublimibus Apostolorum mentibus poni ædificarique conspiceret,* fundamenta ejus, inquit, in montibus sanctis. (Ps. lxxxvi.) *Cum vero in sacro eloquio non fundamenta sed singulari numero fundamentum dicitur, nullus alius nisi ipse Dominus designatur, per cujus divinitatis potentiam nutantia infirmitatis nostræ corda solidantur. De quo et Paulus ait:* Fundamentum aliud nemo potest ponere præter id quod positum est Christus Jesus. *Ipse quippe fundamentum fundamentorum est: quia et origo est inchoantium et constantia robustorum.*"[96]

"By 'foundations' in the Holy Scripture, we are to understand those preachers of God's Word (the Apostles) who were set foremost in the Church by the Lord, and on whom, therefore, was built up the whole structure of the spiritual Building that followed. And

---

[95] St. Gregory the Great, Bishop of Rome from A.D. 590 to 604.

this is the reason that the high-priest, when he enters the Tabernacle, is bidden to wear the twelve stones (of the 'Rationale') on his breast, because our own High-priest, in setting forth at the very first mighty preachers of His Word, carried, as it were, twelve stones, in subjection to the Head, in the forefront of His own Body. And so the Holy Apostles are both stones upon the breast, in accordance with that first setting forth of ornament, and in respect of the first solid grounding of 'the Building' are as foundation-stones laid in the ground. Hence that word of Prophet David as he beheld the holy Church being founded and built up upon the exalted minds of the Apostles, '*Her foundations*,' saith he, '*are upon the holy mountains.*' But when in the Divine Word we hear speak not of 'foundations,' as of many, but of 'the foundation' as of one only, then is none other intended but the Lord alone, by the power of whose divine nature steadfastness is given to the tottering heart of human infirmity. Of Him speaketh Paul when he saith, 'Other foundation can no man lay save that which is already laid, even Christ Jesus.' For He is the Foundation of all foundations, seeing that He is both the beginning of Life to them that begin, and the sustaining strength of them that are strong."[96]

---

[96] This passage is quoted as a strong evidence (to say the least) that to St. Gregory nothing was known in the dress of Christian Bishops that corresponded to the Rational of the Jewish high-priest; and that the idea of any such correspondence being intended never occurred to him. He neither casts about to find any such correspondence, nor thinks it necessary to account for there being none. Compare his own words (quoted below, p. 61), *Vestimenta sacerdotis quid aliud quam recta opera debemus accipere?* "By the vestments of the high-priest what are we to understand but righteous works?"

## XVIII.

## DIVUS GREGORIUS PAPA.

### SYMBOLISM OF THE HIGH-PRIEST'S BREASTPLATE.

Pastoralis Cura, Pars Secunda (Tom. i. p. 1185), Cap. ii.

[In this chapter he is speaking of the purity of thought which becometh them who take upon them the charge of "*carrying living vessels*[97] *into the Temple of Eternity.*" He proceeds as follows:]—

*Hinc divina voce præcipitur ut in Aaron pectore rationale judicii vittis ligantibus imprimatur: quatenus sacerdotale cor nequaquam cogitationes fluxæ possideant, sed ratio sola constringat: ne indiscretum quid vel inutile cogitet, qui ad exemplum aliis constitutus ex gravitate vitæ semper debet ostendere quantum in pectore rationem portet. In quo etiam rationali vigilanter adjungitur ut duodecim nomina patriarcharum describantur. Ascriptos etenim patres semper in pectore ferre, est antiquorum vitam sine intermissione cogitare.* [*Plura et similia in eandem fere sententiam sequuntur.*][98]

"Hence it is that by the voice of God that precept is given that on the breast of Aaron the (breastplate) Rational of Judgment should be closely fastened with attaching bands, forasmuch as it would not be meet that the heart of the priest should be occupied by loose imaginations, but by reason alone be constrained: that nothing indiscreet nor mischievous may fill the mind of one, who, set as he is for an ensample unto others, ought to show plainly how much of reason he beareth on his breast. And of this Rational this, too, is carefully enjoined, that the twelve names of the Patriarchs be thereon inscribed. For by the continual bearing of the fathers graven upon the breast, is meant the remembering without ceasing the lives of them that are of the former times." [*Here follows much more to the same effect, in general, though not verbal, accordance with the comment of S. Jerome already quoted.*][98]

---

[97] In allusion to the words of Isaiah, lii. 11, *Mundamini qui fertis vasa Domini.*

[98] To this passage the same remark applies as to the last quoted. See Note 96.

## XIX.

## DIVUS GREGORIUS PAPA.
### OF THE EPHOD OR SUPERHUMERAL.
Pastoralis Cura, Pars II. Cap. III. p. 1187.

[He is urging upon the Pastor that he should ever lead the way in all good work, that so the Flock, guided at once by the voice of their Shepherd, and by his good life, may make their onward way by example rather than by precept only. In illustration he refers [99] to the setting apart (by Levitical law) of the right shoulder and the breast [100] of the offerings as the priest's portion. He pursues his thought in these words:—]

"*Unde supernæ quoque vocis imperio in utroque humero sacerdos velamine superhumeralis astringitur:* [101] *ut contra adversa ac prospera virtutum semper ornamento muniatur: quatenus juxta vocem Pauli, Per arma justitiæ a dextris sinistrisque gradiens, cum ad sola quæ anteriora sunt nititur, in nullo delectationis infimæ latere flectatur. Non hunc prospera elevent, non adversa perturbent, non blanda usque ad voluptatem demulceant, non aspera usque ad desperationem premant: ut dum nullis passionibus intentionem mentis humiliat, quanta in utroque humero superhumeralis pulchritudine tegatur ostendat. Quod recte superhumerale ex auro, hyacintho, purpura, bis tincto cocco, et tota fieri bysso, præcipitur, ut quanta sacerdos* [102] *clarescere virtutum diversitate debeat, demonstretur. In sacerdotis* [102] *quippe habitu ante omnia aurum fulget, ut in eo intellectus sapientiæ principaliter emicet. Cui hyacinthus, qui aerio colore* [103] *resplendet, adjungitur: ut per omne quod intelligendo penetrat non ad favores intimos sed ad amorem cælestium surgat; ne, dum incautus suis laudibus capitur, ipso*

---

[99] So S. Jerome previously, Epistle to Fabiola.
[100] Compare Note 37, above.
[101] *Velamine superhumeralis astringitur.* [*Superhumeralis* is here a "genitive of apposition."] "He hath the covering of the ephod fastened closely about him on either shoulder." The allusion is to the marked contrast between the close-fitting garb of the Levitical priest (specially noticeable in the ephod), as compared with the more flowing vestments of Christian ministry. See above Note 6, p. 2. In that Note the words quoted from the original text of Josephus should be read as follows: περιγεγραμμένη τῷ σώματι, καὶ τὰς χεῖρας ὑπὸ τοῖς βραχίοσιν κατεσφιγμένης.

[102] *Sacerdos* is here the high-priest. Compare Note 61 a.

[103] *Hyacinthus aerio colore.* See above, Note 33, p. 22.

*etiam veritatis intellectu vacuetur. Auro quoque et hyacintho purpura permiscetur: ut videlicet sacerdotale* (61 ζ) *cor, cum summa quæ prædicat sperat, in semetipso suggestiones vitiorum reprimat, easque velut regia potestate contradicat: quatenus nobilitatem semper intimæ regenerationis aspiciat, et cælestis regni sibi habitum* [104] *moribus defendat. De hac quippe nobilitate spiritus per Petrum dicitur:* Vos autem genus electum, regale sacerdotium .... *Auro autem, hyacintho, bysso ac purpuræ, bis tinctus coccus adjungitur, ut ante interni Judicis oculos omnia virtutum bona ex charitate decorentur: et cuncta quæ coram hominibus rutilant, hæc in conspectu occulti Arbitri flamma intimi amoris accendat. Quæ scilicet charitas, quia Deum simul et proximum diligit, quasi ex duplici tinctura fulgescit. Qui igitur sic ad Authoris speciem anhelat ut proximorum curam negligat: vel sic proximorum curam exsequitur ut a divino amore torpescat: quia unum horum quodlibet negligit in superhumeralis ornamento habere coccum bis tinctum nescit. Sed cum mens ad præcepta charitatis tenditur, restat proculdubio ut per abstinentiam caro maceretur. Unde et bis tincto cocco byssus adjungitur. De terra enim byssus nitenti specie oritur.* [105] *Et quid per byssum nisi candens decore munditiæ corporalis, castitas designatur? Quæ videlicet byssus torta pulchritudine superhumeralis innectitur: quia tunc castimonia ad perfectum munditiæ candorem ducitur cum per abstinentiam* [106] *caro fatigatur. Cumque inter virtutes cæteras etiam afflictæ carnis meritum proficit, quasi in diversa superhumeralis specie byssus torta candescit.* [107]

---

[104] *Cælestis regni habitum*,—the dress of celestial royalty (*regni* = kingship rather than *kingdom*), i.e. the dress proper to one who is a partaker of that "royal priesthood" of which the text goes on to speak.

[105] *Byssus nitenti specie—candens*, &c. For the word *byssus* see Note 5, p. 2; and for the brilliant *whiteness* (*candor*) here attributed to it, compare Note 19, p. 9.

[106] The *maceratio carnis per abstinentiam* is here spoken of as specially typified by the *byssus* of the high-priest's ephod. The reason of this will be made clear by the following quotation. *Sicut byssus vel linum candorem, quem ex natura non habet, multis tunsionibus attritum per artem acquirit, sic et hominis caro munditiam quam non obtinet per naturam, multis castigationibus macerata sortitur per gratiam.* Innocentius III. Mysteriorum Missæ, lib. i. cap. li.

[107] I have thought it unnecessary to translate the above passage at length. It is sufficient to observe upon its general character. It will be seen that throughout a spiritual antitype (not an actual one) is traced, between the literal vestments of the Levitical and the spiritual clothing of the Christian priesthood. The divers colours of the high-priest's ephod are intended to teach *with what variety of virtues* he should be adorned who serves in holy ministry to God. The *gold* is significant of the "understanding of wisdom" (because of its exceeding *preciousness*; he was thinking probably of Job, xxviii. 15–19). The *blue*, of heavenly (Note 33) aspiration. The *purple* of the "power as of a king" wherewith the Christian priest should crush the power of evil thought within his heart. The scarlet is typical of charity, kindled, as he suggests, as into fire, by the flame of holy love. The linen, fine and white, of the subduing (Note 106) of the flesh by Christian abstinence.

## XX.

## DIVUS GREGORIUS PAPA.

### OF THE BELLS UPON THE TUNIC OF THE EPHOD; AND OF THE LEVITICAL VESTMENTS IN GENERAL.

PASTORALIS CURA, PARS II. CAP. IV. p. 1189.

[THE Christian pastor should know both how with discretion to keep silence, and, to the profit of them that hear, *to speak*. In this regard he must be prepared boldly to rebuke if need be. He then proceeds:—]

*Clavis quippe apertionis sermo correptionis est: quia increpatio culpam detegit, quam sæpe nescit ipse etiam qui perpetravit. Hinc Paulus ait* (Tit. i. 9): *Ut potens sit exhortari in doctrina sana, et eos qui contradicunt redarguere. . . . . Hinc per Esaiam Dominus admonet dicens: Clama, ne cesses, quasi tuba exalta vocem tuam. Præconis quippe officium suscipit quisquis ad sacerdotium accedit: ut ante adventum Judicis qui terribiliter sequitur ipse scilicet clamando gradiatur. Sacerdos ergo si prædicationis est nescius quam clamoris vocem daturus est præco mutus? Hinc est enim quod super pastores primos in linguarum specie Spiritus Sanctus insedit: quia nimirum quos repleverit de Se, protinus loquentes facit. Hinc Moysi præcipitur ut tabernaculum Sacerdos ingrediens tintinnabulis ambiatur, ut videlicet voces prædicationis habeat, ne superni Spectatoris judicium ex silentio offendat. Scriptum quippe est* (Exod. xxviii. 35): *Ut audiatur sonitus quando ingreditur sanctuarium in conspectu Domini, et non moriatur. Sacerdos namque ingrediens vel egrediens moritur, si de eo sonitus non audiatur: quia iram contra se occulti Judicis exigit, si sine sonitu prædicationis incedit. Aptè autem tintinnabula vestimentis illius describuntur inserta. Vestimenta etenim sacerdotis quid aliud quam recta opera debemus accipere? Propheta attestante qui ait*

(Ps. cxxxii. 9) : Sacerdotes tui induantur juftitiam. *Veftimentis itaque illius tintinnabula inhærent, ut vitæ viam cum linguæ fonitu ipfa quoque bona opera clament facerdotis.*[108]

---

[108] In this paffage again, as in thofe already quoted, the "bells" of the older facerdotal drefs, and the veftments in general, receive a purely fpiritual interpretation as referred to Chriftian priefthood. The "bells" are the voice of him who in God's Name is both "apt to teach," and "bold to rebuke." And the veftments are good works, the "clothing of righteoufnefs" which becometh the priefts of the Lord.

## XXI.

## DIVUS GREGORIUS PAPA.

### THE USE OF THE PALLIUM, A MATTER OF ROMAN PRIVILEGE.

Epistolarum ex Registro Divi Gregorii Lib. iv. Ep. 2.

[Childebert, king of the Franks, had written to St. Gregory requesting that the *Pallium*, and Vicarial authority from the see of Rome (*vices Apostolicæ sedis*), might be conferred on Vigilius, Bishop of Arles. In writing to Vigilius, and announcing his assent to this, St. Gregory speaks of the sending of this *pallium* as an 'ancient custom.'[109]]

*Quod vero in eis* (sc. *epistolis*) *juxta antiquum*[110] *morem, usum pallii ac vices sedis apostolicæ postulasti, absit ne aut transitoriæ potestatis culmen, aut exterioris cultus ornamentum, in vicibus nostris ac palliis quæsisse te suspicer. Sed quia cunctis liquet unde in Galliarum regionibus fides sancta prodierit,*[111] *cum priscam consuetudinem apostolicæ sedis fraternitas vestra*

---

[109] See Epist. Lib. iv. liii. in which St. Gregory writes to Childebert himself on the same subject.

[110] St. Gregory here states that for Bishops of Arles to receive the privilege of the Roman *Pallium*, and vicarial authority, was in accordance with "ancient custom," or (as the context rather suggests) with "the custom observed in former times." The *Pallium* here spoken of is the *Pallium* worn by archbishops. In St. Gregory's time this had already assumed that later form, in which (with slight modifications only) it has ever since been retained. That is to say, instead of being shaped like a modern stole, as in the pictures of XVSTVS PP. ROM., photographed in this volume, it presented in front the appearance of the English letter Y, and was all but identical with the ὠμοφόριον of the Greek Church, already described (p. 49) by S. Isidore of Pelusium.

As for the "custom of former times" to which St. Gregory refers, full information will be found in *Thomassinus, De Beneficiis*, part ii. lib. ii. cap. liv., where the whole question of the Roman *Pallium* is treated with much learning and considerable candour: and further particulars of importance in Gieseler's Eccl. Hist. vol. i. p. 446.

[111] St. Gregory, in saying this, implies, of course, that the Churches of Gaul owed their Christianity to the Roman Church. It is probable, though not certain, that he was mistaken in so thinking, and that those Churches were by their first origin connected with the Churches of Asia Minor, of which Ephesus was the primatial see. [See Palmer's Pri-

*repetit, quid aliud quam bona suboles ad sinum matris ecclesiæ recurrit?* [118]

"As for the request you have made, in accordance with ancient custom, in your letters addressed to me, that you may be allowed to use the *Pallium*, and be made Vicar of the Apostolic See, I will not for a moment fear that in making this request you have had regard to any exaltation of temporary power, or to the increase of outward adornment. As it is clear to all men from what source [111] the Holy Faith spread in the regions of Gaul, when you ask, as your Brotherhood now does, for the renewal of the customary privilege bestowed of old by the Apostolic See, what is this but the return of a goodly offspring to the bosom of the mother Church?" [112]

---

mitive Liturgies, p. 155, 299.] However this may be, it is noteworthy that St. Gregory here gives as a reason why the Gallic Churches should submit to the patriarchal authority of the See of Rome, that from Rome they had originally received the knowledge of Christian truth. He says not a word of it being the duty of *every* Church to submit itself to the See of Rome as having, by Divine right, a Headship over the universal Church of Christ.

[119] This letter will serve as an example of a great number of others occurring in St. Gregory's epistles, relating to this (then, as now) vexed question of the Papal Pallium. See lib. iv. 53, 54, 55, 56; lib. v. ep. 7, 8, 18, 33; lib. vii. ep. 11; lib. x. ep. 55.

## XXII.

## DIVUS GREGORIUS PAPA.

## THE USE OF THE *MAPPULA* REGARDED AT ROME AS A MATTER OF PAPAL PRIVILEGE, NOT OF GENERAL RIGHT.

Epistola Joannis Episcopi (Ravennatis) ad Gregorium Papam de usu Pallii et diversis ornatibus [tom. 2. p. 1055]
Lib. x. Ep. 55.

*Quod de mappulis a presbyteris et diaconis meis præsumptum Apostolatus vester scripsit, vere fateor, tædet me aliquid exinde commemorare, cum per se veritas, quæ apud dominum meum sola prævalet, ipsa sufficiat. Nam cum hoc minoribus circa urbem*[113] *constitutis ecclesiis licitum sit, poterit etiam apostolatus mei domini, si venerabilem clerum primæ Apostolicæ sedis suæ requirere dignatur, modis omnibus invenire, quia quoties ad episcopatus ordinationem, seu responsi, sacerdotes vel levitæ Ravennatis Ecclesiæ Romam venerunt, quod omnes in oculis sanctissimorum decessorum vestrorum cum mappulis sine reprehensione aliqua procedebant. Quare etiam eo tempore quod (leg. quo) istic a prædecessore vestro peccator ordinatus sum, cuncti presbyteri et diaconi mei in obsequium Domini Papæ mecum procedentes usi sunt.*

---

[113] By *urbem* is of course meant Rome.

## XXIII.

## DIVUS GREGORIUS PAPA.

Lib. ii. Ep. liv. (*apud Labbé Conc.* tom. v. p. 1127) ad Joannem Episcopum Ravennatem.

[After a long and severe reproof of the mode in which the bishop had presumed to wear the *pallium*, on other days, and in other places, than was usual, he adds the following concerning the *mappula*, or maniple]: —

*Illud autem quod pro utendis a clero vestro mappulis scripsistis, a nostris est clericis fortiter obviatum, dicentibus nulli hoc unquam alii cuilibet ecclesiæ concessum fuisse: nec Ravennates clericos illic vel in Romana civitate tale aliquid cum sua conscientia præsumpsisse: nec si tentatum esset ex furtiva usurpatione sibi præjudicium generari. Sed etiamsi in qualibet ecclesia hoc præsumptum fuerit, asserunt emendandum, quod non concessione Romani Pontificis sed sola surreptione præsumitur. Sed nos servantes honorem fraternitatis tuæ, licet contra voluntatem antedicti cleri nostri, tamen primis diaconibus vestris, quos nobis quidam testificati sunt etiam ante eis usos fuisse, in obsequio duntaxat tuo mappulis uti permittimus: alio autem tempore vel alias personas hoc agere vehementissime prohibemus.*

## XXIV.

## DIVUS GREGORIUS PAPA.

### THE PRIVILEGE OF WEARING A DALMATIC, GRANTED TO AREGIUS, BISHOP OF GAP, AND TO HIS ARCHDEACON.

Epist. ex Registro, Lib. vii. Tom. ii. p. 924.

[After writing at some length upon other subjects, he proceeds as follows]:—

Præterea communis filius Petrus diaconus nobis innotuit quod fraternitas vestra, tempore quo hic fuit, poposcerit ut sibi et archidiacono suo utendi dalmaticis licentiam præberemus. Sed quia ita hominum suorum infirmitate compulsus festinanter abscessit, ut nec ipse mæror incumbens diu, ut dignum erat, et res desiderata poscebat, sineret imminere: et nos in multis implicitos ut Ecclesiasticæ rationis consideratio novum hoc inconsulte et subito non permitteret indulgere: idcirco postulatæ rei prolongatus effectus est. Nunc vero charitatis tuæ bona revocantes ad animum, hujus authoritatis nostræ serie, petita concedimus, atque te et archidiaconum tuum Dalmaticarum usu decorandos esse concessimus, easdemque Dalmaticas, dilectissimo filio nostro Cyriaco Abbate deferente, transmisimus.

## XXV.

## S. ISIDORE OF SEVILLE.

### OF THE INSIGNIA OF CHRISTIAN PRIESTHOOD.

[IN the second book of the *De Officiis Ecclesiasticis*, St. Isidore[114] treats at length of the various orders of the Christian ministry. The following passages serve to indicate what in his time were regarded as the characteristic insignia of the clergy]:

#### CAP. VII.

*Quod detonso capite superius, inferius circali corona relinquitur, sacerdotium regnumque ecclesiæ in eis existimo figurari. Tiara enim apud veteres constituebatur in capite sacerdotum. Hæc ex byffo confecta, rotunda erat quasi sphera media; et hoc significatur in parte capitis tonsa. Corona autem, latitudo aurei est circuli quæ regum capita cingit. Utrumque igitur signum exprimitur in capite clericorum, ut impleatur etiam quadam corporis similitudine quod scriptum est, Petro apostolo prædocente, Vos estis genus electum, regale sacerdotium.*

"The cutting off the hair from the upper part of the head, and leaving it in the form of a crown, lower down, is in my judgment a figurative setting forth of the priesthood and royalty of the Church. For with God's ancient people it was customary to place a tiara on the heads of priests. This 'tiara' was made of byffus, and was round like a sphere, divided in twain; and this it is which is signified by the part of the head which is shorn. But the chaplet of hair represents the broad circlet of gold which encompasses the heads of kings. Each of these emblems therefore is expressed on the heads of the clergy, so as by outward similitude to set forth that which is written, in the teaching of the apostle Peter, *Ye are a chosen generation, a royal priesthood.*

---

[114] S. Isidore was born at Carthagena about the year 560 A.D., and died A.D. 636.

## CAP. V.

## THE PASTORAL STAFF AND EPISCOPAL RING.

*Huic ( sc. Episcopo) dum consecratur datur baculus ut ejus indicio subditam plebem vel regat, vel corrigat, vel infirmitates infirmorum sustineat. Datur et anulus propter signum pontificalis honoris, vel signaculum secretorum. Nam multa sunt quæ carnalium minusque intelligentium sensibus occultantes sacerdotes quasi sub signaculo abscondunt, ne indignis quibusque sacramenta Dei aperiantur.*

"To the bishop at the time of his consecration is given a staff, that, as this sign suggests, he may both rule and correct the people committed to his care, and support the infirmities of such as are weak. A ring likewise is given him, for the signifying of pontifical dignity, or to be as it were a seal for guarding of things secret. For many things there are which they who minister unto God keep concealed from the knowledge of carnal men and wanting in wise understanding, lest divine mysteries be laid open to such as are unworthy."

## CAP. VIII.

## OF THE WHITE MINISTERING DRESS WORN BY DEACONS.

*Propterea Altari albis induti assistunt ut cælestem vitam habeant, candidique ad hostias et immaculati accedant, mundi scilicet corpore et pudore incorrupti.*

"The reason why they" (the deacons [115] of whom he is speaking) "assist at the altar clad in white garments is this, that a heavenly [116] life may be theirs, and that bright and pure, and without stain, they may approach unto the holy offerings, being clean in body and in chasteness undefiled."

---

[115] In Cap. vii, when speaking of the second order of the Christian ministry, S. Isidore says nothing of any distinctive dress or insignia specially characteristic of the Presbyter. But I cannot forbear quoting the following expression of half-humorous severity, which he lets fall in passing. "Presbyters," he says, "are so called not from any reference to the decrepitude of old age, but because of the wisdom which is proper to fulness of years. But this being so," he adds, "one cannot but wonder why it is that fools are ordained." *Quod si ita est, mirum cur insipientes ordinentur.*

[116] His thought is of the bright white garments in which angels are described as clad.

XXVI.

## ST. ISIDORE OF SEVILLE.

### ON THE VESTMENTS OF LEVITICAL PRIESTHOOD.

[In Cap. v. of the same book that has been quoted above, viz. *De Eccles. Off.* Lib. ii., St. Isidore treats of priesthood in general, and has occasion to speak of the vestments worn by Aaron and by his sons. He writes as follows]:—

*Veniamus nunc ad sacratissimos ordines clericorum, eorumque originem demonstremus, quod est sacerdotii fundamentum vel quo authore pontificalis ordo adolevit in seculo. Initium quidem sacerdotii Aaron fuit, quanquam et Melchisedech prior obtulerit sacrificium, et post hunc Abraham, Isaac et Jacob. Sed isti spontanea voluntate, non sacerdotali authoritate, ista fecerunt. Cæterum Aaron primus in lege sacerdotale nomen accepit, primusque pontificali stola indutus victimas obtulit, jubente Domino ac loquente ad Moysem,* Accipe, inquit, Aaron et filios ejus, et adplicabis ad ostium Tabernaculi Testimonii: cumque laveris patrem cum filiis indues Aaron vestimentis suis, id est Linea et Tunica et Superhumerali et Rationali, quod constringes balteo, et pones tiaram, et oleum unctionis fundes super caput ejus, atque hoc ritu consecrabitur. Filios quoque illius adplicabis et indues tunicis lineis, cingesque balteo, Aaron scilicet et liberos ejus, et impones eis mitras eruntque sacerdotes mei lege perpetua. *Quo loco contemplari oportet Aaron summum sacerdotem id est episcopum fuisse. Nam filios ejus presbyterorum figuram præmonstrasse. Fuerunt enim filii Aaron et ipsi sacerdotes quibus merito adstare debuissent Levitæ, sicut summo sacerdoti. Sed hoc fuit inter summum sacerdotem Aaron et filios ejusdem Aaron, qui et ipsi sacerdotes fuerunt, quod Aaron super tunicam accipiebat poderem stolam*[17] *sanctam, coronam auream,*

---

[17] It will be seen from the above that the "holy robe" of Aaron was in St. Isidore's judgment something distinct from the white tunic common to Aaron himself and to his sons. And though the mode in which he enumerates the vestments and insignia leaves it open to doubt, whether by 'Stola' he means the vesture of the high-priest taken as a whole, or one particular portion of it, the latter seems on the whole more probable; and if so, the "Tunic of Blue" must be the vestment to which he refers.

*mitram et zonam auream et Superhumerale, et cætera quæ supra memorata sunt. Filii autem Aaron cincti tantummodo et tiarati* [118] *ita adstabant sacrificio Dei.*

---

[118] Note here, that with St. Isidore, the word *corona* (note 54, p. 32) is used in speaking of the distinctive decoration added to the *mitra* of the high-priest, while the sons of Aaron are spoken of as *tiarati*, wearing a "*tiara*." But the same word *tiara* had previously been used (in quoting from Exodus) of the cap, or linen mitre, worn by the high-priest. [See note 84, p. 52, as to the meaning of "*Tiara*." The passage there quoted from the *De Originibus* of St. Isidore will illustrate his usage of *corona* here.]

## XXVII.

## ST. ISIDORE OF SEVILLE.

### ENUMERATION OF THE VESTMENTS OF LEVITICAL PRIESTHOOD.

#### De Originibus, Lib. xix. Cap. xxi.

[He enters in this part of his treatife on the fubject of drefs in general; and after a few introductory lines as to the original invention of the textile arts, he commences with the " eight kinds of facerdotal veftments mentioned in the law."]

*Octo funt in lege genera facerdotalium* [119] *veftimentorum.* Poderis *eft tunica facerdotalis linea, corpori aftricta,* [120] *ufque ad pedes defcendens. Unde et nuncupatur,* πόδας *enim Græci pedes dicunt. Hæc vulgo camifia* [181] *vocatur.* Abaneth *cingulum facerdotale rotundum polimita arte ex cocco purpura hyacinthoque contextum, ita ut flores atque gemmæ in eo videantur effe diftinctæ.* Pileum *eft ex byffo* [182] *rotundum quafi fphæra media, caput tegens facerdotale, et in occipitio vitta conftrictum. Hoc Græci et noftri* tiaram [183] *vel* galeam [184] *vocant.*

Machil *quæ eft tunica talaris, tota hyacinthina, habens ad pedes* LXXII *tintinnabula; totidemque intermixta ac dependentia punica mala.*

Ephod *quod Latine interpretatur fuperindumentum. Erat enim pal-*

---

[119] He ufes the term, inclufively, of both high prieft, and prieft of the fecond order. Compare note 61.

[120] On this clofenefs of fit here noticed, fee above, note 6, p. 2.

[181] He follows St. Jerome in comparing the *tunica talaris* of the Levitical prieft to the *camifia* of ordinary life in his own time. See note 23, p. 13.

[182] On the word *Byffus (βύσσος)* fee note 5, p. 2. The word was never fo naturalifed in the Latin language as to pafs into common ufe. St. Ifidore fpeaks of it as a term whofe real meaning was doubtful. " *Byffina candida confecta ex quodam genere lini groffioris. Sunt et qui genus quoddam lini byffum effe exiftimant.*" Etym. lib. xix. cap. xxii.

[183] For the word *Tiara*, fee note 84, p. 52.

[184] Of feveral various readings which are here found (due to the ignorance of copyifts when claffical terms are concerned), the true one is probably *galerum*. This was a word fpecially ufed of the facerdotal cap of heathen priefthood (fee Index *in voc*). At a later time the fcarlet hat, affigned to the Roman cardinals by Innocent IV. (at the Council of Lyons, A.D. 1244), was known as *galerus rubeus*. See Dufrefne Gloffar. *in voc.*

lium [125] *superhumerale ex quattuor coloribus et auro contextum, habens in utroque humero lapides duos smaragdinos auro conclusos, in quibus sculpta erant nomina patriarcharum.*

Logicon *quod Latinè dicitur rationale, pannus duplex, auro et quattuor textus coloribus, habens magnitudinem palmi per quadrum, cui intexti erant quattuor* [126] *pretiosissimi lapides. Hic pannus super humerale* [Leg. *superhumerali*] *contra pectus Pontificis annectebatur.*

Petalum *aurea lamina in fronte Pontificis, quæ nomen Dei tetragrammatum Hebraicis literis habebat scriptum.*

Batin (sic) *sive feminalia, id est bracæ lineæ usque ad genua pertingentes, quibus verecunda sacerdotis velabantur.*

[Having thus enumerated the vestments of Levitical priesthood, he goes on to describe briefly every other known garment belonging either to male or to female dress. Interspersed among such terms as *Toga, Chlamys, Sagum, Mantum, Prætexta*, we find the following] : —

### Pallium.

Pallium [127] *est quo administrantium scapulæ conteguntur, ut dum ministrant expeditius discurrant.* [128] *Plautus :* Si quid facturus es appende in humeris pallium, et pergat quantum valet tuorum pedum pernicitas. *Dictum autem pallium a pellibus, quia prius super indumenta pellicea veteres induebantur, quasi pellea, sive a palla per diminutionem.*

### Penula.

Penula *est pallium* [129] *cum fimbriis longis.*

---

[125] *Pallium.* St. Isidore generally uses this word as a generic term, nearly equal to our own "garment," requiring some special description to indicate any special article of dress. Thus the *paludamentum* is described as *insigne pallium Imperatorum* ; the *penula* as *pallium cum fimbriis longis* ; the *lacerna* as *pallium fimbriatum quo olim soli milites utebantur.* So again of the *prætexta puerilis*, the *penula*, and many others. A more specific use of the word will be noticed below. See note 127.

[126] We can hardly suppose that this mistake of *four* for *twelve* is due to St. Isidore. Probably the eye of the copyist was caught, or his memory misled, by the *quattuor*, which had just preceded, in speaking of the colours.

[127] The *Pallium* here noticed is the Greek ἱμάτιον, the outer garment or wrapper, worn occasionally at least by persons of all conditions of life, as already noticed in the Introduction (see Index *in voc.*) It corresponded in general use to the Roman *toga*, but in the earlier Roman language (that of republican times) was as distinctly suggestive of a Greek costume as the *toga* of that of Rome.

[128] St. Isidore has been led into error by this particular passage of Plautus. The *pallium* in itself was no more suited for vigorous exertion than the *toga* or the *penula*. And it is precisely for this reason that in this passage of Plautus (Captiv. Act. iv. Sc. 1) Ergasilus, the Parasite, says, *eodem pacto ut comici servi solent conjiciam in collum pallium, primo ex me hanc rem ut audiat*, i.e. he will gather his cloak about his shoulders *to enable him to run the faster*. But so to carry the *pallium* was the exception, not, as St. Isidore seems to think, the rule.

[129] On this generic use of *pallium* see above, note 125.

## Of the Casula.

*Casula*[130] *est vestis cucullata, dicta per diminutionem a casa, quod totum hominem tegat, quasi minor casa. Unde et cuculla quasi minor cella. Sic et Græce planetas dictos volunt, quia oris errantibus evagantur. Unde et stellæ planetæ, id est vagæ suo errore motuque discurrunt.*

## Of the Dalmatic.

[Throughout this portion of his Treatise St. Isidore gives but one slight intimation of any vestment which he regards as belonging to offices of Christian ministry. He is describing various modifications of the *tunic*, and amongst others mentions the Dalmatic.]

*Dalmatica*[131] *vestis primum in Dalmatia, provincia Græciæ, texta est, tunica sacerdotalis candida, cum clavis ex purpura.*

---

[130] This definition of the *casula*, or "chasuble" is quoted by almost all writers on ritual, ancient and modern. But as far as I have observed, none have noticed a remarkable confirmation of the derivation here assigned being really correct. From another passage of St. Isidore (De Off. Eccl. lib. v.) it is clear that in his time, at least, the word *casula* was really used in the sense of a *hut*, or "*minor casa*." He is speaking of Elias and Elisha, and other such, and says, *habitabant in solitudine, urbibusque relictis faciebant sibi casulas prope fluenta Jordanis*.

[131] For further particulars of this vestment see Index *in voc*. It is evident that by *sacerdotalis* reference is here made not to Jewish or to heathen, but to Christian *sacerdotes*. [Compare note 71.] From very early times (those of S. Silvester according to Roman tradition) the Dalmatic had been adopted as a ministering vestment of the Church at Rome. And to this Roman usage St. Isidore probably makes reference in this passage. But it is open to question, as far as this passage is concerned, whether by *sacerdotalis* is meant *episcopal*, or in a more general sense, *sacerdotal*. Compare note 71, p. 46.

## XXVIII.

## ACTS OF THE FOURTH COUNCIL OF TOLEDO.

HELD UNDER THE PRESIDENCY OF ST. ISIDORE OF SEVILLE, A.D. 633.

[THE acts of this Council are throughout of great interest, in their bearing upon questions of ecclesiastical antiquity. The sections of special interest to the question now under discussion are the following] :—

### INSIGNIA OF CHRISTIAN MINISTRY.

§ XXVIII. *Episcopus, presbyter, aut diaconus, si a gradu suo injuste dejectus in secunda synodo innocens reperiatur, non potest esse quod fuerat nisi gradus amissos recipiat coram altario de manu episcopi ; [si episcopus]* [130] *orarium, annulum et baculum : si presbyter, orarium et planetam : si diaconus, orarium et albam : si subdiaconus, patenam et calicem : sic et reliqui gradus ea in reparationem sui recipiant quæ eum ordinarentur perceperunt.*

"If a bishop, presbyter, or deacon, be unjustly deposed, and in a subsequent synod be found innocent, he cannot be what he had previously been, unless he receive again the rank he had lost from the hand of a bishop, before the altar. It he have been a bishop, he must receive *orarium* (*i.e.* stole), ring, and staff; if a presbyter, *orarium* and *planeta* (*i.e.* chasuble) ; if a deacon, *orarium* and alb ; if a subdeacon, paten and chalice ; and so the other minor orders are to receive, with a view to their restoration, what at the time of ordination they originally received."

§ XL. *Orariis duobus nec episcopo quidem licet, nec presbytero uti, quanto*

---

[130] The words *si episcopus*, are not in the present text, though evidently required by the context. The word EPĪ (*i.e. episcopi*) just before would easily be confused in translation with the EPS here required.

*magis diacono qui minister eorum est. Unum igitur orarium oportet Levitam gestare in sinistro humero, propter quod orat, id est prædicat :* [133] *dextram autem partem oportet habere liberam ut expeditus ad ministerium sacerdotale discurrat. Caveat igitur amodo Levita gemino uti orario, sed uno tantum et puro nec ullis coloribus aut auro ornato.*

"Not even a bishop, or a presbyter, is allowed to wear two *oraria* (stoles), how much less a deacon who is their attendant minister. The deacon therefore must wear one *orarium*, as befits his office, and that on the left shoulder. But the right side should remain free, so that he may hasten to and fro in duties of sacerdotal service. The ["Levite"] deacon therefore, from this time forth, must not wear his *orarium* double. He should wear but one, and that plain, not decked out with any colours, nor with gold."

§ XLI. *Omnes clerici vel lectores, sicut Levitæ et sacerdotes, detonso superius toto capite inferius solam circuli coronam relinquant : non sicut hucusque in Galliciæ partibus facere lectores videntur, qui prolixis ut laici comis in solo capitis apice modicum circulum tondent. Ritus enim iste in Hispania hucusque hæreticorum fuit. Unde oportet ut pro amputando ecclesiæ scandalo hoc signum dedecoris auferatur, et una sit tonsura, vel habitus, sicut totius Hispaniæ est usus. Qui autem hoc non custodierit fidei catholicæ reus erit.*

"All clerks, or Readers, as well as Levites and priests, are to cut off the hair from the whole of the upper part of the head, and leave only a circular band of hair beneath; not as hitherto in parts of Gallicia appears to have been done by Readers, who, wearing their hair long like laymen, cut a scanty circle only on the very top of the head. For in Spain this fashion has been confined hitherto to heretics. To remove therefore all occasion of offence in the Church, this mark of unseemliness must be done away, and one mode of tonsure, and

---

[133] *Propter quod orat id est prædicat.* St. Isidore was a student of Etymology, as his xx. books *De Originibus* testify. But with him, as with other ancient writers, whether Greek or Latin, etymology is a weak point. To understand what he means here the reader must bear in mind that he uses *orat* with reference to its (probable) root meaning "speaks;" and that *prædicare* here does not mean "*preach*" in the modern sense of the word, but like κηρύσσειν, "*to make proclamation.*" He alludes to the office of the deacon in "uttering aloud" the various directions to the people which occur in the course of the Liturgy, and more particularly perhaps to the duty, often assigned to a deacon of reading ("*Apostolum*") the Epistle, or the Gospel, of the day.

of drefs, prevail, in accordance with the ufage of the whole of Spain. To difregard this will be an offence againſt the Catholic faith."

It is evident from thefe canons that in Spain, at the beginning of the 7th century, the "orarium," or ſtole, was worn both by biſhops and preſbyters, and by deacons, though, by the latter, in a diſtinctive manner, on the left ſhoulder only. Alſo that the ſtaff and ring were regarded as ſpecial infignia of a biſhop; the *planeta* as the proper veſtment of a Preſbyter; and the Alb, or white tunic, of a Deacon.

## XXIX.

### VENERABLE BEDE.[134]

#### ON THE LEVITICAL VESTMENTS.

Our countryman Bede, writing early in the eighth century, in his treatise *De Tabernaculo* (lib. iii. cap. ii. fqq.), enters at confiderable length upon the fubject of the veftments of the Aaronic priefthood. He lays[135] it down as a general principle that the ordination and the drefs of the Levitical priefthood is in this wife properly applicable to the priefthood of the Chriftian Church, that the outward fplendour which in the former times fhone brightly in an ornate vefture, fhall now, fpiritually underftood, be inwardly confpicuous in the hearts of them who ferve in holy miniftry to God. And in the acts of them who minifter, there fhould be an outward glory alfo,—a glory beyond what is feen in the good works of the faithful generally. He adds,[136] that what is written in Holy Scripture, concerning Aaron, and the veftments of Levitical priefthood, may be underftood primarily in reference to our Lord; but that it becomes us rather to confider therein what pertaineth to our own godly converfation in Him, and alfo what hath regard to correction of life and manners.

In accordance with this general view is the meaning which he attributes to the feveral veftments which he proceeds to enumerate. Thefe are

---

[134] Bede was born (probably) in the year 673 A.D., and died A.D. 735.

[135] Cap. ii. The original is as follows, *Defcripta factura tabernaculi confequenter facerdotes qui in eo miniftrent ordinantur. Quorum quidem ordinatio et habitus recte ecclefiae facerdotibus congruit ita ut omne quod illic in ornatu veftium clarum extrinfecus fulgebat hoc intellectum fpiritualiter in ipfis facerdotum noftrorum mentibus altum intus emineat, hoc in eorum actibus prae ceteris fidelium meritis foris gloriofum clarefcat.*

[136] Ibid. in fin. *Haec quidem ita principaliter de Domino poffunt accipi; fed nos magis in eis quae ad fignificantiam noftra in Domino piae converfationis pertineant, quaeque ad correctionem noftrorum refpiciant morum, decet intueri.*

### 1. THE SUPERHUMERAL OR EPHOD.

This being so worn as to cover *the shoulders*, he regards [cap. iv.] it as typical of the labour [137] of good works, of "the easy yoke, and light burden," spoken of by our Lord.

### 2. THE "RATIONAL," OR BREASTPLATE.

This is interpreted [cap. v.] of the purity of heart and thought which befitteth one highest in holy ministry to God. And whereas *Doctrina et Veritas*,—doctrine and truth,—were to be inscribed either literally or sacramentally upon that "breastplate," this was (so he writes) for this end, that it might the more clearly appear that this ornament was not only a part of the actual vesture of the older High Priest, but was also an announcement beforehand of evangelic truth, having reference either to our Lord Himself, or to His Apostles, or indeed to all who proclaim before men the same grace and the same truth as they.

### 3. THE TUNIC OF BLUE.

He says that this outer tunic of the high-priest's dress was of full length, reaching to the feet, like to the inner tunic of linen. He adds, that to be clothed in a tunic of blue, even to the feet, is to persevere in good works even to our life's end.

### 4. THE PLATE OF GOLD.

The golden plate upon the forehead of the high-priest is significant of the assurance of our "profession," which we bear upon our brow, saying each one in the words of the apostle, "*God forbid that I should glory, save in the cross of our Lord Jesus Christ.*" [138]

### 5. THE INNER TUNIC OF LINEN.

By linen, or byssus, is meant (so all, he says, agree) Christian continence, and bodily chastity. And Christian priests (61 ζ) may then be said to have the close fitting linen vestment, or tunic, of

---

[137] Compare note 35, p. 22.
[138] Compare St. Jerome quoted above, p. 24, *Quod olim in lamina monstrabatur, nunc in signo ostenditur crucis.*

byssus, when they maintain in full vigour the life of continence to which they have devoted themselves.

### 6. OF THE "TIARA," OR PRIESTLY CAP.

"The Tiara, which was also called 'cidaris' and 'mitra,' was at once a covering and an ornament to the head of the High Priest; that by this he might be admonished, that all the senses" (having their seat *in the head*) "should be ever consecrated to God." He goes on to say that after comparing the accounts given in Holy Scripture, and in Josephus, much remains still uncertain as to the material and the colour of these caps or mitres, and of the *coronulæ* or encircling bands, whether of linen or of gold, by which they were encompassed. But their figurative meaning, he thinks, is such as this. "Priestly caps (*mitræ*) and encircling bands of linen, are worn by Christian priests (*sacerdotes*, 61 ζ), who so maintain, in the beauty of chastity, both Sight, Hearing, Taste, Smell, and Touch, as that they may hope in requital thereof to receive from God that crown of life which He hath promised to such as love Him."

### 7. OF THE PRIEST'S GIRDLE.

Whereas, by the wearing of a linen tunic is signified the dedicating the whole body to the bright purity of a chaste life, so may Christian priests (61 ζ) be said to encompass this tunic with a girdle, when with such vigilance and circumspection they guard their purity as that they shall not through self-satisfaction become inactive in good works.

### 8. ON THE LINEN DRAWERS.

These, which are to be worn, as he remarks, both by Aaron and by the other priests, he considers as designating *illam castimoniæ portionem quæ ab appetitu copulæ conjugalis cohibet, sine qua nemo vel sacerdotium suscipere vel ad altaris potest ministerium consecrari, id est, si non aut virgo permanserit aut contractæ uxoriæ conjunctionis fœdera solverit.*[139]

---

[139] The original passage, which I have abbreviated as above, is of very great length. In it Bede follows, and that professedly, "the Fathers;" for so, even in Bede's time, St. Jerome and St. Augustine and other such *Doctores Ecclesiæ*, were styled. Like them, he assigns throughout a figurative meaning to the Levitical vestments, without alluding in any way to any literal vestments, proper to Christian priesthood, which had been modelled upon those described in Exodus and Leviticus.

## 9. THE UNDER GIRDLE OF THE HIGH PRIEST.

Before quitting the subject, he observes that whereas eight vestments are mentioned in Exodus as proper to the high-priest, a ninth seems to be added in Leviticus, viz., a belt (*baltheus*), with which the linen tunic was girt in before the putting on of the tunic of blue. But this belt or girdle he seems to consider as a figurative expression only, not as anything actually worn (cap. ix. *in fin.*).

## XXX.

## GERMANUS PATRIARCHA CONSTANTINOPOLITANUS.[140]

### THE TONSURE, THE CHRISTIAN VESTMENTS, AND THE DRESS OF MONKS.

Μυστικὴ Θεωρία, p. 206.

Τὸ ξύρισμα τῆς κεφαλῆς τοῦ ἱερέως, καὶ τὸ γυροειδὲς αὐτοῦ ἐμῆμα τὸ μέσον τῶν τριχῶν, ἀντὶ τοῦ ἀκανθίνου στεφάνου ὅπερ ὁ Χριστὸς ἐφόρεσεν. Ὁ ἐν τῇ κεφαλῇ τοῦ ἱερέως περικείμενος διπλοῦς στέφανος ἐκ τῆς τῶν τριχῶν σημειώσεως εἰκονίζει τὴν τοῦ ἀποστόλου Πέτρου τιμίαν κάραν, ἣν, ἐν τῷ τοῦ Κυρίου καὶ διδασκάλου κηρύγματι ἀποσταλείς, καὶ κᾳρεὶς ὑπὸ τῶν ἀπειθούντων τῷ λόγῳ, ὡς ἐμπαιζόμενος ὑπ' αὐτῶν, ταύτην ὁ διδάσκαλος Χριστὸς ηὐλόγησε, καὶ ἐποίησε τὴν ἀτιμίαν τιμήν, καὶ τὴν χλεύην εἰς δόξαν, καὶ ἔθηκεν ἐπὶ τὴν κεφαλὴν αὐτοῦ στέφανον, οὐκ ἐκ λίθων τιμίων, ἀλλὰ τῷ λίθῳ καὶ τῇ πέτρᾳ τῆς πίστεως αὐτοῦ ἐκλάμπουσαν, ὑπὲρ χρυσίον καὶ τοπάζιον καὶ λίθους τιμίους. Κορυφὴ γὰρ πικαλλωπισμένη καὶ στέφανος τοῦ δωδεκαλίθου, οἱ ἀπόστολοί εἰσι· πέτρα δὲ ὁ πανάγιώτατος ἀπόστολος ὑπάρχει ἀρχιεράρχης τοῦ Χριστοῦ.

Ἡ στολὴ[141] τοῦ ἱερέως ὑπάρχει κατὰ τὸν ποδήρη Ἀαρών, τουτέστιν ἱμάτιον ὃ ἐστιν ἱερατικὸν ἔνδυμα, τὸ μέχρι τῶν ποδῶν, τὸ τιμιώτατον. Ἔστι δὲ πυροειδὴς κατὰ τὸν προφήτην τὸν λέγοντα· ὁ ποιῶν τοὺς ἀγγέλους αὐτοῦ πνεύματα καὶ τοὺς λειτουργοὺς αὐτοῦ πῦρ φλέγον. Καὶ πάλιν· τίς οὗτος ὁ παραγινόμενος ἐξ Ἐδώμ; Ἐδὼμ γὰρ ἑρμηνεύεται γήϊνος, ἢ ἐκλεκτός, ἢ κόκκινος. Εἶτα ἐπάγει· Ἐρύθημα ἱματίων αὐτοῦ ἐξ ἀμπέλου Βοσόρ. Διὰ τί σου ἐρυθρὰ τὰ ἱμάτια, καὶ τὰ ἐνδύματά σου ὡς ἀπὸ πατητοῦ ληνοῦ; ἐμφαίνοντος τὴν βαφεῖσαι τοῦ Χριστοῦ στολὴν τῆς σαρκὸς ἐν αἵμασιν, ἐν τῷ ἀχράντῳ αὐτοῦ σταυρῷ. Πάλιν δὲ ὅτι καὶ

---

[140] It is matter of question among critics to which of the two patriarchs named Germanus this treatise should be referred. Of these two one was appointed to the See of Constantinople in the year 715 A.D., and was afterwards deposed by the Emperor Leo. The other Germanus was made patriarch of Constantinople A.D. 1222, but resided at Nicæa, the metropolitan city being then in the hands of the Latins. De La Bigne and other editors assign the work to the older Germanus, who lived in the eighth century. A comparison of the present passage with that from the pseudo-Chrysostom given above,

## XXX.

## S. GERMANUS[140] OF CONSTANTINOPLE.

### THE TONSURE, THE CHRISTIAN VESTMENTS, AND THE DRESS OF MONKS.

RERUM ECCLESIASTICARUM THEORIA, p. 135.

The tonsure of the prieſt's head, and the circle cut away in the midſt of the hair, is in place of the crown of thorns worn by Chriſt. The double circlet, marked out by the hair of the head, ſets forth in ſemblance the honoured head of apoſtle Peter, which, when he was ſent forth to preach the Goſpel of His Lord and Maſter, was ſhorn in mockery by them that were diſobedient to the word. But the head that was ſo ſhorn Chriſt did bleſs, and made diſhonour to be unto him for honour, and mockery to be to him for glory; and ſet upon his head a crown, not made of coſtly ſtones, but radiant with light from the ſtone and rock of His faith, above the brightneſs of gold and topaz and precious ſtones. For the adorned head, and the coronal of twelve ſtones, are the apoſtles; and by the rock is meant the moſt holy apoſtle, chief in the hierarchy of Chriſt.

The veſture [141] of the prieſt accordeth with the long tunic (ποδήρης) of Aaron, being an outer garment worn by prieſts, reaching down to the feet, and of higheſt honour. The colour thereof is as of fire, according to the word of the prophet, "*Who maketh his angels ſpirits, and his miniſters a flaming fire.*" And again, "*Who is this that cometh from Edom?*" For this word "Edom" is by interpretation either "earthy," or "elect," or "ſcarlet in colour." And then he addeth, "*The redneſs of his garments is of the vineyard of Boſor. Why are thy garments red, and thy veſture as from the treading out of the*

---

p. 51, and that from patriarch Symeon of Theſſalonica later in this volume, will, I think, confirm their judgment.

[141] ἡ στολή. By the word στολή here uſed, we are to underſtand not the "ſtole" technically ſo called (this is a *weſtern* uſage of "*ſtole*," dating from the eighth century), but what was in the Eaſt regarded as the characteriſtic veſtment of Chriſtian prieſthood, viz. the φαινώλιον (ſee note 143), of which he ſays *that it reſembles the "long tunic" of Aaron in reſpect of its deſcending even to the feet*. [On στολή and *ſtola*, ſee further remarks in note 50.]

κοκκίνην χλαμύδα [142] ἐφόρεσιν ἐν τῷ πάθει ὁ Χριστός, ἐμφαίνουσιν οἱ ἀρχιερεῖς ποίου ἀρχιερέως εἰσὶν ὑπασπισταί. Τὸ δὲ ἀπεζωσμένοις τοὺς ἱεροὺς περιπατεῖν φιλωνίοις,[143] δείκνυσιν ὅτι καὶ ὁ Χριστὸς ἐν τῷ σταυρῷ ἀπερχόμενος οὕτως ἦν βαστάζων τὸν σταυρὸν αὐτοῦ. Ἐν ταῖς ἄνω λαμπρότησι τῶν νοερῶν οὐρανίων λειτουργῶν, προφητῶν καὶ ἱεραρχῶν, εἰσὶ πρεσβύτεροι εἴκοσι τέσσαρες, καὶ διάκονοι ἑπτά· οἱ μὲν πρεσβύτεροι κατὰ μίμησιν τῶν Σεραφικῶν δυνάμεων εἰσι, ταῖς μὲν στολαῖς διπλῆ πτέρυξιν κατακεκαλυμμένοι, ταῖς δὲ δυσὶ πτέρυξι τῶν χειλέων τὸν ὕμνον βοῶντες, καὶ κατέχοντες τὸν θεῖον καὶ νοητὸν ἄνθρακα Χριστὸν ἐν τῷ θυσιαστηρίῳ τῇ λαβίδι τῆς χειρὸς φανερῶς φέροντες.

Οἱ δὲ διάκονοι εἰς τύπον τῶν ἀγγελικῶν δυνάμεων ταῖς λεπταῖς τῶν λεπτῶν ὠραρίων [144] πτέρυξιν, ὡς λειτουργικὰ πνεύματα εἰς διακονίαν ἀποστελλόμενα περιτρέχουσι.

Πρῶτον μὲν τὸ στιχάριον,[145] λευκὸν ὅτι, τῆς θεότητος τὴν αἴγλην ἐμφαίνει, καὶ τοῦ ἱερέως τὴν λαμπρὰν πολιτείαν. Τὰ λωρία [146] τοῦ στιχαρίου εἰσὶ, τὰ ἐν τῇ χειρί, ἐμφαίνοντα τὸν δεσμὸν τοῦ Χριστοῦ· δήσαντες γὰρ αὐτὸν ἀπήγαγον πρὸς Καιάφαν τὸν ἀρχιερέα καὶ τὸν Πιλᾶτον. Τὰ λωρία τὰ εἰς τὰ πλάγια εἰσὶ τὸ αἷμα τὸ ῥεῦσαν ἐκ τῆς πλευρᾶς τοῦ Χριστοῦ ἐν τῷ σταυρῷ.

Τὸ περιτραχήλιόν ἐστι τὸ φακεώλιον,[147] μεθ' οὗ ἐπεφέρετο ἀπὸ τοῦ ἀρχιερέως δεδεμένος, καὶ συρόμενος ἐπὶ τὸ πρόσθεν ἐπὶ τῇ τραχήλῳ ὁ Χριστὸς, ἐν τῷ πάθει αὐτοῦ ἀπερχόμενος. Τὸ δὲ τοῦ ἐπιτραχηλίου δεξιὸν μέρος σήμησιν ὁ κάλαμος ὃν ἔδωκαν ἐμπαίζοντες τῇ δεξιᾷ τοῦ Χριστοῦ. Τὸ δὲ τοῦ ἐξ εὐωνύμου μέρους ἡ τοῦ σταυροῦ βαστάγη ἐπὶ τῶν ὤμων αὐτοῦ.

Ἡ δὲ ζώνη ἣν περιζώννυται σήμησιν ἡ εὐπρέπεια ἣν ὁ Χριστὸς βασιλεύσας εὐπρεπῆ περιεζώσατο δύναμιν τῆς θεότητος.

Τὸ δὲ φιλώνιον ἐμφαίνει τὴν ἀπὸ κοκκίνου πορφύραν, ἥνπερ τῷ Ἰησοῦ ἐμπαίζοντες οἱ ἀσεβεῖς ἐφόρεσαν. Ἔστι δὲ καὶ ἡ στολὴ τοῦ βαπτίσματος.

Τὸ ὠμοφόριον [148] ἐστι τοῦ ἀρχιερέως κατὰ τὴν στολὴν τοῦ Ἀαρὼν ἥνπερ ἐφόρουν

---

[142] Κοκκίνην χλαμύδα. He refers to Matt. xxviii. 28. The χλαμύς of the Greeks answered to the *sagum* (note 5, p. iv.) or *paludamentum* of the Romans, among whom, however, the word *chlamys* itself was naturalised. It was a short cloak, sometimes used by travellers, but in nine cases out of ten spoken of as part of a soldier's dress, and for this reason occasionally also of an emperor's, who was (as his name *Imperator* implies) a king regarded in the character of commander-in-chief. In shape it was not unlike the cavalry cloak worn in our own army.

[143] Φιλώνιον is a later form (note 152) of *φαινόλης*, of which *pænula* is the Latin equivalent.

[144] Ὡράριον, equal to *orarium*, one of the many Latin words which the later Greek naturalised. Compare notes 146, 147, and 151. As an ecclesiastical term, it appears only to be used of the *deacon's* "stole," as we now call it, not as in Latin of the corresponding vestment (ἐπιτραχήλιον) worn by priests. But a passage of Symeon of Thessalonica (De Sacris Ordinationibus, p. 145) seems clearly to show that *the same vestment* which was called ὡράριον, as worn on one shoulder by the deacon (and probably also when named simply as an ecclesiastical vestment), became an ἐπιτραχήλιον or περιτραχήλιον, when worn round the neck, and pendent from it, by a priest. See the passage in Dufresne *in voc.* ἐπιτραχήλιον.

[145] Τὸ στιχάριον λευκὸν ὅν. This στιχάριον of the Greeks corresponds to the *tunica alba* (or "alba" simply) of the Western Church.

*grape?"* By this is signified the vesture of Christ's flesh, dyed red with blood on His immaculate cross. And again, because in His passion Christ was clothed with a scarlet robe,[142] in this too do His chief priests show what manner of High-priest He is under whom they serve.

Then for that of the priests walking with Phelonion[143] unconfined by any girdle, this showeth how that Christ also, when about to depart this life upon the cross, did after the like manner bear His cross. Amid the supernal glories of the unseen heavenly ministry, prophets and hierarchs, there are four and twenty elders (or "presbyters"), and seven deacons. The elders have the semblance of the seraphic powers, and with their robes they cover themselves as with wings; and with the two wings of their lips they lift up the voice of praise, and upon the altar they lay hold upon Him who is the divine and spiritual Coal, even Christ, bearing Him openly in the forceps of the hand. But the deacons, figuring forth the angelic hosts, with the light wings of their light stoles,[144] haste onward, as ministering spirits sent forth for the service of men.

And first the "sticharion,"[145] being white, signifieth the splendour of Godhead, and the bright purity of life which becometh Christian priests. The stripes[146] of the sticharion upon the wristband of the sleeve, are significant of the bands wherewith Christ was bound; for they bound Him and led Him away to Caiaphas the high-priest, and to Pilate. The stripes across the robe itself signify the blood which flowed from Christ's side upon the cross. The Peritrachelion is the band[147] wherewith He was taken bound from the palace of the high-priest, and dragged on by the neck, at the time of His passion. By the right side of the Epitrachelion is showed the reed which they put in mockery into the right hand of Christ. And by the left part thereof the bearing of the cross upon His shoulders.

The girdle, wherewith the priest girdeth himself about, signifieth the beauty wherewith Christ, entering upon His kingdom, did gird Himself withal, even the beauteous majesty of Godhead.

In the Phenolion we may see the scarlet robe which those ungodly ones, in mockery of Jesus, did put upon Him. And this serveth also as the robe of baptism.

The Omophorion[148] belongeth to one chief in priestly ministry to

---

[146] λῶρον. An adaptation, in a late Greek form, of the Latin *lorum*.

[147] φανιώλιον (*aliter* φακιόλιον), probably a Byzantine corruption from *fasciola*. Compare note 152 below.

[148] Assuming that ἐπιριπτούσης is rightly read here, the word can grammatically apply only to ὁ ἐν ἱερᾷ ἀρχιερεύς. But there is no part of the Aaronic vestments which by any stretch of imagination could be described as "put

οἱ ἐν νόμῳ ἀρχιερεῖς, σουδαρίοις μακροῖς τὸν εὐώνυμον ὦμον περιτίθεντες, κατὰ τὸν ζυγὸν τῶν ἐντολῶν τοῦ Χριστοῦ. Τὸ δὲ ὠμοφόριον ὃ περιβέβληται ὁ ἐπίσκοπος δηλοῖ τὴν τοῦ προβάτου δοράν, ὅπερ πλανώμενον [149] εὑρὼν ὁ Κύριος ἐπὶ τῶν ὤμων αὐτοῦ ἀνέλαβε καὶ σὺν τοῖς μὴ πεπλανημένοις ἠρίθμησεν. Ἔχει δὲ καὶ σταυροὺς, διὰ τὸ καὶ τὸν Χριστὸν ἐπὶ τοῦ ὤμου βαστάσαι τὸν σταυρὸν αὐτοῦ. Ἔτι δὲ καὶ οἱ θέλοντες κατὰ Χριστὸν ζῆν ἐπὶ τῶν ὤμων αἴρουσι τὸν σταυρὸν αὐτοῦ ὅ ἐστιν ἡ κακοπάθεια· σύμβολον γὰρ κακοπαθείας ὁ σταυρός.

Τὸ μοναχικὸν σχῆμά ἐστι κατὰ μίμησιν τοῦ ἐρημοπολίτου καὶ Βαπτιστοῦ Ἰωάννου· ὅτι τὸ ἔνδυμα αὐτοῦ ἦν ἐκ τριχῶν καμήλου καὶ ζώνη δερματίνη περὶ τὴν ὀσφὺν αὐτοῦ. Τὸ δὲ κείρεσθαι τὴν κάραν ὁλοτελῶς κατὰ μίμησιν τοῦ ἁγίου ἀποστόλου Ἰακώβου τοῦ ἀδελφοθέου, καὶ Παύλου τοῦ ἀποστόλου καὶ τῶν λοιπῶν. Τὰ δὲ ἀναβόλαιά [150] ἐστι κατὰ τὰ ἀναβόλαια ἅπερ ἐφόρουν ἱμάτια. Τὰ δὲ κουκούλλια [151] κατὰ τὸν λέγοντα ἀπόστολον ὅτι ἐσταύρωται [152] μοι ὁ κόσμος, κἀγὼ τῷ κόσμῳ.

Τὸ δὲ μανδίον [153] ἱμάτιον διὰ τῆς ἀπολελυμένης ἁπλώσεως τὴν πτερωτικὴν [deest ταχύτητα vel simile aliquid] τῆς τῶν ἀγγέλων μιμήσεως καθότι ἀγγέλικον σχῆμα λέγεται.

Ἡ δὲ ὀθόνη [154] μεθ᾽ ἧς λειτουργοῦσιν οἱ διάκονοι δηλοῖ τὴν τοῦ Χριστοῦ ταπείνωσιν, ἣν ἐπεδείξατο ἐν τῷ νιπτῆρι. Τὸ δὲ ἐγχείριον τὸ ἐπὶ τῆς ζώνης ἐστὶ τὸ ἀπομάξαι τὰς χεῖρας αὐτοῦ λέντιον. Καὶ πέφυκε τὸ ἐγχείριον ἔχειν ἐπὶ τῆς ζώνης ἀντίτυπον τοῦ ἀπομάξαντος τὰς χεῖρας καὶ τοῦ Ἀθῶος εἰμι ἐπιφωνήσαντος.

---

about the left shoulder with long bands or kerchiefs." I believe therefore that there is some corruption of the text here, or else some forgetfulness of strict grammatical construction. Reference seems to be made to the way in which the Christian ὠμοφόριον was doubled back over the left shoulder, and hung down the back, while the other end hung pendent (like the extremity of the archiepiscopal pallium) in front.

[149] These words are taken all but verbatim from S. Isidore of Pelusium, quoted above, p. 49.

[150] Τὰ ἀναβόλαια. The diminutive ἀναβολάδιον appears in Latin as anabolodium, which again was corrupted into ambologium. This last is described by Latin writers (see Ducange in voc.) sometimes as covering the head, sometimes as covering the shoulders. He seems to intimate that the ἀναβόλαια here spoken of correspond with the older pallium (note 73.) One end of this was really ἀναβαλλόμενον "thrown up" over the left shoulder.

[151] Τὰ κουκούλλια. Another imported Latin word. It is the Latin cucullus, our own "cowl," which in mediæval writers appears as cuculla. As early as St. Jerome's time this "cowl" is spoken of as worn by monks.

[152] He alludes no doubt to the cross upon the cowl of Eastern Bishops (worn also by the σταυροφόροι, or privileged clergy of the Cathedral Church at Constantinople) which was so placed as to appear upon the forehead, when the cowl was worn upon the head. A similar

God, like to that robe of Aaron which the high-priests wore under the law, putting it about the left shoulder with long bands of linen, even as the yoke of Christ's commandments.

But the Omophorion,[149] wherewith bishops are clad, signifieth the fleece of the sheep which the Lord found wandering, and took it upon His shoulders, and numbered it among them that had not wandered. And this hath crosses marked upon it, because that Christ also bare the cross upon His shoulders. And they that desire to live after Christ's example, they too take up His cross, even the endurance of hardship. For the cross is the symbol of His endurance.

The monastic habit is after the manner of that dweller in the desert, John the Baptist; for his raiment was of camel's hair, and a leathern girdle was about his loins.

They that shave the whole head do it in imitation of the holy apostle James, the "brother of God," and of apostle Paul, and of the rest. And the "anabolæa"[150] are after the manner of the outer garments which they were wont to wear. The Cowls[151] are in accordance with that of the apostle, who saith, "*The world is crucified*[152] *unto me, and I unto the world.*"

The cape,[153] open as it is and simple, is a symbol of the winged speed of angels, and is spoken of commonly as belonging to the dress of angels.

But the vestment of linen[154] wherewith the deacons minister at the altar, is in sign of the humility of Christ which He showed in respect of the Bason (when He washed the disciples' feet). And the napkin upon their girdle is the towel wherewith He dried His hands. And this carrying of a napkin upon the girdle is in antitype of him who wiped his hands and cried, "I am innocent."

---

cowl is to be seen on the head of BENEDICTVS I PAPA ET MONACHVS, in a drawing (unedited as far as I know) in the collection at Windsor.

[153] Τὸ μανδύον. Again, a neuter form, substituted for the older forms μανδύας and μανδύη. This constant obliteration (*following upon confusion*) of the older distinctions of gender is in the later Greek, as in debased Latin, a natural result of barbarous deterioration. The word μανδύας is somewhat vaguely used, sometimes of a garment nearly resembling the Latin *pænula*, sometimes of a kind of cape, shaped much like a *sagum* (note 5, p. iv.) See Ferrarius, De Re Vest. Pars ii, Lib. i. cap. ii. The cloak here described is probably the ordinary walking dress of the clergy in the East.

[154] These words are quoted verbatim from S. Isidore of Pelusium (*supra*, p. 49).

## XXXI.

## RABANVS MAVRVS.[135]

### DE INSTITUTIONE CLERICORUM.[136]

#### Lib. I. Cap. 7. The Alb the characteristic Dress of a Deacon. Pope Sylvester's Ordinances.

Levitæ . . . propterea altari albis induti affiftunt, ut hinc admoniti cæleftem vitam habeant, candidique ad hoftias et immaculati accedant. Quos primus fecit Sylvefter Papa, tricefimus quartus pontifex in Romana ecclefia poft Petrum, Dalmaticis uti, et conftituit ut pallio [137] linoftimo eorum læva tegeretur, ficut in geftis pontificalibus continetur.

#### Cap. 14. The Sacerdotal Habit of the 9th Century compared with the Vestments of Levitical Priesthood.

De vefte ergo facerdotali moderna ad antiquum veteris teftamenti habitum comparationem facientes, fecundum maiorum fenfum, quid myftice fignificet, profequamur.

#### Cap. 15. Of the Superhumeral or Ephod.

Primum ergo eorum [138] indumentum eft Ephod Bad, quod interpre-

---

[135] Rabanus (furnamed "Maurus" by his tutor Alcuin), was born A.D. 785, and in 810 was fet at the head of the fchool attached to the monaftery of Fulda. He was made Abbot of Fulda in 822, and in 847 became Archbifhop of Mayence.

[136] This treatife dates from the year 819 A.D.

[137] This expreffion has caufed difficulty owing to the diverfity of meanings in which the word *pallium* occurs (fee note 125). The pallium (cloth) of linen woof (*linoftimum*) which was to cover *the left hand* of the Roman deacon, is in all probability the *mappula*, which we find the Roman clergy claiming as exclufively their own in the time of St. Gregory. (Cap. fupra, pp. 65 and 66.)

[138] By *eorum* are evidently meant the Levitical priefts. And as Rabanus feems to have known of no actual veftment in ufe by Chriftian priefts which would anfwer to the Ephod Bad, he follows the older writers in giving to this a fpiritual application. The ephod being a covering to the *fhoulders* has reference, he fays, to the activity in good *words* (note 35, p. 22) of one who is to be fet over God's people in the Church.

tatur superhumerale lineum, quod significat munditiam bonorum operum. Hinc bene in lege, cum Dominus de veste sacerdotali Moisen instituit, primum de Superhumerali faciendo præcepit, quia quisquis ad sacerdotium magisteriumque populi Dei promovendus est, primum ejus debent opera cognosci, ut dum hoc, quod foris omnibus patet, inreprehensibile patuerit, convenienter ex tempore et integritas cordis ejus, et fidei synceritas scrutetur.

### Cap. 16. Of the Ποδήρης, or Long Tunic.

Secundum est linea tunica, quæ Græce ποδήρης, Latine talaris dicitur, eo quod ad talos usque descendat. Hanc Josephus byssinam vocat, cujus significatio mystica inpromptu est. Cum enim constet, lino vel bysso continentiam et castitatem significari, strictam[101] habent lineam sacerdotes,[159] cum proposito continentiæ non enerviter, sed studiose conservant. Hæc ad talos usque descendit, quia usque ad finem vitæ hujus bonis operibus insistere debet sacerdos, præcipiente ac promittente Domino, *Esto fidelis usque ad mortem, et dabo tibi coronam vitæ.*

### Cap. 17. Of the Girdle.

Tertium vestimentum est cingulum sive balteum, quo utuntur ne tunica ipsa defluat, et gressum impediat. Hoc nimirum custodiam mentis significat. Qui enim tunica talari indutus absque cingulo incedit, defluit tunica, ac relicto corpore, ventis et frigoribus intrandi spatium tribuit: quin et præpeditis gressibus, incedendi usum retardat, vel etiam calcantibus se, causa efficitur ruinæ. Ergo lineas induunt sacerdotes, ut castitatem habeant: accinguntur balteis, ne ipsa castitas sit remissa et negligens, ne vento elationis animum perflandi aditum impendat, ne crescente iniquitate refrigescere faciat charitatem ipsorum, ne bonorum gressus operum[160] jactantia suæ præsumptionis impediat, ne præpedito virtutum cursu ipsa etiam terrestris concupiscentiæ sordibus polluta vilescat, et ad ultimum, Authorem suum ad ruinam superbiendo impellat.

---

[159] *Sacerdotes.* On the comprehensive meaning of this term see note 61, p. 39.

[160] *Bonorum gressus operum,* "the steps of good works," i.e. the "walk" of the Christian man in all good works for God.

## Cap. 18. Of the Mappula, or Phanon.

Quartum vero, mappula sive mantile, sacerdotis indumentum est, quod vulgo phanonem [161] vocant, quod ob hoc eorum tunc manibus tenetur, quando Missæ officium agitur, ut paratos ad ministerium mensæ Domini populus conspiciat. Mappæ ergo convivii et epularum adpositarum linteamina sunt, unde diminutivum mappula, sicut et mantilia, nunc pro operiendis mensis sunt: quæ, ut nomen ipsorum indicat, olim tergendis manibus præbebantur. Oportet ergo sacerdotes et ministros altaris mappulas manibus tenere, quorum officium est divina sacramenta conficere, ut cum devotione mentis opus spontaneum concordet, digne exerceatur officium, quod pie divino est munere collatum.

## Cap. 19. Of the Orarium, which some call "Stole."

Quintum quoque est quod orarium dicitur, licet hoc quidam stolam vocent. Hoc enim genere vestis solummodo eis personis uti est concessum, quibus prædicandi [162] officium est delegatum. Bene etiam oratoribus Christi orarium habere convenit, quia cum indumentum eorum officio proprio concinat, et ipsi sedulo ad verbi ministerium cohortentur, et plebs ipsis commissa, indicium salutare conspiciens, ad meditationem legis concurrere ferventius admonetur. Apte ergo orarium collum [163] simul et pectus tegit sacerdotis, ut inde instruatur, quod quicquid ore proferat, tractatu summæ rationis attendat, ut illud apostoli semper in eo impleatur quod dicit (1 Cor. xiv. 15): *Orabo spiritu, orabo et mente: psallam spiritu, psallam et mente*; et iterum (2 Cor. vi.): *Os nostrum ad vos, ô Corinthii, cor nostrum dilatatum est*. Ne forte si improvise et irrationabiliter loquatur, damnum patiatur, Salomone attestante, qui ait (Prov. xvi.): *Cor sapientis erudiet os ejus, et labiis illius addet gratiam*. Item (Prov. xxi.), *Qui custodit os suum, custodit animam suam: qui inconsideratus est ad loquendum, sentiet mala*.

---

[161] *Phanon*, also written *Fanon*. Comp. Alcuinus (quoted later in this book), *Sudarium, quod ad tergendum sudorem in manu gestari mos est, quod usitato nomine Fanonem vocamus*.

[162] *Prædicandi officium*. See p. 76, note 133.

[163] *Collum .. pectus .. ore .. rationis*. He connects the neck with the voice (comp. Amalarius De Eccl. Off. cap. 17, quoted p. 96), and the breast (see note 38, p. 22) with reason.

### Cap. 20. Of the Dalmatic.[164]

Sextum namque est quod Dalmatica a Dalmatia Græciæ provincia, in qua primum texta est, nuncupatur. Hæc vestis in modum est crucis facta,[165] et passionis Domini indicium est. Habet quoque et purpureos tramites ipsa tunica, a summo usque ad ima, ante ac retro descendens [*Leg.* descendentes], necnon et per utramque manicam : ut admoneatur minister Domini per habitus sui speciem, cujus muneris particeps est, ut cum per mysticam oblationem passionis Dominicæ commemorationem agit, ipse in eo fiat hostia Deo acceptabilis.

### Cap. 21. Of the Casula, or Chasuble.[166]

Septimum sacerdotale indumentum est, quod casulam vocant ; dicta est autem per diminutionem a casa, eo quod totum hominem tegat, quasi minor casa : hanc Græci planetam nominant. Hæc supremum omnium indumentorum est, et cætera omnia interius per suum munimen tegit et servat. Hanc ergo vestem possumus intelligere charitatem quæ cunctis virtutibus supereminet, et earum decorem suo tutamine protegit et illustrat. Nec enim ullus jam erit virtutum splendor, si non eas charitatis irradiaverit fulgor, quod ostendit Apostolus, dicens (1 Cor. xiii) : *Si linguis hominum loquar et angelorum, charitatem autem non habeam, factus sum sicut æs sonans, aut cymbalum tinniens : Et si habuero prophetiam, et noverim mysteria omnia, et omnem scientiam : et si habuero omnem fidem, ita ut montes transferam, charitatem autem non habuero, nihil mihi prodest. Charitas patiens est, benigna est : Charitas non æmulatur, non agit perperam, non inflatur, non est ambitiosa, non quærit quæ sua sunt, non irritatur, non cogitat malum, non gaudet super iniquitate, congaudet autem veritati. Omnia suffert, omnia credit, omnia sperat, omnia sustinet. Charitas nunquam excidit,* et reliqua. Sine hac, nec sacerdos ipse ad altare adpropinquare debet, nec munus offerre, nec preces fundere. Unde veritas ipsa dicit (Matt. vi.) : *Si offers munus tuum ad altare, et ibi recordatus fueris, quia frater tuus habet aliquid adversum te,*

---

[164] Comp. note 131, p. 74 and the letter of S. Gregory quoted p. 67.

[165] *In modum crucis.* He alludes to the appearance presented by this vestment when the sleeves are stretched out on either side, as in the figures of " *Orantes.*"

[166] Comp. note 130, p. 74.

*relinque ibi munus tuum ante altare, et vade prius reconciliari fratri tuo, et tunc veniens offeres munus tuum.* Et item (Mar. xi.): *Cum ſtabitis ad orandum, dimittite ſi quid habetis adverſum aliquem,* et reliqua. De hoc itaque ſpiritali virtutum indumento, Apoſtolus ad Coloſſenſes ita ſcripſit (Col. iii.): *Induite,* inquit, *vos ſicut electi Dei, ſancti et dilecti, viſcera miſericordiæ, benignitatem, humilitatem, modeſtiam, patientiam,* et cætera: Et de charitatis eminentia paulo poſt ſubjunxit, dicens: *Super omnia autem hæc charitatem habentes, quod eſt vinculum perfectionis.*

### Cap. 22. Of the Sandals.

Induunt quoque ſacerdotes pedes ſandaliis ſive ſoleis, quod genus calceamenti evangelica authoritate eis eſt conceſſum, ut Marci evangelium teſtatur (Mar. vi.): quia hoc calceamentum myſticam ſignificationem habet, ut pes neque tectus ſit, neque nudus ad terram, id eſt, ut nec occultetur evangelium, nec terrenis commodis innitatur. Nam ſcriptum eſt in Apoſtolo (Eph. vi.): *Et calceati pedes in præparatione evangelii pacis.* Sicut ergo ſandalia partem pedis tegunt, partem inopertam relinquunt: ita et evangelii doctores partim evangelium operire, partimque aperire debent: ita videlicet, ut fidelis et devotus ſufficientem habeat doctrinam, et infidelis et contemptor non inveniat blaſphemandi materiam. Admonet etiam et nos hoc genus calceamenti, ut carni noſtræ et corpori in neceſſitatibus conſulamus, non in libidinis laſciviam defluamus, de quibus utriſque nos divina lex inſtruit. Scriptum eſt enim (Iſa. lviii.), *Carnem tuam ne deſpexeris;* et item (Rom. xiii.): *Carnis curam ne feceritis in concupiſcentiis.*

### Cap. 23. The Pallium of an Archbishop.

Super hæc autem omnia ſummo pontifici [167] (qui Archiepiſcopus vocatur) propter Apoſtolicam [168] vicem pallii honor decernitur, quod genus indumenti crucis ſignaculum purpureo colore exprimit, ut ipſo indutus pontifex, a tergo et pectore crucem habeat, ſuaque mente pie

---

[167] *Summo Pontifici.* Note that with Raban *Pontifex Summus,* means not "the Pope," but an Archbiſhop. See above note 45, p. 26.

[168] *Apoſtolicam vicem.* He means either "Apoſtolic Office," *i.e.* office of higheſt authority in the Church, or (and this, I think more probable) "repreſentation of the Apoſtolic See," *i.e.* of Rome. For the phraſe *vices Apoſtolicæ ſedis,* ſee above p. 63.

et digne de passione redemptoris cogitet, ac populo, pro quo dominum deprecatur, redemptionis suæ signaculum demonstret. Condecet quoque bene, ut ipsa Apostolica dignitas Apostolicum virum faciat, ut plena devotione, sano sermone, et digna operatione possit dicere cum Apostolo (Gal. vi.): *Mihi autem absit gloriari nisi in cruce Domini nostri Jesu Christi, per quem mihi mundus crucifixus est, et ego mundo.* Hæc quæque de habitu sacerdotali ad sensum secundum modulum ingenioli [169] nostri breviter diximus, non præjudicantes his, qui congruentius et dignius de eadem re possint scribere et plenius disputare.[170]

---

[169] *Ingenioli nostri*, &c. This is evidently the expression of one who felt that he had not confined himself to the traditionary teaching "of the Fathers" concerning the spiritual significance of the older Levitical vestments (as typifying Christian virtues), but had advanced something of a new theory of his own on a subject which he evidently supposes that others beside himself are likely to discuss.

[170] The passage above given is of special importance to this inquiry, as in the idea here suggested of a correspondence between the seven "sacerdotal vestments" of Christian ministry, and the seven vestments of "the law," we have probably the very earliest example of an attempt being made to draw out in detail a comparison between the two. Raban himself appears to have been conscious how few were in his time the points of resemblance. But the hint which he here throws out was soon improved upon by others, as we shall see in the passages which follow.

## XXXII.

## AMALARIUS METENSIS.[171]

### OF THE VESTMENTS OF CHRISTIAN PRIESTHOOD.

[DE ECCL. OFF. LIB. II. CAP. 15-26.]

#### CAP. 15. OF CLERICAL VESTMENTS IN GENERAL.

PRIMO notandum est, ita esse clericorum habitum constitutum in ecclesiasticis officiis, ut in omnibus Christiano populo possit præbere exemplum bonæ conversationis. Quod quodammodo significat Hieronymus in libro [172] de veste sacerdotali ad Fabiolam: *Legimus*, inquiens, *in Levitico, juxta præceptum Dei Moisen lavisse Aaron et filios ejus. Jam tunc purgationem mundi et rerum omnium sanctitatem baptismi sacramenta signabant. Non accipiunt vestes, nisi loti prius sordibus: nec coronantur ad sacra, nisi in Christo novi homines renascantur.* Ex his verbis intelligimus, vestes sacerdotales ad conversationem populi Christiani pertinere.

#### CAP. 16. SACRED VESTMENTS RESERVED FOR HOLY USE ALONE.

Stephanus [173] natione Romanus ex patre Iobio, ut legitur in gestis episcopalibus, constituit sacerdotibus Levitisque vestes sacratas in usu quotidiano non uti in ecclesia. Tale quid Dominus per Ezechielem loquitur: *Hæc sunt gazophylacia sancta, in quibus vestiuntur sacerdotes, qui appropinquant ante Dominum in sancta sanctorum.* Et paulo post: *Cum autem ingressi fuerint sacerdotes, non egredientur de sanctis in atrium exterius, et ibi reponent vestimenta sua, in quibus ministrant, quia sancta*

---

[171] Amalarius is first heard of as a deacon at Metz, then (A.D. 825) as a bishop sent on a mission from the Council of Paris to the Emperor Lewis; and, lastly, as sent on a mission from the Emperor to Pope Gregory IV. This treatise dates from about the year 824 A.D. Some editors have attributed it to a contemporary archbishop, Amalarius Fortunatus, of Treves.

[172] See above p. 10, sqq. The words quoted by Amalarius will be found at p. 20.

[173] Stephanus I. *sed.* 253-257 A.D. The reference to Ezechiel which follows is to cap. xliv. See above p. 29, sqq.

*Amalarius on Vestments of Christian Priesthood.*

*sunt, vestienturque vestimentis aliis, et sic procedent ad populum.* Et iterum: *Cumque ingrediuntur portas atrii interioris, vestibus lineis induentur, nec ascendat super eos quicquam laneum, quando ministrant in portis atrii interioris et intrinsecus.* Et post pauca: *Cumque egredientur atrium exterius ad populum, exuent se vestibus suis, in quibus ministraverant, et reponent ea in gazophylacia sanctuarii, et vestient se vestimentis aliis.* Quamvis hæc spiritaliter intelligere debeamus, tamen admoniti sumus a supra memorato apostolico,[174] ut mutationem vestimenti juxta literam compleamus. Nobis enim qui spiritu sumus renati, ante oculos bonum est frequentare quod in mentem transeat. Per lineam vestem, qua tantummodo utimur in sanctis, intelligimus subtilem orationem, exutam ab omni carnali cogitatione ante Dominum. Locutio vero ad populum alia debet esse, tamque grossa, ut intelligi valeat a populo. Unde et Hieronymus in libro [175] decimotertio super Ezechielem: *Et quia semel præceperat quibus vestibus uti deberent sacerdotes quando intrinsecus in ministeriis sunt, rursum jubet ut egredientes, in gazophylaciis sive in exedris sanctorum se exuant pristinis vestibus, et induantur aliis, ne si sanctas vestes habuerint, sanctificent populum foris positum, qui necdum fuerit sanctificatus, nec se præparaverit in sanctificatione templi, ut sit Domini Nazaræus. Per quæ discimus, non quotidianis et quibuslibet pro usu vitæ communis pollutis vestibus nos ingredi debere in sancta sanctorum: sed munda conscientia et mundis vestibus tenere Domini sacramenta. Porro religio divina*[176] *alterum habitum habet in ministerio, alterum in usu vitaque communi.* Namque et hic ex verbis Hieronymi admoniti sumus mutationem vestimenti. Sequitur ejusdem in eodem: *Hæc vestimenta proprio nobis labore conficimus, quæ texta sunt desuper, qualem et Dominus habebat tunicam, quæ scindi non potest: quibus induimur, quando secreta Domini et arcana cognoscimus, et habemus spiritum qui scrutatur etiam alta et profunda Dei, quæ non sunt monstranda vulgo, nec proferenda ad populum, qui non est sanctificatus, nec Dei sanctitudini præparatus: ne si majora se audierint, majestatem scientiæ ferre non possint: et quasi solido suffocentur cibo, qui adhuc lacte infantiæ nutriendi sunt.*[177] Inter regulas sacræ scripturæ septem hæc una ex illis constat, ut a litera transeamus ad spiritum, et a spiritu ad literam: Ac ideo non abhorret a vero, quamvis de laneo vestimento accipiamus secundum spiritum, si secundum literam perfecerimus mu-

---

[174] *Apostolico, i.e.* by Stephanus, Bishop of the "Apostolic See."
[175] See above p. 30.
[176] See note 53, p. 31.
[177] For the mystical reference attributed to woollen garments see note 30, p. 20.

tationem vestimenti, quod et secundum literam et secundum spiritum rite possumus intelligere.

### Cap. 17. Of the Amice.

Amictus[178] est primum vestimentum nostrum, quo collum undique cingimus. In collo est namque vox, ideoque per collum loquendi usus exprimitur. Per amictum intelligimus[179] custodiam vocis, de qua Psalmista dicebat: *Dixi, custodiam vias meas, ut non delinquam in lingua mea: posui ori meo custodiam.* Et in alio Psalmo: *Pone, Domine, custodiam ori meo.* Amictus ideo dicitur, quia circumjicitur. In isto primo vestimento admonetur castigatio vocis.[179]

### Cap. 18. Of the Alb.

Postea camisiam induimus, quam Albam vocamus, de qua Hieronymus in epistola memorata de veste sacerdotali ad Fabiolam: *Secunda ex lino tunica, est poderis, id est, talaris,* et in sequentibus, *Hæc adhæret corpori, et ita arcta est et strictis manicis, ut nulla omnino in veste sit ruga, et usque ad crura descendat. Volo pro legentis facilitate, abuti sermone vulgato: Solent militantes habere lineas, quas camisias vocant sic aptas membris et adstrictas corporibus, ut expediti sint vel ad cursum, vel ad prælia, dirigendo jaculo, tenendo clypeo, ense librando, et quocunque necessitas traxerit. Ergo et sacerdotes parati in ministerio Dei utantur hac tunica, ut habentes pulchritudinem vestimentorum nudorum celeritate discurrant.* In eo distat vestimentum illud a nostro, quod illud strictum est, nostrum vero largum. Etenim hi, qui, in veteri testamento spiritu servitutis erant adstricti, de quo dicebat Paulus:

---

[178] The amice was in shape (when opened out square) and in primitive use, nearly the counterpart of our modern "white neckcloth." But instead of being folded several times upon itself, it seems to have been either kept open or doubled but once. Hence it covered both neck and shoulders, and served to keep the outer garment from actual contact with the skin. This mode of wearing it is still preserved in Roman use. See Rock's *Hierurgia*, vol. ii. p. 612, with the plate adjoining. But the thought of making this neckcloth a *helmet* also [by holding it for a few moments upon the head, see Rock, *loc. cit.*] was an invention to which Amalarius and his contemporaries were not prepared. We shall find this, however, in a later author quoted in this work. See the Index *in voc.* Amictus.

[179] *Castigatio vocis.* See above note 163, p. 90.

*Non enim accepistis spiritum servitutis in timore.* Nos vero quia Filius liberavit, liberi sumus; non accepimus spiritum servitutis in timore, sed spiritum adoptionis filiorum. Ac ideo sic illorum strictum,[180] nostrum largum, propter libertatem qua Christus nos liberavit. Quia primum vestimentum diximus esse castigationem vocis, videamus si secundum habeat [181] aliquam castigationem corporis. Dicit Beda [182] in libro de Tabernaculo; *Hæc etenim linea, manus ac brachia debet stringere sacerdotis, ne quid nisi utile faciant: pectus, ne quid inane cogitet: ventrem, ne delicias ultra modum appetendo, deum se gulosis facere præsumat: subjecta ventri membra, ne lasciviendo totam sacerdotalis habitus pulchritudinem corrumpant: genua, ne ab orationis instantia torpeant: tibias et pedes, ne ad malum currant. Induatur ergo sacerdos primo linea stricta, ut et corpus ab iniquis operibus, et a pravis cogitationibus mentem compescat.* Quod ibi significat strictura vestimenti, hoc apud nos lini [183] castigatio. Quia usque ad pedes Beda provenit differendo de lineis vestibus, congruum est, ut nosmetipsos absolvamus de sandaliis, sive ut alio nomine campobis,[184] qui supersunt in pedibus. Sandalia subtus cooperiunt pedem, desuper nudum relinquunt, de quibus dicit idem, qui supra, in tractatu super Marcum: *Marcus dicendo calceari eos sandaliis, vel soleis, aliquid hoc calceamentum mysticæ significationis habere admonet, ut pes neque tectus sit, neque nudus ad terram, id est, nec occultetur evangelium, nec terrenis commodis innitatur.* Sicut per linum, quo pedes vestiuntur, castigatio pedum significatur, ita per sandalia profectus ad prædicandum.

### CAP. 19. OF THE CHASUBLE.

Casulam, quæ est generale indumentum sacrorum ducum,[185] ante cæteras vestes quæ sequuntur, præponimus. In illis quæ supra præ-

---

[180] For the reason why the Levitical vestments were thus "closely fitted" to the body, see note 6, p. 2.

[181] *Videamus si habeat.* To this the same remark will apply that was made above, note 169, p. 93.

[182] The quotation is from the *De Tabernaculo*, lib. iii. cap. 8. See note above, p. 78, sqq.

[183] *Lini castigatio.* See note 106, p. 60.

[184] *Campobis.* The true reading is probably *campagis*. The *Campaga* was a kind of shoe worn at one time by Roman Senators only (Albertus Rubenius *De Re Vest.* lib. ii. cap. 5), and subsequently reserved as a special privilege to the Roman clergy (Divi Gregor. Epist. lib. vii. epist. 28).

[185] The term *sacri duces* seems to be here used nearly as οἱ ἡγούμενοι in H.S. as a general term for the two higher orders of the ministry.

tulimus, castigatio corporis a vitiis designatur, excepto in sandaliis. In sequentibus vero opera justitiæ demonstrabuntur. Dicit Beda in libro memorato de Tabernaculo: *Vestes sanctæ Aaron, quas illi fecit Moises, opera sunt justitiæ et sanctitatis*. Casula vero, quæ pertinet generaliter ad omnes clericos, debet significare opera quæ pertineant ad omnes: hæc enim sunt fames, sitis, vigiliæ, nuditas, lectio, psalmodia, oratio, labor operandi, doctrina, silentium, et cætera hujusmodi. In istis enim nullus sacrorum Dux negligens debet esse. Quando istis operibus vestitur, casula indutus est. Hæc in aperto sunt, et tam ad minores gradus pertinent, quam ad supremos. Casula dupla est post tergum inter humeros, et ante pectus. Per humeros opera exprimuntur. In eis duplex fit vestimentum, quia sic debemus bona opera foris proximis ostendere, ut eadem intus coram Domino integra servemus. In pectore duplex, quia in eo utrunque debet esse, et doctrina et veritas: veritas interius, doctrina ad homines. Hæc duo duplicia sint conjuncta, quia tunc bene ministratur, cum opus et ratio in unum conveniunt. Opus ad humeros, ratio ad pectus.[186]

## CAP. 20. OF THE STOLE.

Stolam[187] accipit diaconus, quando ordinatur ab episcopo. Ipsa enim semper utitur in opere ministerii. Per stolam designatur onus leve ac suave, de quo Dominus dicit: *Tollite jugum meum super vos, jugum enim meum suave est, et onus meum leve*. Per jugum evangelium intelligimus, de quo dicit Hieronymus in commentariis Matthæi: *Quomodo levius lege evangelium, cum in lege homicidium, in evangelio ira damnetur?* Et paulo post: *In lege multa præcepta sunt, quæ Apostolus non posse compleri plenissime docet. In lege opera requiruntur, quæ qui fecerit, vivet in eis: In evangelio voluntas requiritur, quæ si etiam effectum non habuerit, tamen præmium non amittet*. In eo quod stola ad genua tendit, quæ solent curvari causa humilitatis, hoc intelligimus, quod Dominus dicit: *Discite a me, quia mitis sum et humilis corde*. Sciat se diaconus in stola superposita collo, ministrum evangelii esse, non præpositum. Evangelium CHRISTUS est.

---

[186] *Opus ad humeros*, note 35, p. 22; *ratio ad pectus*, note 38, p. 22.

[187] The word *stola* here appears to the exclusion of the older word *orarium*. The vestment here meant closely resembled in shape the stole still worn in the Western Church. See the Plates dating from the 9th century among the Illustrations of this volume.

### Cap. 21. Of the Dalmatic.

Dalmatica a Silvestro Papa instituta est. Per Dalmaticam intelligimus religionem sanctam immaculatam, quæ est apud Deum et Patrem, ut visitentur pupilli et viduæ in tribulationibus eorum, et visitatores immaculatos se custodiant ab hoc seculo. Ipsa Dalmatica duas coccineas lineas habet retro, similiterque in anteriori parte: quia vetus testamentum et novum rutilant dilectione [108] Dei et proximi. Immaculatum esse, ad Deum pertinet: visitare fratres, ad proximum. Per colorem coccineum opera misericordiæ, quæ ex charitate fiunt in pupillis et viduis, intelligimus: per candorem, visitatorum munditia designatur. Ipsa est enim vestis, de qua dicitur in psalmo quadragesimo quarto: *Adstitit regina a dextris tuis in vestitu deaurato, circumdata varietate.* Unde Augustinus in eodem psalmo: *In veste ista varietas sit, scissura non sit. Ecce varietatem intelleximus de diversitate linguarum, et vestem intelleximus propter unitatem.* Et in sequentibus, *Circumamicta varietate. Pulchritudo intrinsecus. In fimbriis autem aureis, varietas linguarum, doctrinæ decus.* Fimbriæ, quæ procedunt de Dalmatica, verba sunt ejus prædicatoris, cujus religio sancta et immaculata est. Sicut verba ab aura aeris raptantur, ita fimbriæ spiramine venti. Profert Paulus candidas fimbrias circa manus ad utilitatem gentium, quando dicit, *Magis autem laboret operando manibus suis quod bonum est, ut habeat unde tribuat necessitatem patienti.* Quod Paulus prædicavit, opere complevit, dicens ad Corinthios de se: *In tribulationibus, in laboribus.* Quod ita Ambrosius in eadem epistola: *Laborare non destitit manibus suis, ne cui gravis esset.* Fert fimbrias candidas in latere, quando dicit: *Castigo corpus meum, et in servitutem redigo;* et in alio loco: *In castitate, hoc est, castitate corporis, et in vigiliis.* Qui hanc custodit, immaculatum se custodit ab hoc seculo. Fert coccineas circa humeros et pectora, quando dicit: *In charitate non ficta.* Ficta charitas est, quæ dimittit viduas et pupillos in tribulatione, et subvenit in prosperitate. Quæ fimbriæ ante sunt et retro, quia mandatum dilectionis et in veteri testamento, et in novo, manet. Unde Johannes: *Charissimi, non mandatum novum scribo vobis, sed mandatum vetus, quod habuistis ab initio. Mandatum vetus, est verbum quod audistis. Iterum mandatum novum scribo vobis.* Quod ita Beda: *Eadem charitas*

---

[108] *Rutilans dilectione.* On the association of red colour with the idea of charity, see above, p. 60, where St. Gregory says that the *bis tinctus coccus* of the Levitical high-priest is typical of charity (note 107 *in fin.*).

*et mandatum vetus est, quod ab initio commendata: et mandatum novum, quia tenebris ejectis desiderium novæ lucis infundit.* Aliquæ Dalmaticæ habent viginti octo fimbrias ante et retro. Ubi est octies repetitus septiformis spiritus propter genera hominum quos replet, ut laudent Deum, hoc est, reges terræ, et omnes populi, principes et judices, juvenes et virgines, senes et juniores : et aliquæ triginta et triginta, singulæ lineæ altrinsecus quindecim ; quia charitas et in veteri testamento et in novo quindecim ramos ex se producit. Quisquis studet prodesse fratribus in adversitate et in prosperitate, iste habet fimbrias coccineas in utroque humero. Hæ duæ fortunæ signantur per sinistrum et dextrum humerum. Quindecim ramos charitatis enumerat : *Patiens est, benigna est: non æmulatur, non agit perperam, non inflatur, non est ambitiosa, non quærit quæ sua sunt, non irritatur, non cogitat malum, non gaudet super iniquitate, congaudet autem veritati. Omnia suffert, omnia credit, omnia sperat, omnia sustinet.* Linea quæ in medio est, est quasi stipes charitatis. Quod enim significant lineæ sive fimbriæ in dextro humero sive sinistro, hoc significant in anteriori parte hominis, quæ pertinet ad novum testamentum. Sinistrum latus habet fimbrias, quia actualis vita solicita est, et turbatur erga plurima : at dextrum latus non habet, quia contemplativa vita quieta est. Per ipsam figuratur regina, quæ stat a dextris. Ipsa est una Columba ; perfecta et proxima stat a dextris, et nihil in se sinistrum habet. Largitas brachiorum, largitatem et hilaritatem datoris demonstrat. Diaconus qui non est indutus Dalmatica, casula legit circumcinctus,[189] ut expedite possit ministrare : vel quia suum est ire ad comitatum propter instantes necessitates. Ipsa habet pertusas subtus alas, quoniam Christum vult imitari, qui lancea perfossus est in latere, et vult ut nos sequamur ejus vestigia, quod significat pertusus in latere.

### CAP. 22. OF THE UPPER TUNIC WORN OVER THE ALB.

Sicut in camisia [190] designatur castigatio corporis, ita in tunica virtutes intimæ, quæ ad solos sublimes pertinent, de qua Hieronymus in epistola ad Fabiolam : *Hæc ipsa hyacinthina tunica, subucula nominatur, et proprie pontificis est, significatque rationem sublimium non patere*

---

[189] It is not easy to give a meaning to these words which will be in accordance with what we know from other sources, and from Amalarius himself, to have been the characteristic dress of the deacon. The meaning, probably, is this, that a deacon, if not dressed in a Dalmatic, wears a Chasuble, but gathered into the waist by a girdle.

[190] For the word *camisia* see note 23, p. 13.

*omnibus sed majoribus atque perfectis.*[191] Ipsa est interior, ipsaque designat virtutes animæ, quæ non multis cognitæ sunt, et quas semper debet habere perfectas. Unde Beda in tractatu super Lucam: *Quis etenim nesciat viscera misericordiæ, benignitatem, humilitatem, patientiam, modestiam, castitatem, fidem, spem et his similia, sine ulla temporum intercapedine a fidelibus esse servanda?* Ipsa non cingitur, sed camisia. Quæ ita est fabrefacta, ut non impediat cursum nostrum ad ministrationem, quoniam memoratæ virtutes liberum nobis iter præbent ad contemplationem Dei. Camisia cingulo continentiæ constringitur, præcipiente Domino: *Sint lumbi vestri præcincti,* ut per duas virtutes, id est, obedientiam Domini, et naturalem disputationem,[192] constringatur omnis voluptas. Hæc sunt vestimenta de quibus scribitur in parabolis Salomonis, *Fortitudo et decor indumentum ejus.* Et in superioribus, *Et cingulum tradidit Chananæo.* Si quis voluerit uti duabus tunicis, ostendet se esse diaconum et sacerdotem, sive [193] ut octo sint vestimenta secundum numerum vestimentorum summi pontificis Aaron, cujus vestimenta narrantur fuisse circa caput et corpus usque ad pedes. De vestimento pedum et manuum reticetur. Ad illius normam, ut dixi, habet summus pontifex noster [194] a capite usque ad pedes octo vestimenta. Primum est amictus, secundum camisia, tertium cingulum, quartum stola, quintum et sextum duæ tunicæ, septimum casula, octavum pallium. Porro vestimentum pedum potius pertinet ad nostros pontifices, quam ad Aaron. Dicitur nostris pontificibus: *Euntes, docete omnes gentes;* Aaron tantum in Judæa versabatur. Sudarium in manu, potius ad nostros quam ad Aaron: quoniam major munditia est in novo testamento, quam esset in veteri: et illa bona habemus, quæ illi habuerunt, et plura per Jesum Christum Dominum nostrum. Sacerdos in suo officio non se exuit casula, quia præcipiente Domino per Moisen non debet exire de sanctis, sicut scriptum est: *Nec egredientur de sanctis.* Ubi intelligi datur, debere eum jugiter in continentia et abstinentia manere.

---

[191] See the passage from S. Jerome at p. 20. The words are quoted *verbatim,* with the exception of the three or four which refer to the LXX usage of ὑποδύτης. The omission somewhat changes the sense of the original text.

[192] *Naturalem disputationem.* He probably means " contending against natural inclination " (the lusts of the flesh.)

[193] *Sive ut octo . . . reticetur.* I must confess that I am unable to follow exactly the thought of the writer in this passage. Two thoughts, however, we may trace. First he hints that the two tunics may in some cases be adopted in order to accommodate the number of the Christian vestments to those of the tabernacle. And again, that in order to preserve this correspondence we must say nothing of what was worn on the hands and the feet of Christian priests.

[194] By the words *summus pontifex noster* we are probably to understand the *pontifex summus* (or chief Pontiff) " *of us Christians,*" in other words, an archbishop. Compare what he says below of *nostros pontifices.* [For the word *pontifex,* see note 45, p. 26.] See also note 167, p. 92.

### Cap. 23. The Pallium worn by Archbishops.

Pallium archiepifcoporum fuper omnia indumenta eft, ut lamina in fronte folius pontificis.[195] Illo difcernitur archiepifcopus a cæteris epifcopis. Pallium fignificat torquem, quem folebant legitime certantes accipere. Quo dono admonentur cæteri ad legitimum certamen. Quod habet duas lineas [196] a fummo ufque deorfum ante et retro. Significat enim fummæ doctrinæ decorem per difciplinam mandatorum Domini acceptabilem. Circulus circa collum, difciplina eft Domini circa fermonem prædicatoris; ut non fit alter fermo prædicationis, et aliud opus, dicente Paulo, *Nemini dantes ullam offenfionem, ut non vituperetur minifterium noftrum.* Quod ita Ambrofius in tractatu epiftolæ ad Corinthios: *Vituperatur enim minifterium ipforum, fi ea quæ verbis docebant, operibus fuis, ut fierent, exempla non darent.* Mandata Veteris Teftamenti, a principio Genefeos ufque finem, in humerali linea operando et docendo portet pontifex: in pectorali Novi, a primitiva ecclefia ufque in finem. De torque dicebat Salomon in parabolis, *Ut addatur gratia capiti tuo, et torques collo tuo.* Quod ita Beda in eodem: *Mos apud veteres fuit, ut legitime certantes, coronam in capite, torquem in collo, acciperent. Et nobis ergo fi difciplinam Conditoris noftri, fi gratiæ matris fcita, cuftodimus, major inde virtutum fpiritalium claritas augetur. Additur gratia capiti, cum charitas quæ principale mentis ornabat, ardentius inflammatur. Additur et collo torques, cum fulgore perfectæ operationis fermo prædicationis, qui per collum procedit, confirmatur: ac ne contemni ab auditoribus debeat, indeficienti virtutum connexione docetur. Sed et his qui Mofaicæ legis decreta Domino veniente fervabant, addita eft gratia novi teftamenti cum fpe regni cæleftis, cujus fplendor eximius ad exemplum coronæ vel torquis, nullo unquam fine claudetur.*

---

[195] *Pontifex* is here the Jewifh high-prieft. Amalarius implies that as the high-prieft was diftinguifhed from other priefts by the golden plate upon his brow, fo are archbifhops diftinguifhed from other bifhops by the wearing of the *pallium*.

[196] The two lines (behind and in front) here fpoken of, and the *torques*, or collar, are evidently a defcription of fuch a later *pallium* (fee note 110, p. 63) as may be feen figured in the reprefentation of Egbertus, Archbifhop of Treves, and in the Mofaic pictures of the popes of the 12th century, given in this volume. He fays the bifhop is to bear upon the fhoulder-line (fee note 35) the precepts of the old covenant of *works*; on the pectoral-line (*i.e.* the part of the pallium which hangs down in front) thofe of the new covenant, "from the firft beginnings of the Church unto the end."

### Cap. 24. Of the Sudarium or Maniple.

Sudario solemus tergere pituitam oculorum et narium atque superfluam salivam decurrentem per labia. Ac ideo sudarium significat isto in loco studium mundandæ cogitationis, quo naturales et velut ingenitas nostras delectationes studemus tergere. Sive propter effusionem lachrymarum tergendam fertur sudarium, ut in martyrologio Bedæ legitur, quod pater noster Arsenius propter redundationem lachrymarum tergendam, sudarium semper in sinu vel in manu habuerit. In manu sinistra portatur, ut ostendatur in temporali vita tædium nos pati superflui humoris, hoc est, carnalis delectationis. Et iterum: Sudarium ad hoc portamus, ut eo detergamus sudorem qui fit ex labore proprii corporis, quod legimus usitatum fuisse circa corpus Christi. Unde legitur,[197] *Et sudarium quod fuit super caput ejus.* Sudor tædium nostro corpori est. Si non esset tædium, non toties tergeretur. Habet aliquoties mens tædium, dicente psalmista: *Dormitavit anima mea præ tædio.* Tædium in anima, quasi sudor in corpore. Tædium animi aliquoties solet fieri ex conscientia peccatorum, aliquoties ex accidentibus, ut est omne flagellum quod patitur ab alieno corpore: aliquoties ex infirmitate proprii corporis, quæ infirmitas aliquoties solet accidere ex peccatis. Quando tædium ex infirmitate peccatorum frontem conscientiæ nostræ tegit, habeamus sudarium ex lino castigatum et mundum, qualia sunt verba David prophetæ: *Cor mundum crea in me Deus, & spiritum rectum innova in visceribus mei.* Et si fuerit infirmitas ex approbatione,[198] sicut in Iob, dicamus quod dixit: *Sicut Domino placuit, ita factum est: sit nomen Domini benedictum.* Munda cogitatio in David fuit, quando dixit, *Cor mundum crea in me Deus:* mundaque in Iob, quando dixit, *Sicut Domino placuit, ita factum est.* Sic et nos, quando tædio aliquo afficimur, ne majore tristitia absorbeamur, in consolationem nostri quasi quoddam sudarium exempla prædicta sanctorum patrum ad corroborandam patientiam, ad detergendum tædium sumamus. Per sudarium intelligimus mundos affectus et pios in labore.[199]

---

[197] *Sudarium, &c.* He alludes (but with a strange misapplication of the original passage) to John, xx. 7, where there is mention of "the napkin" (Gr. σουδάριον) that was laid upon the face of our Lord after His death.

[198] *Ex approbatione:* i.e. sent as a trial of our faith.

[199] *In labore.* In time of trouble or of toil.

CAP. 25. OF THE SANDALS WORN BY BISHOPS, PRIESTS, ETC.

Varietas fandaliorum, varietatem miniftrorum pingit. Epifcopi et facerdotis pene unum eft officium; at quia nomine et honore difcernuntur, difcernuntur etiam varietate fandaliorum, ut vifibus noftris error auferatur, qui poteft intereffe propter fimilitudinem officii. Epifcopus habet ligaturam in fuis fandaliis, quam non habet prefbyter. Epifcopi eft huc illucque difcurrere per parochiam [200] ad regendam plebem: ne forte cadant fandalia de pedibus, ligata funt. Ex eo poteft fciri, quantum neceffe fit ei firmare greffus mentis, qui in turbis populorum verfatur. Prefbyter qui domi [201] hoftias immolat, fecurius incedit. Diaconus quia diffimilis eft epifcopo ab officio, non eft neceffe ut habeat diffimilia fandalia; et ipfe ligaturam habet, quia fuum eft ire ad comitatum. Subdiaconus quia in adjutorio eft diacono et pene in eodem officio, neceffe eft ut habeat diffimilia fandalia, ne forte æftimetur diaconus. Myftice, quia fandalia prædicatoris curfum fignant, folea, quæ fubtus eft, admonet prædicatorem, ut non fe implicet terrenis negociis. Lingua de albo corio, quæ fubtus calcaneum [202] eft, monftrat, debere effe eandem feparationem innocentem et fine dolo, ut poffit de eo dici, *Ecce vere Ifraelita, in quo dolus non eft.* Non fit talis, quales pfeudo-apoftoli errant, qui prædicabant per invidiam et contentionem. Lingua quæ inde furgit, et eft feparata à corio fandaliorum, linguam eorum monftrat, qui prædicatori bonum teftimonium debent proferre, de quibus dicebat Paulus: *Oportet et cum teftimonium bonum habere ab his qui foris funt.* Hi funt in inferiore parte, et funt quodammodo feparati à converfatione fpiritalium. Lingua fuperior, fpiritalium lingua eft, qui prædicatorem introducunt in opus prædicationis. Hæc requiruntur in pofteriore vita prædicatoris. At intrinfecus de albo corio circundata funt fandalia: Ita oportet effe prædicatoris intentionem candidam coram Deo ex pura confcientia: extrinfecus vero nigrum ap-

---

[200] *Parochiam,* i.e. his diocefe. Such was the primitive meaning of the word παροικία in ecclefiaftical Greek (fee Bingham, vol. iii. p. 37), and thence of *parochia* in Latin. The word was ufed, according to its proper meaning, to fignify the "neighbourhood," i.e. the neighbouring diftrict which had its centre in any particular town,—fuch town forming the capital, fo to fpeak, both for civil and for ecclefiaftical purpofes. Our own "counties," each with its "county town," would perhaps be the neareft approach to fuch a παροικία, though as a rule our counties are very much larger than the ancient ecclefiaftical παροικίαι.

[201] *Domi.* Not "at home" in the fenfe of in his "own houfe," but *domi* "ftaying at home," i.e. ftaying in the town wherein he dwelt, and in whofe Church *hoftias immolabat,* to adopt the language of Amalarius.

[202] *Calcaneum,* probably the "tread" of the foot, to ufe a fhoemaker's phrafe. It is a word of the *lingua vulgaris,* and furvives, as moft of fuch words do, in the prefent language of Italy. [*Calcagno,* the heel.]

paret, quoniam videtur prædicatorum vita despecta à secularibus propter multitudinem pressurarum præsentis mundi. Superior pars sandaliorum per quam pes intrat, multis filis consuta est, ut non dissolvantur duo coria. In initio enim debet studere prædicator pluribus virtutibus atque sententiis scripturarum, ut opera forinseca cum his quæ intrinsecus nitent coram Deo, non disjungantur. Lingua sandaliorum quæ super pedem est, linguam prædicatoris potest figurare. Linea opere sutoris facta, præcedens à lingua sandalii usque ad finem ejus, evangelicam perfectionem: lineæ præcedentes ex utraque parte, legem et prophetias, quæ in evangelio recapitulantur. Etenim ipsæ recapitulatæ sunt ad medianam lineam, quæ usque ad finem currit. Ligatura mysterium incarnationis Christi: quæ incarnatio in aliquibus aperta est humanis sensibus humano more, sicuti est poni in præsepio, pannis involvi, et cætera. Et aliter: Dicit Dominus in evangelio: *Quodcunque supererogaveris, ego cum rediero, reddam tibi.* Disponit Dominus his qui evangelium prædicarent, de evangelio vivere: supererogavit Paulus, quia sine sumptu exposuit evangelium, operabatur manibus suis victus sibi necessaria. Opus Pauli quod supererogavit evangelio, possumus intelligere corrigias supererogatas sandaliis, quæ manibus huc illucque ducuntur ut ligentur. Firmo gressu it prædicator, qui nulli onerosus est.

Breviter desideramus recapitulare omnem ornatum clericorum. Caput clerici mens est. In superiore parte disco opertum, ubi est imago Dei, in inferiore parte circundatum capillis, quasi aliquibus cogitationibus de præsenti necessitate. Amictus est castigatio vocis, Alba cæterorum inferiorum sensuum, præsidente magistra ratione, interius per disciplinam continentiæ constringente, quasi quodam cingulo, voluptatem carnis. Calceamenti linea, prohibitio pedum ad malum festinando. Sandalia ornatus, iter prædicatoris, quia cælestia non debet abscondere, neque terrenis inhiare. Secunda tunica, opera mentis sunt: casula, opera corporis pia. Stola, jugum Christi, quod est evangelium. Dalmatica diaconi et sui ministri, quæ est itineri[201] habilis, cura proximorum est. Sudarium, piæ et mundæ cogitationes, quibus detergimus molestias animi ex infirmitate corporis. Pallium archiepiscoporum, torques devotissimæ prædicationis et in veteri testamento, et in novo.

---

[201] *Dalmatica . . . quæ est itineri habilis.* By a dalmatic "suitable for travel," he means a short dalmatic, not reaching lower than the knee. This shortened dalmatic, assigned to deacon and subdeacon (*sui ministri*) is suggestive, he says, of the activity which they should display in work of charitable relief (*cura proximorum*). This will be explained by what has been said in the Introduction, of the various forms of the tunic anciently in use.

## XXXIII.

## WALAFRIDUS STRABO.[904]

### Cap. 24. DE VASIS ET VESTIBUS SACRIS.

#### De Rebus Ecclesiasticis.

Vasa quoque, quibus præcipue nostra Sacramenta imponuntur et confecrantur, Calices funt et Patenæ. Calix dicitur à Græco nomine κάλιξ.[905] Patena à patendo, quod patula fit. Ampulla, quasi parum[906] ampla. Zepherinus[907] Ro. Pontifex XVI patenis vitreis Miſſas celebrare conſtituit. Tum deinde Urbanus[908] XVIII Papa, omnia ministeria facrata fecit argentea, et patenas 25. In hoc ficut et in reliquis cultibus, magis et magis per incrementa temporum decus fuccrevit Ecclefiæ. Bonifacius[909] martyr et Epifcopus interrogatus, Si liceret in vafis ligneis facramenta conficere, refpondit: *Quondam facerdotes aurei ligneis calicibus utebantur: nunc e contra, lignei facerdotes aureis utuntur calicibus.* Sylveſter[910] Papa conſtituit, Sacrificium altaris non in ferico, non in panno tincto celebrari, niſi tantum lineo e terra[911] procreato: ficut corpus Domini Jefu Chriſti in findone munda fepultum eſt. Veſtes etiam facerdotales per incrementa ad eum, qui nunc habetur, auctæ funt ornatum. Nam primis temporibus communi indumento veſtiti, Miſſas agebant, ficut et hactenus quidam Orienta-

---

[904] Walafrid was of German birth, and a pupil of Rabanus Maurus (fee note 155) at Fulda. At a later period he became Dean of St. Gall, and in 842 A.D. was made Abbot of Rofenau (*Augiæ Majoris*) in the diocefe of Conſtance. The text is that of Hittorpius.

[905] Mifprinted in Hittorpius κύαξ.

[906] His etymology is at fault here. The word is probably *amb-olla* or *ambi-olla*. The old Latin *ampulla* was a jar, or bottle, which from its full fwelling fhape came to be ufed metaphorically of anything that was over big or its place [*Projicit ampullas et fefquipedalia verba:* Hor.]. This later ufe is illuſtrated by the verb *ampullari*, to be pompous or bombaſtic, and the *It.* ampolloſità, "bombaſt." Compare the Fr. Ampoulé, bombaſtic. The *It.* Ampolletta, Fr. Ampoulette, an "hourglafs," have preferved the original fignification of the word.

[907] Zephyrinus *fed.* 202–218.

[908] Urbanus *fed.* 223–230.

[909] Our countryman Winifrid was born at *Cridiodunum* (Crediton) in Devon, A.D. 670.

## XXXIII.

## WALAFRID STRABO.[504]

### Cap. 24. OF HOLY VESSELS AND VESTMENTS.

#### De Rebus Ecclesiasticis.

THE veſſels on which for the moſt part our holy oblations (*ſacramenta*) are placed and conſecrated are Chalices and Patens. The Chalice is ſo called from the Greek word κάλυξ.[505] The Paten, from *patere*, in reference to its open flat ſurface. The *Ampulla*, or Flagon, as though from *parum ampla*,[506] in reſpect of its ſmall ſize. Zepherinus,[507] ſixteenth Biſhop of Rome, ordered the celebration of maſſes on patens, made of glaſs. Then again, Urbanus,[508] eighteenth Pope, made of ſilver all the veſſels to be uſed in holy miniſtry, and amongſt theſe twenty-five patens. In this, as in other matters of outward obſervance, the beauty of the church's ornaments increaſed with the increaſe of years. Boniface,[509] martyr and biſhop, was once aſked whether it were lawful to conſecrate the holy elements in veſſels of wood. To this he replied, "*Golden prieſts, and wooden chalices, ſuch was once the rule. Now it is the prieſts that are wooden, while the chalices that they uſe are of gold.*" Pope Sylveſter [510] ordained that the ſacrifice of the altar ſhould be celebrated not in ſilk nor in dreſſes of dyed cloth, but only in linen, which is produced from out the earth;[511] even as the body of our Lord

---

[504] When conſecrated *epiſcopus Germanorum* by Gregory II. in 723, he aſſumed the name of Bonifacius, by which he has ſince been known. A letter of his to Cuthbert, Archbiſhop of Canterbury (Spelman, Concil. p. 241), breathes a ſimilar ſpirit of ſevere condemnation againſt the increaſing luxury in dreſs and ornament of the churchmen of his time. "*Supervacuam et Deo odibilem veſtimentorum ſuperſtitionem omni intentione prohibere ſtude, quia illa ornamenta veſtium, ut illis videtur, quod ab aliis turpitudo dicitur, latiſſimis clavis et vermium imaginibus elevata, adventum Antichriſti, ab illo tranſ-miſſa, præcurrunt. Illius calliditate per miniſtros ſuos introducere intra clauſtra monaſteriorum fornicationem et luxuriem clavatorum juvenum, et fœda conſortia, et tædium lectionis et orationis, et perditionem animarum. Hæc indumenta nuditatem animæ ſignificantia, ſigna in ſe oſtendunt arrogantiæ et ſuperbiæ et luxuriæ et vanitatis; de quibus Sapientia dicit:* Arrogantiam, et ſuperbiam, et viam pravam, et bilinguia detestor."

[510] Sylveſter ſed. 314–335.

[511] He implies a contraſt with the *animæ* origin of woollen garments. See note 30.

lium facere perhibentur. Stephanus[212] autem XXIV conftituit, facerdotes et Levitas veftibus facratis in ufu quotidiano non uti, nifi in Ecclefia tantum.[213] Et Sylvefter ordinavit, ut Diaconi dalmaticis in Ecclefia uterentur, et pallio linoftimo eorum læva tegeretur.[214] Et primo quidem facerdotes Dalmaticis ante Cafularum ufum induebantur: poftea vero cum Cafulis uti cœpiffent, Dalmaticas Diaconibus conceffertunt. Ipfos tamen Pontifices eis uti debere, ex eo clarum eft, quod Gregorius vel alii Romanorum præfules, aliis Epifcopis earum ufum permiferunt, aliis interdixerunt. Ubi intelligitur non omnibus tunc fuiffe conceffum, quod nunc pene omnes Epifcopi, et nonnulli prefbyterorum, fibi licere exiftimant, id eft, ut fub Cafula Dalmatica veftiantur.

Statutum eft autem Concilio Bracarenfi,[215] *Ne facerdos fine orario celebret Miffam.* Addiderunt in veftibus facris alii alia: vel ad imitationem eorum quibus veteres utebantur facerdotes, vel ad myfticæ fignificationis expreffionem. Quid enim fingula defignent, quibus utimur nunc, à prioribus noftris fatis expofitum eft. Numero autem fuo antiquis refpondent: quia ficut ibi tunica fuperhumeralis, linea,[216] fuperhumerale, rationale, balteus, feminalia, tiara et lamina, fic hic dalmatica, alba, mappula, orarium, cingulum, fandalia, cafula et pallium. Unde ficut illorum extremo foli Pontifices, fic horum ultimo fummi tantum paftores utuntur.[217]

---

[212] Stephanus *fed.* 253-257.

[213] Dr. Hefele remarks with truth that fuch a prohibition implies that the veftments of Chriftian miniftry were then fuch as could have been worn for other than ecclefiaftical ufe.—*Liturgifche Gewänder*, p. 153.

[214] *Ut eorum læva pallio linoftimo tegeretur.* Compare note 157, p 88. The interpretation there given (as again here) to the fomewhat obfcure interpretation of the text is fuggefted by the many ancient monuments, in which the left hand of bifhops, priefts, or deacons is feen, covered either with the *orarium* or fome other piece of cloth, when holding facred veffels or facred books. We may not improbably conjecture that this direction to the Roman deacons had reference, in the firft inftance, to the care that was neceffary in the ufe of thofe filver veffels (replacing the earlier glafs veffels), introduced according to Roman tradition by Urbanus, rather earlier in the third century. Hence probably the origin of that *mappula* (the later maniple), the ufe of which was claimed (*fupra*, pp. 65, 66) in St. Gregory's time as an excluſively Roman privilege by the Roman clergy, and only after long debate allowed, under guarded reftrictions, to the principal deacons of the Church of Ravenna. [As to the *privilege* of wearing a Dalmatic noticed by Walafrid, fee above p. 67.]

[215] The fecond Council of Bracara held A.D. 572.

[216] In Hittorpius punctuated thus, "*Tunica, fuperhumeralis linea, fuperhumerale,*" &c. So written it is unintelligible.

[217] Note here that with Walafrid the "*Amice*" is not reckoned among the veftments at all, and he has to make up the number required by adding the *fandals*, which in point of fact conftitute a remarkable contraft to the *bare-footed* miniftrations of the law.

Note alfo that it is clear that no epifcopal mitre (in the modern fenfe of the word) could have been in ufe in Walafrid's time, as it is impoffible to conceive, were it otherwife, that he fhould have failed to notice the coincidence.

Jesus Christ was buried in clean linen. And only by successive additions did the priestly garb attain to that degree of ornament which is now observed. For in the earliest times mass was performed by men wearing the dress of ordinary life, as is said to be done even to this day by some in the Eastern Churches. But Stephanus,[212] twenty-fourth Pope, directed that priests and Levites should not employ their sacred dress for ordinary daily use, but reserve them exclusively for the Church.[213] By order of Silvester, deacons were to use dalmatics in the church, and their left hand was to be covered with a *pallium* (cloth) of linen weft.[214] And in the first instance, before chasubles came into use, those of the priestly order wore dalmatics. But afterwards, when they began to wear chasubles, they left the use of the dalmatic to deacons. Yet that even pontiffs themselves ought to wear it, is clear from this, that Gregory and other Roman primates (*præsules*) allowed the use of the Dalmatic to some bishops, forbade it in the case of others. And by this it is evident that in those days that was not matter of general privilege (the wearing I mean of a Dalmatic under the Chasuble) which now almost all bishops and priests think is permitted them. Then at the Council of Bracara[215] it was prescribed that no priest should celebrate mass without an Orarium (or " stole "). Successive additions were made in this matter of vestments from time to time, partly by way of imitating what was worn by the priests of the old Covenant, partly for the expression of a mystical meaning. What is signified by each of the vestments worn in our own day, those who have preceded me have sufficiently shown. But in respect of their number they correspond with the vestments of the old law. For whereas then there were the tunic of the ephod, the tunic of linen,[216] superhumeral (or ephod), breastplate, girdle, drawers, tiara, and frontlet, so have we now dalmatic, alb, maniple, stole, girdle, sandals, chasuble, and pallium. And as the last named of those older vestments was worn only by high-priests, so is the last of these Christian vestments worn only by chief pastors.[217]

## XXXIV.

## ALBINUS FLACCUS ALCUINUS.[118]

### THE PRIESTLY VESTMENTS OF THE LAW AND OF THE GOSPEL.

#### LIBER DE DIVINIS OFFICIIS.

NUNC dicendum de fingulis veftibus, quibus facerdotes vel reliqui ordines in veteri teftamento utebantur. Erant autem octo fpecies veftium facerdotalium, id eft, tunica linea ftricta, tunica hyacinthina, fuperhumerale, rationale, cidaris, balteum, lamina aurea in fronte pontificis, et feminalia linea. His omnibus pontifex tempore facrificii induebatur: cæteris vero, minoris gradus facerdotibus, folis quatuor licebat uti, id eft, tunica linea ftricta, cidari, balteo, et feminalibus. Reliqua vero quatuor tantum fummi pontificis erant.

Nunc de fingulis explanemus. Tunica linea, veftis erat interior, quam camifiam dicimus vel fupparum. Hæc ftricta dicitur, quoniam adhærebat corpori, et ita erat ftrictis manicis,[119] ut nulla ei omnino ruga ineffet. Sicut folent milites habere tunicas lineas fic aptas membris, ut expediti fint dirigendo jaculo, tendendo clypeum, librando gladium, qualem et Joab habuiffe legitur ftrictam ad menfuram habitus corporis fui : pro qua nunc facerdotes vel clerici albas habent. Tunica tota hyacinthina exterior, nullumque alium colorem recipiens, ufque ad pedes defcendens, ficut et linea, unde et utraque græce podéris, id eft, talaris vocabatur, habens fimilitudinem malorum granatorum aure-

---

[118] This treatife was by the earlier editors affigned, without fufpicion, to Alcuin, our countryman, pupil of Bede, who died A.D. 804. But there is a general agreement now in affigning it to a much later date. Thus Cave (Hift. Lit. tom. i. p. 638) : *Alcuini non effe* (De Divinis Officiis Liber) *et poft annum* 1000 *fcriptum effe, certo certius conftat.* And Dr. Hefele, in referring to the work, writes to the fame effect : " *in dem Werke . . . . das früher Alkuin zugefchrieben, aber neuern Unterfuchungen gemäfs erft in 10ten oder 11ten Jahrhundert verfafst wurde.*"— Liturg. Gewänd. p. 156. [The text is that of Hittorpius, p. 74 *fqq.*]

[119] *Stricta . . . strictis manicis, &c.* See note 6, p. 2.

orum, et tintinnabula aurea. Erat autem fine manicis ad colobiorum [220] similitudinem, et ideo unde manus educerentur, aperta erat. Pro tunica hyacinthina nostri pontifices primo colobiis utebantur. Est autem colobium vestis sine manicis.

Hæ duæ vestes, id est, tunica byssina stricta, et tunica hyacinthina, balteo adstrictæ erant, quod erat cinguli genus ex bysso retorta, hyacintho, purpura ac vermiculo,[221] opere plumari,[222] in similitudinem pellis colubri, latitudinis quatuor digitorum. Pro balteo nunc zonarum, quas Romanas appellant, usus receptus est. Superhumerale,[223] quod Hebraice ephod dicitur, sic vocatum, quod humeros obnuberet: cujus contextus de omnibus coloribus erat, magnitudinis cubitalis, id est, usque ad cingulum pertingens, amplectens omnem locum pectoris, et ad manus ejiciendas hincinde apertum. Cui vestimento locus vacuus dimittebatur in medio pectore, magnitudine palmi, ubi inferebatur rationale, quod Hebraice dicitur essin, et Græce logion. Habebat autem superhumerale in utroque humero singulos lapides onychinos, et in singulis lapidibus erant sculpta singula duodecim patriarcharum nomina. Habent etiam nunc ministri ecclesiæ Christi superhumerale, quod amictum [224] vocamus, quando ad altare ministrant. Rationale [225] opere polymito factum erat, juxta texturam superhumeralis, id est, eisdem coloribus factum erat, quadrangulum, habens mensuram palmi in longitudinem et latitudinem. Erant in eo quatuor ordines lapidum, terni per singulos versus distributi: sculpti erant singulis duodecim patriarcharum nominibus. Erant autem catenulæ aureæ, et uncini aurei: necnon et aurei annuli, tam in quatuor summitatibus rationalis, quam et in summitatibus superhumeralis, quæ catenulæ inferebantur, jungebantque rationale et superhumerale superius, inferius vero vittis hyacinthinis sibi nectebantur. Pro rationali nunc summi pontifices,[226] quos archiepiscopos dicimus, pallio [227] utuntur, quod à sancta Romana sede,

---

[220] *Colobium*, i.e. a tunic without sleeves.
[221] *Vermiculus* [whence the Fr. Vermeil, Eng. Vermilion] the equivalent of *coccus*, or scarlet.
[222] *Opere plumari*, i.e. embroidery.
[223] *Superhumerale* . . . . *ephod*. See above pp. 4, 14.
[224] *Amictum*. See above, note 178, p. 96.
[225] *Rationale*. See p. 22, note 36.
[226] *Summi pontifices*. Note 45, p. 26. Alcuin himself gives a good and pious (but unhistorical) derivation of the word in this same treatise (p. 73), *Pontifex*, he says, *quasi pontem faciens; eo quod pontem, id est, viam aliis præbere debeat, verbo et exemplo, unde homines transeant ad vitam cœlestem*. He probably was not at all aware of the classical usage of the word.

[227] *Pro rationali . . . pallio utuntur*. For the *pallium* here spoken of see note 196, p. 102. Anything less like the "rational" or breast-jewel of the Jewish high-priest, with its twelve precious stones, than the pallium of an archbishop, it would be difficult to conceive. But such comparisons were not too violent for writers of the tenth or eleventh century. And these, I regret to add, have not been without their followers in the nineteenth.

Apostolico [228] dante, suscipiunt. Tiara [229] erat vestis, pileolum videlicet rotundum, quasi sphæra media sic divisa, ut et pars una ponatur in capite, ita ut medii verticis medietatem non excedat, habens vittas, quæ convolutæ sæpius connectuntur, ne facile dilabantur. Et hoc quidem minorum erat sacerdotum: Summus autem Pontifex præter pileum habebat coronam auream, triplicemque, super quam à media fronte surgebat quasi calamus quidam aureus, similis herbæ, quæ hebraice acano, græce autem hios, [229] quæ apud nos latine cidaris. Per circulum vero habebat flores, similes flori plantaginis, ab occipitio usque ad utrunque tempus. In fronte vero erat locus patens, ubi inserebatur lamina aurea, quæ quatuor literis nomen Dei habebat scriptum.

Hujuscemodi vestis non habetur in Romana ecclesia, vel in nostris regionibus. Non enim moris est, ut pileati divina mysteria celebrent. Apud græcos autem hoc dicitur, qui pileos, id est, cuphias [230] gestant in capite dum affistunt altaribus. Lamina aurea in fronte pontificis, in qua sanctum Domino sive sanctum Domini sculptum habebatur, ornamentum erat cæteris sacratius indumentis. Sanctum autem Domino, quod ibi sculptum erat nomen sanctum et venerabile Dei, quod per quatuor literas scribebatur, יהוה scilicet, iod, he, vau, heth; et dicebatur ineffabile, non quod dici non possit, sed quia nec definiri et compræhendi sensu ullius creaturæ, ut digne Deo aliquid dici possit. Ligabatur autem vitta hyacinthina super tiaram, ut totam pontificalis ornatus pulchritudinem Dei vocabulum coronaret ac protegeret. Neque hanc ornamenti speciem Christi accepit ab illis ecclesia. Octavum, id est, novissimum ornamentum seminalia linea, quibus operiebant carnem turpitudinis suæ, ab renibus usque ad femina sive (ut usitatius) femora, cum ad sacrificium accedebant. Hujusmodi habitus ita notus est in nostris regionibus, ut ex eo Gallia bracata cognominata sit.

Compræhensum breviter, quibus vestibus ornarentur sacerdotes et ministri templi Dei, Mosaicæ legis temporibus, quas ad instar illorum, revelata evangelii gratia, suscepit Ecclesia. Sunt tamen alia quæ apud illos non habebantur, ut stola, [231] sandalia, et sudarium, [232] quod ad tergen-

---

[228] *Apostolico*, i.e. the "pope," Bishop of the Apostolic See. For the word *tiara*, which follows, see note 84, p. 52.

[229] *Hios*. He refers to the word δσπυεμος, or *Hpospomos*. The Latin *cidaris* has nothing whatever to do with this plant, but, like the Greek κιδαρις, which it represents, is the proper designation of a *royal* (or of a high-priest's) tiara.

[230] *Cuphias*. The Greek κουφια or ϵκουφια, a skull-cap, a word noticed by Eustathius, on Iliad x, and of not unfrequent occurrence in Byzantine Greek. But it is nowhere used by any classical writer, as far as I am aware.

[231] *Stola*. Here used absolutely for the older word *orarium*. It is of the "stole" as we understand the word, that he is speaking. Compare note 187, p. 98.

[232] *Sudarium*. See above, p. 103, and note 197.

dum sudorem in manu gestari mos est, quod usitato nomine sanonem vocamus.[233]

Verum quia illo tempore figuris omnia et aenigmatibus obumbrabantur, convenit, ut quid illa vestimenta mystice significaverint, quove nomine nunc specialiter in ecclesia venerantur, non verbatim, sed capitulatim ostendamus. Vestimenta illa, quae in sanctis officiis portanda erant, typus erant sanctarum virtutum, unde et sancta dicebantur. Ad haec facienda non tam diversa, quam speciosae species sumebantur, aurum videlicet, quod est splendor sapientiae divinae, cui jungebatur hyacinthus,[234] qui est color aerius, caeleste, videlicet desiderium. Purpura apponebatur, quae sanguinis imitatur colorem, ut per duo genera martyrii noverint se exercendos electi, id est, si necesse sit, non dubitent mori pro Christo, et pacis tempore in seipsis appetitus occidant, mortificantes membra sua cum vitiis et concupiscentiis. Coccus[235] bis tinctus, Dei et proximi dilectionem indicat efficaciter tenendam. Byssus geminam castitatem, corporis scilicet et animae, significat: unde de vere vidua dicit Apostolus, *Ut sit sancta corpore et spiritu.* His ornamentis debet Christi pontifex refulgere, his coloribus exornari. Tunica linea, et byssina stricta, mortificationem[236] carnis pretendit. Byssum enim vel linum, multiplici elaboratum contusione, et naturae subtilitate deductum ac textum, in vestem proficit. Sic nullus Christo ornari poterit, nisi castigatis et mortificatis omnibus carnis passionibus: unde et bene stricta dicitur. Strictum enim, castum dicimus: e contra lascivum, dissolutum vocamus. Tunica tota hyacinthina, quae aerio refulgebat[237] colore, caelestem designat conversationem: quae tota erat hyacinthina, quia sacerdos nihil debet curare terrenum: nemo enim, ait Apostolus, militans Deo, implicat se negociis secularibus, ut ei placeat, cui se probavit. Balteus sive cingulum, quo tunica haec cum interiore, id est, linea, cingebatur, continentiam insinuat, quae mater est et custos pudicitiae, qua maxime ornari pontifices condecet: hanc, qui ingratus est Deo, perdit, sicut Job de talibus dicit: *Balteum regum dissolvit, et*

---

[233] *Fanon.* This word is supposed to be connected with the German *fahne*, meaning a piece of cloth (of wool or of linen), and hence, according to the various uses to which such a piece of cloth may be applied, a banner or ensign; a clerical vestment; a "corporal."

[234] *Hyacinthus* . . . *color aerius.* See note 32, p. 10.

[235] *Coccus* . . . *dilectionem indicat.* See note 188.

[236] Compare note 106, p. 60.

[237] *Refulgebat . . . erat . . . cingebatur . . . induebatur, &c.* From the use of these tenses of past time it is clear that throughout this portion of the treatise the author is speaking of the spiritual significance of the Levitical vestments, not of those worn in Christian ministry. It is not till somewhat later (see below p. 115) that he goes on to speak of these last.

*præcingit fune renes eorum.* Regum enim, id eft, fanctorum facerdotum, balteum, hoc eft, pudicam continentiam diffolvit, id eft, diffolvi permittit, cum de fuis virtutibus extolli cœperint: et præcingit fune afperæ pœnitentiæ renes eorum, ut incipiant fuis cafibus ingemifcere, qui aliorum lapfibus debuerant auxilio fubvenire.

Superhumerale, quod Hebraice ephod dicitur, obedientiam mandatorum Dei fignificat, quo induebatur facerdos, ut meminerit præcepta Dei ftrenue quafi onus humeris impofitum debere portare. Quod vero nomina patriarcharum inter facrificia et in humeris, ficut et in pectore, portabat, monetur per hoc facerdos, ut priorum patrum fidem et exempla fequatur,[520] ut fidelium, qui funt filii apoftolorum, in fuis orationibus meminerit, et ut ipfis eadem exempla fequenda proponat.

Rationale, quod erat in fronte [529] pontificis, defignat, quia paftor fapientia et doctrina debet præditus effe. Nam et ideo rationale judicii dicitur, quia debet rector ecclefiæ fubtili femper examinatione bona malaque difcernere, et quid vel quibus, quando et qualiter conveniat, ftudiofe cogitare. Hoc enim quod dicitur, *Pones in rationale judicii doctrinam et veritatem,* ut videlicet habeat fcientiam fcripturarum, quo poffit alios docere, et contradicentes arguere. Quadrangulum erat, propter quatuor Evangeliorum doctrinam: duplex, propter fcientiæ et operis firmitatem. Menfura palmi, quod eft digitorum extenfio, defignat difcretionem in perfeverantia bonorum operum.

Quatuor ordines lapidum, qui erant in rationali, nominibus patriarcharum infculpti, quatuor exprimunt principales virtutes, prudentiam, temperantiam, fortitudinem, juftitiam. Terni in unoquoque lapides, fidem fanctæ Trinitatis, five fidem, fpem, et charitatem, demonftrant. Quæ omnia in pectore pontificis neceffario effe debere, hujus ornamenti, id eft, rationalis fpecie præmonetur. Tiara, quæ et cidaris et mitra vocatur, et contegebat et ornabat caput pontificis, admonet eum omnes fenfus capitis Deo confecrare debere, ne vel oculi pateant ad videndum vanitatem, vel cæteri fenfus, qui in capite vigent, iniquitati confentiant, et per illos intromiffa delectatio inceftet animi fanctitatem. Lamina aurea, divinæ majeftatis atque potentiæ figura eft, quæ in fronte pontificis deportabatur, quia illa ineffabilis Deitatis potentia cunctis, quæ creavit, fupereminet: et idcirco, quafi cuncta

---

[520] *Ut priorum patrum fidem et exemplum fequatur* ... So St. Gregory, quoted at p. 58.

[529] *Rationale ... in fronte.* By "frons" is here meant not the "brow" or "forehead," but the "front." Compare the expreffion ufed by St. Gregory (*fup.* p. 56) *in prima fui corporis parte.*

sanctificans, eximiam sibi sedem in fronte, hoc est, in mentis principalitate constituit.

Quatuor literæ in lamina scriptæ, quatuor sunt cornua crucis, totum mundum complectentis. Cruci enim Christi in omni creatura apex [840] conceditur, qua omnium fidelium frontes signantur.

Quod lamina semper in fronte pontificis esse videbatur, ostendit, quia dignitatem, quam prætendit in habitu, exercere semper debet in opere, ut Domini placitum semper habere, et subditorum vota Domino idoneus sit semper offerre. Feminalia, quibus pudenda loca corporis tegebantur, continentiam a concubitu designant, quæ magnopere omnibus gradibus observanda præcipitur. Unde dicitur, *ad velandam turpitudinem*. Turpe est enim, sacerdotem nota lascivæ ætatis infamari, quem convenit velut in arce castimoniæ, ab omnibus suspici et venerari.

Quod vero feminalia ipsi sibi imponant, cætera Moises: designat, unumquemque se à carnali concupiscentia refrenare debere. Deinde virtutibus sibi subditos, quasi Moisem ministrum templi vestibus, exornare.

## OF THE VESTMENTS OF CHRISTIAN PRIESTHOOD.

### 1. THE SANDALS.

Sandaliæ dicuntur soleæ. Est autem genus calceamenti, quo induuntur ministri Ecclesiæ, subterius quidem solea muniens pedes à terra, superius vero, nil operimenti habens, patet: quo jussi sunt Apostoli à Domino indui. Significat autem, ministrum verbi Dei non debere terrenis incumbere, sed potius cælestibus inhiare, et prædicationem suam nulli occultare.

### 2. THE SUPERHUMERAL.

Post sandalias in Ecclesiæ vestimentis sequitur Superhumerale, [841] quod sit ex lino purissimo. Per linum quod ex terra sumitur, et per multos labores ad candorem ducitur, designatur corpus humanum, quod ex terra constat. Sicut ergo linum per multos labores ad can-

---

[840] *Apex.* The highest point of anything, and so "the place of highest honour."

[841] *Superhumerale.* He means the "amice" (*amictus*) as he had said above, p. 111, *superhumerale quod amictum vocamus*.

dorem perducitur, ita corpus humanum multis calamitatibus attritum, candidum et purum esse debet ab omni sorde peccatorum.

### 3. THE ALB.

Postea sequitur podéris, quæ vulgo Alba dicitur. Significat autem perseverantiam in bona actione. Hinc Joseph inter fratres suos, talarem tunicam habuisse describitur. Tunica usque ad talum, est opus bonum usque ad consummationem. In talo enim finis est corporis. Ille ergo bene inchoat, qui rectitudinem boni operis usque ad finem debitæ perducit actionis. Qui enim perseverarit usque in finem, hic salvus erit.

### 4. THE GIRDLE.

Deinde sequitur Zona, quæ cingulum dicitur, qua restringitur podéris, ne laxe per pedes diffluat. Per quam designatur discretio omnium virtutum: virtutes enim sine discretione, non virtutes, sed vitia sunt: nam virtutes in quodam meditullio sunt constitutæ.

### 5. THE STOLE.

Sequitur orarium. Orarium, id est, stola, dicitur eo quod oratoribus, id est, prædicatoribus concedatur. Admonet illum, qui illo induitur, ut memor sit, sub jugo Christi, quod leve et suave est, esse se constitutum.

### 6. THE DALMATIC.

Dalmatica quæ sequitur, ob hoc dicitur, eo quod in Dalmatia sit reperta. Usus autem Dalmaticarum à B. Silvestro Papa institutus est: nam antea colobiis utebantur. Colobium vero est vestis sine manicis. Significat autem in eo quod est sine manicis, unumquemque fidelem exercitatum esse debere ad bona opera exercenda. Cum ergo nuditas brachiorum culparetur, ut diximus, à B. Silvestro Dalmaticarum repertus est usus. Est autem vestimentum in modum crucis, monens, indutorem suum crucifixum esse debere mundo, juxta Apostolum, *Mihi mundus crucifixus est, et ego mundo*. Habet etiam in sinistra parte sui fimbrias. Per sinistram partem præsens vita figuratur, quæ diversis curis abundat: quæ curæ significantur per fimbrias sinistræ partis. Per dexteram quæ fimbriis caret, futura vita exprimitur, in qua nullæ curæ solicitant animas sanctorum. Inconsutilis etiam est, quia in Ecclesia vel in corde uniuscujusque fidelis, nulla debet esse scissura, sed indiscissa fidei integritas. Sinistrum latus habet fimbrias, quia actualis vita solicita est, et turbatur erga plurima. At dexterum latus non habet, quia contemplativa vita nihil in se habet sinistrum. Largitas [242] brachiorum, largitatem et hilaritatem datoris significat. Diaconus qui non est indutus Dalmatica, Casula circumcinctus legit, ut expedite possit ministrare, vel quia ipsius est ire ad comitatum propter instantes necessitates.

### 7. The Maniple.

Mappula quæ sinistra parte gestatur, qua pituitam oculorum et narium detergimus, præsentem vitam designat, in qua superfluos humores patimur.

### 8. The Chasuble.

Casula quæ super omnia indumenta ponitur, significat charitatem, quæ alias virtutes excellit. De qua Apostolus, commemoratis quibusdam virtutibus, ait: *Major autem horum est charitas.*

### 9. The Pallium.

Pallium Archiepiscoporum super omnia indumenta est, ut lamina in fronte pontificis. Pallium nihil est aliud, nisi discretio inter Archiepiscopum et ejus suffraganeos. Pallium significat torquem, quem solebant legitime certantes accipere. Hoc etiam erat lamina illa, ut dixi, quam summus pontifex circa tempora ferebat, in qua scriptum erat nomen Dei Tetragrammaton, id est, quatuor literarum, יהוה, Jod, He, Vau, et Heth. Est autem interpretatio, Jod, principium, He iste, Vau vita, et Heth passio, id est, iste est principium passionis vitæ. Passi igitur sunt multi ante Christum, sed nemo eorum per suam passionem hominibus vitam attulit: Christus vero, cujus sanguis in cruce fusus

---

[242] All that follows from here to the end of the chapter is a kind of cento from earlier writers, quoted in this volume, especially (see notes 243, 244) from Amalarius.

est pro totius mundi redemptione, humano generi attulit vitam. Secundum alium doctorem, Jod principium, He iste, Vau et Heth vita interpretatur. Quod ita potest conjungi, Iste est principium et vita Christus. Vocabatur autem hoc nomen sanctum Domini, quod interpretatur ineffabile, non quod non fari, sed quod diffiniri, ut est, minime possit.

Stephanus natione Romanus ex patre Jobio, ut legitur in gestis Pontificalibus, constituit sacerdotibus Levitisque vestes sacras in usu quotidiano non uti nisi in Ecclesia. Hinc Hieronymus in libro 14. super Ezechielem, *Porro religio alterum habitum habet in ministerio, alterum in usu vitaque communi.* Sudario solemus tergere pituitam oculorum et narium, atque superfluam salivam decurrentem per labia: significat studium mundanæ [Leg. mundandæ] cogitationis. In manu sinistra portatur, ut ostendatur in temporali vita tædium nos pati superflui humoris. Varietas [843] Sandaliorum, varietatem significat ministeriorum. Episcopi et sacerdotis pene unum officium est. At quia nomine et honore, discernuntur etiam et varietate sandaliorum, ut visibus nostris error auferatur. Episcopus habet ligaturam in suis sandaliis, quam non habet Presbyter. Episcopi est huc illucque discurrere per parochiam: ne forte cadant sandalia de pedibus, ligata sunt. Presbyter qui domi hostias immolat, sublimius [844] incedit. Diaconus quia dissimilis est episcopo in suo officio, non est necesse ut habeat dissimilia sandalia: et ipse ligaturam habet, quia suum est ire ad comitatum. Subdiaconus qui in adjutorio Diaconi est, et pene in eodem officio, necesse est ut habeat dissimilia sandalia, ne forte Diaconus æstimetur. Sandalia significant, quia prædicator neque cælestia debet abscondere, neque terrenis inhiare.

---

[843] What is here said of the sandals is identical, almost to a word, with a passage of Amalarius already quoted (p. 104). See note in loc.

[844] *Sublimius.* This is scarcely intelligible. In the parallel passage of Amalarius (p. 104) we find *securius*, "more carelessly," "with less of precaution" (i.e. without this *ligatura*). And this probably is the true reading here. A similar comparison supplies the correction, *mundandæ* for *mundanæ*, given above. Probably also in line 16 above, *discernuntur* should be read twice, as in the parallel passage.

## XXXV.

## B. IVO CARNOTENSIS.[245]

## DE ECCLESIASTICIS SACRAMENTIS ET OFFICIIS SERMONES.

### Sermo in Synodo de Significationibus Indumentorum Sacerdotalium.

Quia sanctitas ministerii sanctitatem expetit ministrorum, quales ad sacerdotium promoveri debeant personæ, in superiori sermone breviter ex Apostolica institutione commemoravimus, sed in quo habitu ordinari vel ad altare accedere debeant, illi sermoni non inseruimus. De indumentis ergo sacerdotalibus, vel de pontificalibus, diligenter considerandum est, quid in moribus sacerdotum significet illa varietas vestium, quid fulgor auri, quid nitor gemmarum:[246] cum nihil ibi debeat esse ratione carens, sed forma sanctitatis et omnium imago virtutum. Sicut enim bona domus in ipso vestibulo agnoscitur, sic Christi sacerdos cultu sacrarum vestium ostendit exterius, qualis apud se esse debeat interius. Iste autem sacrarum vestium ritus, per Moisem sumpsit exordium: quamvis Christiana religio, plus intenta rebus quam figuris, sacerdotes suos non omnibus illis veteribus induit ornamentis.

### § 2. The Levitical Vestments and Insignia.

Inspiciamus ergo prius veterum ornamenta pontificum, vel quo ordine illis utebantur, vel cum ordinarentur, vel cum thymiama oblaturi sancta sanctorum ingrederentur. Deinde nostra cum illorum indumentis conferentes, quid simile, quid dissimile inter se habeant, et quomodo etiam in rebus significatis conveniant, attendamus. Duo

---

[245] St. Ivo (or Yvo) was born at Beauvais, and was a pupil of Lanfranc, then Prior of Bec. We first hear of him as Abbot of S. Quintin, in his native town, and afterwards as Bishop of Chartres (*Carnota*). He died A.D. 1115. See Cave, H. L. vol. ii. p. 160. The text is that of Hittorpius. But the division of the text into sections is that of the present editor.

[246] Note that at this period (close of eleventh century) gold and jewels are spoken of as decorations of Christian vestments, for it is of these last, evidently, not of Jewish vestments, that St. Ivo here speaks.

enim Cherubin propitiatorium adspiciunt, quia sacramenta utriusque testamenti ad divinæ propitiationis fidem intendunt; quæ in sacerdotio veteri sub multiplici est sacrificiorum velamine adumbrata, in novo autem testamento per unum verum perfectumque est sacrificium completa. In ornamentis itaque utrorumque sacerdotum et sublimitas sacerdotii commendatur, et sacerdotum casta dignitas significatur, quatenus[947] per exteriorem habitum discant, quales intra se debeant esse, qui vices illius veri summique Pontificis gerunt, in quo fuit omnis plenitudo virtutum, quam profitentur exteriora ornamenta membrorum.

Sed jam ad id, quod proposuimus, veniamus: et primum, qualiter Moises Aaron et filios ejus, Domino jubente, ornaverit, et postea induerit, videamus. Sic enim legitur in Levitico (Lev. viii.): *Et fecit Moises, sicut præcepit ei Dominus: et convocavit synagogam ad januam tabernaculi testimonii, et applicuit Moises Aaron fratrem suum et filios ejus, et lavit eos aqua, et vestivit eum tunica, et præcinxit eum zona, et vestivit eum tunica interiore, et imposuit ei superhumerale, et cinxit eum secundum facturam humeralis, et imposuit super eum logion, et super logion manifestationem et veritatem, et imposuit super caput ejus mitram, et posuit super mitram ante faciem ejus laminam auream, in qua scriptum erat nomen Domini.*

Notandus est ordo verborum. Licet enim de constituendo pontifice præcepisset Dominus, et elegisset, tamen vocatur Synagoga. Idcirco enim requiritur præsentia populi in eligendo sacerdote, ut sciant omnes, quia qui doctior est ex omni populo, qui omni virtute præstantior, hic eligi debet ad sacerdotium, et hoc cum consensu Ecclesiæ, ne qua postea retractatio, ne quis scrupulus remaneat, sed omnium testimonio commendetur, secundum Apostolum (1 Tit. iii.): *Oportet episcopum bonum habere testimonium ab his qui foris sunt.* Ita plebis testimonio approbatos primo lavat, postea induit. Moises quippe in hoc facto typum legis gerit, qui ordinandos sacerdotes prius lavat, antequam induat. Nisi enim quis prius fuerit per legis observationem probatus, non est ad sacerdotium promovendus.

### § 3. First, the Long Tunic of Linen.

Ita vero probatus, induitur tunica, quæ apud eos byssina est, apud nos linea. Byssus enim est genus lini candidissimi, et ad summum

---

[947] *Quatenus* in mediæval writers is nearly equivalent to our own "to the end that."

candorem multa vexatione [248] et ablutione perductum. Significat autem perfectam carnis munditiam, secundum illud quod in Apocalypsi legitur (Apoc. xix.): *Byssus sunt justificationes sanctorum.* Hanc munditiam caro sacerdotis ex se non habet, sicut nec linum ex se est candidum, sed sicut dictum est, multis castigationibus et ablutionibus redditur candidum, ut aptum fiat indumentis pontificum. Forma est sacerdotalis munditiæ, ut secundum Apostolum (1 Cor. ix.), sacerdotes carnem suam castigent, et in servitutem redigant: et præeunte gratia, habeant per industriam, quod non potuerunt habere per naturam. Hæc vestis Græce ποδήρης, id est, talaris, appellatur, quia a collo usque ad talos extenditur: et ita est arcta,[249] et membris corporis contemperata, ut sua forma testificetur, sacerdotem nihil habere dissolutum, nihil remissum, sed ad omne opus bonum esse expeditum.

### § 4. Second and Third, the Girdle and the Linen Drawers.

Hæc eadem vestis circa renes zona fortius adstringitur, ut castitas sacerdotis nullo incentivorum æstu dissolvatur. Quod bene significatur in quatuor coloribus, quibus zona illa variata erat, bysso, purpura, hyacintho, et cocco: quibus coloribus quatuor elementa significantur:[250] quorum complexione natura constat humana, quorum distemperantia fluxus carnis generat, nisi medicinali cohibeatur continentia. Talium enim conjectores[251] naturarum, per byssum, quia de terra oritur, terram; per purpuram, quia sanguine cochlearum marinarum tingitur, aquam; per hyacinthum, quia colorem sereni aeris imitatur, aërem; per coccum, qui colore flammeo rutilat, significari ignem voluerunt. Quorum, ut dictum est, exuberantia in renibus maxime superfluos humores, pravi humores illicitos motus, generant; qui nisi freno parsimoniæ reprimantur, castitatis dignitas in eis facili impulsu periclitatur. Ubi autem major est pugna, major est adhibenda custodia. Inde est, quod inter indumenta pontificalia [252] adhuc circa renes applicantur linea feminalia,

---

[248] *Multa vexatione, &c.* Compare note 106, p. 60.

[249] *Ita est arcta, &c.* It is of the Levitical vestment that he is here speaking, and here (as throughout) he follows closely in the steps of S. Jerome. See the passage quoted in p. 12, *sup.* and compare note 6, p. 2.

[250] *Quatuor elementa.* This symbolism is spoken of by St. Jerome as having been learnt by himself *ab Hebræis. Vid. sup.* p. 19, *in fin.*

[251] *Conjectores,* i.e. Interpreters.

[252] *Pontificalia.* This must refer to the Levitical pontifex (note 45, p. 26), or high-priest, for he says a few lines below, "*feminalibus non utuntur novi sacerdotii pontifices:*" and this being so, *adhuc* must be understood as meaning "furthermore."

non tam ad velandam carnis turpitudinem, quæ jam folitis opertâ eft veftimentis, quam propter fignum caftitatis confervandæ. Unde et Apoftolus dicit (1 Cor. xii.): *Honefta noftra nullius egent: Quæ autem inhonefta funt, his abundantiorem honorem circundamus.* Feminalibus non utuntur novi facerdotii pontifices, quibus eft injuncta fervandæ caftitatis quotidiana neceffitas, ficut eft quotidie offerendi conceffa poteftas: cum pontifices umbræ fervientes, expleta vice fua, feminalia fua folverent, tempore vicis fuæ tamen ea induerent. Reliqua duo, poderis et zona, veteribus et novis facerdotibus fiunt indumenta communia: quamvis zona noftrorum facerdotum non fit quatuor intexta coloribus, aut propter penuriam materiarum, aut propter abfentiam artificum: undecunque tamen fit, et hæc et illa unum gerunt temperantiæ typum.

### § 5. Fourth, the Tunic of Blue.

Sequitur quartum indumentum, tunica interior vel hyacinthina, qua et in veteri et in novo teftamento foli utuntur pontifices. Duabus enim tunicis merito induitur pontifex, quia debet de thefauro fuo proferre nova et vetera, *i.e.* legem intelligere fecundum literam, quemadmodum ante adventum Chrifti obfervabatur, et fecundum fpiritum, quemadmodum poft adventum Chrifti intelligitur. Unde et fecunda tunica, interior appellatur, vel hyacinthina, cujus color cæli ferenitatem imitatur: ut per hoc intelligatur, quia pontifex plus debet de cæleftibus cogitare, quam de terrenis. Rectus quippe ordo eft, ut primum ftudeamus munditiæ carnis, per quam veniamus ad munditiam cordis, quæ nos provehat ad intellectum divinitatis, juxta illud (Matt. v.): *Beati mundo corde, quoniam ipfi Deum videbunt.*

### § 6. Fifth, the Superhumeral, or Ephod.[263]

Quinta veftis eft fuperhumerale quæ Hebraice vocatur ephot. Hæc veftis, facerdotalis fimul et pontificalis apud nos eft: apud Hebræos

---

[263] By the "fuperhumeral" common to priefts and bifhops he means the "amice." Compare Hugo de S. Victor (quoted later in this volume), *amictus fuper humerus, quod nos fuperhumerale dicere poffumus.* The amice (a fquare piece of linen, fee note 178, p. 96) has this in common with the Levitical ephod (*fuperhumerale* of the Vulgate, ἐπωμίς *apud* LXX) that a portion of it lay upon the fhoulders. But in all other refpects the amice and the ephod are as utterly unlike as two garments well could be; the latter being a clofe-fitting coat, fhaped as may be feen in the picture of the Jewifh high-prieft among the illuftrations of this volume. [Even Dr. Bock admits the entire abfence of any refemblance between the two. Vol. ii. p. 20.]

vero, tantum pontificalis, et apud eos eifdem eft variata coloribus, quibus et zona pontificalis, de qua dicitur in ordinatione pontificis: *Et circuncinxit eum (de Moife loquens) fecundum facturam humeralis.* Humeri quippe fortes funt ad agenda opera, et portanda onera, quæ ex circunductione humeralis, fuis ligaturis conftringuntur, quia pontificem et innocentia et operibus juftitiæ oportet effe conftrictum, ut in eo nihil inveniatur diffolutum, nihil remiffum. Quod vero fignificant varii colores in zona, idem fignificant in fuperhumerali: quia quicquid de terrenis operamur, five in largitione, five in reftrictione temporalium, totum fumimus ex contemperantia quatuor elementorum. Unde eft quod quaternarius decies ductus, furgat in quadragenarium, quia elementorum quatuor abundantia legitime difpenfata, quod fignificat denarius, ad verum perducit jubileum, qui exhibitione acquiritur bonorum operum. Quadragenarius enim numerus partibus fuis denominatis quinquagenarium facit. Quo numero in lege fupradictus jubileus (Lev. xxv.), *i.e.* remiffionis annus exprimitur, veram præfigurans libertatem, quam qui adeptus fuerit, nullam timebit ulterius fervitutem. Huic bonorum operum fignificationi concinit, quod in humerali duobus preciofis lapidibus infculpta erant nomina duodecim patriarcharum, fex in uno, et fex in altero: quorum alter fuperpofitus erat dextro humero, alter finiftro. Nihil horum vacat a myfterio. Senarius enim, propter fui perfectionem, opera juftitiæ fignificat: Nomina patriarcharum memoriam fanctorum, quam femper in exemplum bonorum operum habere debemus a dextris et a finiftris, id eft, in profperis et in adverfis, fignificant. Et ideo illa nomina in lapidibus fcribuntur: quia quod in lapide fculpitur, vix aut nunquam inde aboletur. Nec illud vacat a myfterio, quod pontifex cingitur fecundum facturam fuperhumeralis, quia fecundum opera fua unicuique retribuetur. Quod autem noftrorum pontificum fuperhumerale non eft tot coloribus intextum, nec eft tam preciofis gemmis redimitum, nihil refert, cum Chriftiana religio veritati ferviens, compendiofis figuris idem intelligi faciat, quod vetus obfervantia fumptuofis.

### § 7. Sixth, the Rational or "Breastplate."

Poftquam pontificis [254] verenda velata funt fuis indumentis, poftquam

---

[254] *Pontificis*, i.e. the Levitical high-prieft, but not without a reference to thofe Chriftian *pontifices* or bifhops (note 45) to whom the right of wearing a "Rational" (fee note 256) was conceded.

cælestia jam cœpit meditari, postquam justitiæ operibus ornatus est, postquam utroque cingulo, ut in omnibus fortiter et perseveranter staret, confirmatus est, imponitur Rationale pectori pontificis, quod Græce logion dicitur, per quod sapientia, quæ in ratione consistit, indicatur. Imponitur Rationali manifestatio et veritas.[254] Manifestatio ideo, quia non sufficit pontifici habere sapientiam, nisi etiam possit manifestare quæ novit, et reddere rationem de ea, quæ in nobis est, fide et spe. Veritas vero, quia non debet pontifex de suo corde prophetare, sed ea tantum quæ veritas habet, manifestare. Sunt autem adinvicem concatenata Rationale et Humerale: quia cohærere sibi invicem debent ratio et opera: ut quod mentis ratione concepimus, opere impleamus. Et notandus est ordo rerum: quia non prius Rationale, quam Humerale: quia non prius sapientia, quam opera: sed prius opera, deinde sapientia. Unde habetur in psalmo (Psa. cxviii.): *A mandatis tuis intellexi:* et de Domino Jesu dicitur (Act. i.), *Quæ Jesus cœpit facere et docere.* Deinde non prius manifestatio, quam Rationale: quia nemo docere debet quæ non novit. Huic ordini concordat propheta cum dicit (Ose. x.): *Seminate vobis ad justitiam, et metite fructum vitæ, et illuminate vobis lumen scientiæ.* In hoc pectoris ornamento duodecim lapides inserti erant, XII. patriarcharum nomina in se sculpta habentes: quia sanctorum patrum exempla pontifex semper debet habere in memoria, et secundum ea moderari facta sua. In duodenario autem numero lapidum, potest significari apostolica doctrina: quia et ipsi lapides, per quatuor ordines sunt distributi, et terni et terni in singulis angulis Rationalis positi. Quod Apostolicæ doctrinæ bene congruit, quæ fidem Trinitatis per quatuor evangelia in omni parte mundi prædicavit. Hic ornatus solius erat pontificis, sicut et nunc [255] est apud eos, quibus eo uti concessum est, propter distantiam majorum et minorum sacerdotum.

---

[254] *Manifestatio et veritas.* This is the literal rendering of the δήλωσις καὶ ἀλήθεια of the LXX. St. Jerome (quoted at p. 22) translates them by "*doctrina et veritas.*" Our own translators have preserved the original Hebrew words Urim and Thummim, of which "light and perfection" would probably be the nearest translation. See Smith's Dict. of the Bible *in voc.*

[255] *Sicut et nunc est, &c.* By the Rational "conceded" to certain among Christian bishops he means probably the Roman pallium, worn by Western archbishops under privilege of the Roman See. In this comparison he follows the reputed Alcuin. See note 227, p. 111. Amalarius, on the other hand, regards this "pallium" as corresponding in significance to the "golden plate" of the high-priest. See note 195, p. 102. [Dr. Bock thinks that the Rational here spoken of was an actual jewel made in imitation of the Jewish Rational. This is not impossible. See Liturg. Gewänder, vol. i. p. 388, *sqq*; and compare Honorius August. Gemma Animæ. lib. i. cap. ccxliii. *et ibi notata.*]

## § 8. Seventh and Eighth, the "Mitra" and the Golden Plate.

Ita ornato pontifice,[257] superponitur capiti ejus mitra, quæ alio nomine cidaris vel tiara vocatur, quæ regnum quinque sensuum,[258] quo præminere pontifex debet, intelligitur. In capite enim usus habetur omnium corporalium sensuum: quod cum bene regitur, caput viri, id est, Christus decenter ornatur. Et quia caput Christi Deus est, Lamina aurea superponitur, cui insculptum est nomen Dei, quod Hebræi vocant ineffabile (1 Cor. ii.): ut per hoc intelligatur, Deum sicut omnium conditorem, ita esse rectorem: et ad honorem et gloriam ejus esse referendum, quicquid a Domini sacerdotibus bene fuerit dispensatum. Hæc indumenta, octo esse debere constituit Moises in Exodo: sed in Levitico de eisdem indumentis tractans, de octavo, id est, fœminalibus, tacuit. Unde Hieronymus in epistola ad Fabiolam, scribit: Ubi refertur quomodo Moises Aaron fratrem suum vestimentis pontificalibus induerit, de solis feminalibus nihil dicitur, hac, arbitror, causa: quia ad genitalia nostra et verenda lex non misit manum, quia ipsi secretiora nostra confessione digna tegere debemus et velare, et conscientiam puritatis Deo judici servare. De cæteris vero virtutibus, fortitudine, justitia, humilitate, mansuetudine, liberalitate, possunt et alii judicare: pudicitiam sola novit conscientia, et humani oculi certi hujus rei esse judices non possunt, absque his, qui passim in morem brutorum animalium in libidinem feruntur. Unde Apostolus (1 Cor. vii.): *De virginibus autem præceptum Domini non habeo.* Et in Evangelio cum Dominus de eunuchis voluntariis et non voluntariis ageret, addidit in fine (Matt. xix.): *Qui potest capere, capiat.* Tanquam diceretur: Feminalibus ego vos non vestio, nec impono alicui necessitatem. Qui vult sacerdos esse, ipse se vestiat, ipse se castitate muniat. Igitur ipsi assumamus feminalia, ipsi nostra verecunda operiamus, non quæramus alienos oculos: ita tegantur genitalia, ut cum intramus sancta sanctorum, nulla appareat turpitudo, ne moriamur.

---

[257] *Pontifex.* Here again the Levitical high-priest, as is clear from what he says of the "*lamina aurea*" put upon his head, compared with what he says below (§ 9) when speaking of Christian priests and bishops, "*nulli autem lamina aurea.*"

[258] *Regnum quinque sensuum.* Compare Venerable Bede, quoted above, p. 80 (§ 6).

### § 9. DISTINCTIONS IN THE USE OF THESE VESTMENTS.

Notandum vero est, quod minoribus sacerdotibus neque duplex tunica datur, neque humerale, neque rationale, neque lamina aurea, sed tantum poderis, et mitra, et zona, qua stringatur tunica byssina. Funguntur tamen sacerdotio, sed non illa sublimitate, qua funguntur, qui omnibus octo indumentis decorantur. Novi quoque testamenti sacerdotes non omnibus illis utuntur indumentis, quia nec duabus utuntur tunicis, nec rationali, præter solos pontifices : nulli autem lamina aurea, quia sicut dicit B: Hieronymus in supramemorata epistola, *quod olim in lamina monstrabatur, nunc in signo crucis ostenditur. Auro enim legis, sanguis evangelii preciosior est.* [*Supra*, p. 24, note 42.]

### § 10. VESTMENTS OF CHRISTIAN PRIESTHOOD.

Utuntur autem tunica linea, quæ poderis dicitur, vel talaris, quæ omnium figurat castigationem membrorum, et zona quæ tunicam stringit, quæ dissolutam et remissam prohibet esse castitatem. Utuntur et superhumerali,[259] per quod exiguntur opera justitiæ a sacerdote, quia non sufficit temperantia, et a malo abstinentia, quæ superioribus duobus indumentis figurabatur, nisi opera justitiæ et misericordiæ subsequantur. Unde et in Psalmo dicitur (Pf. xxxiii. ; 1 Pet. iii.) : *Define a malo, et fac bonum.* Unde ipsum humerale poderi adstringitur. Utuntur et stola, quæ alio nomine orarium vocatur : qua vetus sacerdotium non utebatur. Hoc tanquam jugum bobus arantibus vel triturantibus collo juxta humeros superponitur, ut illud evangelicum ab eis impleatur (Matt. xi.) : *Tollite jugum meum super vos, et discite a me, quia mitis sum et humilis corde: Jugum enim meum suave est, et onus meum leve.* Hæc a collo per anteriora descendens, dextrum latus ornat et sinistrum, ut doceat sacerdotem, per arma justitiæ a dextris et a sinistris, id est, in prosperis et adversis, debere esse munitum : quod ad fortitudinem pertinet, sine qua cæteræ virtutes facile expugnantur, et minime coronantur.[260] Unde dicit Apostolus (Heb. x.) : *Patientia vobis neces-*

---

[259] *Utuntur et superhumerali.* See above, note 253.

[260] *Minime coronantur, i.e.* win not the vic- tor's crown (compare note 54, p. 32), which the Lord bestoweth on them that are faithful unto the end.

*faria est, ut reportetis repromissiones:* et in evangelio Dominus (Matt. x.; xxiv.): *Qui perseveraverit usque in finem, hic salvus erit.* Inde est quod stola cum zona poderis quibusdam nexibus colligatur: quia virtutes virtutibus adjuvantur, ne aliquo tentationis impulsu moveantur. His omnibus indumentis superponitur casula,[261] quæ alio nomine planeta vocatur: quæ quia communis est vestis, charitatem significat (1 Cor. xii.), quæ universis virtutibus superponitur: quia cæteræ virtutes nihil sine ea utile operantur. Unde dicit Apostolus (1 Cor. xii.): *Et adhuc excellentiorem viam docebo vos. Aemulamini charitatem.* Et quam inutiles absque ea sint cæteræ virtutes, subsequenter approbatur, cum præcipuas virtutes, scientiam scilicet linguarum, distributionem rerum propriarum, ipsum quoque martyrium, sine ea nihil esse confirmat. Et ideo prudentiæ ponitur loco, quia plenitudo legis est dilectio. Et quia mentibus bene compositis, et divino cultui mancipatis, frequenter subrepit acedia,[262] oportet ut ad eam frequenter detergendam diligens adhibeatur vigilantia, qua ab oculis cordis emergens talis sæpe mundetur pituita. Unde in sinistra manu ponitur quædam mappula, quæ sæpe fluentem oculorum pituitam tergat, et oculorum lippitudinem removeat. Hæc quippe ornamenta, ut dictum est, non sunt ipsæ virtutes, sed virtutum insignia, quibus tanquam scripturis admonentur utentes, quid debeant appetere, quid vitare, et ad quem finem sua facta dirigere. Adjiciendum est supradictis, quia Levitæ suo modo utuntur supramemoratis indumentis: idem significantibus, quod significant in presbyteris. Utuntur Levitæ Dalmatica, quæ propter sui latitudinem curam proximorum significat, quod significabat in presbyteris casula: quia utrorunque istorum ministrorum, ad implendam dilectionem, eadem debet esse custodia.

§ 11. SPECIAL VESTMENTS WORN BY BISHOPS AND CARDINALS.

Utuntur episcopi et cardinales presbyteri sandaliis, quæ calceamenta sunt prædicatorum. Habent autem ad terram soleam integram, ne pes tangat terram: supra vero constat ex corio, quibusdam locis pertuso:[263] quia evangelium non debet terrenis commodis inniti, nec omnia evangelica sacramenta omnibus revelari, nec omnibus abscondi. Unde

---

[261] *Casula . . . charitatem significat.* Compare Rabanus Maurus (Cap. 21) quoted above at p. 91.

[262] *Acedia.* An imported Greek word, ἀκηδία, for the older ἀκήδια, "carelessness."
[263] See Bock Liturg. Gewänder, vol. ii. p. 12.

et Dominus discipulis ita dicebat (Matt. xiii.): *Vobis datum est nosse mysterium regni Dei: cæteris autem in parabolis, ut videntes non videant, et audientes non intelligant.* Hanc sandaliorum significationem propheta intelligebat, quando dicebat (Esa. lii.; Rom. x.): *Quam speciosi pedes annunciantium pacem, evangelizantium bona.*

Antequam induantur sandaliis, vestiuntur caligis byssinis vel lineis, usque ad genua protensis, et ibi bene constrictis: per quas significatur, quia debent rectos gressus facere pedibus suis: et genua debilia, id est, negligentiis resoluta, roborare, et sic ad prædicandum evangelium festinare.

### § 12. Unction of Hands and of Head in Ordination.

Unguntur præterea manus [64] presbyteris et episcopis, ut cognoscant se in virtute sancti spiritus hoc sacramento gratiam consecrandi accipere, et opera misericordiæ erga omnes pro viribus exercere debere. Episcopo vero specialiter caput ungitur, ut intelligat se esse illius vicarium, de quo dicitur in Psalmo (Ps. xliv.): *Unxit te Deus, Deus tuus, oleo lætitiæ præ consortibus tuis.* Accipiunt hac unctione claves regni cælorum, ut quæcunque ligaverint super terram, sint ligata et in cælis (Matt. xviii.): et quæcunque solverint super terram, sint soluta et in cælo: et quorum peccata detinuerint, sint detenta, et quorum peccata dimiserint, sint dimissa (Joan. xx.)

### § 13. Practical Exhortation.

His ita de ornatu sacerdotali et pontificali breviter prælibatis, admonendi estis, ut sicut sacramenta profunda audistis, sic ea studeatis et corde intelligere, et opere implere. Non enim auditores legis justi sunt apud Deum, sed factores. Potest enim unusquisque vestrum intra se regale habere sacerdotium et sacerdotales ornatus, si quem abluerit et mundum fecerit legis observatio, et si gratia baptismi et unctio chrismatis illibata permanserit, et si indutus duplicibus indumentis, literæ scilicet et spiritus, fuerit; et si in his fortiter accingatur, ut sit castus

---

[64] *Unguntur manus.* This ceremony is represented in the illustrations from the Pontifical of Bishop Landulfus, given in this volume.

mente et corpore; si etiam superhumerali operum justificetur, si stola fortitudinis a dextris et a sinistris muniatur, si plenitudine scientiæ, quam planeta significat, cumuletur: potest, inquam, ita ornatus intra Dei templum, quod ipse est, verum habere sacerdotium. Qui autem nec sacris vestibus induti, nec honestis moribus ornati, ad altare Dei accedere præsumpserint, sicut filii Aaron, Nadab et Abihu, igne alieno, quem offerebant ante Dominum, consumpti sunt (Lev. x.); ita isti non divina ordinatione, sed sua præsumptione sacerdotium sibi usurpantes, cum his, qui ad regales nuptias sine veste nuptiali intraverunt (Matt. xxii.), æternis ignibus sunt cruciandi. Unde dicitur in Levitico (Lev. xvi.): *Et dixit Dominus ad Moisem: Loquere ad Aaron fratrem tuum, ne intret omni hora in sancta interiora, ut non moriatur.* Unde ostenditur, quod si inordinate intraret sancta sanctorum, non preparatus, non indutus sacerdotalibus indumentis, non propitiato sibi prius Deo, morietur: et merito, tanquam qui non fecerit ea, quæ oportet fieri, antequam accedatur ad altare Dei. Ad omnes enim nos pertinet, nos omnes instruit lex Dei, ut sciamus quod debeamus accedere ad altare Dei, et offerre, scilicet ut deponamus vestimenta sordida, id est, carnis immunditiam, pravitatem morum, inquinamenta libidinum. Unde et in eodem Levitico, cum enumerasset Dominus vestes, quibus induendus erat Aaron et filii ejus, adjunxit (Exod. xxviii.): *Vesties his omnibus fratrem tuum, et filios ejus cum eo, et cunctorum consecrabis manus, sanctificabisque illos, ut sacerdotio fungantur mihi.* Sequitur: *Et utentur eis Aaron et filii ejus, quando ingredientur testimonii tabernaculum, quando appropinquabunt ad altare, ut ministrent in sanctuario, ne iniquitatis rei moriantur.* Ex his omnibus colligitur, quanta sit dignitas sacerdotalis ministerii, et quanta esse debeat sanctitas ministrorum: [265]

---

[265] It will be seen by the passage above quoted, that St. Ivo, writing at the close of the eleventh century, enumerates the following as the vestments of Christian ministry:—1. Linen Tunic. 2. Girdle. 3. Superhumeral (i.e. Amice). 4. Stole. 5. Chasuble (or "Planeta"). 6. Maniple. He mentions also the dalmatic as worn by deacons in place of the Chasuble proper to priests. The vestments worn by bishops only, are the second tunic (§ 9), and (by some at least among them, note 256) the Rational, whether the pallium of archbishops, or a Jewel worn on the Breast. Bishops were distinguished also by sandals of a peculiar shape, and by buskins (*caligæ*) made of linen.

It will be observed that while he mentions the "Mitra," or linen cap of the Levitical priest, he is silent as to any similar ornament among the Christian vestments. The truth seems to be that in the eleventh century the "Mitra" had been already introduced as a distinctive vestment at Rome (Hefele, pp. 230, 231), and through Rome to particular churches in Germany and elsewhere. But it was not in St. Ivo's time regarded as one of the acknowledged vestments of Christian ministry. Of the "golden plate" he says distinctly that it was nowhere worn, "*nulli lamina aurea*" (§ 9).

quam qui habuerit, sacerdotii merito non carebit. Qui vero non habuerit, et sacerdotii officium usurpaverit, merito cum supra memoratis præsumptoribus interibit. Multa de sacerdotii dignitate, multa de indumentorum sacerdotalium mystica pulchritudine, vitantes prolixitatem sermonis, præterivimus: hoc intendentes, quia ad ædificationem morum, et ad utilitatem audientium ista sufficiunt.

## XXXVI.

## HUGO A SANCTO VICTORE.[w]

### THE SACERDOTAL VESTMENTS OF CHRISTIAN MINISTRY.

#### Sermo xiv. [Tom. ii. p. 222].

[He preaches on the words of Pf. cxxxi. "Let thy priests (*sacerdotes*) be clothed with righteousness." He is addressing his brethren of the clergy only.]

Oportet, fratres carissimi, ut nos qui in domo Dei sacerdotio fungimur, dignam sacerdotis justitiam ducamus, et honestis in officio vestibus induamur, immo virtutes quæ per vestes sacerdotales designantur, exerceamus. Quid namque prodest ornari vestibus, nisi ornemur virtutibus? Certe si videremus sacerdotem sine sacerdotalibus vestimentis missam celebrare, sine alba, sine stola, sine infula, multum miraremur, et cum horrore nimio monstrum tale detestaremur. Si ergo detestandus esset qui accederet ad altare sine vestibus, quam detestandus quam horrendus est qui accedere præsumit cum vitiis et sine virtutibus? Quantum distat inter vas quodlibet et cibum, tantum distat inter significans et significatum. Vestes significant, virtutes significantur. Vestes foris coram populo decorant, virtutes intus coram Domino ministrum commendant. Sicut igitur non audemus accedere ad altare sine vestibus, sic non præsumamus accedere sine virtutibus.

Videamus denique quæ sunt istæ vestes, et quæ per eas significentur virtutes. Sunt ergo vestimenta, interior linea, exterior scilicet alba, amictus super humeros, quod nos superhumerale dicere possumus, zona, stola, manipula, infula. Ante omnia debet sacerdos quotidiana vestimenta deponere, deinde manus abluere, et sic candida vestimenta sumere. Depositio quotidianorum vestimentorum significat veteris hominis depositionem; ablutio manuum, criminum confessionem; assumptio novorum vestimentorum virtutum exercitationem.

---

[w] Born 1096, died 1140, a.d. He was Abbot of the Monastery of St. Victor, near Paris. The text which I have followed is that of Hittorpius.

Linea interior interius est, exterior exterius. Ista est in occulto, illa in manifesto. Ista latet, illa patet. Propterea interior significat munditiam cordis, exterior munditiam corporis.

Superhumerale quod supra humeros ponitur, ubi onera solent imponi, tolerantiam praesentium significat laborum, quae nobis necessaria est si veri sacerdotes volumus esse. Unde de illis qui eam perdiderunt scriptum est (Eccl. xi.): *Væ his qui perdiderunt sustinentiam.* Et Dominus de laude patientiæ in evangelio ait: *In patientia vestra possidebitis animas vestras* (Luc. xxi.). Sustineamus ergo, fratres, quicquid nobis acciderit adversum, ut sicut bona suscepimus de manu Domini, ita et mala sustineamus.

Zona, quæ lumbos circumdat, et vestimenta constringit ne diffluant, virtutem continentiæ insinuat, quæ fluxam luxuriæ nostræ lasciviam refrenat.

Stola, quæ collo imponitur, jugum suave Domini exprimit, de quo Dominus in Evangelio ait (Matt. xi.): *Jugum enim meum suave est, et onus meum leve.*

Sequitur manipula, quæ in brachio sinistro dependet, quæ nihil aliud denotat sacramenti nisi quod pro cautela ibi ponitur, ne sacerdos aliquid in officio suo incaute et negligenter agat, sed omnia diligenter, sicut qui in conspectu Domini et sanctorum Angelorum consistit, perficiat. Significat ergo cautelam, per quam cavenda cavemus, et facienda facimus.

His omnibus minister Domini indutus, his omnibus adornatus, nondum est aptus officio sacerdotali, nec illud implere praesumit, nisi septimum, quod infula [a] dicitur, cæteris addatur et superimponatur. Istud vestimentum excellentius est cæteris, eminetque universis. Quam igitur virtutem per hoc significari dicimus nisi charitatem, de qua dicit Apostolus, *Adhuc vobis excellentiorem viam demonstramus. Si linguis hominum loquar et angelorum, &c.*, quæ bene novit fraternitas vestra. Qui cum alia dona spiritualia et virtutes demonstrasset, tandem de charitate intulit dicens, *Si linguis &c.* O beata virtus, Charitas; et beatus solus qui in ipsa usque in finem perseverat. Qui ergo cum aliis virtutibus charitatem habet, sacerdos est. Et qui etiam alias sine ista habet, sacerdos non est.

---

[a] *Infula.* This is one of the few early instances of the use of this word to designate one of the Christian vestments. It here means not a covering for the head (which would be in accordance with the classical usage of the word), but a chasuble. See below, note 268 *in fin.*

Habeamus igitur, si veri sacerdotes volumus esse, quod esse debemus. Habeamus interiorem lineam per munditiam cordis, exteriorem per munditiam corporis; Superhumerale per patientiam: zonam, per continentiam; stolam, per obedientiam; manipulum (*sic*), per cautelam; infulam [208] per charitatem fraternam. His etenim omnibus armati sanctè et relligiose perficiemus holocaustum Domini, et dicetur de nobis quod scriptum est, *Vos estis genus electum, regale sacerdotium.* Tales fuerunt sancti quorum hodie sollennia celebramus. Tales, fratres charissimi, esse studeamus, ut et nos induamur justitiam, et facti cum ipsis participes meritorum, fieri mereamur socii præmiorum. Quod per merita et intercessionem eorum nobis præstare dignetur, qui vivit et regnat.

---

[208] In this passage, written some thirty years after that of St. Ivo last quoted, the enumeration of the Christian vestments corresponds nearly with his, with one apparent exception. He speaks of the two tunics, of the amice (which, he says, may also be called "superhumeral") of girdle, stole, maniple, but the last of the vestments, that which is "more excellent than the rest," which is "added to and superimposed" upon those first mentioned, which is typical of charity, is with St. Hugo not "*casula,*" but "*infula.*" The whole context of this passage points plainly to the conclusion that *infula* is here only another name for the chasuble. Such an interpretation is not in accordance with the classical usage of the term, but another passage of the same writer is conclusive as to his meaning. *Casula, quæ alio nomine Planeta vel Infula dicitur.* [*Speculum Eccl.* lib. i. cap. 6, apud Dufresne.]

## XXXVII.

## HONORIUS AUGUSTODUNENSIS.[269]

### SACRED VESTMENTS AND INSIGNIA.

GEMMA ANIMÆ, LIB. I. CAP. 89.

#### ORIGIN OF THE VESTMENTS.

APOSTOLI et eorum succeffores in quotidianis veftibus et ligneis[270] calicibus miffam celebraverunt: fed Clemens, tradente Petro Apoftolo, ufum facrarum veftium ex Lege fumpfit: et Stephanus Papa in facris veftibus miffas celebrari conftituit.

LIB. I. CAP. 193. OF THE CLERICAL TONSURE.

Tonfura clericorum initium fumpfit ab ufu Nazaræorum. Hi ex juffu legis crines fuos radebant, et in facrificium Domino incendebant. Nazaræi autem dicuntur *fancti*. Unde Apoftoli ad exemplum eorum miniftros Ecclefiæ docuerunt fe ob fignum tondere, quo recordarentur fe Domino in fanctitate fervire debere. Chriftus rex et facerdos fecit nos fibi et facerdotes et reges. Pars capitis rafa eft fignum facerdotale: pars crinibus comata fignum regale. Sacerdotes quippe legis tiaram, id eft, pileolum ex byffo in modum mediæ fphæræ rotundum, in capite portabant: reges aureas coronas geftabant. Ergo rafa pars capitis tiaram, circulus crinium refert coronam.[271]

---

[269] Very little is known concerning this writer, as will appear from the following. "Hiftoire de la Vie d'Honoré. Le titre de cet article énonce prefque tout ce que nous favons de certain fur la perfonne d'Honoré." *Hift. Lit. de la France*, tom. xii. p. 165. "Honorius haud diu poft annum 1152 obiiffe videtur, quod facile conjicias de fcriptore qui jam inter annos 1122 et 1125 fe floruiffe et majorem partem librorum fuorum ediififfe difertis verbis affirmat." Wilman, *apud Patrol.* tom. clxxii. p. 13. Ed. *Migne*.

[270] This probably refers to the fame tradition as that implied in the faying of St. Boniface, quoted at p. 207. See note 209.

[271] In this Honorius follows clofely upon S. Ifidore of Seville, De Off. Ecc. vii. quoted at p. 68.

### Lib. I. Cap. 198. White Garments, why Worn. And why Seven in Number.

Vestes sacræ a veteri Lege sunt assumptæ. Ideo autem ministri Christi vel Ecclesiæ in albis vestibus ministrant, quia angeli,[971] æterni Regis ministri, in albis apparebant. Per albas itaque vestes admonentur ut Angelos Dei Ministros per castitatis munditiam in Christi servitio imitentur. Vestes vero, quibus corpus exterius decoratur, sunt virtutes, quibus interior homo perornatur. Septem autem vestes sacerdotibus ascribuntur, qui et septem ordinibus insigniti noscuntur, quatenus per septiformem Spiritum septem virtutibus resplendeant, quibus cum Angelis in ministerium Christi ornati procedant.

### Cap. 201.

[*After describing the preparatory washing of the hands, and combing of the hair, with the spiritual significance of each act, in capp.* 199, 200, *he proceeds as follows*] :

#### The Amice.

Hinc Humerale,[972] quod in Lege Ephot, apud nos Amictus dicitur, sibi imponit; et illo caput et collum et humeros (unde et Humerale dicitur) cooperit, et in pectore copulatum duabus vittis ad mammillas cingit. Per Humerale, quod capiti imponitur, spes cælestium intelligitur. . . . Hæc vestis est candida. . . .

### Cap. 202. The Alb.

Dehinc Alba induitur, quæ in Lege tunica linea vel talaris, apud Græcos podis (*leg.* poderis) dicitur. Per hanc castitas designatur, qua tota vita sacerdotis decoratur. Hæc descendit usque ad talos, quia usque in finem vitæ debet in castimonia perseverare sacerdos. . . . Hæc vestis albedine candet, quia sanctitas coram Deo inter Angelos splendet.

---

[971] Compare S. Isidore *Hisp. De Off. Ecc.* viii. *supra*, p. 69.
[972] For this identification of the "Amice" with the Levitical Ephod or Superhumeral, compare note 253, p. 122.

### Cap. 203. The Girdle.

Ex hinc Cingulo cingitur, quod in Lege Balteus, apud Græcos Zona dicitur. Per cingulum (quod circa lumbos præcingitur, et, Alba ne diffluat et gressum impediat, astringitur), mentis custodia, vel conscientia, accipitur, qua luxuria restringitur. . . .

### Cap. 204. The Stole, or Orarium.

Deinde circumdat collum suum Stola, quæ et Orarium dicitur, per quam obedientia Evangelii intelligitur. . . . . Cap. 205. Per Stolam quoque innocentia exprimitur. . . . Hac patriarchæ ante Legem utebantur, et primogenita dicebantur. Erat autem vestis sacerdotalis quam majores natu cum benedictione patris, ut Jacob ab Isaac, induebant, et victimas Deo, ut pontifices, offerebant. Unde dicitur, *Vende mihi primogenita tua* (Gen. xxv. 31). Et iterum "*stola Esau*." Stola dicitur missa ;[714] erat enim vestis candida pertingens ad vestigia, sed postquam cæpit portari Alba, mutata est, ut hodie cernitur Stola.[715]

### Cap. 206. The Under-Girdle.

Exhinc Subcingulum, quod perizoma vel Subcinctorium [715a] dicitur, circa pudenda duplex suspenditur. Per hoc eleemosynarum studium accipitur, quo confusio peccatorum contegitur. Hoc duplicatur quia primum animæ suæ misereri peccata devitando, deinde proximo necessaria impendendo, cuilibet imperatur.

### Cap. 207. The Chasuble.

Deinde Casula [716] omnibus indumentis supponitur (*Leg.* superponitur),

---

[714] *Stola dicitur missa.* I can only suppose these words as saying that the word "*stola*" means "sent ;" and as having reference to the Greek origin of the word, viz. στολή, which again is a paronym of στέλλω, "*to send*." Honorius, like most of his contemporaries, was liable to make mistakes when dealing with Greek words.

[715] This passage is somewhat obscurely worded, but its meaning appears to be this. By the word "stola" he thinks was meant originally a full robe (as in fact was the *stola matronalis* of classical times), not a narrow border-like vestment such as was called "*stola*" in his own time. And the change from the primitive "robe" to the later "stola" was made, he thinks, when the "alb" or white tunic became the recognised dress of Christian ministry.

[715a] *Subcinctorium.* On this word see note in the extracts from Innocent III. which follow.

[716] Here again he follows S. Isidore. See note 130, p. 74.

per quam charitas intelligitur, quæ omnibus virtutibus eminentior creditur. Casula autem quasi parva casa [m] dicitur: quia sicut a casa totus homo tegitur, ita charitas totum corpus virtutum complectitur. Hæc vestis et Planeta (quod error sonat) vocatur, eo quod errabundus limbus ejus utrinque in brachia sublevatur. [*He then dwells on the mystical meaning implied in the fact that the Chasuble is gathered in two folds on the breast, and in three upon the arms.*]

### CAP. 208. THE FANON,[ns] OR MANIPLE.

Ad extremum sacerdos fanonem in sinistrum brachium ponit, quæ et mappula et sudarium vocatur, per quod olim sudor et narium sordes extergebantur. Per hoc pœnitentia intelligitur, quia quotidiani excessus labes extergitur.

### CAP. 209. THE SEVEN VESTMENTS WORN BY BISHOPS ONLY.

Episcopus eisdem septem vestibus induitur, insuper et aliis septem redimitur, scilicet Sandaliis, Dalmatica, Rationali, Mitra, Chirothecis, Annulo, Baculo.

### CAP. 210. THE SANDALS.

[*He sets forth the various mysteries to be found in the various parts of the Sandal, in the upper and lower leather, the black and the white leather, the strings, and the seams. He ends all by saying*]: Legis sacerdotes habebant Femoralia, quibus turpitudinem tegebant: Ecclesiæ sacerdotes sandalia portant, quia etiam aliis munditiam prædicant.

### CAP. 211. THE DALMATIC.

Dalmatica a Dalmatia provincia est dicta, in qua primum est inventa. Hæc a Domini inconsutili tunica, et Apostolorum colobio, est mutuata. Colobium autem erat cucullata vestis, sine manicis,

---

[m] See note 130, p. 74.
[ns] *Fanon.* See note 161, p. 90; and note 233, p. 113.

sicut adhuc videmus in monachorum cucullis [279] vel nautarum tunicis. Quod collobium a S. Sylvestro [280] in Dalmaticam est versum; et additis manicis infra sacrificium portari instituta. Quæ ideo ad Missam a pontifice portatur, ubi passio Christi celebratur, quia in modum crucis [281] formatur. Hæc vestis est candida. . . . Hujus vestis manicæ sunt nostræ Gallinæ [282] alæ.

### Cap. 213. The "Rational" worn by Bishops.

Rationale [283] a Lege est sumptum, quod ex auro, hyacintho, purpura, unius palmi mensura erat factum. Huic Doctrina [284] et Veritas, ac duodecim preciosi lapides contexti, nominaque filiorum Israel insculpta erant, et hoc Pontifex in pectore ob recordationem populi portabat. Hoc in nostris vestibus præfert (*Leg.* præfertur) per ornatum qui auro et gemmis summis Casulis in pectore affigitur. Monet autem pontificem ratione vigere, auro sapientiæ, [285] hyacintho [286] spiritualis intelligentiæ, purpura patientiæ, in Christum, qui cælum palma [287] mensurat, tendere debere, Doctrina [288] et Veritate radiare, gemmis virtutum coruscare, duodecim Apostolos sanctitate imitari, totius populi in sacrificio recordari.

### Cap. 214. The Episcopal Cap, or Mitre. [289]

Mitra quoque Pontificis [note 45, *in fin.*] est sumpta ex usu Legis.

---

[279] *Cuculla.* Compare note 151, p. 86.
[280] Compare note 210, p. 107.
[281] Compare note 165, p. 91.
[282] I am unable to explain this allusion. The words seem to point to some provincial use of the term "*Gallinæ alæ*," as a designation for sleeves of a particular shape. [In the following chapter, which for brevity's sake I have omitted, Honorius sets forth the mystical symbolism of the Dalmatic.]
[283] It is clear from what follows that in the time that Honorius wrote, the use of a breastplate, in imitation of the Levitical "breastplate" or "rational," had in some dioceses been introduced. It is also evident that in the time of the reputed Alcuin no such jewel was known to be in use. See note 227, p. 111. The passage of St. Ivo quoted at p. 124, and commented on in note 256, leaves it doubtful whether he knew of any such ornament or no.
[284] See note 255, p. 124.
[285] *Auro sapientiæ.* For this symbolism compare St. Gregory the Great, quoted at p. 59. See note 107.
[286] *Hyacintho . . . intelligentiæ.* This symbolism has its origin in the words of St. Jerome, quoted at p. 20, *in fin.* See note 30.
[287] *Qui cælum palma,* etc. These words have reference, probably, to what he had said of the rational of the high-priest having *unius palmi mensuram.*
[288] Compare note 255, p. 124.
[289] Here for the first time [note 265, p. 129] we meet with mention of a mitra *as one of the vestments of Christian ministry.* It is still a cap made of linen only, as far as from this passage we can judge.

Hæc ex byſſo conficitur, et Tiara [note 84, p. 52], Ydaros,[200] Infula,[200a] Pileum, dicitur. . . . Mitra ex byſſo facta, multo labore ad candorem perducta [note 106, p. 60], caput pontificis exornat. . .

### CAP. 215. THE GLOVES, AND THEIR SYMBOLISM.

Chirothecarum uſus ab epiſtolis[200b] (*Leg.* apoſtolis) eſt traditus. Per manus enim operationes, per chirothecas deſignantur earum occultationes. Sicut enim aliquando manus chirothecis velantur, aliquando exactis chirothecis denudantur, ſic opera bona interdum propter arrogantiam declinandam celantur, interdum propter ædificationem proximis manifeſtantur. Chirothecæ induuntur cum hoc impletur: *Cavete ne juſtitiam veſtram faciatis coram hominibus ut videamini ab iis* (Matt. vi). Rurſus extrahuntur cum hoc impletur: *Luceat lux veſtra coram hominibus ut videant opera veſtra bona, et glorificent Patrem veſtrum, qui in cælis eſt* (ib. v.). Chirothecæ ſunt inconſutiles, quia actiones pontificis debent rectæ fidei eſſe concordes.

### CAP. 216. THE EPISCOPAL RING.

Annuli uſus ex Evangelio acceptus creditur, ubi ſaginati vituli conviva prima ſtola veſtitur, annulo inſignitur (Luc. xv.). Olim ſolebant reges litteras cum annulo ſignare: cum hoc ſoliti erant et nobiles quique ſponſas ſubarrhare. Fertur quod Prometheus quidam ſapiens primus annulum ferreum ob inſigne amoris fecerit, et in eo adamantem lapidem poſuerit; quia videlicet ſicut ferrum domat omnia, ita amor vincit omnia: et ſicut adamas eſt infrangibilis, ita amor eſt inſuperabilis. Quem enim in illo digito portari conſtituit, in quo venam ut cordis deprehendit, unde et annularis nomen accepit. Poſtmodum vero aurei ſunt pro ferreis inſtituti, et gemmis pro adamante inſigniti: quia ſicut aurum cuncta metalla præcellit, ita dilectio univerſa bona

---

[200] *Ydaros. Sic libri impreſſ.* This may have originated in *cydaris*, for the more correct *cidaris*, which is probably the true reading here.

[200a] *Infula.* Here clearly uſed in the ſenſe which in liturgical writers it ſtill retains, that of an epiſcopal cap, or mitre. Compare note 268, p. 153, where *infula* is uſed as the equivalent of *caſula*.

[200b] There can be little doubt that Honorius wrote "apoſtolis." The text (Migne's) which I have here followed ſuggeſts the reading "epiſcopis." But this reading is contrary to ſenſe; the other makes good ſenſe but bad hiſtory, and is therefore probably the true one.

excellit: et sicut aurum gemma decoratur, ita amor dilectione perornatur. Pontifex ergo annulum portat, ut se sponsum ecclesiæ agnoscat, ac pro illa animam, si necesse fuerit, sicut Christus, ponat, mysteria scripturæ a perfidis sigillet, secreta ecclesiæ resignet.

### Cap. 217. The Pastoral Staff.

Baculus ex auctoritate Legis et Evangelii assumitur, qui et "virga pastoralis," et "capuita," et "ferula," et "pedum" dicitur. Moyses quoque, dum oves pavit, virgam manu gestavit. Hanc ex præcepto Domini in Ægyptum pergens secum portavit, hostes signis per eam factis terruit, qui velut lupi oves Domini transgulabant. Gregem Domini de Ægypto per mare Rubrum hac virga eduxit: pastum de cælo, potum de petra, hac produxit; ad terram lac et mel fluentem, velut ad pascua, hac virga induxit. Nihil autem hæc virga fuit quam baculus pastoralis, cum quo gregem utpote pastor minavit (*sic*). Hic baculus apud auctores "pedum" vocatur, eo quòd pedes animalium illo retineantur. Est enim lignum recurvum quo pastores retrahunt pedes gregum. Cap. 218. In Evangelio quoque Dominus apostolis præcepit ut in prædicatione nihil præter virgam tollerent (Marc. vi.; Luc. ix.). Et quia episcopi pastores gregis Dominici sunt, ut Moyses et apostoli fuerunt, ideo baculum in custodia præferunt. Per baculum, quo infirmi sustentantur, auctoritas doctrinæ designatur. Per virgam, qua improbi emendantur, potestas regiminis figuratur. Baculum ergo pontifices portant, ut infirmos in fide per doctrinam erigant: virgam bajulant, ut per potestatem inquietos corrigant: quæ virga vel baculus est recurvus, ut aberrantes a grege docendo ad pœnitentiam trahat; in extremo est acutus, ut rebelles excommunicando retrudat, hæreticos velut lupos ab ovili Christi potestative exterreat. Cap. 219. Hic baculus ex osse et ligno efficitur, quæ crystallina vel deaurata sphærula conjunguntur. In supremo capite insignitur; in extremo, ferro acuitur. . . . Per durum os, duritia Legis; per lignum, mansuetudo ecclesiæ, insinuatur; per gemmam sphærulæ, divinitas Christi. . . . Cap. 220. In sphærula est scriptum, HOMO, quatenus se hominem memoretur. Juxta ferrum est scriptum PARCE, ut subjectis in disciplina parcat, quatenus ipse a summo Pastore gratiam inveniat. Unde et ferrum debet esse retusum, quia judicium sacerdotis per clementiam debet esse delibutum.[191]

### CAP. 221 AND 222. OF THE PALLIUM AND CROZIER.

His Insignibus Archiepiscopus fulget. Insuper et Pallio pollet, ut se Christi Passionem [192] populo præferre demonstret. In duabus quippe lineis Pallii, ante et retro, est purpureum sanctæ crucis signaculum. . . . . Crux ante archiepiscopum portatur, quatenus Christum crucifixum sequi admoneatur. Pallium [193] vero pro aurea lamina est institutum, in qua summus Pontifex in Lege Dei nomen Tetragrammaton, id est quattuor literas, in fronte sua præferebat inscriptum. Quattuor quippe literæ illius Nominis, quattuor cornua crucis præmonstrabant, sicut nunc Pallium crucis modum repræsentat. Et quia hæc lamina aurea cum forma Crucis in fronte Pontificis portabatur, ideo preciosa Crux frontibus Christianorum chrismate impressa portatur. Pallium autem a solo Apostolico [194] datur, quia hæc dignitas a Romano [194] Pontifice jure datur. Quos enim Apostoli provinciis præfecerunt, Archiepiscopi; quos illi paganis prætulerunt, Episcopi, dicebantur; et Apostolorum successores Patriarchæ, Petri vero successor " Apostolicus " [194] nominabatur. Huic collata est potestas ab ecclesia archiepiscopos per provincias constituere, quod per Pallii largitionem accipitur. (Cap. 223.) Patriarchæ quoque et Apostolicus [194] Pallio utuntur, qui eodem officio præditi esse noscuntur.[195]

### CAP. 230. THE DEACON'S DALMATIC, STOLE, AND CHASUBLE.

Diacono . . . Dalmaticæ usus conceditur . . . Huic

---

[191] In the four chapters (or rather sections) occupied in the original by this subject of the "staff," I have omitted a good deal which was of no importance to the present work. Here, as in other parts of this work, any omission of this kind is indicated by a dotted line. For a further account of the staff and its symbolism, see the extracts from Innocent III. which follow.

[192] *Pallium* . . . *Passionem*. This symbolism refers to the purple crosses upon the archiepiscopal pallium.

[193] *Pallium pro lamina*. So Alcuinus quoted at p. 117.

[194] *Apostolicus*. See note 174, p. 95.

[195] From subsequent chapters of this treatise we learn that in Honorius' time the minor orders (below the subdeacon) wore three sacred vestments (*superhumerale, tunica talaris, balteus*: see Cap. 226), and the subdeacon *five*, viz. the three last mentioned and in addition to them, the *subtile, quod et stricta tunica*, and the *sudarium* or maniple, see Cap. 229. And here, too (Cap. 227), we meet with mention of the *cappa* as the proper vestment of the *cantores*. [' Cappa propria est vestis cantorum, quæ pro tunica hyacinthina Legis mutuata est.']

stola in siniftro humero ponitur, et trans scapulas ad dextrum latus reflectitur, quatenus jugo Christi activam vitam subdat, et per pii laboris exercitium ad contemplativam perficiat. Cap. 231. Cum Diaconus casulam [296] portat tunc prædicatores significat. . . .

### CAP. 235. VESTMENTS, WHY LOOSE AND LARGE.

Clericorum . . . vestis est laxa, quia clericalis vita debet esse in eleemosynis et bonis operibus larga.[296 a]

---

[296] With this mention of the chasuble as occasionally worn by deacons, compare note 189, p. 100, and Innocentius III. *Myst. Miss.* lib. i. cap. 5. From the latter we learn that on fast-days the deacon wore a chasuble gathered up in folds (*complicata*) on his left shoulder.

[296 a] In the passage of Honorius above quoted we find proof of a considerable development of the Christian vestments here for the first time (as far as I am aware) formally recognised. The subdeacon has now [note 295] five distinct vestments, the yet inferior orders three; the deacon (as we may gather by inference) six; the priest (Cap. 193, p. 135 *sq.*) seven; the bishop fourteen (Cap. 209, p. 137). St. Hugo, last quoted, speaks only of the priest's vestments, those peculiar to bishops not being then in question, apparently. But St. Ivo [note 265, p. 129], speaks of but six vestments worn by priests, and of three others (second tunic, *caligæ*, and sandals) worn by bishops; some of whom, however, are spoken of as wearing a rational [note 256]. and, if archbishops, a pallium. I may add that the word *infula*, has now (note 290*) acquired its later technical meaning of a mitre; that the mitre itself is now for the first time spoken of as one of the distinctive episcopal vestments (note 289), and that the gloves (which had been worn for convenience, especially in Gaul and Germany, from very remote times) are also now raised to the same dignity.

## XXXVIII.

## INNOCENTIUS III. PAPA.[297]

### VESTMENTS OF THE LAW AND OF THE GOSPEL.

#### De Sacro [298] Altaris Mysterio, Lib. i.

[*In the 9th chapter of this Treatise the Author had spoken of the points of resemblance, and those of difference, in the offices of Bishop and of Presbyter. In the 10th and following chapters he pursues this subject in its application to the distinctions of ministering dress. He writes as follows*]:

##### The Six Vestments worn by Presbyters.

Hæc autem communitas et specialitas potestatum inter Episcopos et Presbyteros ipso numero communium et specialium vestium designatur. Sex autem sunt indumenta communia Episcopis et Presbyteris: videlicet Amictus, Alba, Cingulum, Stola, Manipulus et Planeta.[299] Quia nimirum sex sunt in quibus communis Episcoporum et Presbyterorum potestas consistit, videlicet catechizare, baptizare, prædicare, conficere,[300] solvere et ligare.

##### The Nine Vestments worn by Bishops only.

Novem autem sunt ornamenta Pontificum specialia: videlicet, Ca-

---

[297] "Innocentius III. natione Campanus, patria Anagninus . . . a Clemente III. in cardinalium album cooptatus. Anno 1198 die 8 Januarii Pontifex Romanus electus est, annos natus 37. . . Anno 1215 generale Concilium Lateranum celebravit, in quo monstrosum Transubstantiationis figmentum inter fidei articulos reposuit."—*Cave, Hist. Lit.* vol. ii.

[298] The text is that of the *Opera D. Innocentii Pont. Max.*, published at Cologne in 1552.

[299] He uses here the older name for the vestment, commonly known as the casula or "chasuble."

[300] *Conficere.* The word ordinarily used by Western writers with the meaning "to consecrate" the holy elements, chrism, etc.

ligæ, Sandalia, Succinctorium,³⁰¹ Tunica, Dalmatica, Mitra et Chirothecæ, Annulus et Baculus. Quia munia novem sunt in quibus specialis Episcoporum potestas consistit, videlicet clericos ordinare, Virgines benedicere, Pontifices consecrare, manus imponere, Basilicas dedicare, degradandos deponere, synodos celebrare, Chrisma conficere [Note 300], vestes et vasa consecrare.

### The Pallium, by whom Worn.

Pallium autem Metropolitanorum et Primatum et Patriarcharum est proprium, ut scilicet per illud a cæteris Episcopis discernantur, et privilegiatam obtineant dignitatem. Hoc ergo tam in novo quam in veteri testamento legitur constitutum ut Pontifices præter communes vestes habeant speciales. Sed ibi erant quattuor communes et quattuor speciales, hic autem sex sunt communes, novem autem speciales. Id enim mystica ratio postulabat. Nam illæ datæ sunt carnalibus et mundanis: hæ autem datæ sunt spiritualibus et perfectis. Quaternarius enim convenit carni propter quattuor humores, et Mundo propter quattuor elementa. Senarius autem perfectis, quia numerus est perfectus, qui redditur suis partibus aggregatis.³⁰² Unde sexto die perfecit Deus cælum et terram et omnem ornatum eorum. Novenarius spiritualibus, quia novem sunt ordines qui secundum prophetam per IX species lapidum designantur. Quindecim ergo sunt ornamenta pontificis [note 45, p. 26] quindecim gradus virtutum ipso numero designantia, quos per quindecim Cantica graduum Psalmista distinxit. Vestes enim sacerdotales virtutes significant, quibus debent sacerdotes ornari, secundum illud propheticum: *Sacerdotes tui induantur justitia, et sancti tui exultent.*

[*In the chapters immediately following* (Cap. 11 to 32), *the Writer describes in detail the Levitical Vestments, and states what he believes to be their mystical significance. This done, he proceeds to speak of the Vestments of Christian Ministry, explaining their symbolism under two aspects, first in respect of Christ the true High-priest, and secondly in respect of those who are members of Christ here on earth.*]

---

³⁰¹ *Succinctorium.* Compare note 313, p. 153 and Durandus there quoted.

³⁰² Durandus, who transfers much of this treatise word for word into his own pages, and this about a "perfect number" amongst the rest, adds by way of explanation, "*Nam cum unum duo et tres dicuntur, senarius numerus impletur: vel quia in tribus partibus dividitur, id est, in sexta tertia et dimidia, videlicet in uno, duobus, et tribus.*"—Rat. D. O. Lib. iii.

### Cap. 33. Christian Vestments Generally.

Vestes autem evangelici sacerdotis aliud designant in Capite aliud figurant in Membris. Nam et Caput et Membra sacerdotis nomine nuncupantur. Ad Caput enim dicit Psalmographus: *Tu es sacerdos in æternum secundum ordinem Melchisedech.* Ad Membra vero dicit Apostolus: *Vos estis genus electum, regale sacerdotium, gens sancta, populus acquisitionis.* Prius ergo exponenda sunt earum mysteria juxta quod Capiti congruunt, ac demum secundum quod Membris conveniunt.

### Cap. 35. Of the Vestments in respect of Christ.

Pontifex ergo Altaris officio Capitis sui Christi, cujus membrum est, repræsentans personam, dum pedibus assumit sandalia, illud incarnationis Dominicæ insinuat calceamentum de quo Dominus inquit in Psalmo: *In Idumæam extendam calceamentum meum,* id est, in gentibus notam faciam incarnationem meam. Venit enim ad nos calceata Divinitas, ut pro nobis Dei filius sacerdotio fungeretur. Per ligulas quibus ipsa pedibus sandalia constringuntur illud idem accipimus quod per corrigiam calceamenti Joannes Baptista significavit, cum ait: *Cujus non sum dignus corrigiam calceamenti solvere.* Unionem ergo ineffabilem, copulamque indissolubilem, quibus Verbi Divinitas se carni nostræ conjunxit, per sandaliorum corrigias intelligimus. Mediantibus vero caligis pedes sandaliis conjunguntur, quoniam anima mediante carni Divinitas est unita. Sicut enim pes corpus sustentat, ita Divinitas mundum gubernat. Unde ait Psalmista: *Adorate scabellum pedum ejus, quoniam sanctum est* (Pf. xcviii.).

### Cap. 35. The Amice.

Amictus autem, quo sacerdos caput[303] suum obnubit, illud significat quod in Apocalypsi describitur, Angelum Dei fortem descendisse de cælo amictum nube (Rev. x.). Et in Esaia: *Ecce Dominus*

---

[303] *Amictus quo caput obnubit.* He alludes, apparently, to the mode of putting on the amice referred to in note 178, p. 96. Hence, too, the allusion in Durandus: *Amictus, pro galea, caput contegit.*—Rat. Div. Off. Cap. i. And more to the same effect in Cap. 2.

*afcendet fuper nubem candidam.* Veniens autem ad falvationem mundi Dei Filius, magni confilii Angelus, amictus eft nube dum divinitatem abfcondit in carne. Nam caput viri Chriftus, caput Chrifti Deus. Hoc ergo carnis latibulum amictus facerdotis fignificat. Quod per illam fyndonem expreffius defignatur, qua fummus Pontifex [204] caput obducit. Et pulchre quidem quod per calceamentum pedum hoc ipfum per amictum capitis defignatur, quia divinitas in carne latuit et per carnem innotuit. Nam cum notus effet in Judæa Deus, et in Ifrael magnum nomen ejus, in Idumæam extendit calceamentum fuum, et ante confpectum gentium revelavit juftitiam fuam.

### Cap. 36. The Alb.

Alba lineum veftimentum longiffime diftans a tunicis pelliceis quæ de mortuis animalibus [Note 30, p. 20] fiunt, quibus Adam veftitus eft poft peccatum, novitatem vitæ fignificat, quam Chriftus et habuit et docuit et tribuit in baptifmo, de qua dicit Apoftolus: *Exuite veterem hominem cum actibus fuis, et induite novum hominem qui fecundum Deum creatus eft.* Nam et in transfiguratione refplenduit facies ejus ficut fol, et veftimenta ejus funt facta alba ficut nix. Semper enim veftimenta Chrifti munda fuerunt et candida, quia peccatum non fecit, nec inventus eft dolus in lingua ejus.

### Cap. 37. The Girdle.

Zona facerdotalis illud fignificat quod Joannes Apoftolus ait: *Converfus vidi fimilem filio hominis præcinctum ad mamillas zona aurea.* Per zonam auream perfecta Chrifti charitas defignatur: quam dicit

---

[204] By "*fummus Pontifex*" is here meant the Pope, more exactly defcribed as *Romanus Pontifex* in Cap. 53 below, where fee more concerning the "*orale*" which is the *findon* or veftment of fine linen here referred to. The title, *Pontifex Maximus*, which is now the official title of the Bifhop of Rome, nowhere occurs in the writings of Innocent III. himfelf, as far as I have obferved. The heading of Sermo II. "*In confecratione Pontificis Maximi,*" fo given in the Cologne edition of 1552, is of courfe an *editorial* heading only, and by other Roman writers (as *e.g.* Florovanti), is quoted as *De confecratione fummi Pontificis*. The earlieft medal on which this later title of *Pontifex Maximus* appears, is one of Martin V. [MARTINVS. V. COLVMNA. PONTIFEX MAXIMVS.] *fed.* 1417-1431; the earlieft *coin*, one of Paul II. (1464-1421), ftruck at Avignon [PAVLVS PP. II. PONT. MAX. A. I.] Thefe are reprefented in a work, now of great rarity, the *Antiquiores Pontificum Romanorum Denarii, ftudio et cura Benedicti Florovantis.* 4to, *Romæ*, 1734. For the earlier hiftory of the word *Pontifex*, fee note 45, p. 26.

Apostolus supereminentem scientiæ charitatem Christi, ferventem in corde, radiantem in opere. Cujus succinctorium [305] illud significat quod Esaias de Christo loquens prædixit (Esa. xi.) : *Erit justitia cingulum lumborum ejus, et fides cinctorium renum ejus.* (Pf. l.) : *Nam justus Dominus, et justitias dilexit, æquitatem vidit vultus ejus.* (Pf. cxliv.) : *Fidelis Dominus in omnibus verbis suis, et sanctus in omnibus operibus suis.* Duæ summitates illius duæ sunt partes naturalis justitiæ, quam Christus et fecit et docuit : *Quod tibi vis non fieri, alteri ne feceris ; sed quæcunque vultis ut faciant vobis homines, et vos facite illis.*

### Cap. 38. The Stole.

Stola, quæ super amictum collo sacerdotis incumbit, obedientiam et servitutem significat, quam Dominus omnium propter salutem servorum subivit (Phil. ii.) : *Nam cum in forma Dei esset non rapinam arbitratus est esse se æqualem Deo. Exinanivit enim seipsum, formam servi accipiens, factus obediens usque ad mortem, mortem autem Crucis.* Cautam quippe mortalitatis nec contraxit origine, nec commisit in opere, quia quod non rapuit hoc exoluit [*fort.* exsolvit]. Dedit enim illi calicem pater, non judex ; amore, non ira ; voluntate, non necessitate ; gratia, non vindicta. Hic est ille Jacob qui parens præcepto patris Isaac, et consilio matris suæ Rebeccæ, servivit Laban, ut Rachael et Lyam duceret in conjugium.

### Cap. 39. The (Second) Tunic.

Tunica poderis, quæ hyacinthini coloris erat in veteri sacerdotio, tintinnabulis et Malis Punicis ab inferiori parte pendentibus, ut Pontifex totus vocalis incederet, cælestem Christi doctrinam insinuat. Cujus notitiam habuerunt homines quibus Deus per prophetam ait (Esa. xl.) : *In montem excelsum ascende tu qui evangelizas Sion.* Præcipue tamen hanc habuit tunicam evangelicæ textrix doctrinæ, Sapientia Dei Jesus Christus, et dedit illam Apostolis suis : *Omnia,* inquit, *quæcunque audivi a Patre meo nota feci vobis.* Hanc ergo significavit illa tunica Domini quam milites scindere noluerunt, eo quod esset inconsutilis, desuper contexta per totum : damnum fore maximum existimantes si qui doctrinam evangelicam hæresibus scindere moliantur.

---

[305] *Succinctorium.* See Cap. 52, quoted below, and note 313, p. 153.

### Cap. 40. The Dalmatic.

Super hanc tunicam Pontifex [note 45] veſtit Dalmaticam, quæ ſui orma latam et largam miſericordiam Chriſti ſignificat, quam ipſe præ cæteris et docuit et impendit. *Eſtote*, inquit, *miſericordes ſicut et pater veſter miſericors eſt.* Beati namque miſericordes quoniam ipſi miſericordiam conſequentur. Judicium vero ſine miſericordia fiet ei qui non facit miſericordiam, quia miſericordia ſuperexultat judicium (Jaſ. ii.) : Ergo dimittite et dimittetur vobis; *ſicque*, inquit, *orabitis : Dimitte nobis debita noſtra ſicut et nos dimittimus debitoribus noſtris*. Hic eſt ergo Samaritanus ille, proximus noſter, qui fecit nobiſcum miſericordiam, ſuperinfundens vulneribus noſtris vinum et oleum. Nam per viſcera miſericordiæ ſuæ viſitavit nos Oriens ex alto. Qui non ex operibus juſtitiæ quæ fecimus nos, ſed ſecundum miſericordiam ſuam ſalvos nos fecit. Qui pro peccatoribus venit ut de peccatis veniam indulgeret. *Miſericordiam*, inquit, *volo, et non ſacrificium*.

### Cap. 41. The Gloves.

Chirothecæ ſunt hædorum pelliculæ, quas Jacob manibus Rebecca circumdedit, ut piloſæ manus majoris [205 a] ſimilitudinem exprimerent. Pellis hædi ſimilitudo peccati quam Rebecca mater, id eſt, Spiritus ſancti gratia, manibus veri Jacob, id eſt, operibus Chriſti circumdedit : ut ſimilitudinem majoris, id eſt, prioris Adæ, Chriſtus exprimeret. Chriſtus enim ſimilitudinem peccati ſine peccato ſuſcepit, ut incarnationis myſterium diabolo celaretur. Nam ad ſimilitudinem peccatorum eſuriit, ſitivit, doluit et expavit, dormivit et laboravit. Unde cum jejunaſſet quadraginta diebus et quadraginta noctibus, ac poſtea eſuriiſſet, accedens ad eum diabolus eum ad ſimilitudinem prioris Adæ tentavit. Sed quibus primum vicerat, eiſdem modis victus eſt a ſecundo.

### Cap. 42. The Chasuble.

Caſula vel Planeta magni Sacerdotis eſt univerſalis Eccleſia, de qua dicit Apoſtolus : *Quotquot in Chriſto baptizati eſtis Chriſtum induiſtis.* (Gal. iii.) Hoc eſt illud Aaron veſtimentum cujus in oram deſcendit

---

[205] a *Majoris*, i.e. of the elder brother, viz. Eſau.

unguentum: sed a capite descendit in barbam, et a barba descendit in oram. Quoniam de plenitudine Spiritus ejus nos omnes accepimus, primum Apostoli, postmodum cæteri. Quod autem casula, cum integra sit et integra, extensione manuum in anteriorem et posteriorem partem quodammodo dividitur, designat et antiquam ecclesiam, quæ passionem Christi præcessit, et novam, quæ passionem Christi subsequitur. Nam et qui præibant, et qui sequebantur, clamabant dicentes, *Osanna filio David. Benedictus qui venit in nomine Domini.*

## Cap. 43. The Maniple.

Quod sacerdos manipulum portat in læva, designat quod Christus bravium[306] obtinebat in via. Per manipulum[307] enim præmium designatur, juxta quod legitur (Ps. cxxv., cxxvi.): *Venientes autem venient cum exultatione, portantes manipulos suos.* Per lævam vita præsens accipitur, juxta quod scriptum est, *Læva ejus sub capite meo, et dextra illius amplexabitur me.* Christus autem simul fruebatur et merebatur. Fruebatur in patria,[308] merebatur in via. Nam simul comprehendebat, et stadium percurrebat: quia simul erat in patria et in via. Nemo, inquit (Joan. iii.), *ascendit in cælum, nisi qui de cælo descendit, filius hominis qui est in cælo.*

## Cap. 44. The Mitre.

Mitra Pontificis illud significat quod Propheta loquens de Filio dicit ad Patrem (Ps. viii.): *Gloria et honore coronasti eum, Domine, et constituisti eum super opera manuum tuarum.* Hoc est itaque illud Nomen (Phil. ii.) quod est super omne nomen, ut in nomine Jesu omne genu flectatur,

---

[306] *Bravium*, equivalent to βραβεῖον. The prize of one who conquers in the stadium. *Omnes currunt, sed unus accipit bravium.* 1 Cor. ix. 24. Compare Phi. iii. 14.

[307] *Manipulum.* The primitive meaning of *manipulus* was a handful, and hence various secondary meanings, as, *a.* a bundle of hay, or of corn, "a sheaf" (so in the Psalm above quoted, and again in Ps. cxxvii., cxxviii). β. a "handful" of men, acting together as one body, and so a "company" in the military sense of the word. [Others connect this with what follows.] γ. Any other "handful," as a cloth held in the hand, in which sense *manipulus*, as a later ecclesiastical term, has taken the place of the older *mappula*. [The military sense noticed under β. may have arisen from the use of such a piece of cloth as a *Pennon*. Compare note 233 as to the meanings of *Fanon*.] I know of no instance of the word being used as equivalent to *præmium*, a meaning which Innocent may perhaps have inferred from this Psalm which he quotes.

[308] *In patria*, that is, "in heaven."

cælestium terrestrium et infernorum. Nam et in aurea lamina Cydaris Pontificalis sculptum erat nomen Domini Tetragrammaton, cujus mysterium supra prælibavimus. Per Mitram ergo capitis Christi summam illam honorificentiam intelligimus, quæ propter divinitatem debetur humanitati. Nam propter pedem adoratur scabellum. *Adorate*, inquit (Psf. xcviii.), *scabellum pedum ejus, quia sanctum est.*

### Cap. 45. The Staff.

Virga Pontificis Christi potestatem significat. De qua dicit Psalmista (Pf. xliv. 7): *Virga recta est virga regni tui. Quia dilexisti justitiam et odisti iniquitatem, propterea te unxit Deus, Deus tuus.* Propter quod et alibi dicit: *Reges eos in virga ferrea* (Pf. ii.). Verum potestas Christi non solum virga sed et baculus est; quia non solum corripit sed et sustentat. Unde Psalmista (Pf. xxiii.), *Virga tua et baculus tuus, ipsa me consolata sunt.*

### Cap. 46. The Episcopal Ring.

Annulus digiti donum Spiritus Sancti significat. Digitus enim articulatus atque distinctus Spiritum Sanctum insinuat, secundum illud (Exod. viii.): *Digitus Dei est hic.* Et alibi: *Si ego in digito Dei ejicio dæmonia, filii vestri in quo ejiciunt?* [309] (Luc. xi.) Annulus aureus et rotundus perfectionem donorum ejus significat, quæ sine mensura Christus accepit, quoniam in eo plenitudo divinitatis habitat corporaliter. Nam qui de cælo venit super omnes est. Cui Deus non dedit Spiritum ad mensuram: *Super quem videris Spiritum*, inquit (Joan. i.), *descendentem et manentem, hic est qui baptizat in Spiritu Sancto.* Nam (Esa. xi.) *requiescit super eum Spiritus sapientiæ et intellectus*, etc. Ipse vero secundum differentes donationes distribuit: *Alii*, secundum Apostolum (1 Cor. xii.), *dans sermonem scientiæ, alii gratiam sanitatum, alii operationem virtutum*, etc. Quod et visibilis pontifex imitatur, alios in Ecclesia constituens Sacerdotes, alios Diaconos, alios Subdiaconos, et hujusmodi.

[In Cap. 47 mention is made of the five Psalms (81, 84, 85, 115,

---

[309] The author evidently quotes from memory, and has taken the beginning of his quotation from one verse (ver. 20), and the conclusion from another (ver. 19).

*Innocentius III. on Sacred Vestments.*

and 129 of the Vulgate), and of certain Prayers, to be said by the Bishop when about to celebrate Mass. He then (Cap. 48, *sqq.*) proceeds with the subjects of the vestments, and enumerates then anew, declaring the spiritual significance of each in respect of them who are " members of Christ."]

### CAP. 48. THE SANDALS AND STOCKINGS.[310]

Inter hæc pedes pontificis, in præparatione evangelii pacis, caligis et sandaliis calceantur, quorum pulchritudinem admirabatur propheta cum diceret, *Quam speciosi pedes evangelizantium pacem, evangelizantium bona.* Sandalia vero de subtus integram habent soleam, desuper autem corium fenestratum,[311] quia gressus prædicatoris debent subtus esse meniti ne polluantur terrenis, secundum illud : *Excutite pulverem de pedibus vestris* (Matt. x.), et sursum aperti, quatenus ad cognoscenda cælestia revelentur, secundum illud propheticum : *Revela oculos meos et considerabo mirabilia de lege tua* (Ps. cxviii.). Quod autem sandalia quibusdam locis aperta, quibusdam clausa sunt, designat quod Evangelica prædicatio nec omnibus revelari, nec omnibus debet abscondi. Sicut criptum est (Mar. iv.) : *Vobis datum est nosse mysterium regni Dei, cæteris autem in parabolis.* (Matt. vii.) : *Nolite sanctum dare canibus, nec margaritas spargatis ante porcos.* Prius autem caligis induitur usque ad genua protensis, ibique constrictis, quia prædicator pedibus suis rectos facere gressus, et genua debilia roborare, debet. Nam qui fecerit et docuerit, hic magnus vocabitur in regno cælorum.

[*In Cap. 49 he notices the washing of the hands which forms part of the preparation. He then proceeds as follows*] :

### CAP. 50. THE AMICE.

Lotis itaque manibus assumit Amictum, qui super humeros circum-

---

[310] "Stockings." I have rendered *caligæ* by this term, as more suggestive to English readers than any other word of the real nature of this portion of the episcopal dress. Full details as to their material and ornamentation will be found in Dr. Bock (*L. G.* vol. ii, p. 2, *sqq.*).

[311] *Fenestratum*, i.e. with open spaces here and there. A similar expression (*corio pertuso*) was employed (above p. 127) by St. Ivo. Dr. Bock gives a coloured drawing of a shoe such as that here described, taken from the tomb of Archbishop Arnoldus, of Treves (12th century). In the upper leather "find kleine durchbohrungen (*foramina obtusa*) ersichtlich." *L. G.* vol. ii. p. 14.

quaque diffunditur. Per quem operum fortitudo significatur. Humeri quippe [note 35] fortes sunt ad opera peragenda, secundum illud Patriarchæ Jacob (Gen. xlix.): *Supposuit humerum ad portandum, et factus est tributis serviens.* Duo vasculi quibus ante pectus ligatur signant intentionem et finem quibus informandum est opus, ne fiat in fermento malitiæ et nequitiæ, sed in azymis sinceritatis et veritatis. Sacerdos enim non debet otiosus existere, sed bonis operibus insistere et insudare, secundum quod Apostolus ait ad Timotheum: *Labora sicut bonus miles Jesu Christi.*

### CAP. 51. THE ALB.

Alba membris corporis convenienter aptata nihil superfluum aut dissolutum in vita sacerdotis esse debere demonstrat. Hæc ob speciem candoris designat munditiam, secundum quod legitur (Eccl. ix.): *Omni tempore vestimenta tua sint candida.* Fit autem de bysso vel de lino. Propter quod scriptum est (Apoc. xix.): *Byssum* [*Leg.* byssinum] *sunt justificationes sanctorum.* Sicut enim byssus vel linum candorem, quem ex natura non habet, multis tunsionibus attritum per artem acquirit, sic et hominis caro munditiam, quam non obtinet per naturam, multis macerationibus castigata sortitur per gratiam. Unde sacerdos, secundum Apostolum, castigat corpus suum et in servitutem redigit, ne forte quum aliis prædicaverit ipse reprobus fiat. Hæc vestis in veteri sacerdotio stricta [note 101] fuisse describitur, propter spiritum servitutis in timore. In novo larga est, propter spiritum adoptionis in libertate. Quod autem Aurifrigium [312] habet, et gemmata est in diversis locis, et variis operibus ad decorem, illud insinuat quod Propheta dicit in Psalmo (Ps. xliv.): *Astitit regina a dextris tuis in vestitu deaurato, circumdata varietate.*

### CAP. 52. THE GIRDLE AND UNDER-GIRDLE.

Debet igitur Alba circa lumbos zona præcingi, ut castitas sacerdotis nullis incentivorum stimulis dissolvatur. Unde: *Sint lumbi vestri præcincti, et lucernæ ardentes in manibus vestris* (Luc. xii.). In lumbis

---

[312] *Aurifrigium*, aliter *aurifrisia*, whence the Fr. Orfraie, Eng. Orfrey, an ornamental band attached to the edge, or other portion, of a vestment.

enim luxuria dominatur. Sic Dominus loquens de diabolo manifestat (Job. xl.): *Virtus ejus in lumbis ejus, et fortitudo ejus in umbilico ventris sui.* Debent ergo lumbi præcingi per continentiam. Debet et subcingi [313] per abstinentiam, quoniam hoc genus dæmonii non ejicitur nisi in oratione et jejunio. Hinc etiam Apostolus ait (Eph. vi.): *State succincti lumbos in veritate.*

CAP. 53. SPECIAL INSIGNIA OF THE BISHOP OF ROME.

Romanus autem pontifex post Albam et Cingulum assumit Orale,[314] quod circa caput involvit, et replicat super humeros, legalis Pontificis ordinem sequens, qui post lineam strictam et zonam induebatur Ephot, id est Superhumerale, cujus locum [Note 253] modo tenet Amictus. Et quia signo Crucis [42] auri lamina cessit, pro [193] lamina quam Pontifex gerebat in fronte, Pontifex iste [315] crucem gerit in pectore. Nam mysterium, quod in quattuor litteris auri lamina continebat, in quattuor partibus forma crucis explicuit. Juxta quod inquit Apostolus (Eph. iii.): *Ut comprehendatis cum omnibus sanctis quæ sit longitudo et latitudo et sublimitas et profundum.* Ideoque Romanus Pontifex crucem quandam insertam cathenulis, a collo suspensam, sibi statuit ante pectus, ut sacra-

[313] *Subcingere* is to gird "up" (such being frequently the meaning of *sub* in composition). And the same girdle may be said both *præcingere*, in respect of its girding in the tunic in "front" of which it is fastened, and *subcingere* in respect of its use in gathering up (with a view to active exertion) a garment, which, if worn at its full length, would impede all freedom of movement. When, however, the *zona* and the *succinctorium* are distinguished (as by Innocent himself, *supra*, pp. 143, 144), it seems that by the latter term we must understand the long ends of the girdle which hung down from the waist nearly to the feet. This will explain the language of Durandus (R. D. O. iii. Cap. 4) speaking of the *subcingulum* as double. *A sinistro Pontificis latere duplex dependent subcingulum.* [None of the modern Liturgical works which I have consulted notice the word *succinctorium*.]

[314] *Orale.* In Ciampini (Vet. Mon. l. p. 239) an engraving is given in which a head-dress answering to this description may be seen, on a figure which probably represents Celestine III (*sed.* 1191-1198). This peculiar vestment, retained in the 13th Century by the Roman bishop only, was probably a relic of those earlier times when the "mitre" was what the name μίτρα originally implied, a "cap" made of linen, of wool, or of silk, utterly unlike the modern mitre.

[315] This wearing of a cross (generally containing relics) as an ornament, attached to the neck by a chain, is spoken of here as peculiar to the Bishop of Rome. In Roman theory it was so, but not in fact, even in the Western church. Numerous instances to the contrary are mentioned by Dr. Bock, who has also engraved several ancient "Pectoral Crosses," as they are called, and among them one sent as a present by Gregory the Great to the Lombard Queen Theodolinda. In the East these *εναλπια ἐγκόλπια* were worn both as Imperial and as Episcopal ornaments. At the Council of Florence, no Western bishops were allowed to wear their pectoral crosses in presence of the Pope. The Greeks maintained and exercised their right to do so. [See Bock, *L. G.* vol. ii. p. 213, *sqq.*]

x

mentum quod ille tunc præferebat in fronte, hic autem recondat in pectore:[38] *Nam corde creditur ad justitiam, ore autem confessio fit ad salutem.*

### Cap. 54. The Stole.

Post hæc Stolam,[30] quæ alio modo vocatur Orarium, super collum sibi sacerdos imponit, ut jugum Domini se suscepisse significet; quæ a collo per anteriora descendens dextrum et sinistrum latus adornat, quia per arma justitiæ a dextris et a sinistris, id est, in prosperis et adversis, sacerdos debet esse munitus. Stola quippe significat sapientiam vel patientiam, de qua scriptum habetur: *Patientia vobis necessaria est ut reportetis promissiones* (Heb. x.). Et iterum (Luc. xxi.): *In patientia vestra possidebitis animas vestras.* Hinc est ergo quod Stola cum Zona nexibus quibusdam colligatur, quia virtutes virtutibus sociantur, ne aliquo tentationis moveantur impulsu. Debet autem sacerdos secundum decretum Braccharensis Concilii[316] de uno eodemque orario cervicem pariter et utrumque humerum premens, signum crucis in pectore suo præparare. Si quis autem aliter egerit excommunicationi debitæ subjacebit. Nisi forte quis dixerit hoc decretum per contrariam Ecclesiæ Romanæ[317] consuetudinem abrogatum.

### Cap. 55. The Tunic.

Deinde Pontifex induit Tunicam poderem, id est, talarem, significantem perseverantiam. Unde Joseph inter fratres suos talarem tunicam habuisse describitur. Cum vero cæteræ virtutes currant in stadio, perseverantia tamen accipit bravium [Note 306]: quoniam qui perseveraverit usque in finem hic salvus erit. Unde præcipitur (Apoc. ii.): *Esto fidelis usque ad mortem et dabo tibi coronam vitæ.* Habebat autem hæc vestis in veteri sacerdotio pro fimbriis mala Punica cum tintinnabulis aureis, quorum supra mysterium exposuimus.

### Cap. 56. The Dalmatic.

Super hanc tunicam episcopus vestit Dalmaticam,[131] sic dictam eo quod in Dalmatia fuit reperta. Quæ sui forma figurat largitatem, quia

---

[36] The third Council of Bracara (now Braga, in Portugal) held A.D. 572.

[317] Durandus (R. D. O. lii. v.) transfers the greater part of this chapter almost word for word into his own pages, but makes one important change, "*per contrariam generalis Ecclesiæ consuetudinem.*"

largas habet manicas et protensas. Unde secundum Apostolum (1 Tim. iii.) : *Oportet episcopum non esse turpis lucri cupidum sed hospitalem.* Non ergo habeat manum ad dandum collectam, et ad recipiendum porrectam, sed illud efficiat quod Propheta suadet (Esa. lviii.) : *Frange esurienti panem tuum et egenos vagosque duc in domum tuam. Quum videris nudum operi eum, et carnem tuam ne despexeris.* Ob hoc forte specialiter utuntur Diaconi Dalmaticis, quod principaliter electi sunt ab apostolis ut mensis ex officio ministrarent. Debet autem Dalmatica habere duas lineas coccineas hinc inde, ante et retro, a summo usque deorsum, ut pontifex habeat honorem charitatis,[317a] ad Deum et ad proximum, in prosperis et adversis, juxta Veteris et Novi Testamenti præceptum, quod est: *Diliges Dominum Deum tuum ex toto corde tuo, et proximum tuum sicut teipsum.* Unde Joannes: *Charissimi non novum mandatum scribo vobis sed mandatum vetus, quod habuistis ab initio. Atque iterum mandatum novum scribo vobis, etc.* (1 Joan. ii.). In sinistro quoque latere Dalmatica fimbrias habere solet, id est, solicitudines activæ vitæ signantes, quas Episcopus debet habere pro subditis. Juxta quod dicit apostolus (1 Cor. xi.) : *Præter illa quæ extrinsecus sunt, instantia mea quotidiana, solicitudo omnium ecclesiarum.*

### Cap. 57. The Gloves.

Quia vero plerique bonum opus, quod faciunt, inani favore corrumpunt, statim Episcopus manus operit chirothecis,[598a] ut nesciat sinistra sua quid faciat dextra sua. Per chirothecam ergo congrua cautela designatur, quæ sic facit opus in publico quod intentionem continet in occulto. Nam etsi Dominus dixerit: *Luceat lux vestra coram hominibus ut videant opera vestra bona, et glorificent Patrem vestrum qui in cælis est,* propter quod chirotheca circulum aureum desuper habet, ipse tamen præcepit, *Attendite ne justitiam vestram faciatis coram hominibus, ut videamini ab iis. Alioquin mercedem non habebitis apud Patrem vestrum qui in cælis est.*

### Cap. 58. The Chasuble.

Postremo super omnes vestes induit Casulam [260] vel Planetam,[599] quæ significat Charitatem [Note 261.]. Charitas enim operit multitudinem

---

[317a] He connects "charity" with the colour of scarlet, as do Alcuin (see note 235, p. 113), and Gregory the Great, quoted at p. 60 (see note 107, *in fin.*).

peccatorum, de qua dicit Apostolus (1 Cor. xiii.): *Adhuc excellentiorem viam nobis demonstro. Si linguis hominum loquar et angelorum, charitatem autem non habuero, factus sum velut æs sonans et cimbalum tinniens.* Et hæc est vestis nuptialis, de qua loquitur Dominus in Evangelio: *Amice, quomodo huc intrasti, non habens vestem nuptialem?* Quod autem Amictus [178] super os Planetæ revolvitur, innuit quod omne opus bonum debet ad charitatem referri. Nam finis præcepti Charitas est, de corde puro, conscientia bona, et fide non ficta. Quod autem extensione manuum in anteriorem et posteriorem partem dividitur, significat duo brachia charitatis ad Deum scilicet et ad proximum. *Diliges*, inquit, *Dominum Deum tuum ex toto corde tuo, et proximum sicut teipsum.* In his duobus mandatis pendet tota Lex et Prophetæ. Latitudo Planetæ significat latitudinem Charitatis, quæ usque ad inimicos extenditur. Unde: *Latum mandatum tuum nimis.*

### Cap. 59. The Maniple.

Verum quia mentibus bene compositis et divino cultui mancipatis sæpe subrepit acedia [318] quæ quodam torpore reddit animum dormientem, dicente Psalmista (Ps. cxviii.), *Dormitavit anima mea præ tædio*, in sinistra manu apponitur mappula, quæ Manipulus [307] vel Sudarium [197] appellatur, qua sudorem mentis abstergat, et soporem cordis excutiat, ut depulso tædio vel torpore bonis operibus diligenter invigilet. Per manipulum ergo vigilantia designatur, de qua Dominus ait: *Vigilate quia nescitis qua hora Dominus vester venturus sit.* Unde sponsa dicit in Canticis (Can. v.): *Ego dormio et cor meum vigilat.*

### Cap. 60. The Mitre.

Mitra [190 a] Pontificis scientiam utriusque Testamenti significat: nam duo cornua [318 a] duo sunt Testamenta, duæ fimbriæ spiritus et littera. Circulus aureus, qui anteriorem et posteriorem partem complectitur, indicat quod omnis scriba doctus in regno cælorum de thesauro suo nova profert et vetera. Caveat ergo diligenter episcopus ne prius velit esse magister quam norit esse discipulus, ne si cæcus cæcum duxerit ambo in foveam cadant. Scriptum est enim in Propheta: *Quia tu scientiam repulisti ego te repellam, ne sacerdotio fungaris mihi.* (Ose. iv.)

---

[318] In the text before me *accidia*. The true reading is supplied by a comparison with St. Ivo Carnotensis, quoted at p. 127, from whom these words are taken *verbatim*. On *acedia* see note 262, *in loc.*

[190 a] For details concerning the Mitre, see Bock, *L. G.* ii. 164.

## Cap. 61. The Ring.

Annulus est fidei sacramentum, in quo Christus sponsam suam sanctam Ecclesiam subarravit, ut ipsa de se dicere valeat, Annulo suo subarravit me Dominus meus, id est, Christus. Cujus custodes et pædagogi sunt episcopi et prælati, annulum pro signo ferentes in testimonium. De quibus Sponsa dicit in Canticis: *Invenerunt me vigiles qui custodiunt civitatem.* Hunc annulum dedit pater filio revertenti, secundum illud: *Date annulum in manum ejus* (Luc. xv.).

## Cap. 62. The Staff, and why it is not borne by the Bishop of Rome.

Baculus correptionem significat pastoralem, propter quod a consecratore dicitur consecrato: *Accipe baculum pastoralitatis.* Et de quo dicit apostolus (1 Cor. iv.); *In virga veniam ad vos.* Quod autem est acutus in fine, rectus in medio, retortus in summo, designat quod pontifex debet per eam pungere pigros, regere debiles, colligere vagos. Quod uno carmine versificator quidam expressit: *Collige, sustenta, stimula, vaga, morbida, lenta.*

Romanus autem Pontifex pastorali virga non utitur, pro eo quod beatus Petrus Apostolus baculum suum [319] misit Eucharionis primo Episcopo Trevirorum, quem una cum Valerio et Materno ad prædicandum Evangelium genti Teutonicæ destinavit. Cui successit in episcopatu Maternus, qui per baculum sancti Petri de morte fuerat suscitatus. Quem baculum usque hodie cum magna veneratione Trevirensis servat ecclesia.

## Cap. 63. The Pallium.

Pallium,[110] quo majores utuntur episcopi, significat disciplinam qua se ipsos et subditos Archiepiscopi debent regere. Per hanc acquiritur torques [320] aurea quam legitime certantes accipiunt, de qua dicit Salo-

---

[319] An ancient staff (not, however, by any means of the *most* ancient type) was long preserved at Treves, and shown as the identical staff here spoken of. It is now at Limburg, and is figured by Dr. Bock (vol. ii. Pl. xxx), who out of regard for the traditions associated with it is considerate enough not to pronounce an opinion as to its real date.

[320] *Torques* (a neck chain) is the term ordinarily employed to describe the circular portion of the Papal Pallium. Hence it is compared in this passage to a "chain of gold," such as in the East especially was often bestowed as a mark of special favour upon those whom kings "delighted to honour."

mon in Parabolis: *Audi, fili mi, disciplinam patris tui, et ne dimittas legem matris tuæ: ut addatur gratia capiti tuo, et torques collo tuo* (Prov. i.). Fit enim pallium de candida lana contextum, habens desuper circulum humeros constringentem, et duas lineas ab utraque parte dependentes; quattuor autem cruces purpureas, ante et retro, a dextris et a sinistris: sed a sinistris est duplex et simplex a dextris. Hæc omnia moralibus sunt imbuta mysteriis, et divinis gravida sacramentis. Nam ut scriptura testatur (Eccl. i.): *In thesauris sapientiæ significatio disciplinæ*. In lana quippe notatur asperitas, in candore benignitatis (*Leg.* benignitas) designatur. Nam ecclesiastica disciplina contra rebelles et obstinatos severitatem exercet, sed erga pœnitentes et humiles exhibet pietatem.[321] Propter quod de lana non cujuslibet animalis sed ovis tantum efficitur, quæ mansuetum est animal. Unde Propheta: *Tanquam ovis ad occisionem ductus est, et quasi agnus coram tondente is obmutivit, et non operuit os suum*. Hinc est quod illius semivivi vulneribus, quem Samaritanus duxit in stabulum, et vinum adhibet et oleum; ut per vinum mordeantur vulnera, et per oleum foveantur; quatenus qui sanandis vulneribus præest in vino morsum severitatis adhibeat, in oleo mollitiem pietatis. Hoc nimirum et per arcam tabernaculi designatur, in qua cum tabulis virga continetur et manna. Quoniam in mente rectoris cum scripturæ scientia debet esse virga districtionis, et manna dulcedinis, ut severitas immoderate non sæviat, et pietas [321] plus quam expedit non indulgeat. Circulus pallii, per quem humeri ss constringuntur, est timor Domini, per quem opera ss coercentur, ne vel ad illicita defluant, vel ad superflua relaxentur. Quoniam disciplina sinistram cohibet ab illicitis formidine pœnæ, dexteram vero temperat a superfluis amore justitiæ. Beatus ergo vir qui semper est pavidus. Nam juxta sententiam Sapientis (Eccl. i.): *Timor Domini peccatum repellit, qui vero sine timore existit justificari non poterit*. Hinc est ergo quod Pallium et ante pectus et super humeros frequenter aptatur.[322] Quatuor cruces purpureæ sunt quatuor virtutes politicæ, Justitia, Fortitudo, Prudentia, Temperantia; quæ, nisi Crucis Christi sanguine purpurentur, frustra sibi virtutis nomen usurpant, et ad veram beatitudinis gloriam non perducunt. Unde Dominus inquit Apostolis

---

[321] *Pietas*, though properly used of the mingled love and reverence of children to parents (and hence of subjects to their prince, or of men to God), is occasionally employed in speaking of the tender love of parents towards their children. Such, nearly, is its implication here, "gentleness."

[322] He alludes to the three pins of gold (*acus* or *spinæ*), by which, as he says below, the pallium was formerly fastened to the chasuble. They are now appended to the pallium by loops of silk. Bock, *L. G.* ii. p. 191.

(Matt. v.): *Nisi abundaverit justitia vestra plusquam Scribarum et Pharisæorum, non intrabitis in regnum cælorum.* Hæc est purpurea regis tunica tincta [*al.* juncta *al.* vincta] canalibus quam Salomon [323] commemorat in Canticis Canticorum. Is ergo qui gloria Pallii decoratur, si cupit esse quod dicitur, in anteriori parte debet habere justitiam, ut reddat unicuique quod suum est; prudentiam in posteriori, ut caveat quod unicuique nocivum est; fortitudinem a sinistris, ut eum adversa non deprimant; temperantiam a dextris, ut eum prospera non extollant. Duæ lineæ, quarum una post dorsum et altera progreditur ante pectus, activam et contemplativam vitam significant. Quas ita debet exercere Prælatus ut exemplo Moysi (*leg.* Moysis) nunc in montem ascendat, et ibi philosophetur cum Domino; nunc ad castra descendat, et ibi necessitatibus immineat populorum; provisurus attentius ut, quum sæpe se dederit aliis, interdum se sibi restituat; quatenus et quum (*Leg.* cum) Martha circa frequens satagat ministerium, et quum (*leg.* cum) Maria verbum audiat Salvatoris. Utraque tamen gravat [324] inferius, quia corpus quod corrumpitur [325] aggravat animam, et deprimit terrena inhabitatio sensum multa cogitantem. Quapropter et Pallium duplex est in sinistra sed simplex in dextra. Quia vita præsens, quæ per sinistram accipitur, multis est subjecta molestiis, sed vita futura quæ per dexteram designatur in una semper collecta quiete est. Quod Veritas Ipsa designavit, cum intulit, *Martha, Martha, solicita es, et turbaris erga plurima. Porro unum est necessarium. Maria optimam partem elegit, quæ non auferetur ab ea in æternum.* Pallium duplex est in sinistro, quatenus ad tolerandas vitæ præsentis molestias Prælatus fortis existat. Simplex in dextra, quatenus ad obtinendam vitæ futuræ quietem toto suspiret affectu; juxta verbum Psalmistæ, dicentis: *Unam petii a Domino, hanc requiram, ut inhabitem in domo Domini omnibus diebus vitæ meæ.* Tres autem acus [326] quæ pallio infiguntur ante pectus super humerum et post tergum, designant compassionem proximi, administrationem officii, districtionemque judicii. Quarum prima pungit animum per dolorem, secunda per laborem, tertia per terrorem. Prima

---

[323] Cant. vii. 5, *Comæ capitis tui, sicut purpura regis vincta canalibus.*

[324] *Utraque tamen gravat, &c. Utraque* refers directly to *linea*, indirectly to *vita*. And in saying that "both one and the other is burdensome" (*utraque gravat*), he refers probably to the leaden weight attached to each extremity of the pallium with a view to make it hang properly. For this last see Bock, L. G. vol. ii. p. 193.

[325] *Quod corrumpitur*, *i.e.* which is "subject to corruption." Compare the use of the present participle τοῦ ἀποθνήσκοντος (equivalent to "subject unto death") in the passage of Philo, quoted at p. 8.

pungebat Apostolum cum dicebat: *Quis infirmatur et ego non infirmor?, quis scandalizatur, et ego non uror?* Secunda est: *Præter illa quæ extrinsecus sunt instantia mea quotidiana, sollicitudo omnium ecclesiarum.* Tertia: *Si justus vix salvabitur, impius et peccator ubi parebunt?* Super dextrum humerum non infigitur acus, quoniam in æterna quiete nullus est afflictionis aculeus, nullus stimulus punctionis. Absterget enim Deus omnem lacrymam ab oculis sanctorum, et jam non erit amplius neque luctus, nec clamor, sed nec ullus dolor, quoniam priora transierunt. Acus est aurea, sed inferius est acuta, et superius rotunda, lapidem continens preciosum, quia nimirum bonus pastor propter curam ovium in terris affligitur, sed in cælis æternaliter coronabitur, ubi preciosam illam margaritam habebit, de qua Dominus ait in Evangelio: *Simile est regnum cælorum homini negociatori quærenti bonas margaritas. Inventa autem una preciosa margarita, abiit et vendidit omnia quæ habuit, et emit eam.* Dicitur autem Pallium plenitudo pontificalis officii, quoniam in ipso et cum ipso confertur pontificalis officii plenitudo. Nam antequam Metropolitanus pallio decoretur, non debet clericos ordinare, pontifices consecrare, vel ecclesias dedicare, nec Archiepiscopus appellari.

## Cap. 64. Practical Exhortation.

Ista sunt arma quæ Pontifex debet induere contra spirituales nequitias pugnaturus. Nam ut inquit apostolus, *Arma militiæ nostræ non sunt carnalia, sed ad destructionem munitionum potentia Deo* (2 Cor. x.). De quibus idem Apostolus in alia dicit Epistola (Eph. vi.): *Induite vos armaturam Dei, ut possitis stare adversus insidias diaboli. State ergo succincti lumbos vestros in veritate, et induti loricam justitiæ, et calceati pedes in præparationem Evangelii pacis: in omnibus sumentes scutum Fidei, quo possitis omnia tela nequissimi ignea extinguere: et galeam salutis assumite et gladium Spiritus, quod est verbum Dei.* Provideat ergo diligenter episcopus, et attendat sacerdos studiose, ut signum sine significato non ferat, ut vestem sine virtute non portet, ne forte similis sit sepulchro deforis dealbato, intus autem omni pleno spurcitio. Quisquis autem sacris indumentis ornatur et honestis moribus non induitur, quanto venerabilior apparet hominibus, tanto indignior redditur apud Deum. Pontificalem itaque gloriam jam honor non commendat vestium, sed splendor animarum. Quoniam et illa quæ quondam carnalibus blandiebantur obtutibus ea potius quæ in ipfis erant intelligenda poscebant: ut quicquid illa velamina in fulgore auri, et in nitore gemmarum, et in multimoda operis varietate fignabant, hoc jam in moribus actibusque clarefcat. Quod et apud veteres reverentiam ipfæ fignificationum fpecies obtinent, et apud nos certiora fint experimenta rerum quam ænigmata figurarum. Tunc enim valles abundant frumento, quum arietes ovium funt induti.

### CAP. 65. THE FOUR SACRED COLOURS.

Quattuor autem funt principales colores, quibus fecundum proprietates dierum facras veftes ecclefia Romana diftinguit, Albus, Rubeus, Niger, et Viridis. Nam et in legalibus indumentis quattuor colores fuiffe leguntur, Byffus,[325] et Purpura, Hyacinthus, et Coccus. Albis induitur veftimentis in feftivitatibus Confefforum et Virginum; Rubeis in folemnitatibus Apoftolorum et Martyrum. Hinc fponfa dicit in Canticis (cap. 5), *Dilectus meus candidus et rubicundus, electus ex millibus.* Candidus in confefforibus et virginibus, rubicundus in martyribus et apoftolis. Hi et illi funt flores rofarum et lilia convallium. Albis igitur indumentis utendum eft in feftivitatibus Confefforum et Virginum propter integritatem et innocentiam. *Nam candidi facti funt Nazaræi ejus, et ambulant femper cum eo in albis. Virgines enim funt, et fequuntur Agnum quocumque ierit.* Propter eam caufam utendum eft albis in folennitatibus fequentibus, fcilicet in folennitatibus angelorum, de quorum nitore Dominus ait ad Luciferum: *Ubi eras cum me laudarent aftra matutina?* (Job, xxxviii.) In nativitate Salvatoris et Præcurforis [326]a quoniam uterque natus eft mundus, id eft carens originali peccato. Afcendit enim Dominus fuper nubem levem, id eft fumpfit carnem a peccatis immunem, et intravit Ægyptum, id eft, venit in mundum, juxta quod Angelus ait ad virginem: *Spiritus fanctus fuperveniet in te, et virtus Altiffimi obumbrabit tibi. Ideoque quod nafcetur ex te fanctum, vocabitur Filius Dei.* Joannes autem, etfi fuit conceptus in peccato, fuit tamen fanctificatus in utero, fecundum illud propheticum: *Antequam exires de valva fanctificavi te* (Hier. i.). Nam et angelus ait ad Zachariam: *Spiritu fancto replebitur adhuc ex utero matris fuæ.* In Epiphania, propter fplendorem ftellæ, quæ Magos

---

[325] *Byffus* is here fpoken of as a colour, *i.e.* white. See note 5 (γ).
[326]a *The forerunner, i.e.* John the Baptift.

adduxit, secundum illud Propheticum: *Et ambulabunt gentes in lumine tuo et reges in splendore ortus tui* (Esa. xl.). In Hypopanti,[307] propter puritatem Mariæ, quæ juxta Canticum Simeonis obtulit lumen ad revelationem gentium, et gloriam plebis suæ Israel. In cœna Domini,[308] propter confectionem Chrismatis, quod ad mundationem animæ consecratur. Nam et evangelica lectio munditiam principaliter in illa sollennitate commendat. *Qui lotus est*, inquit, *non indiget nisi ut pedes lavet, sed est mundus totus* (Joan. xiii.) Et iterum: *Si non lavero te non habebis partem mecum.* In Resurrectione, propter angelum testem et nuncium resurrectionis, qui apparuit stola candida coopertus: de quo dicit Matthæus, quod erat aspectus ejus sicut fulgur, et vestimentum ejus sicut nix. In Ascensione, propter nubem candidam in qua Christus ascendit. Nam et duo viri steterunt juxta illos in vestibus albis, qui et dixerunt, *Viri Galilæi, quid statis aspicientes in cælum*, etc. Illud autem non otiose notandum est, quod licet in consecratione pontificis talibus indumentis sit utendum, consecrantibus scilicet et ministris (nam consecrandus semper albis utitur) qualia secundum proprietatem diei conveniunt, in dedicatione tamen Ecclesiæ semper utendum est albis, quocunque dierum dedicatio celebretur. Quoniam in consecratione pontificis cantatur missa diei, sed in dedicatione Basilicæ dedicationis missa cantatur. Nam et Ecclesia virgineo nomine nuncupatur, secundum illud Apostoli: *Despondi enim vos uni Viro virginem castam exhibere Christo.* De qua sponsus dicit in Canticis: *Tota pulchra es, amica mea, et macula non est in te. Veni de Libano, sponsa mea, veni de Libano, veni.*

Rubeis autem utendum est indumentis in solennitatibus Apostolorum et Martyrum, propter sanguinem passionis, quem pro Christo fuderunt. Nam ipsi sunt qui venerunt ex magna tribulatione, et laverunt stolas suas in sanguine Agni. In Festo Crucis, de qua Christus pro nobis sanguinem suum fudit. Unde Propheta: *Quare rubrum est indumentum tuum sicut calcantium in torculari?* Vel in Festo Crucis [309] melius est albis utendum, quia non Passionis sed Inventionis vel Exaltationis

---

[307] *Hypopanti* (a corruption of Ὑπαπάντη, or Ὑπάντη, i.e. ὑπάντησις, Salutation), one of the names by which the Feast of the Purification is designated. See Durandus, *R. D. O.* lib. vii. cap. 7, and Dufresne *in voc.*

[308] *Cœna Domini*, i.e. Thursday in Holy Week. As to the preparation of the Chrism, or holy oil, on this day, see Beleth. *Div. Off. Expl.* cap. 95.

[309] He alludes to the *Inventio Sanctæ Crucis.* "Cruce Domini inventa ab Helena matre Constantini, per Judam, ut narrat historia, festum ejus primo celebratum est Hierosolymæ. Sed Eusebius, Papa trigesimus a B. Petro, illud postea ubique terrarum celebrari præcepit." *Beleth. Div. Off. Expl.* cap. 125.

est Festum. In Pentecoste, propter sancti Spiritus fervorem, qui super Apostolos in linguis igneis apparuit. Nam apparuerunt illis dispertitæ linguæ tanquam ignis, seditque super singulos eorum. Unde Propheta: *Misit de cælo ignem ossibus meis.* Licet autem in Apostolorum Petri et Pauli martyrio rubeis sit utendum, in Conversione tamen et Cathedra [330] utendum est albis. Sicut licet in nativitate sancti Joannis albis utendum, in Decollatione tamen ipsius utendum est rubeis. Cum autem illius Festivitas celebratur qui simul est et Martyr et Virgo, martyrium præfertur virginitati, quia signum est perfectissimæ charitatis, juxta quod Veritas ait: *Majorem charitatem nemo habet quam ut animam suam ponat quis pro amicis suis.* Quapropter et in commemoratione Omnium Sanctorum quidam rubeis induuntur ornamentis, alii vero, ut Curia Romana, candidis: quum non tam in eadem quam de eadem solennitate dicat Ecclesia, quod Sancti, secundum Apocalypsim Joannis, stabant in conspectu Agni, amicti stolis [30] albis, et palmæ in manibus eorum.

Nigris autem indumentis utendum est in die afflictionis et abstinentiæ, pro peccatis, et pro defunctis. Ab Adventu scilicet usque ad Natalis vigiliam, et a Septuagesima usque ad sabbatum Paschæ.[331] Sponsa quippe dicit in Canticis: *Nigra sum sed formosa, filiæ Jerusalem, sicut tabernacula Cedar, sicut pellis Salomonis. Nolite me considerare quod fusca sim, quia decoloravit me sol.* In Innocentum autem die quidam nigris, alii vero rubeis, indumentis utendum esse contendunt. Illi propter tristitiam, quia vox in Rhama audita est, ploratus et ululatus multus, Rachel plorans filios suos, et noluit consolari quia non sunt. Nam propter eandem causam Cantica lætitiæ subticentur, et non in aurifrigio Mitra [332] defertur. Isti propter martyrium, quod principaliter commemorans inquit Ecclesia: *Sub throno Dei Sancti clamabant, vindica sanguinem nostrum qui effusus est, Deus noster.* Propter tristitiam ergo, quam et silentium innuit lætitiæ canticorum, Mitra quæ fertur non est aurifrigio insignita, sed propter martyrium rubeis est

---

[330] *Cathedra*, i.e. Cathedra Petri. "De Cathedra S. Petri Ecclesia sollennizat, quando videlicet apud Antiochiam Cathedrali honore sublimatus esse perhibetur." *Durandus, R. D. O.* lib. viii. cap. 8.

[331] *Sabbatum Paschæ*, i.e. Easter-Eve.

[332] *Non in aurifrigio, &c.* He means that a plain mitre is to be used without any golden or embroidered band. The later Roman Liturgists distinguish three kinds of mitres, the Plain Mitre (*simplex*) made of linen; the Orfreyed Mitre (*Mitra aurifrigiata*, see note 312, p. 152, or *Mitra solennis*); and the Precious Mitre (*Mitra preciosa*), in which the inner Cap (*Mitra*, see note 288\*) is almost entirely concealed by plates made of the precious metals encrusted with jewels.

indumentis utendum. Hodie utimur violaceis: ficut in *Lætare Hieru-salem*,[333] propter lætitiam quam Aurea Rofa fignificat, Romanus Pontifex portat Mitram aurifrifio infignitam, fed propter abftinentiam nigris, immo violaceis utitur indumentis.

Reftat ergo quod in diebus ferialibus et communibus viridibus fit indumentis utendum. Quia viridis color medius eft inter albedinem et nigredinem et ruborem. Hic color exprimitur ubi dicitur (Cant. iv.): *Cypri cum nardo, Nardus et Crocus.*

Ad hos quattuor cæteri referuntur. Ad rubeum colorem coccineus, ad nigrum violaceus, ad viridem croceus. Quamvis nonnulli rofas ad Martyres, crocum ad Confeffores, lilium ad Virgines referunt.[333 a]

---

[333] He alludes to the fpecial obfervances (at Rome) of Mid-Lent Sunday, when the Golden Rofe is carried in folemn proceffion by the Pope. "In hac Dominica (4th S. in Lent) Romanus Pontifex celebraturus ad eccleſiam pergens et rediens ab eadem auream in manu... fert rofam... (*This Rofe is then given to one whom the Pope defires fpecially to honour.*) ... Demum ille cum multo equitatu et lætitia ingenti civitatem cum rofa circuit, *figurans gaudium illius populi in civitatem Hierufalem reverfi.*" *Durandus, R. D. O.* lib. vi. cap. 53.

[333 a] The Veftments of the Roman Church, with the "four Sacred Colours (p. 161) which the Roman Church affigns as proper to various feftivals," are here for the firft time defcribed in their complete development. From the time of this Treatife there have been flight varieties in detail introduced from time to time, in refpect of fhape and ornamentation, but the "*Sacræ Veftes*" of Biſhop, Prieft, and Deacon, proper to the Roman Church, have been accepted, as here defcribed, to this day. [For the "Surplice," which is not mentioned by Innocent III., fee *infra*, p. 166, and Index *in voc.*]

## XXXIX.

## DVRANDI MIMATENSIS EPISCOPI [314] RATIONALE [315] DIVINORVM OFFICIORVM.

### LIB. III. DE VESTIBUS SACRIS.

#### CAP. I. CHANGE IN CLERICAL DRESS IN NINTH CENTURY,

. . . Nota quod tempore Ludovici Imperatoris filii Caroli Magni, Episcopi et Clerici cingula auro texta, exquifitas veftes, et alia fecularia ornamenta depofuerunt.[316]

#### EPISCOPAL VESTMENTS REGARDED AS SPIRITUAL ARMOUR.

. . . Rurfus Pontifex verfus Aquilonem fufpiciens, quamvis verfus Orientem feu verfus altare, fi fit magis accommodum, refpicere poffit, tanquam advocatus feu pugil cum hofte pugnaturus antiquo, veftibus facris quafi armis induitur, juxta Apoftolum, ut jam dicetur. Primo fandalia pro ocreis habet, ne quid maculæ vel pulveris affectionum inhæreat. Secundo Amictus pro galea [note 178, p. 94] caput contegit. Tertio Alba pro lorica totum corpus cooperit. Quarto cingulum pro arcu, fubcingulum [317] pro pharetra affumit: et eft fubcingulum illud quod dependet a cingulo, quo Stola Pontificis cum ipfo

---

[314] Durandus (Gulielmus), born in France circ. 1232 A.D. Bifhop of Mende 1287; died 1296 A.D. The bafis of the text is that of Cellier, Lugduni, MDCLXXII; a very defective one, the punctuation particularly being fuch as often to make nonfenfe of fuch fentences as prefent any difficulties of interpretation. Here, as elfewhere, I have made no alterations, except in punctuation, without notice to the reader.

[315] The third book of this Treatife is entirely occupied with the fubject of veftments. But it confifts in great meafure of large extracts from older writers, many of which have already been before the reader of the prefent work. I have therefore only felected thofe paffages which add to thefe older writers any thing of importance to the fubject of this Treatife.

[316] One effect of the reftoration of an Imperial power in the Weft was that of reftraining the tendency to extravagant fumptuoufnefs and fplendour in the fecular drefs of fome among the Clergy. See, for example, what is faid of Archbifhop Ethelbert by Dr. Hook (*Lives of the Archbifhops of Canterbury*, vol. i. p. 262).

[317] See note 313, p. 153, on the word *fuccinctorium*, which is equivalent to the *fubcingulum* of Durandus.

cingulo colligatur. Quinto, Stola collum circumdans, qua (*Leg.* quasi) hastam contra hostem vibrans. Sexto, manipulo pro clava utitur. Septimo, Casula quasi clypeo tegitur. Manus Libro pro gladio armatur. De singulis etiam aliter dicetur infra. Hæc itaque sunt arma quibus Pontifex vel Sacerdos armari debet contra spirituales nequitias pugnaturus.

## DIFFERENCE IN NUMBER BETWEEN THE VESTMENTS OF THE LAW AND OF THE GOSPEL.

. . . . Quindecim ergo sunt ornamenta Pontificis . . . Sic ergo noster Pontifex [336] plura quam octo induit vestimenta quamvis Aaron non nisi octo habuisse legatur; quibus moderna succedunt. Quod ideo est quoniam oportet justitiam nostram magis abundare quam Scribarum et Pharisæorum; ut intrare possimus in regnum cælorum. Potest etiam dici quod noster Pontifex octo habet a capite usque ad pedes, exceptis vestimentis pedum et manuum; scilicet Amictum, Albam, Cingulum, et Stolam, duas Tunicas, Casulam et Pallium, Vestimentum enim pedum potius pertinet ad nostros quam ad Aaron: quia nostris dictum est, *Euntes docete omnes gentes*, etc.

## THE SURPLICE.

Denique præter præmissas vestes sacris ordinibus et ministris deputatas, est et alia quædam vestis linea, quæ Superpelliceum dicitur, quod quibuslibet servitiis altaris et sacrorum vacantes super vestes communes uti debent: prout in sequente titulo dicetur. Superpelliceum autem primo, propter sui candorem, munditiam seu puritatem castitatis designat: Juxta illud, *Omni tempore vestimenta*, id est, opera tua, *sint candida et munda*. Propter nomen vero suum carnis mortificationem figurat secundo. Dictum est enim Superpelliceum eo quod antiquitus super tunicas pellicias de pellibus mortuorum animalium factas induebatur; quod adhuc in quibusdam ecclesiis observatur, repræsentantes (*sic*) quod Adam post peccatum talibus vestitus est pelliciis. Tertio denotat innocentiam; et ideo ante omnes alias vestes sacras sæpe induitur, quia divino cultui deputati innocentia vitæ cunctis virtutum actibus superpollere debent; juxta illud Psalmistæ, *Innocentes*

---

[336] *Pontifex noster, i.e.* the Pontiff (Bishop) of us Christians in contrast with Aaron the | "*Pontifex in Lege.*" Compare note 194, p. 101.

*et recti adhæserunt mihi.* Quarto propter sui latitudinem congrue charitatem designat. Unde super profanas et communes vestes induitur ad notandum quod Charitas operit multitudinem peccatorum.

Quinto propter sui formam, quia in modum crucis formatur, Passionem Domini figurat, quodque illud gerentes crucifigi debent cum vitiis et cum concupiscentiis.

Fiunt autem Superpellicea in quibusdam locis de crismalibus lineis quæ ponuntur super infantulos baptizatos: exemplo Moisi qui de purpura et bysso, et aliis a populo in tabernaculo oblatis, fecit vestes quibus Aaron et filii ejus induerentur, quando ministrabant in Sanctuario.

### The Pluvial or Cope.

Est etiam et alia vestis quæ Pluviale [339] vel Cappa vocatur, quæ creditur a legali tunica mutuata. Unde sicut illa tintinnabulis, sic ista fimbriis infigitur (*Leg.* insignitur), quæ sunt labores, hujus mundi solicitudines. Habet etiam caputium, quod est supernum gaudium. Prolixa est usque ad pedes, per quod perseverantia usque in finem significatur. In anteriori parte aperta est, ad denotandum quod sancte conversantibus vita patet æterna, seu quod eorum vita patere debet aliis in exemplum . . . Rursus per Cappam gloriosa corporum immortalitas intelligitur. Unde illam non nisi in majoribus festivitatibus induimus, aspicientes in futuram resurrectionem quando electi, deposita carne, binas stolas accipient, videlicet requiem animarum et gloriam corporum. Quæ Cappa recte interius patula est, nisi et [*Leg.* et nisi] sola necessaria fibula inconsuta, quia corpora spiritualia facta nullis animam obturabunt angustiis. Fimbriis etiam subornantur, quia tunc nostræ nihil deerit imperfectioni; sed quod nunc ex parte cognoscimus tunc cognoscemus sicut et cogniti sumus.

---

[339] The name *pluviale* ("parapluie," as it were), and the Cape or Hood from which was derived the name *Cappa*, and our own "Cope," point to the origin of the vestment as originally worn out of doors *for protection from the weather*. The form of the later ecclesiastical cope may be seen in Plate LI., where it is worn by the bishops officiating at the Coronation of Henry VI. The memory of the original hood is still preserved in the peculiar ornament on the back of the Cope, upon which the outline of a small cape or round hood is traced in embroidery. See, for example, Bock, *L. G.* vol. ii. pl. xli. [The Cappa is mentioned as one of the monastic habits early in the eleventh century. See *Thomassinus De Ben.* part i. lib. ii. cap. 48, p. 332.]

## XL.

# SYMEON
# PATRIARCHA THESSALONICENSIS.[340]

Περὶ τῆς ἱερᾶς λειτουργίας.

Κεφ. πι. περὶ τοῦ ἀρχιερατικοῦ Μανδύου [341] τε καὶ τοῦ Ἐγκολπίου [342] καὶ τῆς ποιμαντικῆς ῥάβδου.

Τυθέντος οὖν καὶ θανόντος καὶ ἀναστάντος καὶ ἀπελθόντος Χριστοῦ ὑπὲρ ἡμῶν, τότε τὸ Πνεῦμα κατῆλθε, καὶ τὴν χάριν ἐλάβομεν. Καὶ ἐκ τῆς καρδίας τῶν πιστῶν οἱ ποταμοὶ [343] τῶν δωρεῶν [344] ῥέουσι. Καὶ τοῦτο δηλοῖ ὁ Μανδύας. Καὶ ἡ σφραγὶς δὲ καὶ ὁμολογία τῆς πίστεως ἐν τῷ τοῦ ἀρχιερέως στήθει ἐκκρεμαμένη διὰ σταυροῦ ἢ ἐγκολπίου τινος. Καὶ τοῦτο γὰρ ἐν τῷ στήθει διὰ τὴν ἐκ καρδίας ὁμολογίαν.

Ἡ ῥάβδος [345] δὲ, ἣν κατέχει, τὴν ἐξουσίαν δηλοῖ τοῦ Πνεύματος, καὶ τὸ στηρικτικὸν τοῦ λαοῦ, καὶ τὸ ποιμαντικὸν, καὶ τὸ ὁδηγεῖν δύνασθαι, καὶ τὸ παιδεύειν τοὺς ἀπειθοῦντας, καὶ τὸ συνάγειν εἰς ἑαυτὸν τοὺς μακράν. Διὸ καὶ λαβὰς ὡς ἀγκύρας ἄνωθεν ἔχει. Καὶ τὸ διώκειν τοὺς θηριώδεις τε καὶ λυμαντικούς. Καὶ τελευταῖον τὸν σταυρὸν τοῦ Χριστοῦ δηλοῖ, καὶ τὸ τροπαῖον, ἐν ᾧ καὶ νικῶμεν, καὶ στηριζόμεθα, καὶ ὁδηγούμεθα, καὶ ποιμανόμεθα, καὶ σφραγι-

---

[340] The writer, here quoted, occupied the See of Thessalonica from circ. 1410 to 1429 A.D. This Treatise was first made known in the West by Jacobus Pontanus, a zealous partisan, who, if Cave speak truly (*Hist. Lit.* ii. p. 113), was anything but a trustworthy editor.

[341] In this chapter he describes the ordinary dress of a Bishop; his dress of ministry is spoken of in the chapter following. The Mantle, with its three stripes, technically called ποταμοί, and the Pastoral Staff may be seen in the representation of Patriarch Bekkos among the illustrations of this volume. See Plate LIX.

[342] ἐγκόλπιον. See above, note 315, p. 158.

[343] This is used in allusion to Jo. vii. 38, 39. "*He that believeth on me . . . out of his belly shall flow rivers of living water. This spake He of the Spirit which they that believe on Him should receive.*"

[344] δωρεά is here correctly used of a gift from God to man. Δῶρον, on the other hand, is properly a gift, or offering to homage, from man to God. See *Eirenica*, vol. i. p. 187 (foot-note.)

[345] In the Greek Church the Staff has not the form of a shepherd's crook, as commonly it has in the West, but retains the semblance rather of a staff such as men might use in walking. The handle is set on cross-wise like the horizontal line of the letter T, but the extremities of this handle are generally turned up slightly, and terminate in some carved ornament. See the Figure referred to in note 341.

ζόμεθα, καὶ παιδαγωγούμεθα, καὶ ἑλκόμεθα εἰς Χριστὸν τὰ πάθη νεκροῦντες, καὶ τοὺς πολεμίους διώκομεν, καὶ πάντοθεν φυλαττόμεθα.

### Κεφ. πά. Περὶ τῶν ἱερῶν τοῦ ἀρχιερέως ἐνδυμάτων.

Ὁ δὲ ἀρχιερεὺς ἐνδύεται μὲν ὡς εἰρήκαμεν τὸ Στιχάριον,[346] ὡς ἔνδυμα ἀφθαρσίας φωτεινὸν καὶ ἁγιωσύνης, τὸ καθαρὸν καὶ φωτιστικὸν[347] Ἰησοῦ, καὶ τὸ τῶν Ἀγγέλων ἁγνὸν καὶ λαμπρὸν, δηλοῖ. Καὶ τὴν εὐχὴν φησὶν ἀπὸ τοῦ ψαλμοῦ· Ἀγαλλιάσεται ἡ ψυχή μου ἐπὶ τῷ Κυρίῳ. Εἶτα τὸ Ἐπιτραχήλιον,[348] τὸ ἄνωθεν ἐκ τοῦ οὐρανοῦ ἀπὸ κεφαλῆς δοθεῖσαν χάριν σημαῖνον. Καὶ ἡ εὐχὴ τοῦτο φησίν· Εὐλογητὸς ὁ Θεὸς ὁ ἐκχέων τὴν χάριν αὐτοῦ ἐπὶ τοὺς Ἱερεῖς αὐτοῦ. Εἶτα τὴν ζώνην, τὴν ἀπὸ Θεοῦ ἰσχὺν ἐκτυποῦσαν περὶ τὴν ὀσφὺν τιθεμένη. Καὶ ἡ εὐχὴ μαρτυρεῖ ἐν τῷ περιζωννύεσθαι φησὶ γὰρ, Εὐλογητὸς ὁ Θεὸς ὁ περιζωννύων με δύναμιν. Ἅμα δὲ καὶ τὸ τῆς διακονίας ἔργον δηλοῖ. Ὁ γὰρ διακονῶν περιζώννυται. Καὶ ἔτι τὴν σωφροσύνην καὶ ἁγνείαν, ἐπὶ τοὺς νεφροὺς κειμένη καὶ τὴν ὀσφύν.

Ἔπειτα τὸ Ἐπιγονάτιον,[349] τὸ κατὰ τοῦ θανάτου νίκην δηλοῦν, καὶ τὴν τοῦ Σωτῆρος ἀνάστασιν, ὅπερ καὶ ὡς σχῆμα ῥομφαίας ἔχει. Καὶ ἡ εὐχὴ τοῦτο φησί· Περίζωσαι τὴν ῥομφαίαν σου ἐπὶ τὸν μηρόν σου, δυνατέ. Ἐκ τούτου καὶ τὴν δύναμιν καὶ τὴν νίκην, καὶ τὴν ἔγερσιν τοῦ Χριστοῦ, διὰ τῆς καθαρότητος καὶ ἀναμαρτησίας, δηλῶν (Leg. δηλοῖ.) Διὰ τοῦτο γὰρ καὶ αὐτὸ ἐπὶ τῆς ὀσφύος ἐκκρέμαται. Καὶ τῇ ὡραιότητί σου καὶ τῷ κάλλει σου, φησὶ, καὶ ἔντεινε καὶ κατευοδοῦ καὶ βασίλευε, ἕνεκεν ἀληθείας καὶ πραότητος καὶ δικαιοσύνης. . . .

Εἶτα λαμβάνει τὰ ἐπιμανίκια.[350] Ἃ δὴ τὸ παντουργικὸν σημαίνουσι τοῦ Θεοῦ. Καὶ ἡ εὐχὴ τοῦτο λέγει· Ἡ δεξιά σου, Κύριε, δεδόξασται ἐν ἰσχύϊ.

---

[346] Στιχάριον. The derivation of this word is uncertain. It is the term which in the Greek Church answers to the *alba* (or *tunica alba*) of the West.

[347] The Sticharion as being *white* sets forth τὸ φωτιστικὸν Ἰησοῦ. With this symbolism of white garments compare Clemens Alex *Pædag.* iii. p. 286. εἰρήνεως ἀνέχονται καὶ φωτεινοῖς καπέλλωλως τὸ λευκόν.

[348] Ἐπιτραχήλιον *i. e.* what in the Western Church would be called a stole. See note 144, p. 84.

[349] τὸ Ἐπιγονάτιον. This ornament may be seen in the figures of St. Methodius and St. Germanus among the illustrations of this volume, Pl. LVIII. The germ of this ornament may be seen in the somewhat similar ornaments on the imperial dresses of Justinian and his courtiers, (known in the language of the time as *paragauda*) in the Mosaic of the Church of S. Vitalis at Ravenna. See Pl. XXVIII.

[350] Ἐπιμανίκια. A Byzantine word, half Greek and half Latin, like many others of similar character. By derivation it will mean "what is added to, or set upon, the sleeve;" and hence its actual usage as a designation of the cuffs, worn on either arm, by bishops and priests in the Greek Church. Their form may be seen in those of Bishop Nikitas, figured among the illustrations of this volume. Pl. LVI.

Καὶ τὸ· Αἱ χεῖρές σου ἐποίησάν με καὶ ἔπλασάν με. Ἔτι δὲ καὶ τὸ ταῖς χερσὶν ἱερουργῆσαι τὰ μυστήρια ἑαυτοῦ. Καὶ τὸ τὰς χεῖρας διδῆναι.

Εἶτα τὸ Φαινόλιον,[351] ἢ Σάκκος [352] ὂν ἢ Πολυσταύριον,[353] ἃ δὴ τὴν ἐν τῷ πάθει σημαίνουσι χλαῖναν. Καὶ τὸν Σάκκον μᾶλλον ὁ Σάκκος.[354] Καὶ τὸ Πολυσταύριον δέ. Ἀλλὰ καὶ τὴν προνοητικὴν καὶ φρουρητικὴν ἐν πᾶσι καὶ συνεκτικὴν χάριν τοῦ Θεοῦ, δι' ἣν καὶ καθ' ἡμᾶς ὤφθη, καὶ τὰ πάθη ὑπήνεγκε.

### Κεφ. σβ΄. Τὸ Ὠμοφόριον.

Καὶ τελευταῖον τὸ Ὠμοφόριον,[355] ὃ ἀπὸ τῶν ὤμων ἑλίττων τὴν τοῦ πλανηθέντος προβάτου τῶν ἀνθρώπων ἡμῶν δηλοῖ σωτηρίαν τε καὶ ἀνάκλησιν. Οὗ δὴ καὶ τὴν μορφὴν ἀνέλαβεν ὁ Σωτὴρ, ἐν ᾗ καὶ παθὼν διὰ Σταυροῦ ἡμᾶς ἔσωσι. Οὗτοι καὶ ἐξ ἐρίου. Καὶ ἔμπροσθέν τε καὶ ὄπισθεν καὶ ἐπὶ τοῦ στήθους σταυροειδῶς τέσσαρας ἔχει σταυροὺς τὴν σταύρωσιν ἐκτυποῦντας. Καὶ οὕτω μὲν στολισάμενος ἵσταται ὁ ἀρχιερεύς.

### Κεφ. σγ΄. Τὰ πέντε ἄμφια τῶν ἱερέων.

[*After describing the ceremonies with which the Liturgy begins, he proceeds as follows:*]

Ἀπέρχεται οὖν οὗτος [*sc. ὁ ἱερεύς*] καὶ μετὰ τῶν ἄλλων ἱερέων τὰ ἱερατικὰ

---

[351] φαινόλιον. For the *form* of the word as compared with the older φαινόλης, equivalent to *pænula*, see note 153, p. 86. The primitive forms of this vestment may be seen (Pl. XXVII.) in the figure of Eusebius of Cæsarea (from the Syriac MS. at Florence), or in that of St. Sampson, among the illustrations of this volume, Pl. LVI.

[352] Σάκκος. This is a close-fitting vestment worn in place of the φαινόλιον by Metropolitans, as a mark of distinctive dignity. See Goar, *Euchol. Gr.* p. 113. Its form may be seen in the figure of St. Germanus in Pl. LVIII.

[353] Πολυσταύριον, i.e. a Phænolion marked with crosses over its entire surface. It is worn by Bishops generally, or at least was so in the time of St. Symeon here quoted. In his treatise *De Templo* (quoted by Goar, *Euch. Gr.* p. 113) he says, οἱ λοιποὶ τῶν ἀρχιερέων (i.e. those not having metropolitan dignity) τὸ φιλόνιον πλῆρες σταυρῶν ἐνδύονται· ὃ δὴ καὶ πολυσταύριον ὁ λόγος καλεῖν εἴδε.

[354] These words are explained by what the Patriarch says in another passage (*De Templo*, apud Goar, *Euchol. Græc.* p. 113), ἐξαιρέτως δὲ δι' ἐνδύματος ἱματιζόμενος ὁ Σωτὴρ ἐξεικονίζει σάκκον· διὸ καὶ σάκκον τοῦτον ἔχει. Οὐδὶ γὰρ ἔχει τοῦτο ἃ καλοῦσι μανίκια. Ἀριδηλότερον δὲ τοῦτο παρίστησι καὶ ὁ ἐνδύοντας οἱ ἱερέων τῶν ἀρχιερέων, σάκκον καὶ τοῦτο καλούμενον.

[355] τὸ ὠμοφόριον. This vestment, mentioned first by St. Isidore of Pelusium (see p. 49), and again by St. Germanus (see p. 85), has from the earliest times been worn by all Greek bishops, whether Metropolitans or others. In form, too, it has varied but little, if at all, from the earliest times in which we find it represented, even to the present day. It is worn by all the bishops represented in the picture of the Second Council of Nicæa (Pl. XLI. of the illustrations of this volume), and may be seen also in the figures of St. Methodius and St. Germanus already referred to. An Omophorion of the fourteenth century, that of Archbishop Moses, is figured in Plate LVI.

περιβάλλεται ἄμφια. . . . Ἔκαστον εὐλογεῖ ὡς καὶ ὁ Ἀρχιερεὺς τῶν ἱερῶν ἐνδυμάτων τε καὶ ἀσπάζεται, καὶ οὕτω δὴ περιβάλλεται, δεικνὺς ὡς ἡγιασμένα εἰσι, καὶ ἐν τῷ σταυρῷ τοῦ Χριστοῦ ἁγιάζεται, καὶ ἁγιασμοῦ μεταδοτικά εἰσι πάλιν ἐπενδυόμενα. Περιβάλλεται οὖν πέντε ἐνδύματα, ὡς τέλειος καὶ αὐτὸς, καὶ τελειοποιὸν ἔχων χάριν. Πέντε γὰρ αἱ τέλειαί εἰσιν αἰσθήσεις τοῦ σώματος, καὶ πέντε αἱ δυνάμεις τῆς ψυχῆς ἃς καὶ ὁ Ἰησοῦς ἁγιάζει βαπτίζων καὶ ἁγιάζων τὸν ἄνθρωπον. Ἔστι δὲ ἃ ἐνδύεται, Στιχάριον, Ἐπιτραχήλιον, Ζώνη, Ἐπιμανίκια, καὶ Φαινόλιον. Λευκὰ δὲ ταῦτα, διὰ τὸ καθαρὸν τῆς χάριτός τε καὶ φωτεινόν.

Πολλάκις δὲ καὶ πορφύρεα κατὰ καιρὸν τῶν νηστειῶν, διά γε τὸ πενθεῖν ἡμᾶς ἁμαρτήσαντας, καὶ διὰ τὸν σφαγέντα ὑπὲρ ἡμῶν, ἵν' εἰς ὑπόμνησιν ἐλθόντες τοῦ πάθους αὐτοῦ, αὐτὸν μιμησώμεθα ὃ (fort. ὃν) καὶ μέλλομεν ἑορτάζειν. Τινὲς δὲ τῶν πρώτων πρεσβυτέρων, ἤτοι οἱ Σταυροφόροι,[356] τῶν Ἀρχιμανδριτῶν τε τινὲς, καὶ ἐπιγονάτιον ἔχουσι· τοῦτο γὰρ κατὰ δωρεὰν ἐστιν ἀρχιερατικὴν ὡς καὶ ὁ Σταυρός. Οὐδεὶς γὰρ πλὴν τοῦ Ἀρχιερέως τοὺς σταυροὺς τε ἐν τῷ φαινολίῳ καὶ ἐπὶ κεφαλῆς, καὶ τὸ Ἐπιγονάτιον φορεῖν, δύναται. Τούτοις δὲ ὅμως, διὰ τὸ πρώτους τῶν ἄλλων χειροτονεῖσθαι, τὸ ἐπὶ κεφαλῆς ἔχειν σταυρὸν μόνον, καὶ ἐπιγονάτιον ἐν τῇ ἱερουργίᾳ φορεῖν, δίδοται.[357]

## THE MANDYAS, OR MANTLE, OF THE BISHOP, THE PECTORAL CROSS, AND PASTORAL STAFF.

AFTER that Christ for us had been sacrificed, had died, and risen again, and gone up on high, then did the Spirit come down from above, and we received the grace of God. And now out of the hearts of the faithful flow the rivers [345] of the divine gifts.[346] And this is set forth by the

---

[356] οἱ σταυροφόροι. Certain of the clergy at the principal Church at Constantinople had the privilege of wearing a cross upon their cowls. See above note 152, p. 86.

[357] From this passage we find that in the fifteenth century the recognised vestments of the Greek Church were, with few additions only, identical with those described by St. Germanus seven centuries earlier. St. Germanus mentions Sticharion, Peritrachelion (or Epitrachelion), and Phelonion, adding mention of the Omophorion as a distinctive vestment (τοῦ ἀρχιερέως), worn by bishops. To these we now find added the cuffs (common to priests and bishops), and the " Epigonation," the latter worn by bishops only. On the other hand, the ἐγχείριον, or napkin, mentioned as characteristic of a deacon by Germanus, finds no place in this later notice.

Lastly, the σάκκος (note 352) and the πολυσταύριον (note 353) spoken of in the later treatise, do not appear to have been known to the earlier of the two writers. Nor does St. Germanus make mention of a pastoral staff, or a pectoral cross, as being in his time distinctive insignia of a bishop.

But even with the additions here noticed the seven sacred vestments of the Greek bishop stand contrasted in their greater simplicity and close adherence to antiquity, with the fifteen enumerated by Innocent III., and retained to this day by the Roman Church.

Mantle. The Seal, too, and profession of the Faith, is suspended on the breast of the Bishop by a Cross, or Pectoral ornament. For this also is worn upon the Breast, because of the profession which from the heart is made.

Then the Staff,[145] which he holdeth, showeth forth the power of the Spirit, and what appertaineth to the confirming and pastoral care of God's people, and the power to guide, and the chastising of them that are disobedient, and the gathering unto himself of them that are afar off. Wherefore also it hath handles[148] on the upper part thereof, like unto anchors. It signifieth also the pursuing of them that are fierce in spirit and injurious. And, lastly, it setteth forth the Cross of Christ, and the memorial of victory, wherein we are both conquerors ourselves, and are strengthened, and guided, and shepherded, and sealed, and led by the hand, and drawn unto Christ, mortifying our evil affections, wherewith also we pursue our foes, and are protected on every side.

### CAP. 81. THE SEVEN SACRED VESTMENTS OF A BISHOP.

But the (chief priest) Bishop putteth upon him, as we have said, the Sticharion,[146] as a lightsome garment of immortality and holiness, setting forth the pure and light-giving nature of Jesus, and the holiness and brightness of the angels. And the prayer that he saith is from the Psalm, "*My soul shall rejoice in the Lord.*"

Then he putteth on the Epitrachelion,[148] which is a sign of grace given from above out of heaven, proceeding from the Head. And this doth the prayer express, "*Blessed be God, who poureth out His grace upon His priests.*"

Then the Girdle, setting forth in figure the strength which is from God, in that this is laid about the loins. And to this doth the prayer witness, which at the girding is used, "*Blessed be God who girdeth me about with power.*" By it is likewise signified the work of ministry, for it appertaineth to one who ministers that he wear a girdle. And yet again it is a sign of soberness and chaste purity, resting as it does upon the reins and loins.

After this he putteth on the Genual,[149] which setteth forth Victory over Death, and the Resurrection of the Saviour, which also is worn after the fashion of a sword. And this doth the prayer say, "*Gird thee with thy sword upon thy thigh, thou mighty one.*" And because of this doth it set forth both the power, and the victory, and the rising of Christ from the dead, by the purity and sinlessness thereof. For this is the cause wherefore this vestment also is suspended from the loins. "*In the prime of thy might and in thy beauty,*" saith he, "*hold on thy way, and prosper, and reign, because of Truth, and Meekness, and Righteousness.*"

Next after this he taketh the Cuffs.[350] By these is signified the pervading energy of God. And to this do the words of the prayer apply, "*Thy right hand, O Lord, is glorified in strength.*" And again, "*Thy hands made me and fashioned me.*" By them, too, is figured His consecrating with His hands the mysteries of Himself. And, again, that of His hands being bound.

Next followeth the Phænolion,[351] either Saccos,[352] or Polystaurion,[353] by which is signified the outer robe which He bare at the time of His passion. And by the Saccos that he wears is signified rather the like garment of Christ.[354] And so, too, may we say of the Polystaurion. Though by this is shown also the grace of God, provident and protective in all things, and maintenant, by reason of which He both appeared among us men, and endured those His sufferings.

### CAP. 82. THE OMOPHORION.

Last of all, he taketh the Omophorion,[355] which he rolleth out (unfolds) from his shoulders, and so setteth forth the saving and recalling to the fold of the lost sheep of our Humanity. Of which sheep the Saviour did assume the form; wherein also He suffered, and so saved us by the cross. And this is the reason that it is made of wool. And both behind and in front, and upon the breast, it hath four crosses, arranged crosswise, figuring forth the Crucifixion.

Such is the fashion in which the Bishop doth stand arrayed.

### CAP. 83. THE FIVE VESTMENTS OF THE PRIEST.

[*After describing the ceremonies with which the Liturgy begins, he proceeds as follows:*]

The Priest then goeth thence, and with the other Priests putteth upon him the sacerdotal garments. He blesseth each of the sacred vestments, and kisseth it, even as does the chief-priest (Bishop). And having so done he putteth it about him, showing by that he doeth that they have been consecrated, and are made holy by the cross of Christ, and impart holiness now that again they are put on. Five garments accordingly he putteth about him, as being himself consummate, and endowed with consummating grace. For five is the full number of the bodily senses; and five the powers of the soul, which are sanctified by Jesus when He baptizeth man and sanctifieth him. And the vestments that the Priest putteth on are these, Sticharion [note 346], Epitrachelion, Girdle, Cuffs, Phænolion. And these are white, because of the purity and illumination that belongeth to grace. But oftentimes too they are purple, in times of fast, because of our mourning in respect of sin, and because of Him who on our behalf was slain, in order that being put in remembrance of His passion we may follow the example of Him, whose feast also we are about to keep.

But some of the principal presbyters, the Cross-wearers as they are called, and certain of the Archimandrites, wear a Genual also; for this is a matter of episcopal favour, as is also the wearing of a cross. For none save the Bishop hath power to wear both the crosses (on the Phænolion and the head) and the Genual. Yet, nevertheless, those of whom I now speak, because of their being ordained with precedence over others, have given unto them the right to wear a cross upon the head only, and a Genual, when occupied in the holy office.[357]

# APPENDIX.

## A.

### ASSOCIATIONS OF COLOUR IN PRIMITIVE TIMES, AND MORE PARTICULARLY IN THE FIRST FOUR CENTURIES OF CHRISTIAN HISTORY.

PART I. PASSAGES OF PROFANE AUTHORS QUOTED [358] OR ALLUDED TO IN THE INTRODUCTION.

1. Plato, *De Leg.* xii. p. 956. [He is speaking of the kind of offerings which may with most propriety be offered to the gods: and he says], ὑφὴν δὲ μὴ πλίον ἔργον [359] γυναικὸς μιᾶς ἔμμηνον· χρώματα δὲ λευκὰ πρέποντ' ἂν εἴη θεοῖς, καὶ ἄλλοθι καὶ ἐν ὑφῇ· βάμματα δὲ μὴ προσφέρειν ἀλλ' ἢ πρὸς τὰ πολέμου κοσμήματα.

2. *Ibid.* p. 947. He is speaking of the honours to be paid to the "Most Worthy" citizens in the Commonwealth: that they shall have precedence in all Public Assemblies; shall represent the State in solemn religious Embassies; shall alone among all be crowned with Bay; shall be Priests, all of them, of Apollo and of Helios, and one among them be high-priest in each year, and that by his name (as Eponymus) the year shall be known. He then adds:—

τελευτήσασι δὲ προθέσεις τε καὶ ἐκφορὰς καὶ θήκας διαφόρους εἶναι τῶν ἄλλων πολιτῶν, λευκὴν μὲν τὴν στολὴν ἱσας πάσας κ.τ.λ.

"When they die let them be marked out from all other citizens both by the state in which they are set out, and by their carrying out to burial, and by the tombs to which they are committed; and let their apparel be all of white," etc.

---

[358] Where a translation of any of these passages has already been given in the Introduction, none is given in this Appendix, nor in cases where no difficulty of any kind obscures the meaning of the author. In other passages I have endeavoured to supply, either by full Translations or by Notes, what appeared necessary for the elucidation of meaning.

[359] μὴ πλίον, κ. τ. λ. He means that the labour expended upon it should not be more than would occupy o e pair of hands for a month. See the translation of what follows, and the explanatory note, Introduction, cap. iii. p. xviii. y.

With this of white apparel wherein to array the dead we may compare the passage that follows:—

3. Plutarch, *Quæst. Rom.* τὸ σῶμα τοῦ τεθνηκότος ἀμφιεννύουσι λευκοῖς, ὅτι μὴ δύναται τὴν ψυχήν· βούλεται δὲ ἐκείνην λαμπρὰν καὶ καθαρὰν προπέμπειν, ὡς προειμένην ἤδη, καὶ διηγωνισμένην μέγαν ἀγῶνα [360] καὶ ποικίλον.

"The body of the dead they array in white, seeing that they cannot so clothe his soul; and their desire therein is to attend it, all bright and pure, to the grave, as one already released from the body, and that has contended even to the end in the great and chequered battle of life."

4. Horace, *Sat.* ii. 61. White, the colour of social, and in some sort religious, festival, whether of marriage, birthdays, or the like.

> *Licebit*
> *Ille repotia,*[361] *natales, aliusve dierum*
> *Festos albatus celebret.*

5. Ovid. *Trist.* lib. iii., xii. [He is writing on his Birthday].

> *Scilicet expectes soliti tibi moris honorem*
> *Pendeat*[362] *ex humeris vestis ut alba meis?*

6. Ovid, lib. v. el. 5. [He writes now of his Wife's Birthday],

> *Annuus adsuetum Dominæ natalis honorem*
> *Exigit . . . .*
> *Quæque semel toto vestis mihi sumitur anno*
> *Sumatur satis discolor alba meis.*

"Though because of his unhappy condition he should rather be wearing mourning, yet will he, in honour of this day, put on the white robe (*toga*) of festival."

7. Persius, *Sat.* ii.

> *Negato*
> *Jupiter hoc illi quamvis albata rogarit.*

"Let the gods deny her request, even though (clad in white, *and so*) with all solemnity of outward worship her prayer be uttered."

8. Donatus *on Terence* (apud Wetstenium in Matt. xxvii. 28) *Læto vestitus*

---

[360] An echo one might almost believe of a thought yet finer and more far reaching still: τὸν ἀγῶνα τὸν καλὸν ἠγώνισμαι τὸν δρόμον τετέλεκα· λοιπὸν ἀπόκειταί μοι ὁ τῆς δικαιοσύνης στέφανος ὃν ἀποδώσει μοι ὁ Κύριος ἐν ἐκείνῃ τῇ ἡμέρᾳ, κ. τ. λ.

[361] *Repotia.* The return feast given by the bridegroom on the day after a marriage. *Festus apud Scheller*: "Repotia postridie nuptias apud novum maritum cænatur. Quia quasi reficitur potatio."

[362] *Pendeat ex humeris.* Note this expression as suggesting that it is of the full and flowing supervesture (and here the Toga) that he speaks, not of the Tunic.

*candidus ærumnoso obsoletus: purpureus diviti, phœniceus*[363] *pauperi datur: militi chlamys purpurea induitur.*[364]

"White vesture is for them that rejoice, and sad clothing for them that are oppressed with grief. Purple is bestowed upon the rich, dark red[363] upon the poor. A purple chlamys is the mantle of honour[364] for a soldier."

9. Martial, *Epig.* i. lvi. [After describing the pleasures of the country, where men can do as they like and dress as they like, he adds]:

*Non amet hanc vitam quisquis me non amat opto,*
*Vivat et urbanis albus in officiis.*

The worst he will wish for his enemies is that they may be bored as he had often been, when at Rome, by the ceremonious etiquette of the Capital, on occasions in which the wearing of white dress was a kind of social necessity. To the same effect he expresses himself elsewhere, when describing what to him appear the real blessings of life; one of which is "*toga rara,*" the times few and far between, when one shall need to wear the long white robe of burdensome ceremony. I quote the epigram because of its own worth:—

AD JVLIVM MARTIALEM.

Vitam quæ faciunt beatiorem,
Jucundissime Martialis, hæc sunt:
Res non parta labore, sed relicta:
Non ingratus ager, focus perennis;[365]
Lis nunquam, toga rara, mens quieta;
Vires ingenuæ,[366] salubre corpus,
Prudens simplicitas,[367] pares amici,
Convictus facilis, sine arte mensa:
Mens non ebria, sed soluta curis:

---

[363] *Phœniceus.* There were in Italy common, and not costly, dyes, of home produce, which furnished a colour approaching to purple, but without the lustre and brilliant colour of the more expensive Tyrian or Laconian dye. This is the "*nostra plebeia purpura ac pæne fusca*" of which Cicero speaks (pro Sextio); the μελαῖνα πορφύρα, which Plutarch attributes to Cato, opposing it to the ἐρυθρὰ καὶ ξέα (apud Oct. Ferr. p. 707, 2). Some such cheap and inferior purple is evidently here meant.

[364] *Militi chlamys purpurea induitur.* He does not mean simply "the soldier wears a purple chlamys," but, that a chlamys of purple would be the *dress of honour* put about the shoulders of a soldier, whom an "*Imperator*" desired to honour. For an example, see the passage in Commodus' letter to Albinus, quoted in the Introduction, cap. 3, p. xviii.

This usage of bestowing robes of various kinds as marks of imperial favour was one of the many Eastern customs imported into the West, of which, under the Empire, we find trace, and which in various ways have left their mark upon the usages even of modern society. Witness, for example, the *mantle of purple*, with which a Knight of the Garter is solemnly invested in the presence of his Sovereign. The history of the Papal "*pallium,*" briefly stated in the Introduction (see Index *in voc.*), is a remarkable instance of the same kind.

[365] *Focus perennis* (a permanent hearth, *and so*), a house of one's own.

[366] *Vires ingenuæ* (inborn, or natural, strength, *and so*, with the words that follow), "strength and health."

[367] *Prudens simplicitas.* φρόνιμοι ὡς οἱ ὄφεις καὶ ἀκέραιοι ὡς αἱ περιστεραί. (Matt. x. 16.)

A A

Non tristis torus, attamen pudicus :
Somnus, qui faciat breves tenebras :
Quod sis, esse velis, nihilque malis :
Summum nec metuas diem, nec optes.

(Lib. x. Epig. xlvii.)

10. Artemidori [277a] *Oneirocritica*, lib. ii. cap. 3.

Περὶ ἐσθῆτος καὶ κόσμου παντοδαποῦ ἀνδρείου τε καὶ γυναικείου.

Περὶ ἐσθῆτος καὶ κόσμου παντοδαποῦ ποιούμενος τὸν λόγον πρῶτον περὶ ἀνδρείας σκευῆς, ἐγχωρίου τε καὶ ξένης, ἡγοῦμαι δεῖν διαλαβεῖν. Ἐσθὴς ἡ συνήθης πᾶσιν ἀγαθή· καὶ ἡ κατὰ τὴν ὥραν τοῦ ἔτους. Θέρους μὲν γὰρ ὄντος οὐσία τε καὶ τριβακὰ ἱμάτια δοκεῖν φορεῖν ἀγαθὸν ἂν εἴη καὶ ὑγιείας σύμβολον. Χειμῶνος δὲ ἱερὰ ἱμάτια, καὶ ταῦτα καινά. Μόνῳ δὲ τῷ δίκην ἔχοντι καὶ δουλείας ἀπαλλακτιῶντι πονηρὰ τὰ κατὰ ἱμάτια. Καὶ χειμῶνος βλάπτεται (*Leg.* βλάπτει) διὰ τὸ πολλὴν ἔχειν τρίψιν καὶ ἐπιπολὺ ἀντέχειν. Λευκὰ δὲ ἱμάτια τοῖς ἱερεῦσι μόνοις συμφέρει καὶ δούλοις Ἑλλήνων. Τοῖς δὲ ἄλλοις ταραχὰς σημαίνει, διὰ τὸ τοὺς ἐν ὄχλῳ ἐπιστρεφομένους λευκὰ ἔχειν ἱμάτια. Χειροτέχναις δὲ ἀργίας καὶ σχολῆς. Καὶ ὅσῳ ἂν πολυτελεστέρα ᾖ τὰ ἱμάτια τοσούτῳ πλείονα. Οὐ γὰρ πρὸς ἔργον ὄντες οἱ ἄνθρωποι, καὶ μάλιστα οἱ τὰς βαναύσους τέχνας ἐργαζόμενοι, λευκοῖς ἱματίοις χρῶνται. Δοῦλοι (*Leg.* δούλοις) δὲ Ῥωμαίων μόνοις τοῖς εὖ πράσσουσι· τοῖς δὲ ἄλλοις πονηρόν. Ἐλέγχει γὰρ τοὺς κακῶς πράσσοντας, διά τε (*Leg.* διά τε τὸ) τὴν αὐτὴν τοῖς δεσπόταις ὡς ἐπιπλεῖστον ἔχειν ἐσθῆτα ἐπὶ τούτῳ τῷ ὀνείρῳ οὐ γίνονται ἐλεύθεροι ὥσπερ οἱ τῶν Ἑλλήνων. Ἀνδρὶ δὲ νοσοῦντι λευκὰ ἔχειν ἱμάτια θάνατον προσαγορεύει· διὰ τὸ τοὺς ἀποθανόντας ἐν λευκοῖς ἐκφέρεσθαι. Τὸ δὲ μέλαν ἱμάτιον σωτηρίαν προσημαίνει· οὐ γὰρ οἱ ἀποθνῄσκοντες ἀλλ' οἱ πενθοῦντες τοὺς ἀποθνῄσκοντας τοιούτοις χρῶνται. Οἶδα δὲ ἐγὼ πολλοὺς καὶ πένητας καὶ δούλους καὶ δεσμώτας νοσοῦντας, οἳ καὶ μάλιστα δοκοῦντες ἔχειν ἱμάτια ἀπέθανον· ἦν γὰρ εἰκὸς τούτοις μὴ ἐν λευκοῖς διὰ τὴν ἀπορίαν ἐκκομισθήσεσθαι. Ἔστι δὲ ἄλλως ἡ μελαῖνα ἐσθὴς πᾶσι πονηρά· πλὴν τῶν τὰ λαθραῖα ἐργαζομένων. Ποικίλα δὲ ἱμάτια ἔχειν ἢ ἀλουργίδα ἱερεῦσι μὲν καὶ θυμελικοῖς καὶ σκηνικοῖς καὶ τοῖς περὶ τὸν Διόνυσον μόνοις τεχνίταις συμφέρει. Τοῖς δὲ λοιποῖς ταραχὰς καὶ κινδύνους μόνους ἐπιφέρει, καὶ τὰ κρυπτὰ ἐλέγχει. Τοὺς δὲ νοσοῦντας ὑπὸ δριμέων χυμῶν καὶ πολλῆς χολῆς ἐνοχλεῖσθαι σημαίνει. Πορφυρᾶ δὲ ἐσθὴς δούλοις ἀγαθὴ καὶ πλουσίοις· οἷς μὲν γὰρ διὰ τὸ μὴ μετεῖναι ἐλευθερίας σημαίνει· οἷς δὲ διὰ τὸ μὴ ἐπιτάττειν, καὶ τῷ ἀξιώματι κατάλληλον εἶναι, τιμὴν καὶ εὐδοξίαν προσαγορεύει. Νοσοῦντα δὲ ἀκαιρεῖ καὶ πένητα βλάπτει· πολλοῖς δὲ καὶ δεσμὰ προσήγγειλε. Χρὴ γὰρ τὸν ἔχοντα πορφύραν πάντως διάδημα ἢ στέφανον ἔχειν, καὶ πολλοὺς ἀκολούθους ἢ φύλακας. Τοῖς δὲ περὶ τὸν Διόνυσον τεχνίταις τὰ αὐτὰ τῇ ἀλουργίδι σημαίνει. Κοκκίνη δὲ [ἐσθὴς] καὶ πᾶσα ἡ τοιαύτη ἐσθὴς ἢ πορφυροβαφὴς οἷς μὲν τραύματα, οἷς δὲ πυρετὸν ἐπιφέρει. Γυναικεῖα δὲ ἐσθὴς ἀγάμοις μόνοις συμφέρει, καὶ τοῖς ἐπὶ θυμέλαις ἀναβαίνουσιν· οἱ μὲν γὰρ γαμήσουσιν οὕτω κατανθυμίους γυναῖκας ὥστε τοῖς αὐτοῖς χρῆσθαι κόσμοις· οἱ δὲ διὰ τὸ ἐν τῇ ὑποκρίσει ἔθος μεγάλας ἐργασίας καὶ μισθοὺς λήψονται. Τοὺς δὲ λοιποὺς καὶ τῶν γυναικῶν στερήσει καὶ τόσῳ μεγάλῳ περιβάλλει, διὰ τὸ μαλακὸν καὶ ἀσθενὲς τῶν τὰ τοιαῦτα φορούντων. Ἐν μὲν ταῖς ἑορταῖς καὶ πανηγύρεσιν οὔτε ποικίλα οὔτε γυναικεῖα βλάπτει

---

[267a] See note μ, p. xi., for particulars concerning this Writer.

τινα ἐσθῆς.³⁶⁸ Βαρβαρικὴν δὲ ἐσθῆτα ἔχειν ἐπεσκευασμένην ὅστις οἱ βάρβαροι ἐκεῖ μὲν ἀπιέναι βουλόμενον ὅπου τοιαύτῃ ἐσθῆτι χρῶνται οἱ διατρίβοντες, ἀγαθὰς τὰς ἐκεῖ διατριβὰς σημαίνει. Πολλάκις δὲ καὶ τὸ ἐκεῖ καταβιῶναι προαγγέλλει. Τοῖς δὲ λοιποῖς νόσον καὶ ἀπραγίαν δηλοῖ. Τὰ δὲ αὐτὰ καὶ ἡ Ῥωμαϊκὴ ἐσθὴς ἢν νῦν τήβεννον ³⁶⁹ ⁺ καλοῦσιν. . . .

Μαλακῇ δὲ ἐσθῆτι καὶ πολυτελεῖ χρῆσθαι πλουσίοις μὲν ἀγαθὸν καὶ πένησιν· οἷς μὲν γὰρ ἡ παροῦσα διαμένει τρυφή, οἷς δὲ φαιδρότερα τὰ πράγματα ἔσται. Δούλοις δὲ καὶ ἀπόροις νόσον προαγορεύει. Κολοβὴ δὲ καὶ ἀπρεπὴς ἐσθῆτις ζημίας καὶ ἀπραξίας σημαίνουσι. Χλαμὺς δὲ ἢν ἐνίοι μανδύην, οἱ δὲ ἐφεστρίδα, οἱ δὲ βίρρον, καλοῦσι, θλῖψιν καὶ στενοχωρίαν καὶ τοῖς δικαζομένοις καταδίκην μαντεύεται, διὰ τὸ ἐμπεριέχειν τὸ σῶμα. Τὸ δὲ αὐτὸ καὶ ὁ λεγόμενος φαινόλης· καὶ εἴτι ἄλλο τούτοις ὅμοιον ἴσον ἴσθι ἀπολλύειν τὰ ἱμάτια ταῦτα ἢ ἔχειν βέλτιον. Τῶν δὲ ἄλλων ἱματίων οὐδὲν ἀπολλύμενον συμφέρει, εἰ μή που τοῖς πένησι καὶ δούλοις καὶ δεδεμένοις ἃ καταχρέοις καὶ πᾶσι τοῖς ἐν συνοχῇ οὖσιν. Ἀπολλύμενα γὰρ ταῦτα τῶν περιεχόντων τὸ σῶμα κακῶν ἀπάλλαξιν σημαίνει. Τοῖς δὲ ἄλλοις οὔτε γυμνοῦσθαι οὔτε ἱμάτια ἀπολλύειν ἀγαθόν· πᾶν γὰρ τὸ πρὸς κόσμον τινὸς ἀπολέσθαι σημαίνει. Γυναικὶ δὲ ποικίλῃ καὶ ἀνθηρὰ ἐσθὴς συμφέρει, μάλιστα δὲ ἑταίρᾳ καὶ πλουσίᾳ. Ἡ μὲν γὰρ διὰ τὰς ἐργασίας, ἡ δὲ διὰ τὴν τρυφήν, ἀνθηραῖς ἐσθῆσιν χρῶνται. Τὰ δὲ ἰδιόχροα ἱμάτια πᾶσιν ἀγαθὸν σημαίνουσι, καὶ μάλιστα τοῖς εὐλαβουμένοις ἐλεγχθῆναι γὰρ οὐχ ἱκανὸν τὸ τοιοῦτον χρῶμα. Ἀεὶ δὲ ἄμεινον καθαρὰ καὶ λαμπρὰ ἱμάτια ἔχειν καὶ νενλυμένα καλῶς ἢ ῥυπαρὰ καὶ ἄπλυτα, πλὴν τῶν τὰς ῥυπαρὰς ἐργασίας ἐργαζομένων.

11. Of the entire passage, as given above, I would call more particular attention to the following, as bearing upon questions discussed in the Introduction to this Treatise.

### SIGNIFICANCE OF WHITE GARMENTS.

α. "White garments (seen in dreams) are a sign of good only for priests,³⁶⁹ and for slaves in Greece. To all others they are a sign of troubles, because it is in the busy crowd (of great cities) that men wear white garments. But to artizans they portend idleness, and leisure; and then the more complete in proportion to their greater costliness. For men wear not white garments when at work, especially if engaged in the humble mechanical trades."

### THE DEAD CLAD IN WHITE: MOURNERS IN BLACK.

β. "To a sick man the wearing white garments is an announcement of

---

³⁶⁸ This statement, that a dress like that of women, and of varied colours, is for harm to none in time of feasts or public assemblies, has been already noticed. See Introduction, p. xl, note p.

³⁶⁹ ⁺ Τήβεννος or τήβεννον, a "toga."

³⁶⁹ He does not mean that priests on days of sacrifice wore none but white garments, because, as we shall see below, this was not the case. But days of sacrifice, and of public festivity accompanied by sacrifice, were days on which white dress was assumed by the people generally; and such days were days of profit to the lower order of priests, and of public honour to those higher in station.

death; because it is in white that the dead are carried out to burial. But a black robe is a sign of recovery; for it is not the dead, but they that mourn for the dead, that are so dressed."

### GAUDY COLOURED DRESS.

γ. "The wearing of parti-coloured or of sea-purple dress, bringeth good to priests, to stage-players, and actors, and among artizans to those only who have to do with Dionysus. But to all others they portend trouble and danger only; and serve to the detection of secrets. And for such as are sick they are significant of oppression by acrid humours, and much bile." [To this may be added what follows later in the Chapter.] "To women, parti-coloured garments, coloured like unto flowers, are of good import, especially to harlots, and to the rich. For harlots, because of their occupation, and the rich, out of luxury, wear garments such as these."

### ROBES OF PURPLE, AND SCARLET.

δ. "Robes of purple are of good sign for slaves, and for rich men; to the former because, slaves having no right to such, they are significant of freedom; to the rich, because in respect of wealth alone they have no power to command; and purple, being correlative to official dignity, portendeth to them rank and reputation. But purple is death to a sick man, and harmful to one in poverty. And in many cases they have been found to foretell even bonds. For the wearer of purple must needs have either the band (diadem) that is proper to kings, or a chaplet (στέφανος, note 54) [bound about his brow], and be surrounded with many attendants or guards. But to such as work in matters pertaining to the worship of Dionysus, ordinary purple has the same significance as the sea-purple. Vestments of scarlet and the like, and such as are dyed purple, portend wounds to some, to others fever."

### THE CHLAMYS AND THE PÆNULA.

ε. "The Chlamys, which some call Mandyas, others Epheſtris, others Berion, foretelleth trouble, and difficulty, and to men under trial, condemnation, because of its compassing and confining the body. And like to this is the significance of what is called a 'Pænula,' and of other garments of the same kind."

### VESTMENTS OF HEATHEN PRIESTHOOD.

12. Tyrian Priests wore a χιτὼν πλατύσημος, *i.e.*, a Tunic with a broad band (*clavus*), probably of purple. Herodianus, lib. v. *apud* Ferrar. He is speaking of the honorary Priests of Elagabalus or Heliogabalus, the Syro-Phœnician

Sun-God. τὰ σπλάγχνα τῶν ἱερουργηθέντων τά τε ἀρώματα ἐν χρυσοῖς σκεύεσιν ὑπὲρ κεφαλῆς οὐκ οἰκέται δὲ τινὲς ἢ εὐτελεῖς ἄνθρωποι ἔφερον, ἀλλ᾽ οἵτ᾽ ὕπαρχοι τῶν στρατοπέδων καὶ οἱ ἐν ταῖς μεγίσταις πράξεσιν, ἀνεζωσμένοι χιτῶνας ποδήρεις καὶ χειριδωτοὺς, ὕμνῳ Φοινίκων, ἐν μέσῳ φέροντες μίας πορφύρας.³⁷⁰ Ὑποδήμασι δὲ λίνου πεποιημένοις ἐχρῶντο, ὅπερ οἱ κατ᾽ ἐκεῖνα τὰ χωρία προφητεύοντες.

13. So in Tyrian colonies, as for example, the Priests of Hercules (Melcarth) at Gades: Silius Italicus, *Punica*, lib. iii.

> Nec difcolor ulli
> Ante aras cultus; velantur corpora lino,
> Ex Pelufiaco praefulget ftamine vertex:³⁷¹
> Difcinctis³⁷² mos thura dare, atque e lege parentum
> Sacrificam lato veftem diftinguere clavo.

14. To the fame effect is what Tertullian fays of the Priests of Saturnus at Carthage. *De Pallio*, cap. 4, p. 213.

"Latioris purpuræ ambitio,³⁷³ et Galatici³⁷⁴ ruboris fuperjectio, Saturnum commendat."

In the fame place he fpeaks of the Priests of Ceres as dreffed wholly in white, thofe of Bellona in dark and gloomy garb.

"Cur . . . non fpectas . . . illos habitus qui novitati fuæ ftare religionem mentiuntur, cum ob cultum omnia candidatum, et ob notam vitæ, et privilegium galeri,³⁷⁵ Cereri initiantur; cum ob diverfam affectionem tenebricæ veftis, et tetrici fuper caput velleris, in Bellonæ mentes (*al.* montes) fugantur."

15. Priests of Dionyfus wore purple. See Artemidorus, quoted above, No. 10, and Clement of Alexandria, *Pæd.* lib. ii. cap. 9, quoted later in this Appendix. See No. 39.

16. At Rome the *Pontifices* wore a *Toga prætexta* (*i.e.*, bordered with purple). See Lampridius, quoted in note 1, p. xi. And to the fame effect is that of Livy (xl. 42), when, in fpeaking of the *Triumviri Epulones*,³⁷⁶ he fays that to them *idem ut Pontifici lege datum togæ prætextæ habendæ jus*.

---

³⁷⁰ μίαν πορφύραν, *i.e.* a fingle band or ftripe (*clavus*) of purple. Compare Silius Italicus in No. 13.

³⁷¹ That is, they wear a cap, or μίτρα, made of fine Egyptian linen.

³⁷² This points to the *long* tunic, not girt up by any *cingulum*.

³⁷³ *Latioris purpuræ ambitio*. This laft word (*ambitio*) may poffibly be ufed with reference to its literal meaning, "going round," and fo of "the compaffing" of the veftment, on its border, by a broad purple ftripe. But the more probable meaning (as the previous context fhows) is "the ambition of wearing a broad purple ftripe" correfponding to the *latus clavus* of Roman ufe. The words here commented on refer to the *Tunica*; the *fuperjectio*, &c. (ἐπίβλημα) to the Super-veftment.

³⁷⁴ *Galaticus rubor, i.e.* fcarlet. Plinii *Hift. Nat.* xxii. cap. 11. *Infci veftes fcimus admirabili facco. Atque ut fileamus Galatiæ, Africæ, Lufitaniæ cocci granum Imperatoriis paludamentis dicatum, &c. &c.*

³⁷⁵ Note 124, p. 72.

³⁷⁶ *Triumviri Epulones*. Commiffioners who regulated the public facrificial feafts.

17. When sacrificing, the Pontiffs commonly covered the head with a portion of this *Prætexta*. To this Virgil alludes, when he represents Helenus giving directions to Æneas as to the ceremonial dress of sacrifice : Æn. iii. 404.

> Quin ubi transmissæ steterint trans æquora classes,
> Et positis aris jam vota in littore solves,
> Purpureo velare comas adopertus amictu,[277]
> Ne qua inter sanctos ignes in honore Deorum
> Hostilis facies occurrat, et omina turbet.

18. So also Flamens wore purple (Servius on Æneid iv.), and Augurs a *Trabea* of purple and scarlet, known as δίβαφος. Hence the allusion of Cicero when writing to Atticus (*ad Att.* ii. 9), he says:—

"Proinde isti licet faciant quos volent Consules, Tribunos plebis ; denique etiam Vatinii strumam sacerdotii διβάφῳ vestiant" (*i.e. let them make Vatinius an Augur.*).

PART II. ASSOCIATIONS OF COLOUR IN HOLY SCRIPTURE.

19. White Robes are symbolic of joy, Eccl. ix. 8 : of purity and cleansing from sin, Is. i. 18; Dan. xii. 10; Rev. iii. 4, 5; Rev. vii. 13, 14: of righteousness, Rev. xix. 8.

20. In white angels are clothed, Matt. xxviii. 3; Mark, xvi. 5; Acts, i. 10. In white, too, our Lord was seen in vision at the Transfiguration, Matt. xvii. 2; Mark, ix. 3. In white "The Ancient of Days" was seen in vision by Daniel, Dan. vii. 9.

21. White are the robes of Levites at the Dedication of Solomon's Temple, 2 Chron. v. 12. White (because made of *Linen*, note 16) the robes of Priests. White the robes with which the High-priest entered the Holy of Holies, on the Day of Atonement. See Philo Judæus, quoted at p. 8, and see note 17, p. 7.

RED.

22. Red is the colour of wine (*the blood of the grape*), Gen. xlix. 12; Ps. lxxv. 8; Prov. xxiii. 36; If. lxiii. 2.

23. Red is the colour of blood (2 Kings, iii. 22, &c.), and so associated with the idea of battle, Nahum, ii. 3; Zech. i. 8; Rev. vi. 4.

24. Red is also a royal colour, and used in the decoration of kings' palaces (Esther, i. 6). And as such probably used in the decoration of the "House of God," King of kings, and Lord of lords.

25. But at other times red is associated with the idea of sin ("Thy sins,

---

[277] This line is quoted by St. Jerome, on Ezek. xliv. See above, p 30, *in fin.*

though they be red like crimson"), If. i. 18; or with the impersonation of Sin described, in Rev. xii. 3, as a great dragon having seven heads and ten horns.

### BLUE.

26. Blue is (like red) a royal colour, Esther, i. 6, used especially in "royal apparel," Esther, viii. 15. Compare Ezek. xxiii. 6.

27. It was used (compare No. 24) in the decoration of the Tabernacle and Temple (Exod., Numb., 2 Chron., *passim*) and in the vestments of the High-priest, Exod. xxviii. 31, &c.

28. We also find it mentioned as one of the products of "Tyrus," Ezek. xxvii. 7, 24; and associated with purple in the clothing of idols, Jer. x. 9.

### SCARLET.[378]

29. Scarlet is a royal colour, 2 Sam. i. 24; Lam. iv. 5; Dan. v. 7, 16, 29.

30. As such, probably, it was used in the decoration of the Tabernacle (compare Nos. 24 and 27) and of the Temple, 2 Chron. ii. 7; and in the vestments of the High-priest, Exod. xxviii. 6, &c.

31. From its resemblance to the colour of blood it has a symbolical use in "cleansing from sin" ("*without shedding of blood there is no remission*"). Lev. xiv. 4; Heb. ix. 19.

32. As being a brilliant and very costly colour it was rarely used by unofficial persons, as an ordinary colour of dress, save by the very wealthy, or by immodest women. (See above, No. 11, γ.) Hence it is sometimes spoken of in Scripture (as elsewhere) as a meretricious colour, Rev. xvii. 4, 5, or as symbolical of sin generally, If. i. 18; Rev. xvii. 3.

### PURPLE.

33. Purple is a royal colour, Judg. viii. 26; Esther, i. 6; viii. 15; Mark, xv. 17.

34. As such (compare Nos. 27, 30) it had its use in the Tabernacle, Numb. iv. 13.

---

[378] Scarlet was attainable, from its great costliness, only by the wealthy. This probably explains the phrase employed in Prov. xxxi. 21, where, in speaking of the "virtuous woman," it is said that "all her household are clothed with scarlet," *i.e.* by her prudence and wise management there is abundance of clothing, even the most costly, for all that need.

35. And for a similar reason, when used by private persons, it is regarded as a proof, sometimes of abundant wealth, Prov. xxxi. 22 (where the clothing of "the virtuous woman" is silk and purple), more often of luxury and self-indulgence, as in Luke, xvi. 19.

### Part III. ASSOCIATIONS OF COLOUR IN EARLY CHRISTIAN WRITERS.

36. Clemens Alexandrinus, *Pædag.* lib. ii. p. 233.

"I honour that ancient Lacedæmonian people, who allowed none but harlots to wear garments wrought like unto flowers, and ornaments of gold."

#### SELLERS OF INCENSE AND DYERS OF WOOLS SHOULD BE BANISHED FROM THE COMMONWEALTH OF TRUTH.

37. *Ibid.* p. 208. [He had been speaking with strongest condemnation of the use of unguents, and scents, and incense, and the like (for purposes of luxury), and he adds]:

"With good reason, to my judgment, did they act, who, indignant at seeing pains bestowed on things like these, held scents and unguents in such ill esteem, as emasculating all manliness of character, that they banished the makers of them from well-ordered states, and did treat no otherwise the dyers of various wools. An unrighteous thing it were that garments full of deceit, and unguents, should find their way into the city of truth. . . . And if perchance it should be said, that the Lord, the great High-priest, offereth the incense of sweet savour unto God, let them learn that this is no sacrifice and sweet savour of (actual) incense, but that which the Lord doth offer is the acceptable oblation of holy love, the spiritual sweet savour, upon the altar."

#### DYED GARMENTS SIGNS OF AN EVIL DISPOSITION.

38. *Ibid.* p. 234.

"All dyed colours should be avoided in dress; for these are far away both from man's need, and from truth; and beside this they give proof of evil in the inward disposition."

#### GARMENTS DYED LIKE UNTO FLOWERS, FIT ONLY FOR WORSHIPPERS OF BACCHUS, FOR HEATHEN PRIESTS, AND STAGE PLAYERS.

39. *Ibid.* p. 235. "For men that are pure and unadulterate in heart a white and simple garb is the most fitting for their use. Plainly and purely speaketh Daniel the prophet. *Thrones,* saith he, *were set, and one took his seat thereon as it were the Antient of Days: and His raiment was white like snow.* And the Revelation speaketh of beholding the Lord in the like vesture. "I saw at the foot of the altar the souls of them that had testified for Christ, and there was given unto each one white raiment." But if need should be for seeking

any other colour, that natural colour which is of truth, sufficeth. But garments coloured like unto flowers are fit only for Bacchic rites, and for the mummeries of heathen priests. Purple, too, and silver tissues, are 'for tragedy players, not for real life,' as the comic poet writes. Whereas the life of us Christian folk should be anything rather than a vain pomp."

### THE SPIRITUAL MEANING OF THAT WHICH IS WRITTEN CONCERNING " THE RAIMENT OF GOLD WROUGHT ABOUT WITH DIVERS COLOURS."

40. *Ibid.* p. 236. He had been speaking in strong condemnation of women wearing gaudy colours, such as those above spoken of. And lest any should defend this by alleging words of Scripture, which, as he judged, were to be spiritually understood, he writes as follows:

"What though the word of God by the mouth of David speaketh in Psalm concerning the Lord, saying, *Kings' daughters were among thine honourable women: on thy right hand stood the queen in a vesture of gold, and with garments fringed with gold was she compassed about.* [379] In this he would have us to understand not raiment of luxurious softness, but that which is wrought of faith, the incorruptible adornment of them that have received mercy, the adornment of the Church; wherein Jesus, the guileless one, shineth out as gold, and the fringes, made of gold, are the elect."

### IN WHITE TRUE BEAUTY IS TO BE FOUND.

41. *Ibid.* p. 239. "Why is it then that ye are attracted by that which is rare and costly, rather than by that which is ready to your hand and of easy purchase? It is because ye know not what is the truly beautiful, and the truly good; and, in place of realities, bestow your pains upon what is esteemed only among men of no understanding, to whose imagination, as with men mad, white and black seem both alike."

### TERTULLIAN.[380]

#### DYED COLOURS DISPLEASING TO GOD.

42. De Habitu Muliebri, cap. 8. "Quis est vestium honor justus de adulterio colorum injustorum? Non placet Deo quod non ipse produxit, nisi si non potuit purpureas et aerias [381] oves nasci jubere. Si potuit, ergo jam noluit: quod Deus noluit, utique non licet fingi." [382]

---

[379] In this prophecy, Amalarius (quoted at p. 99) sees a reference to the dalmatic. The two comments, those of Clement and Amalarius, present an instructive contrast.

[380] Born at Carthage, *circ.* A.D. 150. Embraced Christianity A.D. 185. Died A.D. 220. His middle life was spent partly at Rome, and partly (at a later period) at Carthage.

[381] *Aerias*, i.e. of the colour of the sky.

[382] Whatever may be thought of the logic of this argument, the passage is good evidence as to the feeling of Tertullian in respect of the costly colours of which he is speaking.

### Dyed Colours Meretricious.

43. *Ibid.* p. 68. "Illa civitas valida quæ super montes septem et plurimas aquas præsidet, cum prostitutæ appellationem a Domino meruisset, quali habitu appellationis suæ comparata est? Sedet certe in purpura cum coccino et auro et lapide pretioso."

### The true Purple of the Christian Man.

44. *De Corona Militis,* cap. 13. [He is addressing the Christian man as at once a soldier of Christ, and a citizen of the Jerusalem that is above.]

"Coronant et publicos ordines laureis publicæ causæ, magistratus vero insuper aureis. . . . . Sed tui ordines et tui magistratus, et ipsum Curiæ [383] nomen, Ecclesia est Christi. Illic purpuræ tuæ, Sanguis Domini; et clavus latus, in Cruce ipsius: illic securis,[384] ad caudicem arboris posita: illic virgæ,[385] ex radice Jesse."

---

# APPENDIX B.

## PASSAGES OF EARLY WRITERS INDICATIVE OF A LEVITICAL ORIGIN FOR CHRISTIAN VESTMENTS.

The monuments, whether of literature or of art, during the first eight hundred years of Christian history, point with an overwhelming weight of concurrent testimony to the conclusion, that the vestments of Christian ministry were not modelled upon those of Levitical priesthood.

In all those monuments, as far as we have seen hitherto, there has been no indication of any but white [386] vestments being worn; no trace anywhere

---

[383] He alludes to the etymological connection between *Curia* and *așușand*.

[384] This points probably to the blood that flowed from the pierced side.

[385] *Securis,* and again *virga,* in allusion to the axe and rods borne by the lictors of the higher magistrates.

[386] The only exception to this, of which I am aware, is one of those exceptions "that prove the rule." We learn incidentally from a notice in the *Gesta Pontificum Romanorum,* quoted by Walafrid Strabo (p. 106), and by Anastasius, that attempts were made at Rome, in the pontificate of Sylvester (314–335), to introduce the use of coloured cloth, and of silk, in the vestments of Christian ministry. For

of any intentional imitation of the distinctive characteristics of the dress of Levitical priesthood, viz. the coloured girdle, and the priestly cap, of priests of the second order; the gorgeously coloured super-vestments, the jewelled "rational," the cap with its golden plate, worn by the high-priest.

But it is desirable to notice, and to give all due weight to, a few facts that may be alleged as pointing to an opposite conclusion. It should not be forgotten, in dealing with questions such as those now before us, that between the Aaronic priesthood and the priesthood of the Christian Church, there are many points of close analogy, though there are also points of important difference. These points of analogy, suggested as they are by many passages of Holy Scripture, were recognised from the very earliest times by ecclesiastical writers. One effect of this was, that titles, properly applicable to the older priesthood, were, sparingly at first, but with an ever-increasing freedom as time went on, applied to the several orders of the Christian ministry. And this being the case, it would be strange if we did not find here and there some recognition, in like manner, of certain features of analogy [386a] between the vestments of the Christian bishop or priest, and the Levitical vestments of the older Church.

Some [387] passages, of the kind now spoken of, have already been quoted, and their language carefully considered. And I take this opportunity of adding thereto such other passages of early writers as might be thought to invalidate the general conclusions, as to the origin of Christian vestments, which have been set forth in the Introduction to this treatise.

1. The first in date occurs in the well-known sermon, or rather oration, pronounced by Eusebius of Cæsarea, at the opening of the great Church at Tyre, after the public recognition of Christianity by Constantine the Great. It is given at full length by its author in the tenth book of his Ecclesiastical History. Written in a style of florid rhetoric from first to last, the leading thought that pervades it is that of a comparison between the magnificent church, for the consecration of which they were assembled, and the Temple of Solomon. Addressing the Bishop of Tyre, Paulinus, the speaker knows not whether to regard him as a second Bezaleel, or as another Solomon, king of a new and better Jerusalem, or as the Zorobabel of their own day, crowning

---

Sylvester found it necessary to forbid their use. His *constituit ut sacrificium altaris non in serico neque in panno tincto celebraretur, nisi tantum in lineo ex terreno lino procreato, sicut corpus Domini Nostri Jesu Christi in sudone lintea munda sepultum est, et sic Missa celebraretur.* [Anastasii V. P. R. in S. Sylvestro, p. 105.] There are abundant proofs (especially in the notices preserved by Anastasius) of a vast accession to the splendour of divine service generally, at Rome and elsewhere, from the time of "the conversion of Constantine." But it is plain from this passage, and from the evidence of subsequent centuries, that little if any change was then permitted in the simple but dignified dress of Christian ministry.

[386a] As in S. Germanus quoted above, p. 82, note 141. With his expression closely agrees, that of Martinus, Bishop of Braga (circ. 572 A.D.), in the collection known as the Capitula Martini Episcopi. Labbe, tom. v. p. 912, Canon lxvi. "Non oportet clericos comam nutrire, et sic ministrare, sed attonso capite, patentibus auribus; *et secundum Aaron talarem vestem induere, ut sint in habitu ordinato.*"

[387] See note 59, p. 37; note 62, p. 39; note 65, p. 41.

the temple of God with that glory, better than the former, which belongeth to these last times. And it is in accordance with this strain that he addresses the assembled clergy as "friends of God, and priests (ἱερεῖς) clad in the holy vesture that reacheth to the feet, and with the heavenly crown of glory, and with the unction of inspiration, and the priestly vesture of the Holy Spirit."[388]

Now I am free to confess that I can only understand these words as highly figurative throughout. The "sticharion," white and glistening, which was no doubt worn both by bishops and priests there assembled before him, was, in point of fact, a feature in common between the Jewish and the Christian dress. But precisely for the reason (so at least it seems to me) that in all the other, and more distinctive, features of the Jewish sacerdotal dress, *no counterpart was to be found in the actual dress of those before him*, he speaks of "the glory," and the "unction," and the "Holy Spirit," as spiritual robes, which the priesthood of the new covenant may rightly claim as their own.

But among modern writers there are some who see the matter in a very different light, and find in this passage proof that the bishops of that day wore mitres (κιδάρεις) or priestly caps, after the model of the Jewish priests, and had also sacerdotal robes modelled upon the same style.

I leave it to my readers to decide between the two interpretations.

2. Another passage, closely resembling this, is to be found in the fourth discourse of Gregory Nazianzen.[389] The passage referred to is the following. He is addressing his father, then Bishop of Nazianzum, who had been desirous of associating his son with himself in the duties of the episcopal office, for which at his greatly advanced age he felt himself unequal. St. Gregory says, (referring to this), "Thou soughtest that a second Barnabas might be joined, as helper, to thyself a second Paul; that to Silvanus and Timotheus, a Titus also should be added, that so the gift of God that is in thee might have free course, by means of them that naturally have care for thee, and that from Jerusalem round about unto Illyricum thou mightest fulfil the work of an evangelist.' For this cause it is that thou bringest one forth, and settest him in the midst, and layest hold on him, though he would draw back, and settest him beside thyself ('This,' you will perhaps say, 'is my only wrong'); and makest him partaker both of the cares of thine office, and of its crowns. Therefore,[390] it is that thou anointest the chief priest, and puttest about [him]

---

[388] Ὦ φίλοι Θεοῦ καὶ ἱερεῖς, οἱ τὸν ἅγιον ποδήρη, καὶ τὸν εὐράνιον τῆς δόξης στέφανον, τό τε χρῖσμα τὸ ἔνθεον, καὶ τὴν ἱερατικὴν τοῦ Ἁγίου Πνεύματος στολὴν περιβεβλημένοι. By ἱερεῖς here mentioned we should probably understand *bishops*. See note 61. The passage will be found in Euseb. H. E. lib. x. cap. 4.

[389] Born A.D. 324, Bp. of Constantinople in 378, died in 389. See vol. i. of his collected works (Moreli), p. 136, Oratio v. *in fin*.

[390] The original is as follows. διὰ τοῦτο τὸν μύστην ἄγεις, καὶ ὑπεχωροῦντος λαμβάνῃ, καὶ παρὰ σαυτῷ καθίζεις. Τοῦτο τὸ ἐμὸν ἀδίκημα, φαίης ἂν καὶ κοινωνὸν ποιῇ τῶν φροντίδων καὶ τῶν στεφάνων. διὰ τοῦτο χρίεις τὸν ἀρχιερέα, καὶ περιβάλλεις τὸν ποδήρη, καὶ περιτίθης τὸν κίδαριν, καὶ προσάγεις τῷ θυσιαστηρίῳ τῆς πνευματικῆς ὁλοκαυτώσεως, καὶ θύεις τὸν μόσχον τῆς τελειώσεως, καὶ τελεῖς τὰς χεῖρας τῷ πνεύματι, καὶ εἰσάγεις εἰς τὰ ἅγια τῶν ἁγίων λειτουργήσοντα, καὶ πᾶσιν λειτουργὸν τῆς καινῆς τῆς ἀληθινῆς, ἧς ἔταξεν ὁ Κύριος οὐκ ἄνθρωπος.

the (ποδήρη) priestly robe, and settest the priest's cap about his head, and bringest him unto the altar of the spiritual burnt sacrifice, and flayest the calf of consecration, and dost consecrate his hands with the spirit, and bringest him into the holy of holies, as one that shall see the hidden things of the Lord, and makest him a minister of the true tabernacle, which the Lord pitched and not man. But whether he [91] be worthy both of you that anoint him, and of Him for whom, and unto whom, is that anointing, this He only knoweth who is the Father of the true 'anointed one' (Χριστός), whom He anointed with the oil of gladness above His fellows, bestowing upon humanity the unction of divinity, so as to make of these twain one."

Upon this passage I need add little to what I have said above upon the similar language of Eusebius. It is evident that many of the expressions (such as that of "*slaying the calf of consecration*"), cannot by any possibility be regarded as more than figurative phrases, drawn from the analogies of the rites of consecration under the Levitical law. And this fact is enough to mark the character of the whole passage. On the other hand, it is only right to say, that there is a strong probability that in pursuing this comparison into detail, as he does, the writer would fix upon such points in the older rites as had something analogous to them in Christian consecration. The "sticharion," or long white tunic of the Christian ministry, offered a point of comparison with the ποδήρης of Levitical ministry. And the mention of the κίδαρις which follows, would lead one to suppose that among the ministering vestments of St. Gregory's time, there might be something corresponding to the cap or mitre of the Levitical priest.

But the more direct evidence of antiquity points, as in the Introduction has been shown, to a directly opposite conclusion. And if St. Gregory really had present to his mind any episcopal vestment (so to call it), which he regarded as correspondent to the Levitical κίδαρις, I should suppose that it was either a close fitting skull-cap, such as that which Eusebius of Cæsarea is represented as wearing, in Pl. XXVII., or some such distinctive head-dress as that, with which, at a later time certainly, the *out-door dress* of bishops and patriarchs was distinguished.

Dr. Hefele, who has examined this question at some length, after referring briefly to the two passages above quoted, goes on to speak of the following passages, which he thinks point to an early use of a distinctive head-dress by Christian bishops.

3. Ammianus Marcellinus, lib. xxix. cap. 5. He describes the submission of Firmus to Theodosius, the general sent into Mauritania against him. He says that, *Ne quid ultimæ rationis omitteret, Christiani ritus antistites oraturos pocem cum obsidibus misit.* These being kindly received, two days later, *militaria signa et coronam sacerdotalem cum cæteris quæ interceperat, nibil cunc-*

---

[91] St. Gregory is alluding throughout to himself, as the person who had been made bishop against his own will. But he avoids direct mention of himself in the first person.

*tatus restituit, ut praeceptum est.* The historian, who writes about this *corona sacerdotalis* is himself a heathen; and it is in the highest degree improbable, even on this ground only, that he should use the term *sacerdotalis* thus absolutely in speaking of Christian bishop or priest. There can be little, if any, doubt, that this was one of those richer crowns, made of precious metal, which we know [393] to have been worn by the priests of some among the heathen gods.

4. Dr. Hefele also lays great stress (but I venture to think, without strong ground for so doing) on passages [393] in which the word *infula* occurs in connection with Christian vestments. According to *classical* usage one meaning of *infula* undoubtedly was that of a long band, made either of linen or of wool, which was fastened about the head of priests, or hung round the neck, or the body, of victims [394] to be offered in sacrifice. But the word was not confined to this meaning, but was often used of the insignia of imperial or magisterial rank, and had nearly the meaning (in some instances) of an "official vestment," context alone determining what the nature of that vestment might be. And I am confirmed in the belief that, in the passages quoted by Dr. Hefele, *infula* has this wider meaning, by finding most certain proof that, even as late as the twelfth century, the word was used as a synonym for the *casula* or *planeta*. (See note 268, *in fin.* p. 133.)

5. Another passage is quoted from Ennodius, a Christian poet (his Christianity better than his poetry, we may charitably hope, after reading the lines that follow). He wrote about the close of the fifth century. Speaking in praise of St. Ambrose, he expresses himself as follows [Epig. 77]:

> *Roscida regifico cui fulsit murice lingua,*
> *Vere suo pingens germina quae voluit.*
> *Serta redimitus gestabat lucida fronte;*
> *Distinctum gemmis ore parabat opus.*

Dr. Hefele quotes the third line of this passage, without its context, as

---

[391] See, *e.g.* the quotation from Tertullian, *De Cor. Mil. supra*, p. xiv.

[392] Such are Prudentius Clemens, *Peristephanon*, iv. 9. He is singing the praises of the city of Saragossa (Cæsar-Augusta), and of the martyrs of whom it could boast. He adds, "*Hinc sacerdotum domus infulata Valeriorum.*" He writes about the year 400 A.D., and refers in these words to Valerius, Bp. of Saragossa, and to others of the same family.

Again, Pope Gelasius speaks in one of his letters of a bishop as being *clericalibus infulis reprobabilis* (unworthy to wear the dress of a cleric). Here the use of the plural confirms the interpretation given above.

In like manner in a life of St. Willibald, written in the eighth century, his consecration as bishop is spoken of as the time when he had bestowed upon him *sacerdotalis infulae honorem.*

And St. Boniface (note 209, p. 106) is represented (in a biography dating from the eleventh century) as writing to the Bishop of Rome concerning Burchard of Wurzburg, to say that he was *pontificali infula dignus.*

[394] See, for example, Pl. III., where the bull, being led away for slaughter, has such *infulae* hung about him:

Stans hostia ad aram,
Lanea dum nivea circumdatur infula vitta.
                                    Virg.

a proof that bishops in the days of St. Ambrose wore a distinctive head-dress.³⁹⁵ But a moment's reference to the context is sufficient to show how entirely ungrounded is such an inference.³⁹⁵ᵃ Throughout these lines it is of the eloquence of St. Ambrose that Ennodius is speaking; and the "*bright garlands which crowned his brow*," are no more to be taken literally, than is the "*royal purple*," with which "*his tongue glowed*," or the "*work bedecked with jewels*," which he "*fashioned with his lips*."

Other authorities quoted by Martene in support of the antiquity of the episcopal "mitra," are the following:

6. Theodulfus, Bishop of Orleans, writing *circ.* A.D. 800, is describing the "*Ornamenta Pontificis*" (so Martene writes), and employs the following expression (lib. iii. carm. 5):

*Illius ergo caput resplendens mitra tegebat.*

In this, Martene sees proof of the early use of the mitre by Christian bishops. This, again, is a curious instance of the mistakes to which even men of great learning are liable, when they quote, without reference to context, single lines, or it may be half-sentences, out of ancient authors, in support of preconceived conclusions.

The quotation is from lib v. carm. 3 (Sirmondi Opera, ii. p. 1106), part of a poem called *Paraenesis ad Episcopos*, written by Theodulph while yet a deacon (*Parva sed in magna cum sim Levitide turba Pars*, is his expression in referring to himself). In the poem, as it stands in the edition of Sirmondus, the order of the verses has evidently become confused. But there is a long passage in which a comparison is made between the outward splendour of the *pontifex*, or Jewish high-priest, and the ornament of diverse virtues which should be conspicuous in the Christian "pontifex," or bishop.

> *Illius insignis radiabat lumine vestis,*
> *Blanditiasque hominum visibus illa dabat:*
> *At tibi virtutum dent ornamenta decorem,*
> *Atque oculis cordis, qua potes, usque fove.*
> *Illi erat in sacro pollens reverentia cultu,*
> *Et decus in habitu pontificalis opis.*
> *Sancta est in sancta tibimet reverentia Matri,*
> *Et vitae studiis, actibus inque piis.*
> *Aurea Pontificis cingebat lamina frontem,*
> *Quae bis binus apex Nomen Herile dabat.*
> *At tibi frons mentis cingatur sensibus almis,*
> *Christum Evangelico vox et ab ore sonet.*
> *Sint manifesti actus Fidei, probitatis, et aequi,*
> *Qui sit virtutum quattuor ordo tibi.*

---

³⁹⁵ Beiträge, s. i. w. p. 227. *Aliquando bonus dormitat Homerus.* Dr. Hefele's criticism is generally very accurate, and very unprejudiced, as far as I have had opportunities of judging. The passage here commented upon must not be regarded as a typical specimen of the author, but quite the reverse.

³⁹⁵ᵃ So Hugo Menardus pointed out long ago. See his notes to the Sacramentary of St. Gregory, p. 363.

Then after about hundred lines come in the two following verses, in a context to which they have no reference whatever:

> *Illius ergo caput refplendens mitra tegebat :*
> *Contegat et* (at ?) *mentem jus pietafque tuam.*

So far from proving, as Martene thought, the ufe of an epifcopal mitre in France at the clofe of the eighth century, the evidence of this paffage (when examined with its context) points, as will now be feen, to a directly oppofite conclufion. The lines I have quoted are nothing more than a reproduction, in Latin verfes, fuch as were written in thofe times, of the language of Venerable Bede, quoted in p. 78, and commented on in the Introduction. And Theodulphus probably owed the idea, which he has here amplified, to the fame fource as did Bede, viz, to the prayer ufed in the confecration of bifhops, quoted above, Introd. note *s*, p. li.

It is inftructive, on many accounts, to the ftudent of antiquity, to fee in the examples above given, how plaufible a cafe may be made out in favour of any preconceived conclufion, by dint of mutilated quotations fet forth without reference to context. Inftructive, too, to mark (I am obliged to add), how little weight fhould be given, in difputed queftions fuch as thefe, to the reputation, even though deferved, of great and varied learning, on the part of thofe who write concerning them. Erudition, fuch as that of Edmond Martene; accurate fcholarfhip, thorough impartiality, careful refearch, fuch as are confpicuous in Dr. Hefele; may all be employed in laborioufly building up arguments, which fall to the ground, as in a moment, when the witneffes, to whom they appeal, are allowed to tell their own tale in full.

I fay this of archæologifts, to whom it applies in fome meafure. But I commend the remark to theologians, to whom, unfortunately, it applies much more.

---

# APPENDIX C.

## PASSAGES FROM ANCIENT AUTHORS ILLUSTRATING THE HISTORY OF THE PÆNULA, CASULA, AND PLANETA.

### PART I. THE PÆNULA.

1. Plautus (born *circ.* 254 B.C.), *Moft.* iv. 11, 74. [Theuropides fays, angrily, to a flave with whom he is difpleafed]:

> *Jamne abis ? Libertas pænula eft tergo tuo.*

"It is only that big cloak of yours that saves your back." Literally, Thy pænula is liberty (*i.e.* the privileges of a free man) to thy back.

2. Lucilius (born B.C. 148), *Sat.* lib. xv. Fr. 6.

*Pænula, si quæris, cantherius, servus, segestre,*
*Utilior mihi, quam sapiens.*

3. Cicero (born 106 B.C.), *Pro Milone*. He is shewing from the mode in which Milo travelled that he could not have set out with the intention of attacking Clodius. He states (p. 524, 20) that while Clodius (really bent on violence) had left the city *expeditus, in equo, nulla rheda, nullis impedimentis,* Milo, on the contrary (who had been falsely accused of treacherous and intended violence) "*cum uxore veheretur in rheda pænulatus.*" Accordingly, as soon as the followers of Milo attacked him, the first thing he did was *rejicere pænulam,* which, by its form and its weight, confined his arms and prevented his defending himself. *Cum hic (sc.* Milo) *de rheda, rejectâ pænulâ, desiluisset, seque acri animo defenderet*. And these circumstances, he argues (p. 518, 40), proved of themselves, "Uter esset insidiator, uter nihil cogitaret mali; cum alter veheretur in rheda pænulatus, una sederet uxor. Quid horum non impeditissimum, vestitus (*sc.* pænula) an vehiculum, an comes? Quid minus promptum ad pugnam, cum pænula irretitus" (entangled in his pænula as in a net), rheda impeditus, uxore pene constrictus esset?"

4. From another passage, *pro P. Sestio*, p. 444 (70), we learn that a rough pænula was commonly worn by mule-drivers, and the like.

"Sensit rusticulus . . . suum sanguinem quæri . . . mulioniam pænulam arripuit, cum qua primum Romam ad comitia venerat, messoria se corbe contexit."

5. From its being commonly worn in travelling, *pænulam attingere alicui* seems to have been a proverbial phrase, for what we should call "keeping a man by the button."

*Cic. Ad Atticum*, lib. vi. p. 288 (113). *Paullo post C. Capito cum T. Carrinate. Horum ego vix attigi pænulam, et tamen remanserunt.* And to the same effect just before: "*De Varrone loquebamur. Lupus in fabula*" ("Talk of the devil!"), "*venit enim ad me, et quidem id temporis ut retinendus esset. Sed ego ita egi ut non scinderem pænulam.*" In other words, he was not *over pressing* in his expressions of civility, when he inquired whether he would not stay. He did not "tear his cloak" rather than let him go.

6. Varro (born B.C. 82), *apud Nonnium*, 14, n. 3.

"Non quærenda est homini, qui habet virtutem, pænula in imbri."

7. Horace (born 65 B.C.), 1 Ep. xi. 18.

*Incolumi Rhodos, aut Mitylene pulchra facit, quod*
*Pænula solstitio, campestre nivalibus auris.*

"If not compelled to live at Rhodes, or at Mitylene, by ill health, a man would no more take up his abode there for good, than he would wear a thick cloak, such as the pænula, at midsummer, or the dress of the exercise ground (scarcely to be called dress) in midwinter."

8. Seneca (born 61 B.C.) *Epist.* lxxxvii. He is describing a little riding tour which he had taken with his friend Maximus, and the manner in which they bivouacked.

*Culcita* (a mattrass) *in terra jacet, ego in culcita. Ex duabus pænulis altera stragulum, altera opertorium facta est.*

"One pænula served the purpose of a blanket under him; the other that of a coverlet to throw over him."

9. *Martial* (43 to 104 A.D.) To him, writing at Rome towards the close of the first century of our era, *pænulatus* is an epithet implying a position below that of a gentleman; while *togatus* (see above, p. 177, No. 9) means a "*needy* gentleman," one not altogether independent of others, and obliged therefore to pay ceremonious court to the rich and influential, to whom he is under obligation. Epig. lib. v. 27.

> *Quod Alpha dixi, Codre, pænulatorum*
> *Te nuper, aliqua cum jocarer in charta ;*
> *Si forte bilem movit hic tibi versus,*
> *Dicas licebit Beta me togatorum.*

10. But people of all ranks would wear a *pænula* (as we should carry an umbrella) when on a journey. Hence the allusion in the following lines, where "*scortea*" means a rough pænula made of sheep-skin or the like. Compare No. 7:

> *Ingrediare viam cælo licet usque sereno,*
> *Ad subitas nunquam scortea desit aquas.*

11. Another kind of *pænula* known as *gausapina* was of fine and white wool, and so handsome withal, that people who were vain of their dress are represented as wishing for cold weather *that they might have an excuse for wearing them*.

> *Et dolet et queritur sibi non contingere frigus,*
> *Propter sexcentas Baccara gausapinas.*
>
> Epig. lib. vi. 59.
>
> *Pænula gausapina.*
> *Is mihi candor inest, villorum gratia tanta est,*
> *Ut me vel media sumere messe velis.*
>
> Epig. lib. xiv. 145.

12. Juvenal (writing *circ.* 100 A.D.) *Sat.* v.

> *Scilicet hoc fuerat, propter quod sæpe relicta*
> *Conjuge, per montem adversum gelidasque cucurri*
> *Esquilias, fremeret sæva cum grandine vernus*
> *Jupiter, et multo stillaret pænula nimbo.*

13. Emperor Adrian (Imp. 117 to 138 A.D.). Lampridius in *Adriano.* "Tribunus plebis factus est, in quo magistratu ad perpetuam tribunitiam po-

teftatem (*i.e.*, to *imperial* power) omen fibi factum afferit, quod pænulas amiferit, quibus uti Tribuni plebis pluviæ tempore folebant, Imperatores autem nunquam. Unde hodieque Imperatores fine penulis ac togati videntur."

14. Emperor Commodus (Imp. 180 to 192 A.D.) Lampridius in *Commodo*. [He is fpeaking of a fhow of gladiators (*munus*) exhibited in the circus.] "Ipfe prodigium non leve fibi fecit. Nam cum in gladiatoris occifi vulnere manum mififfet, ad caput fibi deterfit; et contra confuetudinem pænulatos juffit Senatores, non togatos, ad munus convenire, quod in funeribus folebat, ipfe in pullis veftimentis præfidens."

15. Emperor Alexander Severus (Imp. 222 to 235). Lampridius in *Alexandro*. "Pænulis intra urbem frigoris caufa ut Senatores uterentur permifit." *Ibid.* "Matronas intra urbem pænulis ubi vetuit, in itinere permifit."

16. Julius Pollux, tom. ii. lib. vii. cap. 13, p. 729. [*Floruit circa* 185 A.D.] ἡ δὲ μανδύη ἔμοιδο τι τῇ καλουμένῃ φαινόλῃ· Τίνων δὲ ἐστιν, ὡς μὴ περιεχόμεθα (*fort.* περιεχόμενα, Salmas. vel περιεχόμενα, *i.e.*, ne oberremus Kuhn), Κρέσσαις ὁ Πέρσαις Αἰσχύλος ἐφῆ· Λιβυστικὰς μέμηκα μανδύας χιτών· Καὶ αὐτὸς δὲ ὁ φαινόλης·[390] ἐστὶν ἐν 'Ρίνθωνος 'Ἰφιγενίᾳ τῇ ἐν Ταύροις· ἐχοῦσα (*leg.* ἔχουσα) καινὸν φαινόλαν.[391]

From this paffage we learn that the Greek *pænula* in the fecond century was fomewhat like in fhape to the μανδύη (note 153). This agrees with what we have already quoted from Artemidorus (*fupra*, Appendix A, No. 11 *c*, p. 180). We learn, too, that the φαινόλη was as old, at leaft, as the time of Rhinthon (*circ.* 320 B.C.). But there are reafons for thinking that it was very much older than this.[392]

17. Tertullian (died *circ.* 230 A.D.) *De Oratione*, cap. 12 (tom. iv. p. 14). [He had been fpeaking of the fuperftitious ufe of various ablutions practifed by fome in his time, and faying that "*satis mundæ funt manus, quas cum toto corpore in Chrifto femel lavimus*" (his thought being of John, xiii. 10). He follows out his fubject as follows:]

"Sed quoniam unum aliquod attigimus vacuæ obfervationis, non pigebit

---

[390] Compare alfo the expreffion ufed in the *Dialogus de caufis corruptæ eloquentiæ* (probably Quintilian's). *Quantum humilitatis putamus eloquentiæ attuliffe pænulas iftas, quibus adftricti ac velut inclufi, cum judicibus fabulamur?*

[391] We have here two forms, φαινόλης and φαινόλη (here quoted from Rhinthon, a dramatic poet, in its Doric form φαινόλαν). In the older Greek, the feminine form φαινόλη was ufed in fpeaking of the finer and lighter garment worn by women, the mafculine φαινόλης of that worn by men. The later Byzantine Greek, obliterating, as was its wont, thefe finer diftinctions, merged them both in the neuter φαινόλιον.

[392] Tertullian ftates (Apolog. adv. Gentes) that the pænula was "invented" by the Lacedæmonians, to enable them, as fpectators, to enjoy, even in cold weather, the fpectacles of the ftadium. *Ne voluptas impudica frigeret, Lacedæmonii pænulam ludis excogitarunt.* But an unfupported ftatement of this kind does not carry much weight.

cetera quoque denotare, quibus merito vanitas exprobranda eſt, ſiquidem ſine ullius aut Dominici aut Apoſtolici præcepti auctoritate fiunt. Hujuſmodi enim non religioni ſed ſuperſtitioni deputantur, affectata et coacta, et curioſi potius quam rationalis officii, certe vel eo coercenda, quod gentilibus adæquent. Ut eſt quorundam poſitis pænulis orationem facere: ſic enim adeunt ad idola nationes. Quod utique ſi fieri oporteret, Apoſtoli, qui de habitu orandi docent, comprehendiſſent; niſi ſi qui putant.[399] Paulum pænulam ſuam in oratione penes Carpum reliquiſſe. Deus ſcilicet non audiat pænulatos; qui tres ſanctos in fornace Babylonii regis orantes cum Sarabaris et Tiaris ſuis exaudivit."

[This is a very inſtructive paſſage concerning the Pænula. From it we learn that heathen worſhippers, in Tertullian's time, thought it indecorous to wear a Pænula when engaged in public prayer, that on ſuch occaſions therefore they put them off. We learn, too, that many Chriſtians had adopted the ſame cuſtom, and that ſuch ſcruples were regarded by Tertullian as favouring of ſuperſtition rather than of religion. He then puts it as an abſurd (note 399) ſuppoſition, which ſome might poſſibly adopt, that St. Paul loſt his Pænula in conſequence of his taking it off when about to engage in prayer at the houſe of Carpus. As to St. Paul's Pænula being itſelf a "ſacrificial veſtment," it is evident that ſuch an idea had never entered Tertullian's head. No one having any real acquaintance with antiquity could ſuppoſe ſo now. The "ſuperſtition," in Tertullian's time, was that of ſuppoſing that it was ſuch a garment as none could fitly appear in church at all.

18. From another paſſage of Tertullian (*De Cor. Mil.* p. 346) we find that, in his time, the Pænula was worn by ſoldiers, not of courſe when actively engaged (compare No. 3), but much as our own ſoldiers wear "great-coats" for protection againſt the weather. He is ſpeaking of a Chriſtian ſoldier, who had refuſed to wear the *corona* of heathen ſacrificial rites. *Reus ad præfectos. Ibidem graviſſimos pænulas poſuit, relevari auſpicatus.* A ſimilar uſe of the Pænula by ſoldiers appears in a paſſage of Suetonius (in Galba). Speaking of Ser. Sulpicius Galba (afterwards emperor) in the year 45 A.D., he ſays, " A Caio Cæſare Gætulico ſubſtitutus, poſtridie quam ad legiones venit, ſollenni forte ſpectaculo plaudentes inhibuit, data teſſera ut manus pænulis continerent."

19. St. Jerome, ad *Damaſum*, Epiſt. cxxv. 9, 2. " Volumen[400] Hebræum replico, quod Paulus Φαιλόνη juxta quoſdam vocat." [Compare No. 21, below.]

20. *Ibid.* in 2, Epiſt. ad Timoth. iv. 13.[401] " *Pænulam quam reliqui, &c.* Non dixit pænulam meam: potuit enim converſus aliquis, ad pedes ejus, inter cætera, impoſuiſſe vendendum." [Ed. Benedict. vol. v. p. 1100.] *He ſuppoſes*

---

[399] *Niſi ſi qui putant.* This is a formula with which Tertullian introduces a hypotheſis, the abſurdity of which he deems to be ſelf-evident. Compare the paſſage quoted above, Appendix A, No. 42, *niſi ſi non potuit Deus* etc.

[400] He uſes the words *volumen* and *replico* in their technical ſenſe. See note 79, p. 50.

See, too, the words of Theodoret (on 2 Tim. iv. 13) quoted under No. 21, note 403.

[401] This commentary on 2 Ep. Tim. is regarded as ſpurious by the Benedictine editors. But the authorſhip is not, to the preſent queſtion, a matter of primary importance.

*that this Pænula may have been brought by some convert, as a superfluity of which to make an offering to God,* " laying it at the apostles' feet " (Acts, iv. 35), *that it might afterwards be sold, and the proceeds made use of as St. Paul should think fit.*

21. St. John Chrysostom (born *circ.* 347, died 407 A.D.) Tom. xi. p. 780 A, in 2 Tim. iv. 13. Τὸν φελόνην ὃν ἀπέλιπον ἐν Τρῳάδι παρὰ Κάρπῳ, ἐρχόμενος φέρε, καὶ τὰ βιβλία, μάλιστα τὰς μεμβράνας. Φελόνην ἐνταῦθα τὸ ἱμάτιον λέγει. Τινὲς δὲ φασὶ τὸ γλωσσόκομον,[402] ἔνθα τὰ βιβλία ἔκειτο. Τί δὲ αὐτῷ τῶν βιβλίων ἔδει μέλλοντι ἀποδημεῖν πρὸς τὸν Θεόν; Καὶ μάλιστα ἔδει, ὥστε αὐτὰ τοῖς πιστοῖς παραδοῦναι, καὶ ἀντὶ τῆς αὐτοῦ διδασκαλίας ἔχειν αὐτά . . . . . . Τὸν δὲ Φελόνην ζητεῖ ὥστε μὴ διεθῆναι παρ' ἑτέρου λαβεῖν.

" By the word φελόνης, here used, is meant the outer garment so called. But some think that it was the case (*capsa*) in which lay the Books.[403] But for what could he need these Books, when he was about to depart hence unto God? Nay, he had in truth the greatest need of them, that so he might commit them into the hands of the faithful, to be to them in place of his own teaching. . . . And his inquiring for this cloak was for this cause, that he might not need to receive one (as a gift) from some other. For thou seest that this is a matter about which he is specially careful, saying, as he does, in another place, when discoursing to them of Ephesus, *Ye know that these my hands did minister to my necessities, and to them that were with me.* And again, *It is blessed to give rather than to receive.*"

It is evident from the above that St. Chrysostom regarded the φελόνης of St. Paul as an ordinary ἱμάτιον; and that the *membranæ*, or parchments, were in his judgment MSS. containing St. Paul's own teaching.

22 The Theodosian Code, published in 438 A.D., and that simultaneously for the Eastern and the Western empire, furnishes us with an important indication of the changed use of the Pænula established by that time. In lib. i. *De Habitu,* we read as follows:

" Nullus senatorum habitum sibi vindicet militarem, sed chlamydis terrore deposito, quieta colobiorum ac pænularum induat vestimenta. . . . officiales quoque per quos statuta complentur ac necessaria peraguntur, uti quidem pænulis jubemus, verum interiorem vestem admodum cingulis observare."

The chlamys being (note 142) a military garb, is unsuited for senators when at Rome. In earlier times their proper garb would have been the *tunica laticlavia* and the *toga.* The corresponding vestments are now (fifth century) the *colobium* and *pænula.*

---

[402] That is a case for books, such, perhaps, as is represented in Pl. XII., XIV.

[403] For this interpretation of τὰς μεμβράνας, compare Theodoret on this passage. He follows St. Chrysostom closely as was his wont. Μεμβράνας τὰ εἰλητὰ αἴσαλεῖ· (εἰλητὸν i.e. volumen) οὕτω γὰρ Ῥωμαῖοι καλοῦσι τὰ δέρματα. Ἐν εἰλητοῖς δὲ εἶχον πάλαι τὰς θείας γραφάς. Οὕτω δὲ καὶ μέχρι τοῦ παρόντος ἔχουσιν οἱ Ἰουδαῖοι. [This may be said with truth of the Jews even to the present day.]

23. St. Isidore of Seville, *circ.* 600 A.D. See the quotation at p. 72 and note 130 *in loc.* This passage, however, does not prove any *contemporary* usage of the word Pænula, either in Spain or in other parts of the West. For the gloss in question is simply transferred (as was St. Isidore's wont) *totidem verbis* from a *vetus interpres* on Persius.

24. St. Germanus, Patriarch of Constantinople, *circ.* 715 A.D. See his words quoted at p. 84, l. 4. From another mention of the Phænolion at p. 86, l. 1, we learn that in the eighth century, at Constantinople, if not elsewhere, this vestment was either of a purple or a scarlet colour, or at least of a colour which served to recall the "scarlet (or purple) robe" put in mockery upon our Lord.

25. Patriarch Nicephorus of Constantinople writes (in the year 811) to Leo III., *inter alia:*

"In signum mediatricis inter nos in Domino dilectionis, misimus vestræ fraternæ beatitudini encolpion [404] aureum, cujus una facies cristallum inclusum, altera picta nigello [404] est, et intus habet alterum encolpion, in quo sunt partes honorandi ligni in figura Crucis positi: tunicam candidam, et pænulam castaneam inconsutilem (*leg.* inconsutiles); stolam et semicinctium,[405] auro variata."

The word *pænula,* here used, represents the φαινόλης (or more probably φαινόλιον) of the original text. The description of this φαινόλιον as ἄῤῥαφος (*inconsutilis*) may be regarded as probably pointing to those words of St. John, ἧν δὲ ὁ χιτὼν ἄῤῥαφος (*al.* ἄῤῥαφος) ἐκ τῶν ἄνωθεν ὑφαντὸς δι' ὅλου.

### PART II. THE CASULA.

26. The earliest notices of the Casula are two following from St. Augustine (born 354, died 430).

#### THE CASULA AS AN OUT-DOOR DRESS FOR WORKING MEN, *circ.* 350 A.D.

*a. De Civit. Dei,* lib. xxii. cap. 8, § 9. "Erat quidam senex Florentius, Hipponensis noster, homo religiosus et pauper; sartoris se arte pascebat. Casulam perdiderat, et unde sibi emeret non habebat. Ad [406] Viginti Martyres, quorum

---

[404] Ἐγκαύσεως. Enamelling. Baronius edits the letter from the Latin of Anastasius Bibliothecarius. The original Greek text will be found in Harduin's Concilia, vol. iv. p. 1000.

[405] Ἐγχείριον. A handkerchief. Here, probably, something resembling the *sudarium* or *mappula* of the Latin Church. *Stola* is here used as the Latin rendering of ἐπιτραχήλιον, which corresponded (see note 144 p. 84) to the Orarium or Stola of the West.

[406] *Ad viginti, &c.* "At the chapel of the twenty Martyrs." The word "memoria," which follows is here used in its technical sense of a "memorial chapel," or church. St. Augustine's Sermon CCCXXV. is on the "birthday" (day of martyrdom) of these "twenty martyrs," whose number "cœpit ab Episcopo Fidentio, clausit ad fidelem feminam sanctam Victoriam. Initium a fide. Finis ad victoriam."

memoria apud nos est celeberrima, clara voce, ut vestiretur, oravit. Audierunt eum adolescentes, qui forte aderant, irrisores; eumque discedentem exagitantes prosequebantur, quasi a Martyribus quinquagenos folles, unde vestimentum emeret, petivisset. At ille tacitus ambulans ejectum grandem piscem palpitantem vidit in littore, eumque illis faventibus atque adjuvantibus apprehendit, et cuidam coquo, Catoso nomine, bene Christiano, ad coquinam conditariam, indicans quid gestum sit, trecenis follibus vendidit; lanam comparare inde disponens, ut uxor ejus, quomodo posset, ei, quo indueretur, efficeret. Sed coquus, concidens piscem, annulum aureum in ventriculo ejus invenit; moxque miseratione flexus, et relligione perterritus, homini eum reddidit, dicens, Ecce quomodo Viginti Martyres te vestierunt."

### THE CASULA AN ORDINARY OUT-DOOR GARB, *circ.* 400 A.D.

27. β. *Ibid.* Sermo CVII. cap. 5 (tom. v. p. 530). "Quid est iniquius homine qui multa bona habere vult, et bonus ipse esse non vult? Indignus es qui habeas, qui non vis esse quod vis habere. Numquid enim vis habere villam malam? Non utique, sed bonam. Numquid uxorem malam? Non, sed bonam. Numquid denique casulam malam? Numquid vel caligam malam? Quare animam solum malam?"

### THE CASULA WORN BY MONKS (AND BY BISHOPS IN MONASTIC LIFE), *circ.* 500 A.D.

28. Of Fulgentius, Bishop of Ruspa (*circ.* 507), his disciple and biographer Ferrandus writes as follows, l. 18 (*apud Thomassinum, Vet. et Nov. Ecc. Disc.* lib. ii. cap. 47):

"Nunquam pretiosa vestimenta quæsivit: una tantum vilissima tunica, sive per æstatem, sive per hiemem, est patienter indutus. *Orario quidem sicut omnes episcopi nullatenus utebatur. Pellicio cingulo* (note 74) *tanquam monachus utebatur* . . . . *Casulam pretiosam vel superbi coloris nec ipse habuit, nec suos monachos habere permisit.*[407] . . . . In qua tunica dormiebat in ipsa sacrificabat; et in tempore sacrificii mutanda esse corda potius quam vestimenta dicebat."

### A CASULA WORN (AS A CLOAK) BY AN ARCHBISHOP.

29. Extracts from the last will and testament of S. Cæsarius, Archbishop

---

[407] Compare what is said, by Ven. Bede, of S. Cuthbert and the monks of Lindisfarne (Vita S. Cuthberti, cap. 16, Bedæ Opera, tom. iv. p. 262). "Vestimentis utebatur communibus, ita temperanter agens, ut horum neque munditiis neque sordibus esset notabilis. Unde usque hodie in eodem monasterio exemplo ejus observatur, ne quis varii aut pretiosi coloris habeat indumentum, sed ea maxime vestium specie sint contenti, quam naturalis ovium lana (note ʒ, p. xviii) ministrat."

of Arles, † 540. [A copy of this will was obtained for Baronius, from the archives preserved at Arles. See the *Annal.* tom. vi. p. 602, *sqq.*] " Sancto et domino meo archiepiscopo, qui mihi indigno digne suscesserit, licet omnia in sua potestate sint, tamen, si lubet, et dignum ducit, indumenta paschalia [408] quæ mihi data sunt, omnia illi serviant, simul cum casula villosa [409] et tunica vel galnape quod melius dimisero. Reliqua vero vestimenta mea, excepto birro amiculari, mei tam clerici quam laici, cum gratia vel ordinatione domini archiepiscopi, sibi ipso jubente, immo donante, dividant."

30. [In the life of the same Archbishop Cæsarius, we find mention of his wearing a Casula both in his ordinary walks about the city, and in processions.] "Ambulans per plateam civitatis, vidit contra in foro hominem qui a dæmonio agebatur. In quem cum attendisset, *habens manum sub casula, ut a suis non videretur, crucem contra eum fecit*." And again:

31. Lib. ii. cap. 19. [A poor man begs of him, and the bishop having no money to give him] "*casulam qua in processionibus utebatur*, et albam paschalem [408] profert, datque egeno, jubetque ut vendat uni ex clero."

THE CASULA A DRESS FOR PEASANTS, *circ.* 530 A.D.

32. Procopius (Fl. *circa* 530 A.D.) *De Bello Vandalico*, lib. ii. cap. 26. He is describing the abject submission of Areobindus when defeated by Gontharis. He speaks of him as ἱμάτιον ἀμπιχόμενος οὔτε στρατηγῷ οὔτε ἄλλῳ στρατευομένῳ ἀνδρὶ ἐπιτηδείως ἔχον, ἀλλὰ δούλῳ καὶ ἰδιώτῃ παντάπασι πρέπον, Κασοῦλαν αὐτὸ τῇ Λατίνων φωνῇ καλοῦσι 'Ρωμαῖοι.[410]

CASULA AS AN OUT-DOOR DRESS AT ROME, *circ.* 600 A.D.

33. *S. Gregorii Vita* a Joanne Diacono conscripta, lib. iv. cap. 63. The biographer quotes a story of St. Gregory told by Abbot John, a Persian. "Olim ivi Romam ad adorandum loculos sanctorum apostolorum Petri et Pauli: et una dierum cum starem in medio civitatis, video Papam Gregorium per (prope?) me transiturum: et cogitavi me mittere ante eum. Cum ergo appropinquasset mihi Papa, videns quia pergerem ut mitterem me ante eum,[411] sicut coram Deo dico, fratres, primus misit se ante me super terram: et non

---

[408] By the *alba paschalis*, here mentioned, we are probably to understand an alb of some more than usually rich material to be used at the Easter festival. Dr. Hefele, however, interprets the parallel expression *indumenta paschalia*, (*supra*, No. 29) as " Sonntagsgewänder." I can hardly suppose this to be correct.

[409] Dr. Hefele observes (D. L. G. p. 196) that this *casula villosa*, or long-napped cloak, is here distinguished from the *indumenta paschalia*

(note 409), and is a garment for out-door wear, not an ecclesiastical " vestment," properly so called.

[410] Procopius evidently considers the *casula* to be a garb fit only for peasants. It is assumed on this occasion as a *vestis sordida*, in token of abject humility and subjection.

[411] *Me mittere ad eum*, i.e., " bowing himself to the ground before him," as is the wont of Eastern people.

ante furrexit, quam ego prior furgerem; et amplexatus me cum multa humilitate, *tribuit mihi per manum numifmata tria: et juffit mihi dari cafulam et neceffitates meas omnes.*"

### A CASULA SENT AS A PRESENT TO A KING.

34. Bonifacii III. PP. Epift. iii. (*apud O. Ferrarium*, D. R. V. p. 685,) A.D. 606. "Litteras et munufcula parva tranfmitto vobis, id eft, Cafulam non holofericam, fed caprina lanugine miftam, et villofam, ad tergendos pedes [414] dilectionis veftræ."

35. St. Ifidore, *Hifp. De Originibus*, lib. xix. (quoted above, at p. 74), *circ.* A.D. 620. He does not mention the Cafula as in any way a *facred* veftment, but merely defcribes it as a *veftis cucullata*.

### A CASULA THE OUT-DOOR DRESS OF THE CLERGY.

36. Concilium Germanicum I. Celebratum xi. Kal. Mai, A.D. 742. Sub Carlemanno Majore Domus Regiæ, auctoritate S. Bonifacii, Can. vii. "Decrevimus [415] quoque ut presbyteri vel diaconi non fagis laicorum more, fed cafulis utantur, ritu fervorum [416] Dei." [Labbe, Concil. tom. vi. p. 1533, *fqq.*]

37. To the paffages above given may be added a reference to a fingular fragment, illuftrating the old Gallican ufe, and which may poffibly date from the eighth [417] century, though it would feem to belong rather to the ninth. See Appendix E. The fecond paragraph, there quoted, contains not only a

---

[414] This letter is addreffed to king Pepin. It is difficult to underftand how a cafula fhould be ufed *ad tergendos pedes*. Either therefore *villofa* muft here be taken as a virtual fubftantive (compare *linea, alba, gaufapina, fcortea*), or we muft fuppofe fome word fuch as *mappam* to have been dropped.

[415] It is worth noting as a characteriftic feature of thefe times, that the decrees of this Council iffue in the name of "*Ego Carlemannus Dux et Princeps Francorum*," acting "*cum confilio fervorum Dei et optimatum meorum;*" and in purfuance of fuch counfel, decreeing (*ftatuimus*) that fynods fhould be held, yearly, "*ita ut nobis præfentibus canonum decreta et ecclefiæ jura reftaurentur, et religio Chriftiana emendetur.*"

[416] In fpeaking of the Cafula as befitting thofe who are "*fervi*" of God, St. Boniface may not improbably have had in view the lowly origin of this garb, as worn by peafants and by monks. The *fagum*, which presbyters and deacons in Germany are forbidden to wear, is the fhort military cloak which in the eighth century had come into general fecular ufe. Some (as Dr. Hefele) underftand the words *ritu fervorum Dei* to mean "as do monks." But in the Preface, quoted in note 415, the words evidently are ufed of "the clergy."

[417] There is mention made of the *cafula* as the veftment of a presbyter in the Sacramentary of St. Gregory, and from this fome writers have carelefsly inferred that the cafula muft *in his time*, i.e., *circ.* 600 A.D., have been recognifed as a veftment of Chriftian miniftry. But, as Profeffor Hefele remarks, the Sacramentary proves nothing of the kind, feeing that it dates, *in its prefent form*, from a period confiderably later than St. Gregory, probably not earlier than the ninth century. The words occur in the *Ordinatio Presbyteri*, p. 238, when, juft before the bleffing is conferred, the direction following is given: *Hic veftis et cafulam, i.e.* At this point thou art to inveft him with the chafuble.

reference to the Chasuble as a vestment of holy ministration, but a description of its form. *Casula . . . sine manicis, unita prinsecus, non scissa non aperta.* See p. 204, below.

### PLANETA TOO COSTLY TO BE WORN BY MONKS.

38. Cassianus (*circ.* 418 A.D.) *De Habitu Monachorum,* lib. i. cap. 7. "Post hæc angusto palliolo tam amictus humilitatem, quam vilitatem pretii compendiumqne sectantes, colla pariter atque humeros tegunt quæ mafortes tam nostro quam ipsorum nuncupantur eloquio, et ita Planeticarum simul atque birrorum (note *w,* p. lvi) pretia simul et ambitionem declinant."

### THE PLANETA WORN BY LAYMEN OF RANK.

39. Vita S. Fulgentii († 533) *Acta Sanctorum,* tom. i. Januar. p. 43. [The writer, Nolanus, a contemporary of Fulgentius, is describing the return of Fulgentius to Carthage after his exile.] "Tantum fides Nobilium crevit, ut Planetis suis super B. Fulgentium gratanter expansis, repellerent imbres, et novum tabernaculi genus artificiosa caritate componerent."

### PLANETA WORN BY THE ATTENDANTS OF A BISHOP OF ROME.

40. Joan. Diac. Vita D. Gregorii, lib. ii. cap. 43. [The writer is speaking of a plot laid by certain sorcerers (*magi*) to throw St. Gregory off his horse as he rode through the city.] "Cumque magi ex planetatorum[418] mappulatorumque processionibus magnum pontificem cognovissent," &c., &c.

### PLANETA WORN BY A ROMAN SENATOR, AND A ROMAN BISHOP.

41. Joan. Diac. Vita D. Gregorii, lib. iv. cap. 83. [Describing the dress of Gordianus, a senator, father of St. Gregory, he says,] "Gordiani habitus castanei coloris planeta est, sub planeta dalmatica, in pedibus caligas habens."

And in cap. 84, speaking of St. Gregory himself, "Planeta super dalmaticam castanea."

### THE PLANETA NOT TO BE WORN BY MONKS.

42. St. Isidore (*circ.* 620), *in Regula,* cap. 13 (*apud Ducange*). "Linteo non licet Monachum indui. Orarium, birros, planetas, non est fas uti, neque illa indumenta vel calceamenta quæ generaliter cætera monasteria abutuntur" (" do not use ").

---

[418] The people dressed in *planetæ* are probably presbyters, and high officials; the mappulati, deacons, and sub-deacons.

## THE PLANETA WORN AS A DISTINCTIVE VESTMENT BY BISHOPS AND PRESBYTERS.

43. *Concil. Tolet.* iv. ann. 634. See p. 75, *sqq*.

## A PLANETA ONE OF THE VESTMENTS OF A POPE.

44. *Ordo Romanus* i. (eleventh century), *apud Mabillon, Museum Italicum*, and Martene *De Antiq. Eccl. Rit.* tom. ii. lib. iii. cap. 11.

In § 6 the vestments of the Pontifex Romanus are enumerated:

"Subdiaconi regionarii secundum ordinem suum accipiunt ad induendum Pontificem ipsa vestimenta: alius lineam, alius cingulum, alius anagolaium, id est amictum, alius lineam dalmaticam, et alius majorem dalmaticam, *et alius planetam*; et sic per ordinem induunt Pontificem. . . . Novissime autem, quem voluerit Dominus pontifex de diaconibus, vel subdiaconibus, cui ipse jusserit, sumit de manu subdiaconi sequentis pallium, et induit super Pontificem, et configit eum cum acubus in planeta retro et ante, et in humero sinistro et salutat Domnum et dicit," &c.

## PLANETA WORN BY DEACONS, SUB-DEACONS, ACOLYTES.[419]

45. *Ibid.* §§ 7 to 11. From a variety of notices in this portion of the *Ordo Romanus I.*, it is clear that at Rome, in the eleventh century (and probably at a somewhat earlier time also), deacons, sub-deacons, and other of the inferior orders, wore a planeta when in attendance on a pope at a solemn function.[420]

---

[419] Compare Ordo Rom. viii., where an acolyte, at his ordination, is described as invested with *orarium* and *planeta*. Dr. Hefele, referring to this, conjectures (p. 201), that the *planeta* of the minor orders was a scantier and shorter vestment than that worn by bishops and presbyters, resembling the little phænolion so called, worn by ἀναγνῶσται in the Greek Church. But he has apparently overlooked the passage in the Ordo I., which is inconsistent with his explanation. For the sub-deacon is there described (§ 7) as carrying the mappula of the pontiff on his own left arm, *super planetam revolutam*. A vestment such as Hefele describes could not be rolled (folded) back upon the arm, and then have a mappula resting upon it. But these are minor matters, of antiquarian interest only.

[420] From the close of the eighth century the terms *Planeta* and *Casula* ceased to be distinguished the one from the other. See Rabanus Maurus (quoted p. 91, "Casula . . . hanc Græci planetam vocant"); Honorius of Autun (quoted p. 137, "Casula . . . hæc vestis et Planeta . . . vocatur"); Innocent III. (quoted p. 155, "Casulam vel Planetam.") To these passages may be added the following from the life of Abbot Ansegisus (written in the ninth century), edited by Mabillon in the *Acta Sanctorum Ord. Benedict.* Sæc. iv. p. 945. Mention is made of various gifts to the church made by St. Ansegifus, and amongst them of *Planetas casulas quatuor . . . mappulas duas . . . . stolas duas*. And so Luitprand (Hist. vi. cap. xi). Cui (sc. Benedicto Pseudo-Papæ) "Casulam quam Planetam vocant, cum stola pariter abstulit."

# APPENDIX D.

## VESTMENTS WORN IN THE GALLICAN CHURCH.

### From a MS. of Uncertain Date Edited by Martene.[421]

*Epist. Secunda De Communi Officio.* . . . "Pallium in pascha cum tintinnabulis Eucharistia velatur, instar veteris testamenti ubi tonica [h. e. tunica] sacerdotis plena tintinnabulis, signans verba prædicationis, ostenditur. Præcinctio autem vestimenti candidi, quod sacerdos baptizaturus præcingitur, in signa sancti Joannis agitur, qui præcinctus baptizavit Dominum. Albis autem vestibus in pascha induetur, secundum quod angelus ad monumentum albis vestibus cerneretur. Albæ etinim vestis exaltationem significant.

"Casula, quam amphibalum vocant, quod sacerdos induetur, tota unita, per Moysem legiserum instituta primitus demonstratur. Jussit ergo Dominus fieri dissimilatum vestimentum, ut talem sacerdos induerit quali indui populus non auderetur. Ideo sine manicas, quia sacerdos potius benedicit quam ministrat.[422] Ideo unita prinsecus, non scissa, non aperta: quia multæ sunt Scripturæ sacræ secreta mysteria, quæ quasi sub sigillo sacerdoti doctus debet abscondere, et unitatem custodire, non in hæresi vel schismata declinare.[423]

"Pallium[424] vero quod circa collo usque ad pectus venit, rationale vocabatur in vetere testamento, scilicet signum sanctitatis super memoriam pectoris, dicente propheta ex persona Domini, 'Spiritus Domini super me.' Et post pauca, 'ut ponerem gloriam lugentibus Sion, et darem eis coronam pro cinere, oleum gaudii pro luctu' (Is. lxi. 3). Pallium laudis pro spiritu mœroris. Quod autem collo cingit, antiquæ consuetudinis est, quia reges et sacerdotes circumdati

---

[421] These extracts are from a MS. edited by Martene (*Thesaurus Anecdotorum*, tom. v). He describes it as follows; *Sancti Germani Parisiensis episcopi expositio brevis antiquæ Liturgiæ Gallicanæ*; and gives it as his opinion that *this work was written* (hoc opus scriptum) about the middle of the sixth century. This, he says, because St. Germanus was Bishop of Paris from 556 to 576 A.D. The only link of connection, however, between this anonymous MS. (found in the Monastery of St. Martin at Autun) and St. Germanus, is the fact that the writer begins by referring to (and quoting) what *Germanus episcopus Parisius scripsit de Missa*. Internal evidence points to the ninth or tenth century as the earliest at which the MS. could have been actually written. [The spelling of the original is preserved throughout.]

[422] He refers to the fact that the form of the Casula was inconsistent with the use of the arms for anything like *active ministration*.

[423] This furnishes, as will be seen, a new mystical meaning for the *Casula*.

[424] The word Pallium is probably not used here in the technical sense of an archbishop's Pallium. In early representations (ninth century) of Gallican Bishops, the older form of the Pallium is seen, resembling that of Pl. XXX., XXXI., but meeting it at a point at the breast. And so the words here commented on may point to the *Pallium Gallicanum* (so called), of which more in Appendix E.

erant pallia veste fulgente, quod gratia præsignabat. Quod autem fimbriis vestimenta sacerdotalia adnectuntur, Dominus Moysi præcepit in Numeris, ut per quattuor angulos palliorum filii Israel fimbrias facerent, ut populus Domini non solum opere, sed etiam et vestitu, mandatorum Dei signum portaret.

"Manualia vero, id est manicas,[425] induere sacerdotibus mos est, instar armillarum quas regum vel sacerdotum brachia constringebantur. Ideo autem ex quolibet pretioso vellere, non metalli duritia, extant, vel ut omnes communiter sacerdotes etiam minoris dignitatis in sæculo facilius inveniant.

"Vestimentum parvolum [425a] quod non sit in alio uso nisi ad frequentandum sacrificium, vel significat quod non graventur manus nostræ honoribus seculi, sed circumdentur subtilia exercitia mandatorum Dei. Prohibet autem manica, tonica, ne appareat vile vestimentum, aut quocunque indignum tactum sordium super divina sacrificia, quo manus immolantis discurrunt.

"Albas vero quas levitæ utuntur ideo statuerunt Patres, quia in vestimento tincto non sic apparet cito macula quomodo in albo: et minister altaris ideo utitur, ut observet et caveat omnem maculam et nullatenus vestimenta ministrantium vel leviore tactu appareant sordida; sed candida sint, exterius veste, interius mente. Sirico aut vellere fictur, quia Dominus sacerdotibus ideo exinde habere indumenta mandavit, ut eorum vestis spem resurrectionis ostenderet. Sirico enim de ligno per verme fictur. Vermis post mortem procedit in alate, et post occasum et volatum figurans Christum, qui ex ligno crucis quiescens in sepulchro, tanquam vermis clausus in sæculo angusto, surrexit de tumulo, et ad cælos sumsit volatum. Alterius vero velleris albi innocentiam tantum vitæ demonstrant. Alba autem non constringitur cingulo, sed suspensa tegit levitæ corpusculum, quia omnis conversatio Levitica in desiderio cælestis patriæ a terrenis operibus debet esse suspensa, nec cingulo peccatorum constricta.

"Stola autem, quam super alba diaconus induit, significat subtilitatis intelligentiam in divina mysteria, licet veteri (h. e. veteres) stola induentes gaudium sollennitatis se habere monstrabant. Et pro hac causa in quadragesima pro humiliatione non utitur, sicut nec alleluia in nostra ecclesia, sanctus, vel prophetia, hymnum trium puerorum, vel canticum rubri maris, illis diebus decantantur. Stola alba namque angelus præcinctus apparuit, quando sedens in monumento Domini sollennitatem resurrectionis illius nunciavit. Ideo in quadragesima prohibendum hæc cantica, quia cælestia et angelica sunt."

---

[425] The *manicæ*, here mentioned, "*instar armillarum*," seems to point to a vestment resembling the Greek *ἐπιμανίκια* (note 350, p. 169).

[425a] This "small vestment" is evidently the maniple.

# APPENDIX E.

## PASSAGES FROM EARLY WRITERS ILLUSTRATING THE HISTORY OF THE ORARIUM ("STOLE,") AND THE PAPAL PALLIUM.

### THE ORARIUM OF SECULAR USE.

1. The following passages will indicate the form, and usage, of the Orarium in ordinary life. *a.* St. Jerome, *ad Nepotianum*, 529. *Plenum dedecoris est, referto marsupio, quod sudarium orariumque non habeas gloriari.* β. St. Ambrose, *De Resurrect. Et facies ejus (sc. Lazari) orario colligata erat.* γ. St. Augustine, *De Civit. Dei*, lib. xxii. cap. 8, § 7. [An Orarium used as a bandage to tie up a wounded eye.] *Tunc, sicut potuit, oculum lapsum atque pendentem loco suo revocatum ligavit orario.* δ. Prudentius (fifth century), *Peristeph.* 1, 86. [Speaking of two martyrs, Hemeterius and Celedonius, he says that the ring worn by one, and the handkerchief of the other, were miraculously carried up to heaven.] *Illa laus occulta non est, nec senescit tempore, missa quod sursum per auras evolarunt munera. . . . Illius fidem figurans nube fertur annulus; Hic sui dat pignus oris, ut ferunt, orarium.* ε. With this last compare St. Gregory of Tours, *De Glor. Martyr.* cap. 93, where he relates the same tale. In another passage of the same author we read of the son of Sigismund being strangled by means of an *Orarium. Hist. Franc.* lib. iii. cap. 5. *Sopitum vino dormire post meridiem filium jubet: cui dormienti orarium sub collo positum ac sub mento ligatum, trahentibus ad se invicem duobus pueris, suggillatus est.* [This was in the year 522 A.D.] ζ. St. Gregory the Great (close of the sixth century), writing to a friend at Constantinople, a *vir religiosus*, but not a priest, sends him as a present *duas camisias et quattuor oraria*, much as the Emperor Gallienus had done when writing to Claudius, three centuries earlier. [Epist. lib. vii. xxx. Indict. xv.]

### ORARIA AS IMPERIAL PRESENTS.

1 *b.* Trebellius Pollio in *Claudio* (*prope finem*). He is quoting a letter of the Emperor Gallienus in which he enumerates the presents (chiefly plate and rich garments) which he had sent to Claudius (afterwards emperor from 268 to 270). "Albam subsericam, paragaudem triuncem unam. Zanchas de nostris Parthicis paria tria, . . . Penulam Illyricianam unam . . . Oraria Sarabdena quatuor."

*Appendix E.*

Flavius Vopiscus in *Aureliano* (*Imp.* 270-275), *prope fin.* (p. 428). "Sciendun ... illum ... donasse populo Romano tunicas albas manicatas ex diversis provinciis, et lineas Afras atque Ægyptias puras; *ipsumque primum donasse oraria populo Romano quibus uteretur populus ad favorem.*" [On this use of *oraria*, "ad favorem," see F. B. Ferrarius, *De Veterum Acclamationibus*, lib. ii. cap. 7, p. 63.]

### THE ORARIUM, AS A SACRED VESTMENT, NOT TO BE WORN BY ANY BELOW THE RANK OF A DEACON.

2. Council of Laodicea, A.D. 327. [Harduin *Concil.* tom. i. p. 786.] Can. xxiii. οὐ δεῖ ὑπηρέτας ὀράριον φορεῖν, οὐδὲ τὰς θύρας ἐγκαταλιμπάνειν. Ibid. Can xxiv. ὅτι οὐ δεῖ ἀναγνώστας ἢ ψάλτας ὀράριον φορεῖν, καὶ οὕτως ἀναγινώσκειν ἢ ψάλλειν.

### ORARIUM WORN BY DEACONS, *circ.* 467.

3. St. Chrysostom († 407). In *Parab. de Filio Prodigo. Inter opera spuria.* [Though probably not St. Chrysostom's, it is of a date not much later than his]. Tom. viii. p. 655. Μεμνημένοι τῶν φρικτῶν μυστηρίων τῶν λειτουργῶν τῆς θείας λειτουργίας, τῶν μιμουμένων τὰς τῶν ἀγγέλων πτέρυγας ταῖς λεπταῖς ὀθόναις ταῖς ἐπὶ τῶν ἀριστέρων ὤμων κειμέναις, καὶ ἐν τῇ ἐκκλησίᾳ περιτρεχόντων.

### THE SAME, *circ.* 412.

4. St. Isidore of Pelusium, *circ.* 412 A.D. He speaks (see above, p. 49) of ἡ ὀθόνη μεθ' ἧς λειτουργοῦσιν οἱ διάκονοι ἐν ταῖς ἁγίαις; and he adds that this ὀθόνη, or piece of fine linen, recalls the humility of our Lord in that of His washing, and wiping dry, the feet of His disciples.

### ORARIUM FORBIDDEN TO MONKS, A.D. 511.

5. Concil. Aurelian. (anno 511) Canon xx. "Monacho uti orario [426] in Monasterio, vel tzangas [427] habere non liceat." [Labbe, Concil. tom. iv. p. 1407.]

---

[426] All commentators on this passage consider the word Orarium to be here used with its older meaning of a "pocket hankerchief."

[427] *Tzangæ.* A kind of boot. τζάγγα or ἐζάγγια in Byzantine Greek. As being of barbarous origin they were not allowed to be worn at Constantinople, *intra urbem,* even by laymen. [Codex Theod. *De Habitu,* &c. 14, 10. *Usum Tzangarum atque braccarum intra urbem venerabilem nemini liceat usurpare.*] Nearly four centuries later Charlemagne interdicted their use by the Clergy. *Capitul.* lib. vii. cap. 314. *Ut clerici pampis* [*al.* pompis] *aut tzangis vel armis non utuntur.* The passage in the letter of Emperor Gallienus quoted in p. 206 (overlooked by Ducange), determines their origin. *Zanchas de nostris Parthicis paria tria.*

### DEACONS ARE NOT TO HIDE THEIR ORARIA.

6. Concil. Bracar. II. A.D. 563, capitulum ix. "Item placuit ut quia in aliquantis hujus provinciæ ecclesiis diaconi absconsis infra tunicam utuntur orariis, ita ut nihil differre a subdiacono videantur, de cetero superposito scapulæ utantur orario." For Concil. Bracar. III. A.D. 572, see Innocent III., *sup.* p. 154.

7. Concil. Tolet. IV. A.D. 633. [See above, p. 76.] Bishops and presbyters alike wear *Oraria*, but not more than *one*. Deacons also are to wear but one, and that upon the left shoulder only. They are to wear it plain (*purum*), not decked out with colours nor with gold.

8. Concil. Bracar. IV. A.D. 685 [Labbe, tom. vii. p. 581] Can iv. "Cum antiqua ecclesiastica noverimus institutione præfixum ut omnis sacerdos, cum ordinatur, orario utroque humero ambiatur, scilicet ut qui imperturbatus præcipitur consistere inter prospera et adversa, virtutum semper ornamento utrobique circumseptus appareat; qua ratione tempore sacrificii non assumat quod se in sacramento accepisse non dubitatur? Proinde modis omnibus convenit ut quod quisque percepit in consecratione, hoc et retentet in oblatione, vel perceptione suæ salutis; scilicet ut cum sacerdos ad solemnia missarum accedit, aut pro se Deo sacrificium oblaturus, aut sacramentum Corporis et Sanguinis Domini nostri Jesu Christi sumpturus, non aliter accedat quam orario utroque humero circumseptus, sicut et tempore ordinationis suæ dignoscitur consecratus: ita ut de uno eodemque orario cervicem pariter et utrumque humerum premens signum in suo pectore præferat crucis. Si quis autem aliter egerit, excommunicationi debitæ subjacebit."

9. St. Germanus of Constantinople, *circ.* 715 A.D. [See the passage quoted, *supra*, p. 84.] He speaks of the deacons as distinguished by the light wings of their light oraria.

10. Concil. Moguntiacum (Mayence), A D. 813, Can. xxviii. [Labbe, vol. xi. p, 336, Venet.] "Presbyteri sine intermissione utantur orariis propter differentiam sacerdotii dignitatis."

### ORARIUM AND OTHER VESTMENTS, NINTH CENTURY.

11. Riculfus, Bishop of Soissons [† 902] Statutum vii. "Studere etiam debetis ut digne atque honeste vestra ecclesiastica vestimenta præparata habeatis; Albam videlicet ad divinum mysterium unam vel duas nitidas, cum orariis, id est, stolis duabus nitidis, et amictus duobus nitidis, corporalibus quoque totidem nitidis, item zonis duabus, id est cinctoriis, ac manipulis totidem nitidis; ac linteamina altaris habeatis nitida, et casulam sericam, cum qua missa celebretur. Hoc autem omnimodis prohibemus, ut nemo illa alba utatur in sacris mysteriis, qua in quotidiano vel exteriori usu induitur."

### ORARIUM TO BE WORN WHEN TRAVELLING.

12. From the *Capitula* of Hincmar, Archbishop of Rheims († 882), and from the *Disciplina Ecclesiastica* (lib. i. 62) of Regino, Abbot of Prume, in the following century, we find that a priest, when on a journey, was bound to wear his *stola* or *orarium*, that his sacred character might be known. If he were robbed, or murdered, *non stola vestitus*, the crime was to be atoned *simplici emendatione*, but if *cum stola*, then *emendatione triplici*. This last provision was made by a council held at Tribur, near Mayence, in 895.

### THE PALLIUM (PAPAL OR ARCHIEPISCOPAL).

13. The political history (so to call it) of the "Pallium Pontificium" in the West, may be briefly summed up as follows:

It was at first [408] conferred on archbishops [409] and metropolitans, not as a necessary qualification for that dignity, but as a symbol of accession of honour and of authority through *vicarial powers* (vices Apostolicæ Sedis), bestowed by the Roman See. Arles,[410] for example, had been an archiepiscopal See long before Symmachus bestowed the Pallium on Cæsarius. See note *t*, p. lviii. And when, nearly a century later, another Archbishop of Arles, Virgilius, applied (by letter) to St. Gregory the Great, for a similar privilege, he had been already for four years in possession of his See, and in the full exercise of his office.

This being so, a question of some difficulty arises out of the language of the first Council of Macon, A.D. 581, which in its sixth canon directs that no archbishop shall celebrate mass *sine Pallio*. Interpreted by the later discipline of the Western Church, when the power of the Papacy had been firmly established,

---

[408] Anastasius, in the *Gesta* of Marcus, Bp. of Rome, A.D. 336, writes as follows: "Hic constituit ut episcopus Ostiensis, qui consecrat episcopus Urbis,[408] tunc pallio uteretur, et ab eodem Urbis[408] episcopus consecraretur. Hic fecit constitutum de omni ecclesiastico ordine. If the "Pallium" here spoken of is the Papal pallium, which is open to doubt, we have here the first instance of its being conferred by favour of the Roman See, but only for this special occasion of the consecration of the *Urbis episcopus*.

[409] Millin, Voyage en Italie, tom. i. p. 108, speaks of a sarcophagus of S. Celsus, Archbishop of Milan, on which the Archbishop is represented wearing a Pallium marked with a single cross. [Martigny, D. J. A. C., *in voc.* Pallium.]

[410] "Primate and Metropolitan had been synonymous terms applied to the first Bishop of a Province" [*Primæ sedis episcopus* is the only term allowed by Concil. Carth. iii. A.D. 397], "and so they continued to be for some time: subsequently the heads of the nations, or exarchs of a diocese, monopolised the title. Conc. Chalced. can. 9 et 17. Thus there were three Gallican primates over Celtica, Belgica, and Aquitania, respectively, whose Sees were Lyons, Treves, and Bourges. Again, the Bishop of Arles was styled Primate after that city had been made the residence of the prætorian Prefect; and hence the frequent contentions between him and the Bishop of Vienne about the primacy, in which the Roman bishops interfered, constituting themselves, as it were, primates over primates." Foulkes' *Manual of Ecc. Hist.* Oxford, 1851.

this might be supposed to mean *till he had been to Rome and there received the Pallium*. But such an interpretation in regard of the churches of Gaul in the sixth century would be altogether an anachronism, as well as a forcing of the language of the canon itself. Hence some ritualists [431] have supposed that in the sixth century a Pallium (but not necessarily the Roman Pallium) was worn by all archbishops as the symbol of their office, in the Gallican churches, as in the East, whose customs in many particulars they followed. It is believed, accordingly, that there was a *Pallium Gallicanum*, such as Gallican archbishops wore, existing side by side with the *Pallium Romanum*, worn by such bishops only as had the *vices Apostolicæ Sedis*. Hence the language of the canon will imply that an archbishop must wear a *Pallium*, when celebrating mass, just as a priest was bound at such time to wear an "orarium" (see Appendix E, No. 8). Compare note 424.

A further point of great interest in the history of the Papal Pallium is that of the joint action in regard to it of the chief powers in church and state. With regard to this there are some points which are absolutely beyond question,—others upon which Roman and Gallican (or German) authorities are at issue. It is admitted that at the close of the sixth century St. Gregory the Great speaks of himself as sending the Pallium with vicarial authority, to an archbishop of Arles, *with the assent of the Emperor* [432] (*i.e.* of the Byzantine Emperor, Maurice), and in compliance with the request (*petitio*) of the King. It is admitted, too, that at a somewhat earlier date (A.D. 545), Pope Vigilius, when conferring similar privileges on Auxanius, Bishop (really Archbishop) of Arles, did so *pro gloriosissimi filii nostri Regis Childeberti Christiana devotione mandatis*, "as our most glorious son, King Childebert, with Christian devotion, has commissioned us to do." But when, going back yet a hundred years earlier, a rescript of the Emperor Valentinian is produced, which purports to confer, by exclusively imperial authority, archiepiscopal powers, and the right of wearing the Pallium, upon one Joannes, Bishop (thenceforth archbishop) of Ravenna, and attaching these privileges to that see in perpetuity, we reach ground which is, naturally, intolerable to some. Hieronymus Rubeus, who was the first to publish the document, sought to evade the difficulty by supposing, that the Pallium spoken of by Valentinian was an imperial (or secular) Pallium, not the Pallium of an archbishop. Cardinal Baronius shows conclusively that the whole context is such as to exclude such a meaning. And he intimates, what is evidently true, that even were it otherwise, the really important question would be left untouched, that of the power of an emperor to constitute, by his own act and authority, a metropolitan province,

---

[431] See Hefele, L. G. p. 217; Ruinart. Dissertatio de Palliis Archiepiscop., printed among the Opera Posthuma of Mabillon.

[432] But on other occasions, in dealing with Churches, which were created by the missionary zeal of the Roman See, St. Gregory acts upon the principle alluded to in Note 216. And so (knowing nothing of the older *British* Church in the *Anglia* of his day) he created in England the two Archiepiscopal Sees of Canterbury and York, and sent over two Pallia for their use.

and assign archiepiscopal powers. He maintains therefore (followed in this by Cardinal Bona) that the entire document is a forgery. Dr. Hefele, a Roman Catholic, but not an Ultramontane, points out a fatal flaw in *one* of Baronius' arguments, viz. his assuming (what is notoriously [433] contrary to fact) that the conferring of such powers was *in those days* a matter of *exclusively* ecclesiastical jurisdiction, pertaining to the See of Rome. But I cannot help observing that he has not dealt with a far stronger argument, with which the Cardinal backs up his first. If such a rescript as this had been in existence among the archives of Ravenna (or even kept in memory by tradition), in the time of another John of Ravenna (see above, p. 66), contemporary of St. Gregory the Great, how came it that when there was a warm dispute, as in his time there was, concerning the nature and extent of the privileges of the Pallium attaching to the See of Ravenna, *no reference was made to this rescript* either by John himself (as far at least as we can judge from the correspondence), or by St. Gregory?

On the whole, I incline to think the Cardinal's theory probable, viz. that at some subsequent time of division between the Bishops of Ravenna and of Rome, this document was forged, in order to support the claims to independence put forward by the Northern See. Well would it be if Christian historians could say with truth, that such politic forgeries were without precedent elsewhere in Mediæval times.

Such is the earlier history of the Roman Pallium. If we turn to later history, we shall find another phase of thought concerning the Pallium, symbolised by the interesting historical monument reproduced in Plates XXXII. and XXXIII., and with more exactness of representation at p. lii. And some fifty years after the date of Leo III., and of Charlemagne (the embodied "Church and State" of those Mosaics), we find Pope Nicholas I., in his *Responsa ad Bulgaros*, laying down (for the first time) the rule which, whenever possible, has been adhered to ever since by the Roman Curia, viz. that no archbishop shall venture to exercise any of his functions, even after consecration, till he has received the Pallium from the tomb of the chief of the apostles. Labbe, Conc. tom. viii. p. 541; Innocent III., quoted at p. 160.

Those who would pursue this subject further will find the materials for doing so in the treatises named in note 110, p. 63; and in the passages of ancient authors quoted or referred to in the later editions of *Du Cange* (G. M. et I. L. *in voc.* Pallium), and of *Meursius, in voc.* Ὠμοφόριον.

---

[433] In the Codex Theodosianus, for example, we find an imperial rescript (lib. xvi. tit. ii. No. 45) addressed to the Prefect of Illyricum, which places all ecclesiastical affairs in the Illyrian Provinces under the jurisdiction of the "*vir reliogissimus, sacrosanctæ Legis Antistes*," the Bishop of Constantinople. With this compare the rescript of Gratian, giving jurisdiction over other metropolitans to Damasus Bishop of Rome. [Gieseler, E. H. p. 434.]

# APPENDIX F.

## THE SACRED VESTMENTS OF THE ROMAN CHURCH.

### 1. THE AMICTUS, OR AMICE.[434]

The Amice is described in note 178, p. 96. It is nowhere mentioned as a vestment till the ninth century. Walafrid Strabo, even in that century, is silent with regard to it. Note 217, p. 108. There is no corresponding vestment in the Greek Church.[435]

But though not named in the first eighth centuries as a sacred vestment, we can trace its origin in some expressions of St. Jerome, which suggest also the reason of its late appearance among church vestments. In a letter to his friend Nepotianus (a priest), he is warning him not to think that there is any merit in being dirty, and bids him not to take pride, *quia linteolum*[436] *in collo non habeas ad detergendos sudores*, i.e. because, following monastic rule, you wear no linen between the neck and the outer woollen garments. As long as church vestments were themselves *of linen*, such a *linteolum* was not needed *in Church*. But when silk and rich ornaments (especially about the *upper border* of the planeta) came to be worn, it was necessary to prevent their actual contact with the skin, and hence the introduction of the "Amice."

The mystical meanings attached to it may be seen detailed at p. 88 (Ephod Bad), 96, 111,[226] 115,[241] 122, 126, 128, 132, 135.

Dr. Bock gives a plate (vol. ii. Pl. II.) showing the mode of wearing the Amice, both on the shoulders, and (in passing) as a *galea* (note 178, and Durandus, quoted at p. 167) on the head. The same writer furnishes details as to the *parurae*, or ornamental borders, sometimes attached to the Amice, from the tenth century onward (as he thinks). Weiss (*Kostümkunde*, p. 667) dates these a full century later. [The former is right. See note 441, below.]

### 2. THE ALB.[437]

The history of the Alb during the first eight centuries has been already given. See Introduction, Chap. vii. p. liv.

---

[434] Other names are *Humerale*, i.e. shoulder-piece, *Superhumerale* or *Ephod* (so, perhaps, Rabanus, p. 88); *Anabolagium* (i.e. ἀναβολάδιον or ἀναβολαῖον) or *Anagolaium*.

[435] M. Victor Gay admits that the Amice cannot be traced back farther than the 8th century; A. A. vol. vi. p. 158. He adds (p. 161), "Les Orientaux plus stricts observateurs des traditions du costume primitif ne l'ont jamais adopté."

[436] When in the same letter (Ep. 52) St. Jerome speaks of one who *absque amictu lineo incedit*, the word *amictus* is probably used in its older classical sense. *Non absque amictu lineo incedere, sed pretium vestium linearum non habere, laudabile est. Alioquin ridiculum est et plenum dedecoris, referto marsupio, quod sudarium orarium-que non habeas gloriari.*

[437] *Tunica linea*, or *tunica talaris, linea, ca-*

Like other vestments which in primitive times, and even till the close (or nearly so) of the eighth century, were of white linen only, the Alb became enriched in the later centuries,[458] both in respect of material and of ornament. See Bock, L. G. vol. ii. p. 33, *sqq.*, and Hefele, p. 171, *sqq.* Their ornamentation was effected by adding *parura*, the position of which may be seen in Pl. LXI., on the Alb worn by the priests. Such Albs were known in France as *Albæ Romanæ* (V. Gay in Didron, A. A.).

The mystical meanings attached to this vestment may be seen on reference to pp. 69, 89, 95, 96, 110, 116, 135, 165.

The full and flowing shape of the Christian *Alba* was contrasted in the ninth century (see Amalarius, p. 96) with the closely fitting (note 6, p. 2) tunic of Levitical priesthood. But as super-vestments were multiplied in the tenth and eleventh centuries, the Alb was necessarily more and more confined, and the modern Alb is almost as closely fitting as was that of the Levitical priest. Compare Pl. IX. and LXI. Even in St. Hugo's time (see p. 132, l. 4) the *linea interior*, corresponding to the original Alb, was altogether hidden (*latet*) by the additional vestments worn.

### 3. THE GIRDLE.

*Cingulum, Zona, Balteus.*

The Girdle was almost universally worn in ancient times as a matter of convenience, to fasten up the tunic, and in that case, generally, so worn as not to be visible. Exceptionally, too, by kings (note 81, p. 51) and other great personages in the East, it was worn as a distinctive ornament, and in such cases was richly ornamented. Such was the Girdle (see Pl. VIII. and IX.) of the Levitical priesthood.

Hence a double significance of the Girdle, α. as a symbol of *activity* (so, generally in Scripture, and in classical authors); β. as a symbol of royal or priestly dignity.

A third symbolism, that of chastity, which in ecclesiastical writers has almost exclusive place, is to be referred to associations of idea in regard to the Girdle sufficiently familiar to scholars, and upon which it is not necessary to dwell.

These considerations will explain the mystical significance attached to the Girdle from the ninth century onwards. These may be seen in pp. 89, 113, 116, 122, 132, 136.

Till, in the eighth or ninth century, the idea of an intended resemblance

---

*mifa, fupparus, linea interior,* are various names used in speaking of this vestment.

[458] "After the 10th century," says Weifs (K. p. 667). The two kinds of albs were distinguished as "*Alba pura*" (the "white alb *plain*" of Edward's first Prayer-book), and the *Alba parata*.

in detail between the Christian and the Levitical vestments was first broached, the Girdle, naturally, was either not [429] worn at all (with the *tunica talaris* it was not necessary), or, when worn, was not visible, and was thought of only as a matter of convenience. In none of the early monuments of the West before A.D. 800, is any trace of it to be seen. But in the East we have mention of a Girdle as worn by deacons, early in the eighth century. (See p. 86, *in fin.*)

The mode in which the Girdle was worn in the ninth century is well illustrated in Pl. XXIII., where the priest is in an alb, with close-fitting sleeves (for obvious reasons of convenience in the administration of baptism by immersion) without chasuble.[440] And the alb is evidently girt in at the waist, though no pendent ends are visible. The mode in which these ends appear in the later Roman costume may be seen in Pl. LXI., where they hang down beside the stole. These pendents probably correspond to the *subcingulum*, or *succinctorium* of Honorius, p. 136, note 275 *a*; Innocent III., p. 144, note 301; and Durandus, p. 165, note 337.

It will readily be understood that a richly ornamented girdle, like that of Levitical priesthood (see Pl. VIII. and IX.) would be out of place (because wholly unseen) in the primitive dress of Christian ministry. Hence the *cingula auro texta* worn by bishops and others of the clergy in the ninth century were, as Durandus says (p. 165, note 336), *secularia ornamenta*, worn as part of the splendid secular dress then in fashion.

A variety of documents dating from the ninth century lead to the conclusion, that the Zona, *as a sacred vestment*, was not then in *general* use, but that costly Girdles (Zonæ Romanæ, p. 111) were in some cases used by bishops, as, for example, by Riculfus [441] of Soissons († 915 A.D.). These could

---

[429] Note, as bearing upon this, the reproof given by St. Celestine ( *sup.* p. 45), to certain Bishops in Gaul, who sought " by wearing a girdle (Note 74) round their loins to fulfil the truth of Scripture, not in the spirit, but in the letter."

[440] Curiously parallel to this are the words, quoted at p. 204, where the priest is described as dressed *in albis*, and wearing a girdle *when about to baptise.*

[441] The Will of Bishop Riculfus is a complete inventory of Church vestments such as were used in the wealthier Churches of the 10th century. I subjoin those portions of it which refer to this subject, from the text of Migne (P. C. C. tom. cxxxii. p. 468). For the credit of the Bishop's Latin I will add that such expressions as *capas duas, una purpura,* &c., may arise simply from copyists not recognising the abbreviation commonly employed for the accusative case in MS.

Among the various things *quæ in cultu Dei pertinent,* which he leaves for the use of his Church, and of his successors in the See, he names—

" Caligas et sandalias paria duo, amictus cum auro quattuor; albas quinque, tres claras et planas duas; roquos quattuor, unum purpureum cum auro, et alium palleum Græco, et alios duos in Græcia factos; zonas quinque, una cum auro, et gemmis pretiosis, et alias quattuor cum auro; stolas quattuor cum auro, una ex illis cum tintinnabulis; et manipulos sex cum auro, unum sex [*leg.* ex] iis cum tintinnabulis; casulas episcopales optimas tres, unam dioprasiam, et alias duas de orodenas; annulum aureum unum cum gemmis pretiosis, et urantos paria unum; camisas ad textum et missalem quattuor, unum cum auro purpureum, et alios palleos corporales quattuor; palleos quattuor, e brosdo unam; dalmaticas tres; capas duas, una purpura et alia blition " (*blatteos ?*). [For *de orodenas* above, Dr. Hefele reads *diarodinas, i.e., ῥαγαδίνας,* " rose-coloured."]

be worn *so as to be seen* with a *copa* or cope (two of which are mentioned among the bishop's vestments), though not with a *casula*.

Full details as to the later forms of the Girdle, and the changes in it at various times, will be found in Bock, L. G. tom. ii. p. 50, *sqq*. Compare Hefele, L. G. p. 78.

### 4. THE STOLE [ORARIUM OR STOLA].

For the earlier history see Introduction, p. lxii., *sqq*. and Appendix D. And for the two names see note 144, p. 84.

No satisfactory [442] account has yet been given of the introduction of this later term *Stola*. I venture to think that it is to be accounted for by the fact that the word, *as employed in the Vulgate*, is suggestive of a vestment of solemn state or dignity, particularly of "a priestly robe." And as in the eighth century the *Orarium* was regarded as *the special vestment of Christian priesthood*, to be worn *hora sacrificii* under pain of excommunication, it seems not improbable that the *Orarium* may then have been called, *by certain persons*, as Raban says, "the Stole," or, as we might now say, "the vestment" of the priest. The technical terminology of the Mediæval Church in the West was formed not upon classical Latin, still less upon classical Greek, or, indeed, any Greek at all, but upon the Latin of the Vulgate,[443] and of the Latin fathers. We find, accordingly, some indications that the word *stola* was occasionally used in early writers, as it is occasionally in Scripture, of a long white garment, "a priestly robe," as the *tunica talaris*. Such probably is the meaning of the word in the only passage in which *stola* is expressly distinguished from the *Orarium* by any of the mediæval writers. [Acta Sanctorum, Maius xxvi. p. 393, "*Addit Stolam et Orarium*."]

This vestment was originally of white linen. But so early as the beginning of the seventh century we find that some of the younger clergy of Spain had taken to "coloured oraria," decked out with gold; and were not even content with *one* only. Hence the Canon of the Fourth Council of Toledo, quoted at p. 75.

---

[442] The supposition that it was the *border* of a long and full garment called "stola" (such as the older *stola matronalis*), is deservedly rejected by most writers on this subject. The suggestion made by Honorius (see p. 136), points rather to such an explanation as that made in the text, in this, at least, that he traces back the ecclesiastical use of "*stola*" to the scriptural (Vulgate) use of the same word. See next note.

[443] Thus Honorius (*supra*, p. 139, l. 17) speaks of the *prima stola* "the best robe," with which the prodigal on his return was clad. And Innocent III., in like manner, quotes the words of the Apocalypse, "*stabans . . . . amicti stolis albis*" (p. 163, l. 15), without any thought whatever of the "*Stole*" technically so called. Compare the passage of Ezekiel, xliv., quoted at p. 29, where see note 50. And that of Honorius (p. 156) referred to in last note.

By the ninth century we find such coloured stoles, bedecked with gold, represented both in Italy and in Gaul.[444] In the Pontifical of Bishop Landulfus, some of the presbyters wear *two* Stoles, differing in pattern one from the other, one being white, with black crosses, the other gold colour.

For notices of the Stole (other than those in Appendix E), see pp. 126, 129, 132, 136, 142, 147, 154, 165, 166, 207.

For representations of it, Pl. XXIII., XXXV., XXXVI., XLIV., XLV., LXI. In the three last, only the lower [445] extremity of the Stole is visible under the dalmatic.

## 5. THE MANIPLE.

[*Pallium Linostimum, Mappa, Mappula, Manipulus, Sudarium, Phanon* [61] *or Fanon,*[233] *Mantile, Manutergium.*]

The earlier history of the Mappula has been already touched upon. Introduction, p. lxx.

Till the close of the eighth century, we hear of it only as a processional vestment, distinctive of the Roman clergy. But from the beginning of the ninth it has been recognised as one of the *sacræ vestes*. See pp. 65, 90, 101 (*sudarium in manu*), 103, 113 (note 233), 117, 127, 137, 149, 156, 161, (*manipulo pro clava utitur*).

The ἐγχείριον, or ὀθόνη, which in the eighth century was carried suspended from the Girdle by *deacons* in the East, constituted, in all probability, a real parallel to this vestment. But the episcopal ἐπιμανίκια (see note 350, and Pl. LVI.), differ from it in origin, in shape, in symbolism, as they do in name.

For representations of the Maniple, see Plates XLIII., XLVIII., LXI.[446]

---

[444] In the Pontifical of Landulfus, and in the illuminations, dating from the ninth century, published by Louandre et Maugé, L. A. S. vol. ii. "Le Prince Franc." In this picture the ends of the Stole (which alone are visible) in two figures of bishops, are decked with gold.

[445] In this we see the reason for the concentration of ornament in the *ends* of the Stole, in mediæval times, and for their gradual enlargement consequent upon this.

[446] In a French MS. of the ninth century (subsequent to the adoption of the Roman ritual), bishops and priests are represented *holding* a Maniple, generally in the right hand (not wearing it pendent from the left wrist as in later use). See Louandre et Maugé Les A. S. vol. ii. Les Chanoines de St. Martin. So Amalarius (*sup.* p. 112, 113) *writing in Gaul,* "sudarium quod . . . . *in manu gestari mos est.*"

But in the Pontifical of Landulfus, assigned by all Roman antiquaries to the ninth century (see Pl. XXX. to XXXIII. of this work) none of the priests have Maniples. In No. 3, 5, 9, the bishop has on his right hand what might be mistaken for a Maniple, but which on close examination of the facsimiles (drawn and coloured from the originals) now before me, appear rather to be the extremity of a kind of pallium, worn by the bishop over his chasuble; and which appears to be a detached vestment, not a mere " orfrey " (note 312) of the chasuble itself.

## 6. The Chasuble.

[*Planeta, Casula, Infula, Amphibalum.*]

For earlier history, see Introduction, p. lxiii, *sqq.*, and Appendix C.

For subsequent notices see Rabanus, p. 91; Amalarius, p. 97; Walafrid, p. 108; Alcuinus, p. 117; St. Ivo, p. 127, (note 217); St. Hugo, p. 132, 133 (note 268); Honorius, p. 136; Innocent III., pp. 148 and 156; Durandus, p. 166, l. 3 (casula quasi clypeo tegitur).

For representations, see Pl. XXVIII., XXX., XXXI. (all these, however, *Planetæ* rather than *Casulæ*), XXXIII. (but ?), XXXIV., XXXV., XXXVI., XXXVII., XXXIX., XL., XLII., XLIV., XLV., XLVI., XLVIII., LXI.

With these compare the Greek φαινόλια, both secular, as in Pl. XVIII., XIX., XX., XXI., XXVII., and liturgical, as in Pl. XLI. and LVIII.

For details of ornamentation at various times, see Bock, L. G. p. 101 to 128; Hefele, L. G. p. 199, 200; and Pugin G. G. A. *in voc.*

This vestment is utterly unlike any of those of Levitical priesthood. And as long as the humble origin of the vestment (see Appendix C, No. 32) was remembered in the church, and it was regarded as common to all clerics, and to monks also (Appendix C, No. 33, 34, 35), as a secular dress, there was of course no special association of ideas of "sacrifice" with this vestment. Accordingly we find the earlier writers speaking of it as typical either of "charity," the symbolism [447] which it has retained through all the later liturgical writers, or of those good works and duties which are "*common to all of the clerical order,*" hungering, thirsting, watching, nakedness; reading, singing of psalms, prayer; activity in good works, teaching, silent meditation, and the like (Amalarius, p. 98). But as time went on, and the secular [447*] dress of the clergy no longer resembled the *casula* in form or in name, the chasuble came to be regarded as *the* distinctive vestment of Christian priesthood, and *therefore* (according to the prevailing idea of mediæval times) became specially associated with the idea of sacrifice. See Appendix G, No. 2, and note 458.

## NINE ADDITIONAL VESTMENTS PROPER TO BISHOPS ONLY.

### 7. The Caligæ, Leggings or Stockings.

First mentioned among the sacred vestments by St. Ivo, p. 128, l. 6. He describes them as made of linen, and *reaching* (from the foot) *to the knee,*

---

[447] See Rabanus, p. 91. The passage there quoted will show the fanciful ground on which this symbolism was originally based.
Compare St. Ivo (p. 127). *Casula quæ quia communis est vestis charitatem significat.*

[447*] On the secular dress of the clergy, both in East and West, from the ninth century downwards, see Thomassinus, *De Ben.* part i. lib. ii cap. 48, 50, 51. *Cappa* was, as we shall see, the prevailing name for the out-door dress both of clergy and monks.

*where they are closely fastened.* Hence the symbolism which he gives them. Compare Innocent III., p. 150. In later times the *tibialia* [446] of a bishop were always made of silk. — Of this regulation we retain, by custom, some traces among ourselves.

### 8. THE SHOES.

#### *Sandalia, Soleæ, Campagæ or Campobi.*

First noticed *as a sacred vestment* by Rabanus (*supra*, p. 92). Compare Amalarius, p. 97, l. 15, and p. 104 (where every minute part of the Shoe has its special symbolism assigned); Alcuinus, p. 112 (*in fin.*), 115, 118, and note 243; St. Ivo, p. 127; Innocent III., pp. 150 and 157.

Even at an earlier time we find that the kind of Shoes to be worn by ecclesiastics was matter of strict regulation in churches subject to the Roman See. Note 184, p. 97. Such matters had not been thought unworthy of imperial legislation, in reference to the etiquette of dress at Rome and at Constantinople. See note 427, p. 207, and Plates XXII., XXIV., XXV., XXVIII., XLIII.

### 9. THE UNDER-GIRDLE.

#### *Subcingulum, Succinctorium.*

This vestment has been already noticed, in connection with the Girdle, and in note 313.

But since that note was written I have discovered what appears to be the real explanation of what is written about the Under-Girdle, by Honorius (p. 136); Innocent III. (pp. 143, 144); and Durandus (quoted in note 313). They all speak, directly or by implication, of *two* Girdles. And though the language of Durandus and of Innocent III. in p. 153, might admit of the explanation given in note 313, that of Honorius seems inconsistent with it. But the Ordo Romanus V., when describing the vestments of the *Pontifex* (*i.e.* the Pope),[449] shows that there really were two

---

[446] *Tibialia* is another name for the *caligæ*. The *caligæ* of a bishop, wearing ecclesiastical dress, are, of course, not visible. Similar *caligæ* worn by Charlemagne are seen in the woodcut at p. lii.

[449] Though in the language of the Western Church *generally*, Pontifex has the meaning "bishop," as pointed out in note 45, yet *at Rome itself* (to which, as shown in that note, the word *Pontifex* has a special relation), this title was distinctively used of the Pope, while to other bishops was given the ordinary title of *episcopus*. Both these usages of Pontifex are illustrated by John the Deacon (*circ.* 875). He sometimes uses it of ordinary bishops, as in lib. iii. cap. 15, 33, 33, or of archbishops, as of John of Ravenna. But in lib. iv. cap. 91, he speaks of Bishop (*episcopus*) Lucidus, *then resident at Rome*, going up to dine in full dress (*sacerdotalibus infulis redimitus*) at the patriarchium, with the *Pontifex*, St. Gregory. In accordance with this, the Ordo Romanus V. distinguishes between the *Vestimenta Pontificalia*, and the *Vestimentum alii* (*i.e.* alios) *Romani Episcopi*. [See Mabillon's Preface, p. 63.]

distinct Girdles, as indicated by Honorius. The vestments are enumerated as follows: *De Vestimentis Pontificalibus. In primis eam* (i.e. camisia) *et cingitur supra. Dein linea cum cottis, serica, et cingulum. Post hæc mittitur anagolai* (i.e. amictus); *exinde dalmatica minore, postea majore dalmatica, et supra orarium. Post hæc planeta, et supra mittitur pallium.* The inner Girdle over the *camisia,* or shirt, represents the older Girdle of primitive usage, without ornament, and altogether out of sight. The *cingulum,* afterwards spoken of, is an ornamented girdle, introduced among the " vestments " at a much later period, in imitation of the ornamented Girdle of Levitical priesthood.

### 10. THE EPISCOPAL TUNIC.

*Tunica Pontificalis, T. poderis, T. interior vel hyacinthina.*

Innocent III., in his enumeration of the pontifical (*i.e.* episcopal) vestments, distinguishes between the Alb, p. 145, *sqq.,* the Tunic, and the Dalmatic. All these are really Tunics, the two latter having been superadded one after the other for richer ornament. The process was probably this. The *tunica alba,* made of linen, of the more primitive dress, was replaced by one of silk, often of *blue* silk, in imitation of the *tunica hyacinthina* of the Levitical high-priest. A rich vestment of this kind required *an under tunic,* for obvious reasons. And, accordingly, that under Tunica was now called *alba* simply, the second Tunic (which was *talaris,* but not quite so long as the alb) followed; and the Dalmatic, shorn now of its ancient length, *in order to leave the second tunic visible,* followed third in order. All this will readily be understood by reference to the figure of the bishop in Pl. LXI. The gradual addition of one Tunic after another may be traced from the ninth century downwards in Pl. XXXVII. (one only); XXXIX. and XLIV. (two); XLVIII. and LXI., (three). The Ordo Romanus V. (*sup.* § 9) enumerates three Tunics in all, besides the *camisia.*

The language of St. Ivo (see p. 122), and previously of Amalarius (p. 100, 101), fully confirms this supposition. St. Ivo says, that both in the old and the new covenant, only *Pontifices* (high-priests in the one case, bishops in the other), wear two Tunics, the second Tunic, the *tunica hyacinthina,* being that which was exclusively theirs. This Tunica he calls *interior,* as does Amalarius (p. 101), not of course in reference to the *alba* [450] (or to the *tunica talaris* of the high-priest), but in reference to the dalmatic. Alcuinus, on the other hand, speaks of the Levitical Tunic of blue (p. 110) as *tunica exterior,* an *outer* Tunic, in respect of the white Tunic of linen beneath it. St. Hugo varies yet again from these. The *two Tunics* are to him the *linea interior*

---

[450] Hence Amalarius speaks of the alba as *camisia,* and of the two others as *duæ tunicæ.* See p. 101, and note 194. And what Amalarius calls *duæ tunicæ,* appear in the fifth of the *Ordines Romani* as *dalmatica major* and *minor.*

(answering to our shirt), which (*latet*) is unseen, and the *linea exterior* or alb, which was visible. See pp. 131, 132.

## 11. THE DALMATIC (OF THE BISHOP).

The general history of the Dalmatic has already been fully investigated See Introduction, p. lv, *sqq.*

But the Dalmatic now in question is not the full and flowing white linen vestment of primitive times (with simple stripes for ornament, see Pl. XVII., XXXIII.), but the highly ornamented vestment worn by bishops and other high officials of the Church, immediately under the *casula* or *planeta*. In some instances (Ordo Rom. V. quoted in § 9) two such Dalmatics are spoken of. Representations of this vestment may be seen (immediately under the chasuble) in Pl. XXXIX., XLII., XLIV., XLV., XLVI., LXI., in which last is seen the deacon's Dalmatic also.

## 12. THE MITRA.[431]

First mentioned among the *Sacræ Vestes* by Honorius of Autun, about the middle of the twelfth century. See p. 138. But it had been in use, in some parts at least of the West, some time previously. The figure of St. Dunstan (Pl. XL.) in a MS. of the eleventh century, shows him wearing a cap *ex byssō confecta*, much such as that to which the language of Honorius points, and this is the earliest example of the kind which I have seen. I should except, perhaps, one of the bishops represented in the Benedictional of St. Ethelwald, belonging to the Duke of Devonshire. This is of the tenth century. The figure is represented with a kind of diadem, a narrow circlet of gold, with jewels round the head. This, however, is not really of the nature of a "Mitra," and may not improbably be suggestive of royal rank, to which church dignitaries could then not unfrequently lay claim. Some ritualists have sought to assign a much earlier date to the "Mitra." The passages they allege have been already considered (Appendix B, No. 1 to 6). If we omit these (for the reasons given in that Appendix) we shall find that the earliest mention of the Mitra, which Dr. Hefele can adduce as genuine,

---

[431] The word μίτρα (*quasi* μιτιρὰ from μίτος thread), was probably by origin an adjective. Hence its double use in classical Greek, meaning a woman's cap (ὀυπάρη being understood), or a girdle, when ζώνη is the word to be supplied. In the LXX it is used as the rendering of Misnepheth, the priest's cap (Exod. xxviii. 33; xxix. 6; xxxix. 31), for which elsewhere (Exod. xxviii. 4, 35, and 36; xxix. 9; xxxix. 27) μίδαρις is employed. The Vulgate has in corresponding passages either *cidaris* (Exod. xxviii. 4) or *tiara* (see note 84, p. 52), as in Exod. xxviii. 37, 40; xxix. 6; or *mitra*, as in xxix. 9; xxxix. 26 and 20. In St. Isidore, *mitra* (as in classical Latin) means a cap worn by women. *Orig.* xix. 31, and *De Off. Ecc.* lib. ii. cap. 17. So in Tertullian, *De Virg. Vel.* (vol. iii. p. 32).

Other names for the Mitra are Tiara (note 84, p. 52), Pileus, Cidaris, Infula (note 296 a, and Appendix B, No. 4) Phrygium (Menardus in *Lib. Sacram. S. Gregor.* p. 212).

is of the eleventh century, where in 1049 A.D. mention [452] is made, on more than one occasion, of a *Mitra Romana*, a kind of Mitra specially characteristic of the Roman Church. And to the same effect, Peter Damian, writing *circ.* 1073, to Cadalous, then "antipope," says, "*Habes nunc forsitan mitram, habes juxta morem Romani pontificis rubram cappam* (opp. tom. i. p. 121, Epist. lib. i. 20); "It may be that you now are wearing the vestments which properly belong to the pope, the mitre and red cope." Menardus states that in all the ritual books before 1000 A.D. which he had examined, there was no mention of the *Mitra*, and that he believes *vix ante annum post Christum natum millesimum mitræ usum in ecclesia fuisse*. The documents quoted in this work all point to the same conclusion. See the language of Alcuinus, quoted at p. 112. *Tiara* (that of the Levitical priest) *erat vestis, pileolum videlicet rotundum. . . . . . habens vittas. . . . . Summus Pontifex* (the high-priest) *præter pileum habebat coronam auream triplicemque.*[453] *. . . Hujuscemodi vestis non habent (leg.* habetur) *in Romana ecclesia vel in nostris regionibus*, and then again, after speaking of the *lamina aurea*, he adds, *Neque hanc ornamenti speciem Christi accepit ab illis ecclesia.* This treatise dates (note 218) from late in the tenth century. Compare note 217, *in fin.*

Various forms of the Mitra will be seen in Plates XLIV., XLVI., XLVII., XLVIII., L., LI., LII. to LV., LXI. And see description of Pl. XXXIX.

For details as to the ornamentation of the Mitra, and its varieties of form at different periods, see Bock, L. G. tom. ii. p. 153, *sqq.*

---

[452] In a charter of Leo IX., conferring privileges on Eberhard, Archbishop of Treves: *Quapropter omnibus ipsis laudantibus et respondentibus* [respondentibus?] *pro investitura ipsius Primatus, Romana mitra caput vestrum insignimus, qua et vos et successores vestri in Ecclesiasticis officiis Romano more semper utemini, semperque vos esse Romanæ sedis discipulos reminiscamini.* [*Apud* Dufresne *in voc.*]

[453] Among the expressions in ancient writers alleged as bearing upon this point, are some few, from which it appears that *corona vestra* (literally "*your chaplet*") was a term of formal courtesy in addressing bishops and others of the clergy as early as the fourth century. The only *corona* of Christian ministry known to antiquity, even as late as St. Isidore's time (see p. 68, above), was the chaplet or circle of hair beneath the tonsure. Tertullian, as is well known, regards *coronæ* as essentially symbols of heathenism, and asks (after his rhetorical manner), *Quis Patriarcha, quis Propheta . . . . vel postea Apostolus . . . aut Episcopus invenitur coronatus?* De Cor. Mil. 350. I can only suggest that "*corona vestra*" may have been, in the conventional language of Rome in the fourth century, an expression of courtesy answering to "Your Reverence," "Your Grace," and the like in modern times; and *imported into Christian usage from an idiom, which originally had reference to the coronæ of heathen priesthood.* The passages, of which I speak, are, α. Hieronymus ad Augustinum, No. 26. "*Fratres tuos, dominum meum Alypium et dominum meum Evodium, ut meo nomine salutes, precor coronam vestram;* and β. St. Augustine, ep. 147, ad Proculianum. *Per coronam nostram nos adjurant vestri* (h. e. the Donatists); *per coronam vestram vos adjurant nostri.* Many passages to the same effect are quoted by Dufresne, *in voc.*, and he adds that the phrase ἡ ὑμετέρα κορυφή is used in the same sense by some of the Greek Fathers.

## 13. THE GLOVES.

*Chirotbecæ, Guanti,*[454] *Uvanti.*

Like many other parts of the full episcopal costume as developed in the twelfth century, the Gloves (*chirothecæ*) had long been in use, for practical purposes, before they were exalted to the rank of "sacred vestments," and invested with a symbolism of their own. The first writer who so mentions them is Honorius (note 296ª), early in the twelfth century.

Full details concerning these will be found in Bock, L. G. ii. 131, *sqq.*

## 14. THE EPISCOPAL RING.

In Roman usage, of the classical times, Rings were used as insignia of rank, and a Ring of a particular kind was exclusively appropriated to those of the equestrian order.

Early in the seventh century we find mention (see p. 75) of a Ring as one of the distinctive insignia of a bishop. When the coffin of Bishop Agilbert of Paris (seventh century) was opened, De Saussay, who was present, saw on his finger a gold ring, with a jewel on which was a likeness of our Lord and St. Jerome. Other similar instances are referred to by Bock, L. G. ii. p. 207, *sqq.*

That no mention of the Ring, as one of the insignia of a bishop, should be made by any of the writers of the ninth, or even tenth century, quoted in this volume, may be accounted for by the fact, that they occupy themselves more particularly with those vestments which resembled (or were thought to resemble) those of Levitical priesthood. Of the later writers, Honorius is the first to speak of it (see p. 139); and he is followed by Innocent III., p. 149 and 157; as afterwards by Durandus, and all the later ritualists.[455]

## 15. THE STAFF, AND THE CROZIER.

*Baculus, Pedum, Virga, Cambuca, Ferula.*

The Staff, as a distinctive mark of a bishop, is mentioned in the Acts of the Fourth Council of Toledo. The allusion to the Baculus in the letter of Celestine, Bishop of Rome (quoted at p. 45), is such as to indicate that the carrying of a *Baculus*, by bishops, as matter of ceremonial, was an innovation peculiar to certain parts of Gaul at that time (*circ.* 430 A.D.). The earliest

---

[454] These forms, which with *Wantus, Quanto, Gantus* (whence the French "gant"), are all of German origin, and indicate the source from which the use of gloves was introduced into Europe.

[455] For this see Innocent III., quoted at p. 147, and p. 155; and Honorius, p. 139.

representation of a Staff in art-monuments, that I have seen, are those in Pl. XLII. and XLIII. But a "cross," somewhat resembling the later Crozier of an archbishop (see Pl. XLVIII.), is attributed both to St. Peter and to St. Laurentius, in the mosaic dating from the time of Pelagius II. (*sed.* 578 to 590), reproduced from a drawing in the collection at Windsor in Pl. XXIX. The same plate represents a *Virga* in the hand of our Lord, the symbolism of which, as the "rod" or "sceptre" of *divine power*, has already been noticed. (Introduction, p. xl.) For the later forms of the Staff and Crozier, appropriated to bishops and archbishops respectively, see Plates XLII., XLVII., XLVIII., LI., LXI; and for the abbot's Staff, Pl. XLVII. and XLIX. For the Pallium, see Introduction, p. lxxi, *sqq.*, and Appendix E, No. 13, to end. For the Orale (or *Fanon*) of the Pope, note 314, p. 153; and for the Pectoral Cross, note 315. To this last ornament answers the ἐγκόλπιον (note 342), worn by bishops in the East.

# APPENDIX G.

### THE VESTMENTS PRESCRIBED IN THE FIRST PRAYER-BOOK OF EDWARD VI., AND IN THE LATER BOOKS.

The vestments ordered in the Prayer-book of 1549, are at the holy Communion, *a*. "for the priest that shall execute the holy ministry, the vesture appointed for that ministration, that is to say, *a white alb plain, with a vestment or cope;*" *β*. where there are priests or deacons, ready to help, these are to wear "albs with tunacles."

1. The first-named is the "*white Alb plain.*" By the Alb, when distinguished, as here it is, from the surplice, is meant a white tunic, of much scantier [436] dimensions than the surplice, and, as such, suited for wearing under a super-vestment, such as the "vestment or cope." By plain (*pura*) is meant without the "apparels" (note 438, p. 213), which, in mediæval times, had been adopted as ornaments to the Alb.

For the earlier history of the Alb, see Introduction, p. liv, *sqq.* and Appendix F. No. 2.

2. The "*vestment.*" In strictness of grammar, one who speaks of wearing

---

[436] See p. 213, l. 10, *sqq.*

"*a vestment or cope,*" would be understood to mean but *one* vestment, of which "cope" was an alternative name. But it appears clear that in the fifteenth and sixteenth centuries, the word "*vestimentum*" was often [457] used, with a limited meaning, of that which was *then* regarded as *the* special vestment of Christian ministry, viz. the chasuble.

It is clear that the last-named vestment was in the later pre-Reformation times regarded as specially appropriate to "the sacrifice of the altar." This will appear first from the language of the older Inventories, quoted and examined below (p. 226). And the inference thence made is curiously confirmed by another rubric of the same first Prayer-book. Though an option is given (in the rubric already quoted) between "vestment or cope," for the priest *at holy communion*, yet in the rubric providing for services on Wednesdays and Fridays, when there is no communion, a "cope" is prescribed without any alternative.[458]

3. The vestment next named is the Cope (Cappa or Capa). A representation of the Cope, dating from the time of Henry VII., will be seen in Pl. LI. An earlier example at Pl. XLVII., and XLVIII.

The word *capa* is first met with in the *Origines* of St. Isidore. And the two definitions which he gives to the word (answering, respectively, to our "cape," or hood," [459] and "cope"), serve to cover the whole range of meanings attached to the word even to the present time. "*Capa*," he says, in one place, "*dicta, quod capitis est ornamentum;*" and then again, "*capa . . . quia quasi totum capiat hominem.*"

It is with the second of these two meanings that we are now concerned. The Cope was originally a garb for out-door use, and was therefore furnished, as were almost all such garments in primitive times, with a "hood," for protection of the head against cold or rain.[460]

---

[457] It was also used as an inclusive term, for a complete set of vestments for "Celebrant, Epistoler, and Gospeller," with altar-hangings to match (*ejusdem sectæ*). See passages to this effect quoted below in note 463.

[458] I have to thank Mr. Droop for calling my attention to this. He adds, as further, and very conclusive proof of the distinctive position then assigned to the chasuble, a reference to a kind of "*directorium*," in the Lutheran Church in Brandenburg, published in MDXL. Provision is there made for part of the communion office being performed *when there are no communicants*, but with the direction appended, that the priests are in that case *not to wear a chasuble*, but a cope (korkappe) only, or in village churches where there are no copes, a common surplice (ein schlechten Corrock), *left simple folk should suppose that it was intended to celebrate mass*, after the former fashion, *without communicants*. [Kirchen Ordnung in Churfürstenthum der Mareken zu Brandenburg u. s. w. Berlin, MDXL. In the British Museum under "Liturgies." Brandenburg, c. 47, d.]

[459] For this we have direct authority at a later time. Theodemarus, writing *from Italy* to Charlemagne, and speaking of the dress of the monks of Monte Cassino (Dufresne, *in voc. Capa*). *Illud indumentum quod a Gallis monachis cuculla dicitur, nos Capam vocamus.* We may trace the same meaning of *Cope* as equivalent to "hood" in the eleventh century (Concil. Metense, A.D. 888). when the use of *Cotti* and *Mantelli*, with *Capa*, was forbidden to laymen, and prescribed to monks.

[460] Hence the name *Pluviale*, by which the cope is often known. See p. 167, and note 339, *in voc.*

Such a garment, it is obvious, admits of every possible variety in material, and colour, and ornamentation. And we find, accordingly, that the *Cappa* was used by laymen, by monks, by the clergy of all orders.[460 a] But even the richest Copes were for the most part considered as vestments of stately dignity to be worn *in processions*, and on ceremonial occasions, not as having any especial relation to the *ministerium Altaris*.

One very common usage of the simpler *Cappa* was that of a choir-vestment for the *Cantores*. See note 295, p. 141. Being made of a thick woollen material, and furnished with a hood, it was well suited for such a purpose as a protection from cold.[461]

4. The *Tunacle*.[462] The rubrics of 1547 were written so as to be understood by persons who, with very few exceptions, were neither scholars nor antiquaries, but who were acquainted with the conventional meaning of terms in common use in this country at the time. That common use we may now trace in the barbarous Latin, or the Latinised English, of church Inventories. And in these we find that *Tunicæ* are distinguished, as in this rubric, from *Albæ*. And it is clear that the direction given in this rubric of the first Prayer-book of 1549, is based throughout upon the old arrangement. Such lists as those given below,[463] when carefully examined with special reference to the *numbers* of each separate vestment named, will at once illustrate, and be illustrated by, the rubric we are now considering. In each case the "*vestimentum*," spoken of (the word here meaning a *complete set of vestments for three* persons, the Celebrant, Epistoler, and Gospeller), contains *three* of all such vestments as in pre-Reformation use *would be worn by all three*, but has *one* Casula only, and *two* Tunicæ. In mediæval times, these *Tunicæ*,

---

[460 a] A *cappa rubra* is spoken of as one of the distinctive marks of a pope in a letter of Peter Damianus, quoted at p. 221. A *cappa paonacea* (violet colour) is worn by Roman cardinals.

[461] For detailed information as to the shape, size, and ornamentation of the Cope, see Bock, *L. G.* ii. 287 sqq. or Pugin's *Glossary*, *in voc.*

[462] The very form of the word Tunacles (instead of the more correct Tunicles) indicates the debased period from which the word dates. Properly speaking, the diminutive *Tunicule* answers to the χιτωνίσκος of the Greek Church, and is correctly used of any of those *shorter* forms of the Tunic, which from early times, and from associations of idea which were all but universal, served to mark *inferiority of dignity* on the part of those who wore them. They were also suggestive of the more *active ministration* required of the inferior orders of the clerical body.

[463] *Inventory of St. George's Chapel, Windsor.* "Item de dono Regis Henrici quarti unum vestimentum blodii coloris intextum cum albis canibus, viz., duabus frontellis, duabus ridellis [Fr. *rideaux*] una casula, duabus tunicis, tribus amictibus, cum stola et fanone ejusdem sectæ. Item unum vestimentum album bonum de panno adaurato pro principalibus festis beatæ Mariæ, cum casula, duabus tunicis, tribus albis, tribus amictibus, cum stola et fanonibus, quattuor capis ejusdem sectæ, cum diversis orfreis, et quatuor aliis capis diversæ sectæ de panno adaurato, cum duabus ridellis et toto apparatu Altaris sive frontello." [In another "vestimentum," three Casulæ are mentioned without any mention in detail of other vestments.] Quoted by Pugin, *G. G. A. in voc.* "vestment."

which in English [464] Inventories appear as "Tunacles" (note 462), were in many cases of costly material, and richly embroidered. Their shape resembled that of the later Dalmatics, and may be seen in the representation of the deacon in Pl. LXI.

## 2. Ministering Vestments of a Bishop, A.D. 1548.

In the last page of the Liturgy authorised by the Act of 1548, occurs the following rubric:

"In the saying or singing of Mattins and Evensong, baptizing and burying, the minister in parish churches, and chapels annexed to the same, shall use a surplice. And in all cathedral churches and colleges the archdeacons, deans, provosts, masters, prebendaries, and fellows, being graduates, may use in the quire, beside their surplices, such hood as appertaineth to their several degrees. And whensoever the bishop shall celebrate the holy communion in the church, or execute any other public ministration, he shall have upon him, beside his rochette, a surplice or albe, and a cope or vestment, and also his pastoral staff in his hand, or else borne or holden by his chaplain."

Taking these in their order, we have,—

1. The Rochette [465] [*Rochetum*, or *Roquetum*, It. *Rochetto*, Fr. *Rochet*.]

This is by origin a German word, of which *Rock* (a coat) is the modern form, appearing, in respect of Church usage, in the form *roquus*, as early as the tenth century, in the will of Bishop Riculfus above quoted (p. 214, note 441); and in modern German in the word "*chorrock*," i.e. quire dress, or surplice. The Rochet answers to the *colobium* of primitive use, being a *tunica talaris* without sleeves.[466] It came to be assigned more especially to episcopal use, because it was suited, as the full surplice is not, to be worn under a supervestment, such as the cope.[467]

2. A Surplice or Alb. These two vestments are (as their juxtaposition in this rubric intimates) slight variations of what was by origin one vestment.

---

[464] "Item, a Chasuble of green bauiekin, with tunacles of one suit, . . . . with three albes of divers sorts with their apparel." "A Chasuble of purple velvet . . . with two tunacles and three albes of the same suit." From Dugdale's Inventory of vestments belonging to Lincoln Cathedral, quoted by Pugin *in voc.* "Chasuble."

[466] In Anglo-Saxon, *Roc.* Leofric, Bishop of Exeter, in the eleventh century, bequeathed to the use of the cathedral church, *inter alia*, (ii *dalmatica*, and iii *pistel roccas, i.e.* Epistoler's rochets). [Dr. Rock, *C. O. F.* vol. i. p. 385.]

[465] Lindwodus (*apud* Dufresne) ad Provincial. Eccl. Cantuar. lib. iii. tit. 27. "Rochetum differt a superpelliceo quia superpelliceum habet manicas pendulas, sed Rochetum est sine manicis, et ordinatur pro clerico ministraturo sacerdoti, vel forsan ad opus ipsius sacerdotis in baptisando pueros ne per manicas ipsius brachia impediantur."

[467] The Chimere [It. Zimarra, Sp. Chamarra, Fr. Chamarre, or Cimarre] is itself probably a modification of a Cope. See mention of the Chimere in the *Ordo*, &c., of Archbishop Parker's consecration, quoted at p. 229, No. 3.

One of the earliest notices of the *Superpelliceum*,[468] [O. Fr. Sourpelis] has been already quoted (p. 166). The first in date to speak of the *Superpelliceum* is Stephanus [469] Tornacensis, towards the close of the twelfth century (born 1135 A.D., Bishop of Tournay 1192). The allusions he makes to it imply that the vestment was one which had long been in use. It was of linen, and *talare* of full length, while the *cappæ* mentioned by the same author are of wool.

It is impossible to say how long this name may been in popular use before it appeared in ecclesiastical literature. But in shape and general arrangement it is a combination into one vestment of the *tunica* and super-vestment of the primitive Christian dress, as shown in the earliest monuments of the West. [Plates XIV., XV., XVII.] And it still more closely resembles the dress which by the traditions of the Eastern Church was assigned as a sacred vestment to the Apostles. See the figure of St. James in Pl. LXIII.

The surplice is, in point of fact, a *tunica talaris*, made full and flowing, as was the primitive *tunica alba* of Christian ministry, and with sleeves which correspond to the early *Greek* type just spoken of, rather than to the comparatively small sleeve of the Roman dalmatic.

The difference between the Roman and English Surplice may be seen in Pl. LXIII. And the all but exact correspondence in appearance between our present English Surplice and Stole, of ordinary usage, and the primitive dress attributed to apostles, may be seen on reference to the central figure of the right-hand group (*spectator's* right) in Pl. XV.

3. The Alb has been already noticed. *Sup.* p. 223, No. 1.

4. The Vestment or Cope. *Sup.* pp. 223, 224, No. 2 and 3.

5. The "Pastoral Staff." See above, p. 222, No. 15. In the *Ordo*, &c., quoted at p. 229, it is made matter of special remark that there was no ceremonial *traditio* of a pastoral staff to the archbishop. In mediæval times this [470] constituted a special ceremony of which a full account is given by Gervase of Canterbury [Rock, *C. O. F.* p. 226] at the close of the twelfth century.

6. The *Hood*. Both the *Casula* and the *Cappa* were originally furnished with a hood (*cucullus, capitium, cappa*) for the protection of the head. So were the Pænula and Caracalla,[85] of still earlier use.

Our own word *Hood* is derived from the Anglo-Saxon *Hod*, virtually identical with the German *Hut*, and our own more modern "hat."

---

[468] So called as being worn *over* the *pelliceum*, the woollen or furred coat.

[469] In his 106th letter (Migne, *P. C. C.* tom. ccxii. col. 394), which he sends with a present of a new surplice to Cardinal Albinus, and with it a sermon which he had preached shortly before " *de mystica superpellicei confectione*." In another form (*linea superpelliceolis*) the word occurs in reference to the vestment of John, Archbishop of Rouen († 1076). Dufresne *in voc.*

[470] Or rather the delivery of the *Crosier*. See p. 222, No. 15.

The Hood which in primitive times formed part of the super-vestment, was afterwards separated from it. Thus separated, it was lined with fur for the greater comfort (and with *costly* fur for the greater dignity) of them who wore it. The material of which it was to be made, the lining with which it was to be furnished, became matters of minute regulation. Hence the various Doctor's, Master's, Bachelor's hoods, of our present Universities.[471]

## 2. THE PRAYER-BOOK OF 1552.

In the first Prayer-book, authorised by the Act of 1548, the more important of the older vestments were retained, no mention, however, being made of Amice, Girdle, or Under-Girdle, Stole, Maniple, Caligæ, and Sandalia, Mitre, Gloves, or Ring.

In the second Prayer-book a further change[472] was made. The second rubric before Morning Prayer runs as follows:

"The minister at the time of the Communion, and at all other times in his ministration, shall use neither alb, vestment, nor cope, but, being archbishop or bishop, he shall have and wear a rochette, and being a priest or deacon, he shall have and wear a surplice only."

## 3. INJUNCTIONS OF QUEEN ELIZABETH, A.D. 1559.

In the injunctions issued in the first year of Queen Elizabeth no mention is made of vestments. But in the interpretations appended to them by the archbishop and bishops (Cardwell, *Doc. Ann.* p. 203, *sqq.*), there occurs the following direction:

"That there be used only but one apparel; as the cope in the ministration of the Lord's Supper, and the Surplice in all other ministrations."

## 4. PRAYER-BOOK OF 1559.

This book, the use of which was enjoined by the Parliament of 1558–1559, has the following rubric on vestments:

"And here is to be noted, that the minister at the time of the communion, and at all other times of his ministration, shall use such ornaments in the church, as were in use by authority of Parliament in the second year of the

---

[471] Of similar origin is the Amess (often confused with the Amice). The word Amess appears in its earliest form in the Provencal *Almusse*, in which the Arabic article is combined (as in many words dating from after the Saracen conquests in Europe) with a European word, the German *Mutse* (a cap) Sp. *Mozeo*. In mediæval Latin it is *Almutium*, in O. Fr. *Aumuce*, now *Aumusse*. In Spanish and Italian we find two sets of derivates, some from the compound form, as Sp. *Almucio*, It. *Almucia*; others from the simple word, as Sp. *Muceta*, It. *Mozzetta*.

[472] The question of the vestments had in the interval been brought prominently into discussion in consequence of Bishop Hooper refusing to be consecrated unless the use of the Pontifical vestments were dispensed with.

reign of King Edward VI. according to the act[473] of parliament set in the beginning of this book."

### 5. VESTMENTS[474] WORN BY THE BISHOPS AT THE CONSECRATION OF ARCHBISHOP PARKER, DEC. 16, 1559.

1. At Morning Prayer (*mane, circiter quintam aut sextam*) and Sermon, the archbishop elect wore his doctor's gown and hood (*toga talari coccinea caputioque indutus*).

2. Sermon ended, the archbishop, and the four bishops, *sacellum egrediuntur . . . . se ad sacram communionem paraturi*. They return vested as follows:

α. The archbishop (elect) *linteo superpelliceo (quod vocant) induebatur*.

β. The Bishop of Chichester in a Cope: *capa serica ad sacra peragenda paratus utebatur*.

γ. Two chaplains of the archbishop who assisted at holy communion wore silk copes also.

δ. The Bishop of Hereford (elect)[475] and the suffragan Bishop of Bedford *linteis superpelliceis induebantur*.

ε. *Milo vero Coverdallus non nisi toga lanea talari utebatur*.

3. After the Consecration Service, and the Communion, the archbishop went out, accompanied by the four bishops, and speedily returned, "*alba episcopali, superpellicea, chimeraque*[477] (*ut vocant*) *ex nigro serico indutus, circa collum vero collare quoddam ex preciosis pellibus sabellinis (vulgo 'sables' vocant) consutum gestabat. Pari quoque modo Cicestrensis et Herefordensis suis episcopalibus amictibus, superpelliceo sc. et chimera*[467] *uterque induebatur. D. Coverdallus vero, et Bedfordiæ suffraganeus, togis solummodo talaribus utebantur*. The archbishop then formally delivered the white wands of office to the principal persons of his household, and then left the chapel attended by them, and accompanied by the bishops.

### 6. THE ADVERTISEMENTS[476] OF 1564.

"Item. In the ministration of the holy communion in cathedrall and

---

[473] This refers to the Act for the Uniformity of Common Prayer (1 Elis.), re-enacting the second Prayer-book of Edward VI., but with certain specified alterations, whereof this of the vestment is one. The direction, however, is thus modified, "until other order shall be therein taken by the authority of the Queen's Majestie, with the advice of her commissioners appointed and authorised under the great Seale of England, for causes ecclesiastical, or of the metropolitan of this realme."

[474] Rituum et ceremoniarium Ordo in consecratione, &c. Cardwell, *Doc. Ann.* i. p. 243.

[475] John Scory, late Bishop of Chichester, but now of Hereford elect.

[476] Put forth, at the Queen's injunction, by the Archbishop of Canterbury, Metropo-

collegiate churches, the principall minister shall use a cope, with gospeller and epistoler agreably; and at all other prayers to be sayde at the communion table, to use no copes, but surplesses.

"Item. That the deane and prebendaries weare a surplesse with a silk hood in the quyer; and when they preach in the cathedrall or collegiate churches to weare their hood.

"Item. That every minister saying any publique prayers, or ministringe the sacraments, or other rites of the churche, shall wear a comely surples with sleeves. . . . ."

### 7. CANONS OF 1603.

XVII. "All masters and fellows of colleges or halls, and all the scholars and students in either of the universities, shall in their churches and chapels, upon all Sundays, holy days, and their eves, at the time of Divine Service, wear surplices according to the order of the Church of England; and such as are graduates shall agreeably wear with their surplices such hoods as do severally appertain unto their degrees."

XXIV. and XXV. By the terms of these canons, the "principal minister" at the holy communion, in cathedral and collegiate churches, is to wear a decent cope. But "when there is no communion, it shall be sufficient to wear surplices. Saving that all deans, masters, and heads of collegiate churches, canons, and prebendaries, being graduates, shall daily at the times both of prayer and preaching, wear with their surplices such hoods as are agreeable to their degrees."

### PRAYER-BOOK OF 1604.

In this Book the ornaments of the first Prayer-book of Edward VI. are re-enacted as follows:

"And here is to be noted, that the minister at the time of the communion, and at all other times in his ministration, shall use such ornaments in the Church, as were in use by authoritie of Parliament in the second yeere of the reigne of Edward the Sixt, according to the Acte of Parliament [477] set in the beginning of this booke."

### 8. PRAYER-BOOK OF 1662.

To this are prefixed, α. The Act I. Eliz. (see note 473); β. The Act of

---

litan, the Bishops of London, Ely, Rochester, Winton, and Lincoln, "Commissioners in causes ecclesiastical with others." See Note 473 above. As to their authority, see Cardwell, *Doc. Ann.* vol. i. p. 287.

The same advertisements contain some-what minute directions for the "outwarde apparell of persons ecclesiasticall," i.e. for their secular dress.

[477] This Act being 1 Eliz. For the uniformitie, &c., containing the modifying clause, "*until other order shall be taken,*" &c.

Uniformity, XIV. Carol. II. "Whereas in the first year of the late Queen Elizabeth," &c.

The rubric as to vestments is as follows:

"Here is to be noted, that such ornaments of the church and of the ministers thereof, at all times of their ministration, shall be retained and be in use, as were in this Church of England, by the authority of Parliament, in the second [478] year of the reign of King Edward the Sixth."

---

[478] The Parliament which authorised the first Prayer-book of Edward VI., met Oct. 15, 1548; was prorogued till Nov. 24 by reason of the Plague. The Bill for confirming "the order of divine worship," which had been drawn out "by the Archbishop of Canterbury, with other learned and discreet bishops and divines," was brought in Dec. 9 to the Commons, Dec. 10 to the Lords, and was agreed to Jan. 15, 1549. The Parliament was not prorogued till March 14. And as Edward's accession dates from Jan. 28, 1547, the session is technically described as 2 and 3 Edward VI., and yet the "authority of Parliament" is said to be given to this book "*in the second year of King Edward VI.*"

# PART III.

# PLATES AND DESCRIPTIONS.

*Frontispiece.* DIPTYCH OF S. PAUL.[479] Photographed from a facsimile in fictile ivory in the British Museum. Imperfectly represented, and wrongly described, as a *Consular* diptych, by Duval.

In the centre compartment is the scene described in Acts, xxviii. 1 to 6. The viper is falling from St. Paul's hand; the "fire of dried wood" is at his feet; the πρῶτος τῆς νήσου, the chief officer of the island, is looking on in astonishment; a soldier (the dress marks him as a "barbarian") is in attendance upon him.

In the lower compartment are some of those "which had infirmities in the island," whom the soldier, mentioned above, is directing to St. Paul for healing.

In the upper compartment St. Paul[480] is seated on an apostolic throne, and giving his blessing to a bishop.[481] In this we may probably see a trace of an early Roman tradition, coinciding with the conclusions to be drawn from Scripture, and from the epistle of St. Clement of Rome. From these it appears clear that St. Paul, and not St. Peter,[482] was the first "apostle and bishop" of Rome; though St. Peter no less than St. Paul witnessed there, by his death, for Christ. Compare p. xlii. l. 1, *sqq.*

PLATES I. TO VII., ILLUSTRATIONS OF CLASSICAL COSTUME.

Pl. I. *The Monument of Caius Sestius.* The father (dressed in *tunica talaris* and *toga*) bids " Farewell, for ever," to his daughter.

---

[479] The original was at one time in the possession of Baron Denon, and belongs now to M. Carrand of Lyons.

[480] This is plain from a comparison of this figure with that of St. Paul in the central compartment. Contrast the figures of consuls in Plates XXII., XXIII.

[481] So I infer from the book of the Gospels held in the left hand, this having been in early times the distinguishing *insigne* of a bishop. See p. xlii, and compare Plates XXX., XXXI., XLIV., XLV., XLVI , and, for the East, the figure of St. James in Pl. LXIII.

[482] This will account for the fact that in very many of the early monuments at Rome precedence is given to St. Paul over St. Peter; the former being often placed on the *right* hand of our Saviour, St. Peter on the left.

Pl. II. *From the Arch of Titus.* The Emperor, in the long garb of peaceful (p. ix, 1) rule, gives audience [463] to his people. The figures standing around and below him illustrate the various types of dress described in Introduction, Chap. ii. p. vii, *sqq.*

Pl. III. *From the Column of Trajan.*[464] The Emperor, before the Prætorian tent, offers the sacrifice known as the *Suovetaurilia.* He is clad in a *toga* (see p. xiv), and has the head covered (p. 182, No. 17); in his hand a *patera.* The actual sacrificers are *nudi* (note π, p. xxi), naked to the waist.

Pl. IV. *From the Arch of Constantine.* The Emperor, in the garb of war [465] (p. xl, 1), addresses the people of Rome.

Pl. V. *The Ornamented Planeta*[466] *and the Dalmatic.*[467] The first of these figures is by most antiquaries described as dressed in a Pænula.[468] There is little doubt that in *form* it resembles the Pænula, and it may be such a Pænula as in the fifth century (p. 197, No. 22) was worn even *intra Urbem* by senators. The ornamental *clavi* worn, as here, *upon a super-vestment,* are of very rare occurrence.

The other figure is clad in a Dalmatic.

Both figures are "*orantes*," in what was in early times the attitude of prayer.

Pl. V. *bis. Roman Dress*[469] *of the Imperial times.*

1. A Roman marriage, as generally described, but rather perhaps a betrothal (*sponsalia*). For the dress of the man, see pp. x, xi. The head-dress of the bride may either be the (*Flammeum*) bridal veil, or a *Mafortis*, if the ceremony be not a marriage.

2. A mode of wearing the *Pallium*,[470] common in works of late Greek or Roman art, and reproduced in many of the early frescoes and mosaics in representations of Apostles. Plates XXIX., XXXVIII., XLV.

---

[463] This sculpture is intended to represent the blessings of peace and plenty restored by the emperor to Italy. FEMINARVM FOECVNDITATI GENITORVMQ SPEI CONSVLVIT PVBLICVS PARENS PER VNIVERSAM ITALIAM PVERIS PVELLISQ VLPIIS (?) ALIMENTARIIS INSTITVTIS. See Bellori (*Vet. Arc. Aug*), by whom the reliefs of this arch are fully described and figured. Compare Pliny, *Paneg.* cap. 26. *Adornanto congiarii die . . . labor parentibus erat ostentare parvulos, impositosque cervicibus adulantia verba blandasque voces edocere.*

[464] For a full description, see Bellori, *Colonna Traiana.*

[465] Because he is here represented at the moment of his entering Rome, *immediately after his victory* over Maxentius, Oct. 28, A.D. 312. See Bellori, *Vet. Arc. Aug.*

[466] For the Planeta, see Appendix C, No. 38, *sqq.*

[467] See Introduction, p. lv, *sqq.*

[468] See Appendix C, Nos. 1 to 25; Introduction, p. lx. *sqq.*

[469] These outlines are from Weiss, K. Abt. ii. fig. 376, 423; K. i. M. fig. 3, 8.

[470] This term is here used, as by the Romans under the empire, as the equivalent for the Greek ἱμάτιον, a general term for a super-vestment, as distinct from the χιτών.

H H

3. The Toga, with a sketch showing its supposed form and proportion when opened out.

4. The Pænula, with its hood attached. An outline appended, showing its *cucullus* (or "hood") as worn upon the head.

5. The *tunica talaris* (p. viii, and note λ, p. ix) *manicata*.

Pl. VI. *Greek Dress.* From Montfaucon, A. E. tom. iii. Pl. I. The smaller groups are from the Parthenon, and of the time of Pericles. The larger figures (wearing ἱμάτιον and χιτών) are of the Roman Period. See Boissard, Pl. 51, 123.

Pl. VI. *bis* and VII. *Roman and Greek Sacerdotal Costume.* The figures here given (from Montfaucon and Boissard) will serve to show the conventional modes of designating official priesthood in classical art. See p. xxxix, *sqq.*

Pl. VIII. and IX. *Dress of Jewish Priesthood.* These Plates, which are reproductions of those given by Dr. Bock[491] (*L. G.* vol. i. Pl. III., IV), are probably near approaches to those of actual Levitical priesthood. Compare the accounts of Josephus (p. 2 to 7), and of St. Jerome (p. 10 to 19). But the mitre of the Levitical priest was probably very different from that here represented. Braunius himself, whom Dr. Bock here follows, speaks with great diffidence upon this point, and expresses his opinion that if we could determine what was the *pileolum* assigned to Ulysses[492] in works of ancient art, this would determine the real form of the Levitical cap. Such a cap is in point of fact seen in several works of art still existing,[493] and is what we should call a "skull-cap," of the shape of the head, and "*like a sphere divided in twain,*" as St. Jerome described it. Such a cap as that attributed to the high-priest in Pl. IX., was probably common to both orders, the difference consisting only in the insignia (pp. 6 and 19), proper to the high-priest, the additional overing, *coloris hyacinthini*, and the *lamina aurea.*

Pl. X. *The Holy Family.* From the chromolithograph of De Rossi [I. S. D. V.] This fresco, in its original place in the cemetery of S. Priscilla, occupies, strange to say, a wholly subordinate position amongst a number of unimportant figures. It is probably the oldest picture of the subject now extant. [For a very early *Eastern* representation, see Texier and Pullan, B. A. Pl. V.] The Star of Bethlehem is seen above. And De Rossi very ingeniously (but somewhat fancifully) suggests, that the standing figure is not that of St. Joseph, but the embodiment of the Jewish prophet of the older

---

[491] Dr. Bock's authority is Braunius *De Hab. Sac. Hebraeorum*, a very learned writer, but one who has followed Maimonides, and other late Jewish authorities, upon some points in which they differ from Josephus and St. Jerome.

[492] *Pileolum quale pictum in Ulysse* (al. Ulysseo) *conspicimus, quasi sphæra media sit divisa.* St. Jerome, *ad Fabiol.* quoted at p. 14.

[493] See, for example, Gell's *Pompeii*, Pl. XV., vol. ii.

covenant, pointing to that star as the symbol of the fulfilment, in the Nativity, of the great subject of Old Testament prophecy. A comparison of this with Plates XXXVIII., XL., XLV., and XLVI., will show at a glance the difference of belief at Rome in the third or fourth century (from which, if not from an earlier time, this first representation dates), and in the ninth, and eleventh, and twelfth, to which those later pictures belong.

Pl. XI. *Our Lord blessing a young child.* From the Cemetery of SS. Marcellinus and Peter. Aringhi, R. S. tom. ii. p. 71. For the *virga* in the hand of our Lord, see p. xl.

Pl. XII. *Our Lord as the giver of the Divine Word.* Cemetery of St. Agnes. Aringhi, R. S. tom. ii. p. 213. On either side are two Apostles, who, as well as our Lord, have the nimbus, indicating a somewhat late date for this picture. The two *capsæ*, on either side, filled with *volumina*, are intended (almost without doubt) as representations of the Old and New Testament respectively. The open *codex* in the hand of our Lord shows the later form of Book.[94]

Pl. XIII. *Our Lord as the Good Shepherd.* [Aringhi, R. S. tom. ii. p. 111.] From a drawing made for me by a valued friend, and most accomplished artist, the late Mrs. C. Newton.

For the type of dress represented, see pp. viii and ix.

Pl. XIV. *Our Lord with Six Apostles.* From the Cemetery of St. Agnes at Rome. Aringhi, R. S. tom. ii. p. 195. On the dress here attributed to our Lord and to the Apostles, and with very slight variations perpetuated in much later monuments, see Introduction, Chaps. IV. and V.

Pl. XV. *Our Lord with the Twelve Apostles.* From the Cemetery of S. Callixtus at Rome. Aringhi, R. S. tom. i. p. 529.

Pl. XVI. *A Passover Celebration.* The *lamb* (as I suppose it to be) dressed whole, which is upon the table, the cup, and the youth, dressed, not as a slave, but as a son of the house (compare Exod. xii. 26), all indicate such an interpretation as is implied by the title I have given to this picture. Aringhus (R. S. ii. p. 119) regards it as an *Agape Funeralis.*

Pl. XVII. *The Ordination of a Deacon.* From the Cemetery of St. Hermes. Aringhi, R. S. ii. p. 329. Anastasius states (D. V. P. in Pelagio II.) that Pope Pelagius II. " made " (*fecit*) this cemetery, and held ordinations there. The style of a mosaic (Pl. XXIX.), which Pelagius constructed elsewhere, confirms the probability of the conjecture, that the fresco reproduced in this plate dates from his time. It may probably be regarded as an ideal

---

[94] In accordance with this somewhat late date, probably the fifth century, is the curious fact that in this picture our Lord is distinguished from the two Apostles by an *Orarium*, corresponding in arrangement to those shown in Pl. IV.

reprefentation of ordination, as proceeding ultimately from our Lord. If fo, the two figures on either fide will reprefent St. Peter and St. Paul, as the joint founders, under Chrift, of the Church at Rome.

Pl. XVIII. ΡѠΜΑΝΟΥ ΠΡΕСΒΕΥΤΟΥ (probably the Prefbyter Romanus, martyred Nov. 17, A.D. 303) and ΕΥΚΑΡΠΙѠΝΟС СΤΡΑ-ΤΙѠΤΟΥ St. Eucarpion, foldier and martyr in the Reign of Diocletian. This and the three plates which follow are from chromolithographs publifhed by Texier and Pullan ("from careful drawings coloured on the fpot") in their "Byzantine Architecture." The mofaics reprefented decorate the vault of the Church of St. George at Theffalonica, and are among the very few early Greek mofaics which efcaped deftruction either from the Iconoclafts, or at the hands of the Turks. The learned authors of the work above mentioned give reafons for their belief, that this church was built by Conftantine himfelf during his firft fojourn at Theffalonica. The drefs feen in all thefe plates is not the drefs of holy miniftration (which would have been white), but the drefs of folemn ceremonial, fuch as could appropriately be attributed, as here it is, to laymen, as well as to bifhops and priefts.[195] For details concerning this, fee Introduction, Chapters II., III., IV., and for the queftion of colour, Appendix A.

Pl. XIX. ΚΟСΜΟΥ ΙΑΤΡΟΥ and ΔΑΜΙΑΝΟΥ ΙΑΤΡΟΥ SS. Cofmas and Damianus, natives of Arabia. They practifed Medicine at Ægæ in Cilicia, A.D. 283.

"They traverfed the country curing difeafes, and demanded no other recompenfe from thofe whom they cured than that they fhould embrace the Chriftian faith. But the partifans of idolatry, believing that they worked by magic, denounced them to the Emperor (Carinus). When arrefted they were ordered to deny Chrift; upon their refufal they were about to be conducted to execution, when, through divine infpiration, the emperor was convinced of his error by means of a cure effected by thefe two Chriftians. The emperor and all his fervants thenceforth believed in Chrift; but the honours rendered to the two phyficians excited the jealoufy of the courtiers, and one day, when Damian and Cofmas were gathering plants upon a mountain, they were furprifed and put to death." *Byz. Archit.* p. 141.

Pl. XX. ΦΙΛΙΠΠΟΥ ΕΠΙСΚ and ΘΕΡΙΝΟΥ СΤΡΑΤ *i.e.* Philip, Bifhop of Heraclea; Therinus, foldier and martyr.

"Philip was Bifhop of the town of Heraclea, in the fourth century. . . . . Baffus, being Governor of Thrace, fent the procurator Ariftomachus, to clofe the church and feize the treafure. Philip ftill perfifted in performing fervices under the portico, and in exhorting Chriftians to remain fteadfaft in the faith: for this he was fent to the ftake. . . ." *Ibid.*

---

[195] Slight variations may, however, be noticed as between the drefs attributed to a bifhop (Pl. XX) and a prefbyter (Pl. XVIII.), compared with that of the laymen.

Of Therinus nothing is known with certainty, save what the title of "soldier," here given him, indicates. His position relatively to St. Philip makes it probable that he was of the same province (Macedonia) and probably an officer, or soldier, of the Macedonian Legion.

Pl. XXI. ΟΝΗCΙΦΟΡΟΥ CΤΡΑΤC and ΠΟΡΦΟΙΡΙΟΥ.

"Onesiphorus and Porphyrius . . . . suffered martyrdom on the same day. Onesiphorus was a native of Iconium, and a relative of the Empress Tryphæne. He lived at Iconium, and having received there the Apostle Paul, he was instructed by him, and baptized with his whole household. Having become a Christian he quitted Iconium and went to dwell at Paros, where he preached the Christian doctrine; but having been seized by the order of the Archon, at the same time as his servant Porphyrius, he was tortured and afterwards put to death by being tied to the tail of a spirited horse, and dragged over a stony road. Porphyrius suffered the same torture, and died with his master." Texier and Pullan, B. A. p. 140.

Pl. XXII. *Diptych of Boethius, Consul of the West*, A.D. 510. For the history of the diptych, and a statement of the various questions suggested by it, see Gori. Thes. Diptych, tom. i. p. 137, *sqq*. A comparison of this with Pl. XXIII. will show the identity (with very slight modifications only) of official costume in New and Old Rome, in the sixth century, and will indicate the probable source of the Omophorion, worn (as matter of privilege) by Patriarchs and Metropolitans in the East, and, out of usage rather than of theoretical right, by almost all bishops.

Pl. XXIII. *Diptych of Clementinus, Consul of the East*, A.D. 513. For a description of this diptych, see M. D. Wyatt, *Notices of Sculpture in Ivory*, p. 6; Gori, *Thes. Dipt*. i. p. 229, *sqq*. This, and the following Plate, are photographed, by permission, from the facsimile, in fictile ivory, published by the Arundel Society.

Pl. XXIV. *Diptych of St. Gregory the Great, in the Costume, and with the Insignia*,[96] *of a Consul*. This singular monument, assigned by antiquaries to the year 700, or thereabouts, now forms the cover of an antiphonary, presented by St. Gregory to Theodolinda, Queen of the Lombards. It is preserved in the Treasury of the Cathedral at Monza.[97] The received opinion among the older antiquaries was, that this was originally a consular diptych, *converted* into a representation of St. Gregory. Fuller information, however, has led the most eminent modern antiquaries to regard this as an original work. The inscription above the bishop's head is thus worded: GREGORIUS PRÆZVL MERITIS ET NOMINE DIGNV VNDE GENVS DVCIT MERITVM CONSCENDIT HONOREM.

---

[96] The *Mappa* in the r. h. of a consul (thrown into the arena as a signal for the games to commence), as in Plates XXII., and XXIII., may here perhaps be interpreted as a *Μαππυλα*, or Maniple.

[97] Photographed, by permission, for this work, from the facsimile of the Arundel Society.

Pl. XXV. *Picture of St. Gregory the Great, of his Father Gordianus, and his Mother Sylvia.* This picture corresponds with the description [498] given of the original by Joannes Diaconus, in the tenth century. Roman antiquaries constantly refer to it as authentic; and Cardinal Baronius, who had opportunities of knowing its history, and Papebrochius (AA. SS. Maius Propyl. p. 177) publish it as such. Reference is made to a *tabula æri incisa* used by Baronius, but the actual drawings (if any), of older date, from which this derived, are not specified.

Pl. XXVI. *The Ascension.* Facsimile of an illustration in a Syriac MS. of the Gospels, written A.D. 586, at Zagba, in Mesopotamia, and acquired for the Library of the Medici, at Florence, A.D. 1497. The picture represents the Ascension. The dresses of the Apostles correspond exactly with those assigned to them in early Roman frescoes and mosaic pictures. It is noticeable that in this picture we have already traces, slight in themselves, of a tendency to exalt the blessed Virgin to a position beyond that assigned to her in Holy Scripture, or in the earlier monuments of Christian antiquity. She here occupies the central place amid the Apostles, as present at the Ascension, an event with which, in the narrative of Scripture, she is not in any way connected. And to her, as to our Lord and to the angels, the nimbus is assigned, though the Twelve have it not. In these respects this picture forms a connecting link, in the thought implied, as in the time from which it dates, between Pl. X., and XXXVIII. [From Seroux d'Agincourt, Histoire, &c., vol. v. Pl. XXVII.]

Pl. XXVII. *Eusebius, Bishop of Cæsarea, and Ammonius of Alexandria.* [From the same MS. as No. XXVI.] After Asseman. Bib. Med. Pl. III.

Pl. XXVIII. *The Emperor Justinian, and Archbishop Maximianus, at the Consecration of the Church of S. Vitalis, at Ravenna.* From a mosaic dating, probably, from the close of the sixth century. The Archbishop wears a Dalmatic under a Planeta.[499] Over the Planeta is a Pallium of the older [480] form and arrangement, and in his hand a jewelled cross. The two personages

---

[498] Joan. Diac. D. G. P. lib. iv. cap. 83. 84. In this description, note particularly the following concerning St. Gregory's dress: " Planeta super Dalmaticam castanea: evangelium in sinistra, modus crucis in dextra: pallio mediorici, a dextro videlicet humero sub pectore super stomachum circulatim deducto: deinde sursum per sinistrum humerum veniens propria rectitudine non per medium corporis sed ex latere pendet: circa verticem vero tabulæ " (the "*square nimbus*," so called) " similitudinem, quod viventis insigne est, præferens, non coronam " (the "*nimbus*"). The *Pallium* described is evidently such as that ascribed to Leo III. in the drawing at p. lii. The language of John the deacon implies that in his own time (tenth century) the form and arrangement of the pallium had undergone a change. Compare cap. 80 of the same book, whence it appears that the pallium was in St. Gregory's time of *linen* and *sullis accubiis* (i.e. *acubus* [add.]) perforatum.

[499] As to the colour of this Planeta it is difficult to speak with authority. Ciampini speaks of it as *aurea*. Hefner-Altenek (Pl. XCI) in his coloured drawing represents it as a very dull green, the Dalmatic white, with black stripes; and Gally Knight (E. A. Pl. X.) both figures and describes the whole dress as white. All the coloured drawings that I have seen represent the *lora* (or *clavi*) as black.

on his left (probably archdeacon and deacon) wear Dalmatics of the older form, with black *clavi* (not clearly shown in this Plate), and corresponding stripes at the edge of the sleeve. [After Gally Knight, E. A. Pl. X ]

Pl. XXIX. *A mosaic, dating from the close of the Sixth Century, from the Church of S. Laurentius, at Rome.* The figures represented are our Lord, S. PETRVS and S. PAVLVS, S. LAVRENTIVS and S. STEPHANVS, S. YPPOLIT (St. Hippolytus) and PELAGIVS EPISC. (Bishop of Rome from 578 to 590). Pelagius is without the nimbus assigned to the other six personages, and wears the dress traditionally attributed to our Lord and the Apostles. [From a drawing in Her Majesty's Collection.] The figure of Pelagius has been in great part destroyed by accident, and is here represented as restored by Roman antiquaries. In one particular,[500] not of importance to this inquiry, the arrangement of the two figures on the spectator's left is probably incorrect.

Pl. XXX. SCS CORNELIVS PP. (Bishop of Rome A.D. 251–252), and SCS CIPRIANVS (Bishop of Carthage A.D. 248–258). [From a fresco lately discovered by Chevalier De Rossi, and dating[501] (probably) from the close of the eighth century.]

Pl. XXXI. Fresco of the same date[501] as the above, in which are represented S. XVSTVS [Bishop of Rome from A.D. 257 to A.D. 259], and a contemporary Bishop [SCS. O. perhaps St. Optatus] of some unknown see.

Pl. XXXII. *The TRICLINIVM LATERANVM.*[502] A portion of the Banquet-room of the Lateran Palace, built and decorated with mosaics by Leo III., at the beginning of the ninth century.

Pl. XXXIII. *Two groups from the Mosaics of the TRICLINIUM LATERANUM.*[502] In the one our Lord bestows a Pallium (symbol of ecclesiastical authority), upon St. Sylvester, and a *Vexillum* (symbol of imperial rule) upon CONSTANTINVS REX. In the other, St. Peter gives a Pallium to D. N. SCTISSIMVS LEO PP. (Dominus noster Sanctissimus Leo Papa); and a *Vexillum* to CAROLVS REX (Charlemagne). By these two groups is symbolised the Divine origin of both spiritual and temporal power; and the alliance, and partition of the two, in the person of the Pope and the Emperor. A more exact representation of this Plate, photographed

---

[500] According to one restoration the model of the church is held in the hands of Pope Pelagius, so as to designate him as the restorer of the church.

[501] As to the date of these monuments see De Rossi, R. S. p. 298 to 304. He pronounces them to be "certainly not older" than the seventh century, and mentions various reasons for attributing them to the pontificate of Leo III.

[502] For full details concerning this monument see Alemannus, *De Parietinis Lateranis*, from which the above drawings are taken. The first is altogether, and the second in great part, a restoration, authority for which was found in drawings preserved in the Vatican, after the original itself (even as restored by Leo IV.) had been in great part destroyed.

from a drawing in Her Majesty's collection, will be found at p. lii. See description of woodcuts below.

Pl. XXXIV. to XXXVI.[503] A series of illustrations from the Liber Pontificalis of Landolfus, a MS. of the ninth century, in the Library of S. Minerva, at Rome. These represent the Costume and Insignia, and the modes of Ordination, regarded as proper to priests, deacons, sub-deacons, exorcists, and the other minor orders, at the period in question.

Pl. XXXIV. *Ordination of Ostiarii* (doorkeepers) *and of Lectores* (readers).

1. The Bishop delivers to the Doorkeepers the keys of the Church. *Tradendo eis claves ecclesiæ Dei.*

2. The *Ostiarii* prostrate themselves before the Bishop to receive his blessing. *Prosternuntur ante pontificem.*

3. Ordination of Readers. *Tradidit eis episcopus codicem.*

4. The Bishop gives his blessing to the Readers. *Deinde prostratis in terram (benedicit).*

Pl. XXXV. *Ordination of Exorcists, Acolytes, Sub-deacons, and Deacons.*

5. The Bishop gives a book to the Exorcists. *Exorcistis tradit episcopus libellum.*

6. The Bishop hands a candlestick to the Acolyte. *Acolitis tradit episcopus cerostatam.*

7. The Sub-deacons receive the Paten and the Chalice. *Subdiaconi patenam et calicem.*

8. The Bishop lays the *Orarium* (Stole) on the left shoulder of the Deacon. *Ponens oraria super humeros.*

Pl. XXXVI. *Ordination of Deacons and Priests.*

9. The Bishop bestows Benediction on the Deacons. *Dum in terram prostrati fuerint.*

10. Ordination of Priests. The Bishop places the *Orarium* (Stole) about their necks. *Oraria super colla eorum.*

11. They bow the head to receive imposition of hands, and episcopal Benediction. *Super quos inclinatis capitibus* (benedicit).

12. The Bishop anoints their right hands, tracing thereon the sign of the Cross. *Cum pollice dexteræ faciens crucem.*

---

[503] From the outlines published by Seroux d'Agincourt. Facsimiles of the original drawings are in the author's possession.

Pl. XXXVII. *A Bishop giving the Chrism to a newly baptized Infant.* From a Latin MS. of the ninth century, in the Library of the S. Minerva, at Rome.[504]

Pl. XXXVIII. *The Virgin Mother and Holy Child.* The former wears a royal diadem, and a dress of purple and gold, with scarlet shoes (insignia of royalty). On either side are, *r.* S. IACOBVS and S. IOANNES; *l.* S. PETRVS and S. ANDREAS. This mosaic dates from *circ.* 848 A.D. [Photographed from a drawing in Her Majesty's Collection.]

See above on Plates X. and XXVI.

Pl. XXXIX. *Pope Nicholas I.* [*sed.* A.D. 858–867] *and the Emperor Lewis II.* [*regn.* A.D. 843–876.] From the *Chartularium Prumiense*, a MS.[505] partly of the ninth century, partly of later date, in the Stadtbibliotek, at Treves. The Cap here worn by the Pope is not a *Mitra*, but a *Camelaucium*, so called. Compare Florovantes, *Ant. Pontif. Rom. Den.* p. 37. He is speaking of a coin of Hadrianus I. *Figura in medio Pontificali habitu et bireto, quod Camelaucium ab Anastasio in Constantino, hodie vero Camaurum dicitur.* The first change of head-dress on the coins is early in the tenth century. Describing a coin of Sergius III. (*sed.* 904–911), Flor. says, p. 63, *Sergium III. pontificia veste indutum, et mitra ornatum, hic exhibet nummus;* at in superioribus nummis Pontificum capita camelaucio tantum tecta visuntur: *quæ res mire favet eorum sententiæ qui Pontifices serius mitram gestasse arbitrantur.* These facts bear out the opinion already expressed (note 265, p. 129), that the Mitra had been introduced at Rome before the time (close of eleventh century) of St. Ivo's writing. Compare Appendix F, No. 12. But they throw back the *Mitra* at Rome itself to a somewhat earlier date than most modern antiquaries have assigned to it. [The book above quoted is of great rarity. But these coins are figured in another work, the *Memoria di Domenico Promis. Monete dei Rom. Pontef.* Torino, 1858.] See further on Pl. XLVII.

Pl. XL. A fresco from the hypogene Church of S. Clemente, at Rome (lately discovered). It presents a picture of the Assumption, and contains a representation of Leo IV., and S. Vitus. This picture, when first discovered, was supposed, by such of the Roman clergy as were not antiquaries, to prove the recognition of the doctrine of the Assumption as early as the second or third centuries. They forgot that, though the walls on which these frescoes are painted are undoubtedly very ancient, it by no means follows that the paintings upon them are of the same date. The square nimbus (*quod viventis insigne est*, Joan. Diac. note 498) on the head of Leo IV., *and the position assigned him in the picture*, indicate that he was the giver of this fresco. SANCTISSIMVS DOM. LEO QRT. PP. ROM. may be seen inscribed about his head. The signature QVOD HÆC PRÆ CVNCTIS FVLGET PICTVRA COLORE COMPONERE HANC STVDVIT PRESBYTER ECCE LEO shows that he gave the picture before he became Pope, and that the smaller inscrip-

---

[504] Photographed from a drawing in Her Majesty's collection.

[505] This Plate is from Ramboux (Beiträge zur Kunstgeschichte, u. s. w).

tion was added somewhat later, probably soon after his death. A.D. 855. [On the title *Papa Romanus*, derived from the earlier times of the Church, when there were other "Papæ" even in the West, beside the Bishop of Rome, see De Rossi, R. S. p. 303, and Dufresne, *in voc.*]

Pl. XLI. The Emperor Constantine VI. presiding at the Seventh General Council (so called), held at Nicæa, A.D. 787. From a Greek MS. of the tenth century, the *Menologium Græcorum*, &c., in the Vatican Library. This Plate is from the outline published by Seroux d'Agincourt. An accurate copy of the original is in the author's possession. The Sticharia of the bishops, as well as their Phænolia, are coloured. The Phænolion of the bishop on the emperor's left (Tarasius, Patriarch of Constantinople), is lavender purple; the others (apparently) black and gold. Two of the patriarchs here represented, though *supposed to be present* (by their deputies), had not even heard of the Council, the occupation of the country by the Saracens preventing communication. The prostrate figure represents the "defeated party," in this case the Iconoclasts. The determinations of this Council were fully sanctioned by the Pope (Hadrian I.), as before by his legates. But Charlemagne summoned another Council of three hundred bishops, at Frankfort, A.D. 794, at which the authority of this Nicene Council (claiming to be the Seventh General Council) was rejected, and its decrees reversed. [An entirely different account is given by most of the Roman authorities. For the above, and the evidence on which it rests, see Cave, *Hist. Lit.* i. 652.]

Pl. XLII. Egbertus, Archbishop of Treves (*sed.* 975 to 993), receives a book offered to him by Keraldus Augiensis and another Benedictine Monk. This picture forms the title-page of an Evangeliarium, written at the close of the tenth century. [From the drawing of Ramboux.]

Pl. XLIII. *St. Clement at the Altar.* The miraculous blinding of Sisinnius. [The same subject in one of the frescoes of the Church of St. Mark, at Venice. Kreutz, *Mos. Sec.* &c., tav. xxiii.] The donors of this fresco, Beno de Rapiza, and Maria his wife, are represented *de more* at the left of the picture; and *of small size* (compare Pl. XLI.) in token of humility. There is strong internal evidence, to an antiquarian eye, of the late date of this picture. And I hear that diplomatic evidence, lately discovered at Rome, shows that Beno de Rapiza and his wife lived in the eleventh century.

Pl. XLIV. *St. Gregory the Great and St. Dunstan.* From a MS. of the eleventh century, in the British Museum. St. Gregory wears a Mitre of the earliest form, the *tæniæ* or *fasciæ* of which hang down on either side, so as to appear like large earrings. The archbishop (who also wears a Mitre) is kneeling, with two monks, at St. Gregory's feet, and embracing them. The dove whispering, as it were, into the ear, is an emblem of divine inspiration. For further details, see the great work of Professor Westwood (*Miniatures and Ornaments*, &c., p. 126) to which I owe this more correct description of the picture.

Pl. XLV. The Blessed Virgin, as the Queen of Heaven, seated on the same throne with our Lord. In her hand a scroll (painted black in the drawing at Windsor, from which this is photographed) on which in the original are inscribed the words *Læva ejus sub capite meo* (Cant. ii. 6; viii. 3). The figures on either side are (on the spectator's left) INNOCENTIVS PP., (Innocent II. *sed.* A.D. 1130-1143, the donor of this mosaic), LAVRENTIVS (St. Laurence carrying a cross, as in Pl. XXIX.) CORNELIVS PP. On the *r.* PETRVS, CALIXTVS PP. IVLIVS PP. and CALEPODIVS PRESBYTER. [From a drawing in Her Majesty's collection, as is Pl. XLVI. which follows.]

Pl. XLVI. PRÆSIDET ÆTHEREIS PIA VIRGO MARIA CHOREIS. [A mosaic[506] in the apse of the Oratory of St. Nicolaus, at Rome, commenced by Calixtus II., and completed[507] by Anastasius II.] The inscription on this mosaic is too characteristic of the times to be omitted :

SVSTVLIT HOC PRIMO TEMPLVM CALLIXTVS AB IMO
VIR CLARVS LATE GALLORVM NOBILITATE.
VERVM ANASTASIVS PAPATVS CVLMINE QVARTVS
HOC OPVS ORNAVIT VARIISQVE MODIS DECORAVIT.

Pl. XLVII. Pope Innocent II. giving Benediction to Abbot Adalbero. From an *interpolated* copy of the *Chartularium Prumiense*, now in the Stadt-Bibliothetek, at Treves. For the History of the MS., see Ramboux. The greater part of it dates from 1222 A.D. But there have been additions to it, of which this picture must be one. For the *triple* crown, here shown, points to the fourteenth century. According to Roman antiquaries of the highest repute, the *double* crown (significant of spiritual and temporal power combined) was introduced by Boniface VIII. A.D. 1299-1303, (Alemannus, *De P. L.* cap. 13, p. 129; and Florovantes, *Ant. Pont. Rom. Den.* p. 57); and the *triple* crown by Urbanus V. (A.D. 1362-1370). Compare AA. SS. Maius. Propyl. p. 419.

Pl. XLVIII. From a MS. written by Matthew Paris (*circ.* 1250) in the British Museum. Cotton MSS., Nero D. I.

α. Pope Adrian I. receives a letter from Offa II., King of Mercia.

β. The Pope's sanction having been obtained, the archiepiscopal see is transferred from Canterbury, in the " Kingdom of Kent," to Lichfield, in the " Kingdom of Mercia." Eadulfus is consecrated the first Archbishop of Lichfield.[508]

This transaction here recorded had an important influence on the subsequent history of the English Church in its relation to the Roman See. Cf. Hook, *Lives of the Archbishops*, vol. i. p. 243, *sqq.*

---

[506] Compare AA. SS. Maius Propyl. p. 320, where this mosaic is figured and described; and Muratori, R. I. S. tom. ii. p. 417.

[507] In this I follow Papebrochius (AA. SS. *ubi supra*), who further expresses his belief, that the principal figure in this group was intended by Calixtus for our Lord, but that this was considerably altered by Anastasius, and *changed into the figure of the Virgin* here exhibited. A similar change has been made in a mosaic of the fifth century. The original state of this is delineated by Ciampini, M. V. i. p. 200, the Saviour (with the *nimbus*) being seated on a throne, whilst the Virgin mother stood near. " As this group is *now* before us, the erect figure is left out ; the seated one is converted into that of Mary, with a halo round the head, although in the original even such attribute (alike given to the Saviour and to all the angels introduced) is *not* assigned to her." Hemans' History, &c., p. 207. With what he says of the nimbus, compare what is said above on Pl. XXVI.

[508] The crowns of the two principal personages in this picture have been deliberately

Pl. XLIX. [From the same MS.]

α. King Offa gives investiture to Willegoda, first Abbot of St. Albans.

β. The King and the Abbot kneel on either side of the altar, on which is laid the charter bestowed by the king.

Pl. L. *The Council of Constance.* "Erle Richard (of Warwick), and Robert Halain, Bishop of Salisbury, with other worshipful persones, ambassiatours of king Henry the Fifth to the general counsell of Constance, are honourably and honestly received by the pope and the clergy, by the Emperor Sygesmonde and the temporalte." [From a MS. of the fifteenth century. Cotton MSS. Julius, E iv.] The inscription is of later date than the MS.

Pl. LI. "Howe kyng Henry the VIth, beyng in his tender age, was crowned kyng of Englond at Westminstre with great solempnytie." [From same MS. as Pl. 6.]

The bishops all wear copes.

Pl. LII. *The Coronation of the Emperor Sigismund.* α. He is crowned by Pope Eugenius IV., β. The solemn cavalcade of the Pope and the Emperor, γ. The governor of the Castle of St. Angelo awaits their approach.

Pl. LIII. to LV. Bassi Relievi commemorative of the Council of Florence, A.D. 1440.

Pl. LIII. The Emperor Palæologus, accompanied by the Patriarch of Constantinople, and attended by the officers of his household, α. Embarks at Constantinople, β. Crosses the Adriatic in the Venetian Galleys, γ. Lands at Venice, δ. Is publicly received by Pope Eugenius IV., to whom he makes submission. [*This last Scene is wholly imaginary, nothing of the kind having really occurred.*]

Pl. LIV. Pope Eugenius IV. and the Emperor Palæologus at the Council of Florence, July 6, A.D. 1440. The Cardinal Presbyter, Julianus Cæsarinus, and other great Roman officials, are to the right of the Pope, Bessarion (Archbishop of Nicæa) and others of the Greeks on the Emperor's right. The Emperor, α. Leaves Florence in State, attended by his Court; and β. Embarks at Venice for Constantinople. [The figure standing on the left of the Emperor represents the Patriarch of Constantinople, who died before the Council separated.]

Pl. LV. Envoys from Æthiopia and from other Eastern Churches, deputed (A.D. 1441) to attend the Council of Florence, and make submission to the Pope. They are received by Eugenius IV., who hands to Abbot Andreas, their spokesman, the definitions agreed to by the Council.

The four Relievi above described have been copied at Rome for the illustration of this work. They were executed by Antonio Philarete, of

---

defaced, and redrawn in ink, within a comparatively recent period. They are restored here to their original state by comparison with the engravings of Strutt, M. and C. vol. ii. and with other drawings in the same MS.

Of three crowns figured above (copied from later drawings in this MS), two (No. 2 and 3) are assigned to the Emperor, the third (No. 1) to the Empress.

Florence, at the command of Eugenius IV., and now form part of the great Gates of St. Peter's. In some important particulars they represent events not as they really did occur, but as according to Roman theory they ought to have occurred. For further particulars concerning them, see the Basilica Vaticana, of Valentini, Pl. XXII., &c. And for the true history of this Council, see Ffoulkes, *Divisions of Christendom*, part ii. p. 332, *sqq.*

Pl. LVI. 1. The Epitrachelion[348] of Bishop Nikita, † 1167 A.D. 2 and 3. The ἐπιμανίκια[350] of the same Bishop. 4. The ὁμοφόριον[355] of Archbishop Moses, † 1329 A.D.

Pl. LVII. A leathern breastplate[509] ("Rational") and girdle, found in a coffin in the Church of the Passion at Moscow. [This cannot be older than the tenth century, when Christianity was first introduced into Russia. From what later time it dates I have not the means of knowing. This is a wholly exceptional instance in the Greek Church of a direct imitation of the Jewish "Rational." But King (*Greek Church*, p. 39) states, that in Russia, two jewelled ornaments are worn upon the breast by Metropolitans, which "are imagined to be taken from the Urim and Thummim, on Aaron's breastplate." For a similar (local) usage in the West, in the twelfth century, see notes 256 and 263.]

Pl. LVIII. *Costume of the Greek Church.*

1. St. Sampson. He wears a φαινόλιον,[351] answering to the Latin chasuble, over the Sticharion (p. LXIII. v.), or white tunic. The ends of the Peritrachelion[144] (answering to the Latin Stole) are seen pendent under the Phænolion.

2. St. Methodius. In this Figure the Polystaurion[351] takes the place of the plain Phænolion: the Genual[510] is seen pendent (as in the next figure, that of S. Germanus) on the right side; and on the outside of the Polystaurion is seen the Omophorion,[355] which corresponds to the Pallium of the Roman Church, but is worn in the East by almost all bishops.

3. St. Germanus. The Sticharion, or Alb, is here distinguished by the λῶρια,[146] or stripes proper to a bishop (Goar, *Euchol.* p. 110). He wears a Sakkos in place of the ordinary Phænolion, and thus marks[356] his dignity as a Metropolitan. In other respects he wears the same vestments as those last described. [In Russia the Saccos is now worn by all bishops, See King's *Greek Church*, p. 40.]

Pl. LIX. 1. *The Patriarch Bekkos, in Walking Dress.* He wears on his head the outer and the inner καμηλαύχιον; and in his left hand carries the καπόνιον (also known as κέπελλις), the strings of which (καμίλαβα) are seen pendent below it.

---

[146] This and the Plate last described are from the *Antiquités de l'Empire de Russie*, lately published by the Russian Government. The first volume of this work contains many ecclesiastical monuments of great interest.

[510] *Genuale* is the rendering given by Latin writers to ἐπιγονάτιον[510] as "hanging down to the knee," a distinctive ornament outside the Saccos,[357] worn by Patriarchs and metropolitan.

The long-sleeved coat, worn as a body-dress, corresponds to the cassock of an English clergyman. The outer garment is the Mandyas, with its three stripes (ποταμοί, see Note 343, p. 168). In his right hand he holds the δικανίκιον, or ῥάβδος. See Note 345, p. 168.

2. St. Macarius. This figure shows the characteristic ministering dress of a Deacon, viz. a close-fitting Sticharion (answering to the Alb of the Latin Church) and an Orarion (ὀράριον), or Deacon's Stole, having the word ΑΓΙΟC, thrice repeated, embroidered upon it. [This and Pl. LIX. are from Goar's *Euchologion*.]

Pl. LX. *Patriarch Nicon* (circ. 1650, A.D.) *in his Cowl.* This Plate is from the same source as Pl. LVI. and LVII. The accompanying woodcut shows the back of the same Cowl.

Pl. LXI. This Plate is given with a view to the readier understanding of the shape, and relative position, of the various vestments and insignia now worn in the Roman Church, and described in Appendix F. The central figure is from Bock *L. G.* Band ii. The figures of the Priest and Deacon from Pugin's *Glossary*.

Pl. LXIII. Four figures illustrating the variations in the white dress recognised at various times, and in various branches of the Church, as specially appropriate to offices of Holy Ministry. That on the left is the figure of an Apostle from the Roman Catacombs.[511] The next of St. James (wearing an Omophorion), from the Church of St. Sophia, at Trebizond, dating from the 14th century,[512] accidentally discovered not long since, by the fall of the plaster with which it had been overlaid by the Turks. The third is from a fresco

---

[511] After Aringhi *R. S.* tom. ii. p. 213.
[512] Texier and Pullan B.A. Pl. LXV. They attribute the Church (though upon no very certain *data*) to the Emperor Alexis III., *circ.* 1350.

at Florence, a group in which a priest (here represented) is saying the last office beside a dying man. The fourth is a canon of an English Collegiate Chapter, and, as such, has the Scarf (or broad Stole) worn, out of customary usage, by Doctors of Divinity, cathedral dignitaries, and others. This prepared the way for the use of the Stole, which for the last twenty years, or thereabouts, has been very generally adopted in the English Church, presenting nearly the appearance of the black *clavi* on the Tunic of the Apostle in this Plate, and in others figured in this Volume.

## LIST OF WOODCUTS.

P. vi. The Adoration of the Magi. From the Cemetery of SS. Marcellinus and Peter. Aringhi, *R. S.* tom. ii. p. 117.

P. xv. A figure in the attitude of Prayer (comp. Mark, xi. 25 (ὅταν στήκητε προσευχόμενοι): Matt. vi. 5; Luke, xviii. 11, &c.), wearing a short Tunic and a supervestment of peculiar shape. From the Cemetery of SS. Marcellinus and Peter. Aringhi, *R. S.* tom. ii. p. 111.

P. xxvi. Our Lord administering the Bread and the Cup to the Eleven Disciples. From a Syriac MS. of the year 586, A.D. See description of Pl. XXVI.

P. xliii. The Prophet Malachi. From the same MS. as Pl. XXVI. above described. For the " roll of a book " in the hand see p. xl., *sqq*.

P. lii. [From a Drawing in Her Majesty's Collection.] This represents the actual state of the mosaic nearly two hundred years ago. A comparison with Pl. XXXIII., already described, will be suggestive of the manner in which, as regards minor details, antiquaries vary in their representation of the same objects. The *keys* in St. Peter's lap, for example, figured by Alemannus, are nowhere to be seen here. And the Pallium of Leo, arranged *more Romano* by Alemannus, has the older form (preserved by the Greek ὠμοφόριον), as depicted in the present woodcut. And there are slight variations in the inscription [513] (DN. CAROLVS REX in one; DN. CAROLO REGI in the other).

P. lxxvi. An " Orante " (Female) in Dalmatic, and veil (*mafortis*). From the same source as the woodcut in p. xv, already described.

P. lxxxiv. Ancient Glass. From the Roman Catacombs.[514] This specimen is figured and described by Garrucci (*V. A.* tav. xxv. fig. 3), as follows:

A man, and a lady at his left hand, are here figured. They have their hands raised in prayer. Between them is the monogram; and below this a "*volumen*," or scroll. On the spectator's left is a bishop's throne, or chair of state (*una cattedra*); above this, another monogram (which he describes);

---

[513] BICTORIA is for VICTORIA, according to a variation of very frequent occurrence in Roman inscriptions.

[514] From an engraving kindly lent to me by the present possessor of the specimen, Mr. C. Wilshere.

behind it a mountain coloured green, from which flows a golden stream. On the top of this mountain is a tree, with fruit thereon. There is a superscription DIGNTIAS AMIC.[514a] Then after describing the dress, he goes on to say, that this had once been supposed to represent SS. Perpetua and Felicitas. But one of the figures, which, as he says, is clearly that of a man, he thinks is very like that of S. Laurentius, in tav. xx. 7 (it is difficult to trace the resemblance); and the female figure, he adds, may be St. Agnes. The dress does nearly resemble that attributed to St. Agnes in other specimens of glass, the fact being that it is the rich costume worn by Roman ladies of high rank at that time. A comparison of tav. xxvi. No. 11 and 12, in the same volume, suggests what I venture to think is the real explanation of the figures before us. They are man and wife, people of high rank: the "scroll" between them represents the *tabulæ matrimoniales*;[515] the coin just below the roll, the marriage dowry: the bishop's chair[516] is suggestive of the Church, and more particularly of the *Cathedral* Church, as we should call it; and the tree with its fruits, probably of the Tree of Life. I have a third explanation to mention, not my own, but that of a gentleman who, at a recent Church Congress, referred to this glass as an undoubted representation of *a priest vested in a Chasuble*. It is to be regretted that he did not give an explanation of the lady at "the priest's" side, or of the DIGNTIAS AMIC of the inscription. For myself I confess to some surprise, that anybody, having the slightest acquaintance with antiquity, should have ventured to assert, without any doubt or hesitation, that "*on this glass is depicted a priest, vested in just such a Chasuble as may now be seen in Ritualistic Churches.*"[517]

---

[514a] A mistake of the original workmen for DIGNITAS AMIC. The full inscription (for which these words stand representative) is DIGNITAS AMICORVM VIVAS CVM TVIS FELICITER. So in tav. ii. Or as on yet another specimen, DIGNITAS AMICORVM PIE ZESES CVM TVIS OMNIBVS BIBE ET PROPINA. By the phrase *Dignitas Amicorum*, we may understand either "*digni amici*," or "honoured by all thy friends," ("Orgueil de tes amis." Gar).

[515] S. Augustine's Serm. xxxviii de Proverb. c. 31 (*apud Garrucci*) " Unaquæque conjux bona . . . . tabulas matrimoniales instrumenta emptionis suæ deputat." Compare Martigny, D. A. C. *in voc.* "mariage."

[516] In the other specimens (figured by Garrucci, as above) in which man and wife are represented, the Church (and through this their Christian faith) is typically suggested by a pillar or column. [So Garrucci, a very learned author, whose work will repay a careful study.]

[517] Dr. Littledale. Report of Wolverhampton Church Congress (1867), p. 279. I have reproduced the engraving above described, that my readers may form their own opinion upon the matter.

---

N.B.—*The Plates, above described, as being from Her Majesty's Collection at Windsor, are from Coloured Drawings by Santo Bartoli and others, in which the Mosaic Pictures of the Roman Churches, and other objects of antiquarian interest, are depicted as they existed more than 150 years ago. The Collection was originally made for Cardinal Albano (afterwards Clement XI.), and is now the property of Her Majesty. These Drawings bear marks of having been very accurately copied, and contain a number of important details which are not to be found elsewhere.*

# INDEX.

## WORDS AND SUBJECTS.

*N.B. Roman Numerals refer to the pages, and Greek Letters to the Notes, of the Introduction.*

*The larger Arabic Numerals refer to the pages of the later portions of this Treatife; and the fmaller Arabic Numerals to the correfponding Notes.*

Acedia, 127 262
Accidia, 156 318
Acus (palli), 158 322, 236 498
Aerius, 185 381
Alb, liv. App. F, No. 2; App. G, 226
Alcuin (reputed), 110 218
Almutium. See "Amefs."
Amefs, 228 471
Amice. App. F, No. 1.
Amphibalum = Cafula, 204, *l.* 11
Ammonius, Pl. xxviii. 238
Ampolla, 106 206
ἀμφίμασχον, 66 130
ἀνάσυρμα, 50 79
Angel's drefs, liv π, 69 116
Animal origin (garments of), 20 30
Antiftes, 27 45
Apoftolicæ vices, 92 168
Apoftolicus = Bp. of Rome, 95 174, 141 294
Artemidorus, xi μ
Affumption, doctrine of the, p. 241, *l.* 33
Auguftine, St. 44 ; App. C, No. 26, 27
Aurea Rofa, 164 333
Aurifrigium, 152 312

Bells on Tunic, 4, 15, 62 108
Blue (hyacinthus), fymbolifm of, 20 32, 59 103, 138 286
——— cap of, 6
——— in H. S., 183, No. 26 to 28
——— tunic of, 4, 79
Boniface, St., on Veftments, 78 135
Bracæ, 11 21
Braviam, 149 306
Breaftplate. See "Rational."
Brilliant colours, xx λ. App. A.
Βύσσος (byſſus), 2 5, 7 16, 60 105, 72 122
——— as a colour, 161 326
Byrrhus, lvi ω

Cœna Domini, 162 328

Cæfarius of Arles, his will, 199, *in fin.*
Calcaneum, 104 202
Caligæ, lxxx, 128, 217
Camifia, 13 23
Campobi (campagæ), 97 184
Capitium, 14 24
Cappa. See "Cope."
Capfa, xl, 197 402
Caracalla, 16 25
Cardinal's hat, 72 124
Cafula, lxiii, *ſqq.* 74 130, 198, *ſqq.*, 217
Cathedra Petri, 163 330
Celeftine (Pope), on Veftments, 45
Chafuble. See "Cafula."
Chimere, 226 467
Cidaris, 32
Clofely fitted veftments, 2 6, 59 101, 121 249
Coccus-ineus. See "Scarlet."
Colobium, lv, lvii, 111 220
Colour, xvi. *ſqq.* 53. App. A.
——— of wool, xviii β, 199 408
Concilium Aurelian. 207
——— Bracar. II. 208
——— Bracar. III. 154
——— Bracar. IV. 208
——— Carthag. III. 209 430
——— Carthag. IV. liv.
——— Chalcedon. 209 430
——— Germanicum I. 201
——— Laodic. 207
——— Lugdun. 72 124
——— Matifcon. 209
——— Mogunt. 208
——— Narbon. liv
——— Nicæn. li, p. 242, *l.* 5
——— Toletan. IV. 74, 208
——— Tribur. 209
Confecration of bifhops, 53, 89
Cope, 224, No. 5
Corona, xiv, xlii, 32 54, 71 118
——— veftra, 221 453

Corona, facerdotalis, 189, *in fin.*
Coronari, 126 260
Crofs (fign of), 24 42, 86 152, 115 *l.* 3, 126, *l.* 10, 171 356
—— (pectoral), 153 315, 168 342
Crozier, 141, 222, No. 15
Cowl, Greek, 246
Crown (triple) of high-prieft, 6 13
—————— of Pope, 243 *l.* 20
—————— of emperor, 243 508
—————— double, of pope, 243, *l.* 22
Crucis feftum, 162 329
Crux = Crozier, 141
Cuphia, 112 230
Cuthbert, St., his drefs, 199 408
Cyprian, St., his drefs, lvi

Dalmatic, lv, *fqq.*, 67, 74 131, 91
———— (of Bifhop), 220, No. 11
———— (of Deacon), 141, *in fin.*
———— (*itineri bobilis*), 105 203
δελματικιον, lv, *v.*
δαδημα, 6 13
διβαφος, 182, No. 18
λααιτιον, 246
Diptych (confular), 237
———— of St. Paul, 232
———— of St. Gregory, 237
Domi, 104 201
Drefs of activity, viii
———— Chriftian priefthood, l, *fqq.* and *paffim*
———— heathen priefthood, xx, App. A, No. 12 to 18
———— Jewifh priefthood, xlix, 1, 2, 10, 21, 51 to 62, 70, 72, 234
———— royal priefthood, 60 104
———— laity in church, xxv
———— minor orders, 141 295, 203, No. 45
———— monks, 46 72 74, 202, No. 38
———— peace, ix 1, 233 483
———— folemn ftate, viii
———— war, xlv, 233
Dunftan, St., 220, No. 12, 242
Durandus, 165 334
Dyed garments, xviii, xx, xxii, 180 § γ, 184, No. 37 to 39, 185, 186

ἐγχείριον (napkin), lxxvi
ἐγκόλπιον, 168 342
Edward VI. (Prayer-book of), App. G.
Elements (fymbolifm of), 121 250
Ennodius, 190, No. 5
Ephod, 4, 15, 23, 28, 59
———— girdle of, 5
ἐπιγονάτιον, 169 349
ἐπωμίδιον, 169 350, 245
Epiphanius, 40 63
ἐπιτραχήλιον, 169 349, 245
Epulones, 181 376
Ethelwald (Benedictional of), 220
Eufebius of Cæfarea. Pl. xxvii. 238

Fanon, 112 233, 137 278
Feminalia, 11 21, 80, 115, 125, *in fin.*
*Frons* = fore-part, or "front," 114 239
Fulgentius, Bp., his drefs, 199, No. 28

Galaticus rubor, 181 374
Galerus, 14, 72 124
Gallinæ alæ, 138 282
Gallican Church, veftments of, App. D.
Germanus, Patriarch, 82 140
Germanus, St. of Paris, 204 421
Girdle (in the Weft), App. F, No. 3
———— Greek, lxxv.
———— Levitical, 80, 89, 113
———— monaftic, 46, 72 74
———— royal, 51 81
Gloves (apoftolic origin of), 139 290 *b*
———— fymbolifm of, 148
———— of Roman ufage, 222, No. 13
Gold, its fymbolifm, 138 285
Golden drefs, xix *t*, 60 107, 119 246, 184, No. 36
———— plate (high-prieft's), 19, 24, 44, 79, 114, 126
———— of St. John, 38 62
———— of St. James, 41 65
"Golden Priefts," 106
Golden rofe, 164 313
Gordianus, his drefs, 202, No. 41.
Gofpels (book of), in Ordination, 53 89
Gregory the Great, xlvi, xlviii, 238 498
———— of Nazianzum, 188 389

Holy family, 233

James, St. (traditions concerning), 36, 40 65
ἱερὰ στολή, xxxi, 1 1, 42 67
ἱερεὺς (meaning of), 39 61
—— = bifhop, xlii *a*, 54 90
Jerome, St., 10 to 35
Jewels, 119 246
Jewifh priefthood. See "Drefs."
Imperial drefs, rationale of, xlv
Infula = chafuble, 131 267, 133 268, 190, No. 4
———— = mitra, 139 290 *e*
Infulæ facerdotales = Epifcopal robes, 190 393
Innocent III., 143 297
Infignia of office, xxxiv, *fqq.*
Ifidore, St., of Pelufium, 49 76
———— of Seville, 68 114
———— his quotations, lx *μ*
Ivo, St., 119 245

χιτὼν ποδήρης, 12 22
χλαμύς, 84 142
κόμης, 49 77
ἀκροβάττυς, 52 85
μανδύλλιον, 86 151

Lacerna, xii *a*, xlii *ε*
λαμπρὸς = white, xxxi, xxxiii *a*, 9 19
Leaden weights to Pallium, 159 324
Levitical origin of Chriftian veftments, 1 *a*, App. B
Levitical priefthood, fymbolifm of drefs, 62 108, 78, 113 237
Linen (veftments of), 36 (Chriftian), 107 211
———— not allowed to monks, 202, No. 42
———— , cap of, 39
———— , fymbolifm of, 60 106, 79, 97 183, 113 236, 121 248

Liturgies (additions to), xxxii ζ
Long garments, xi n, μ, 135 *in fin.*
Loose vestments, 142
λώρον, 84 146 245

Majoribus atque perfectis, 22 34
Manikin, 86 153
Maniple, App. F, p. 216
Manifestatio et Veritas (Urim and Thummim), 124 255
Manipulus, meanings of, 149 307
Mappa (consular), 237 496
Mappula, lxx, 65, 66, 90
Marcus, Bp. of Rome, 209 428
Martinus, Bp. of Braga, 187 386 a
Mitre (the word), 220 451
——, Jewish, 80
——, Christian, 108 217 (App. B), App. F, No. 12 (p. 220) p. 241, *l.* 18.
—— in the eleventh century, 29 265
—— in the twelfth century, 138 288 a
——, three kinds of, 163 332

Nimbus, 235 238, 243 507
—— square, 238 498, p. 241 *l.* 37
Nudus, technical meaning of, xxi v

Omophorion (ὠμοφόριον), lxxiv, 49, 170 355
Opera togata, xiii v
Orale, lxxx, 153 314
'Ωράριον, 84 144
Orarium, lxviii, *sqq.* 75 132, 90, App. E
Ordination, representation of, Plates XVII., XXXIV. to XXXVI
Orfrey, 152 312
Ornament of ancient dress, xxxv, *sqq.*
*item*, 49 78

Pænula, lxx, *sqq.* App. C, 1 to 25
—— of St. Paul, App. C, No. 17, 19, 20, 21
Pallia linostima, lxix
Pallium, the word, 73 125, 233 490
—————— Gallicanum, 204 424, 210
—————— linostimum, 88 157, 108 214
—————— Græcum, xii v, xv, 73 127, 128, 233 490
—————— monastic, 46 73
—————— Pontificium, lxxi μ, 63, 102 196, App. E, 238 498
Papa Romanus, p. 242, *l.* 2
Parochia = diocese, 104 200
Pastoral staff, xliii, 69, 140
—————— St. Peter's, 157 319
—————— English, p. 227, No. 5
—————— Greek, 168 345
—————— Roman, p. 222, No. 15
Patria = heaven, 149 308
Pectoral Cross. See "Cross."
Pectus = understanding, 22 38, 90 163, 98 186
Pelliceum cingulum, 46 72
Phænolion (φαινόλιον), lxxix ξ, lxxv, 169 351
φαινόλη and φαινόλης, 195 397
φαινόλιον, 84 147
σιμερφαιχέλιον, 84 144
Phanon (fanon), 90 161
φιλώνιον, 84 143

Pietas, 158 321
πίλος ἄπειρος, 3 7
Planeta, lxvi, *sqq.* App. C, 38 to 45, 238 499
Plumare opus, 111 222
Pluviale, 167 339. See "Cope."
ποδέρης, 12 22, 89
ποδυσταύριον, 170 353
Polycrates, Bp. of Ephesus, 38 60
Pontifex, the word, 27 45, 111 226
—— Jewish high-priest, 102 195, 123 254, 125 257
—— Maximus, title when assumed by Pope, 147 304
—— noster, 166 338
—— summus = archbishop, 92 167
—— *at Rome*, not = episcopus, 218 448
ποταμοί, 168 341
Præcursor, 161 326 s.
Prayer-book of 1549, 223 to 228
—————— of 1552, 228
—————— of 1604, 230
—————— of 1662, 230
Prædicare, 76 133
Præsul, xlviii, ?
Prætexta, xiv, xix
Presbyter, the name, 69 115
Priesthood, dress of. See "Dress."
Primates and metropolitans, 209 430
Prudentius Clemens, 196 393
Purple, xviii, 1 ζ, xix a, xxi, 60 107, 113 *l.* 10, 186
—— in Holy SS. App. A, No. 33 to 35
—— in mourning, xix a, 180 ?
Purpura latior, 181 373

Rabanus Maurus, 88 155
ῥάβδος, 52 82
Rational, 5, 17, 22 36, 57 96, 58, 79, 111 227, 114 229
—————— (Christian), 124 256, 138 283, 245
Red, symbolism of, xviii γ, 99 188
—— in Holy SS. 182, No. 22 to 25
Regino, Abbas, 209
Relligionis divinæ habitus, xxix, 31 53
Ricculfus, Bp., his *Statuta*, 208, No. 11
—————— his will, 214 441
Ridellæ (curtains or hangings), 225 463
Ring, episcopal, 222 No. 14
Roccus. See "Rochet."
Rochet, 226 (No. 1) 465, 466
Roman fashions imitated, xlviii γ

Sacerdos = bishop, 22 39, 39 61, 46 71
—————— high-priest, 59 102
σάκκος, 170 352, 245
Sacramentary of St. Gregory, date of, 201 417
Sagum, ix i, lxv, 201 416
Sandalia (soleæ) 92, App. F, No. 8
—— pertusa, 127 263
—— fenestrata, 151 311
Scarf (English), p. 247, *l.* 5
Scarlet, xix, 60 107, 113 235, 155 317
—— in Holy SS. 183, No. 29 to 32
Secular dress of clergy, 165 336
Shoulder, in symbolism, 22 35, 55 92, 79, 98 186
Sirmondus (Jacobus), 47 75

σαθνσςεν, xxxix v
Splendour of bright white, xiii v, xxxiii, 135 *in fin.* See "λαμπρόν."
Staff. See "Pastoral."
σταυροφόρει, 86 152, 171 356
Stephanus, Papa, 94 173
——— Tornacensis, 227 469
στιχάριον (or στοιχάριον), xxxvii v, 84 145, 169 347
Stola, 29 50, 70 117, 98 187, 112 231, 136 275, 215 442, App. F, No. 4.
στολὰ not = Stole, lxx, 29 50, 83 141
Stole (English), p. 247, *l. 7*
——— (Greek). See ὀράριον
Subcingulum, 165 337
Succinctorium, 144 301
Sudarium, 103 197
Superhumerale = ephod, 15, 23, 79, 88
——— = amice, 115 241, 122 253
Surplice, 166, App. G, p. 226, *sqq.*
Symeon, Patriarch, 168 340

τιλαμὸν χρύσεον, 8 14
Theodoret, 42 66
Theodulfus, Bp., 191, No. 6
Tiara (τιάρα), 15, 52 84, 85, 71 118
——— papal. See "Triple Crown."
Tibialia, 218 447
Toga, ix ι, xii ξ, xiii, xlvi β
Tonsure, 30 52, 82, 134 271
Torques, 157 320
Tricliniam Lateranum, 239 502, 247
Triple crown of high-priest, 6 13

Triple crown of emperor, 243 508
——— of pope, 243, *l.* 20
Tunacle, 225 462
Txangx, 207 427

Ulysses, cap of, 234 492
Unction of hands, 128 264

Vestimentum (meanings of word), 223 457
Vestments, English, App. G
——— Greek, 171 357
——— Roman, lxxxi, *sqq.* 164 333 *b*, App. F
Viginti Martyres, 198 406
Virga, xl
Virgin Mary, representations of, p. 235, *l.* 2, 241, *l.* 4, 243 507
Vitalis S., mosaics in Church of, 238
Volumen (εἴλητον), 198 400, 197 403

Walafrid Strabo, 106 204
Wanti, 222 454
White, in Holy SS. App. A, No. 19 to 21
——— dress of high-priest, 7 17, 9
——— of Christian ministry, xxx, *sqq.* 34, 135
——— of deacons, 69
——— associations of idea, App. A, 1 to 11, 19 to 21, 41
Winifred (St. Boniface), 106 209
Wool, natural colours of, xviii 2, 199 408

Zanchæ, 206 *prope fin.* and 207 427

THE MONUMENT OF CAIUS CESTIUS.

Google

FROM THE ARCH OF TITUS

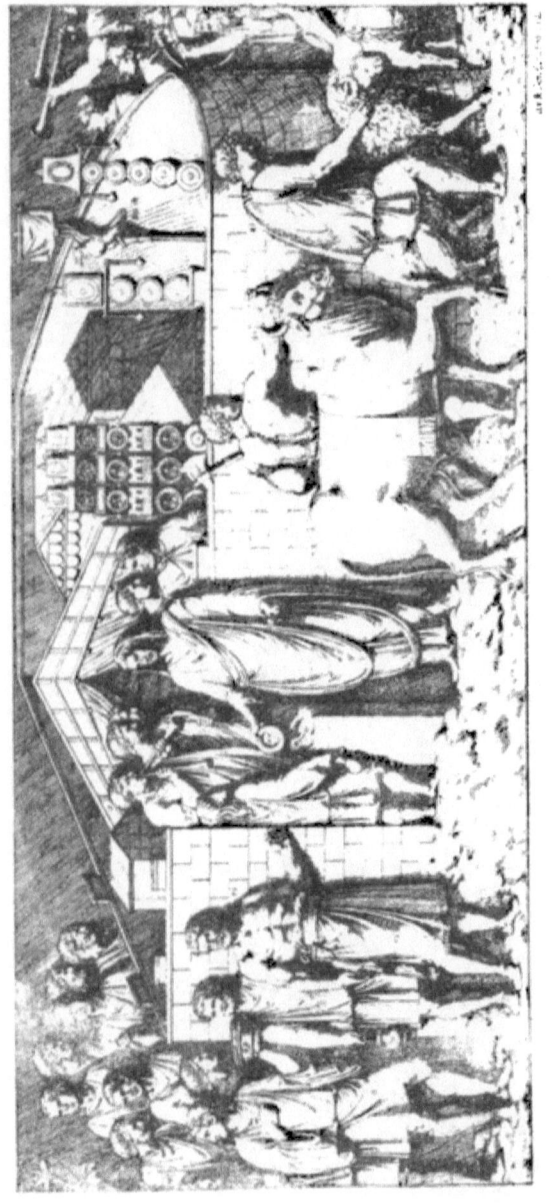

THE EMPEROR SACRIFICING.
From the Column of Trajan

Google

FROM THE ARCH OF CONSTANTINE.

Google

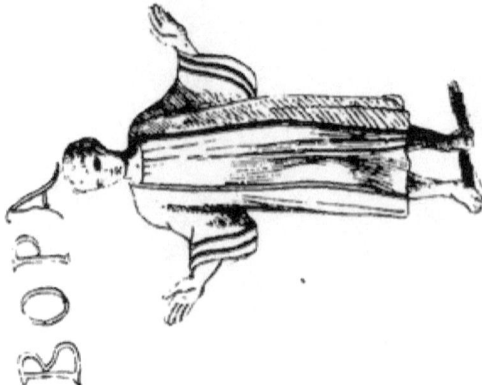

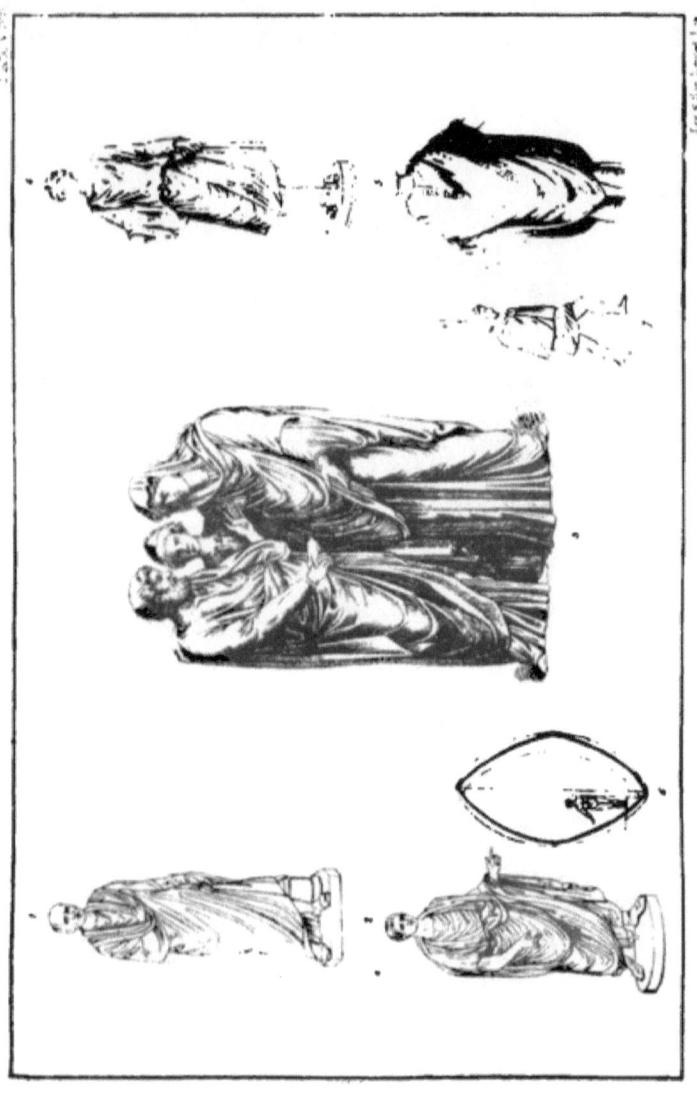

ROMAN DRESS

Google

Google

Plate VI bis

Google

TOMB OF DEMETRIUS,
A Greek High Priest.

Google

Plate VII.

Google

Plate IX

THE HOLY FAMILY
From the Cemetery of Priscilla at Rome

Google

Plate XI.

FROM THE CEMETERY OF MARCELLINUS AND PETER
At Rome

OUR LORD AS THE GIVER OF THE DIVINE WORD.

Google

Plate XIII

FROM THE CEMETERY OF MARCELLINUS AND PETER
AT ROME

FROM THE CEMETERY OF ST AGNES AT ROME.

Google

Plate XV

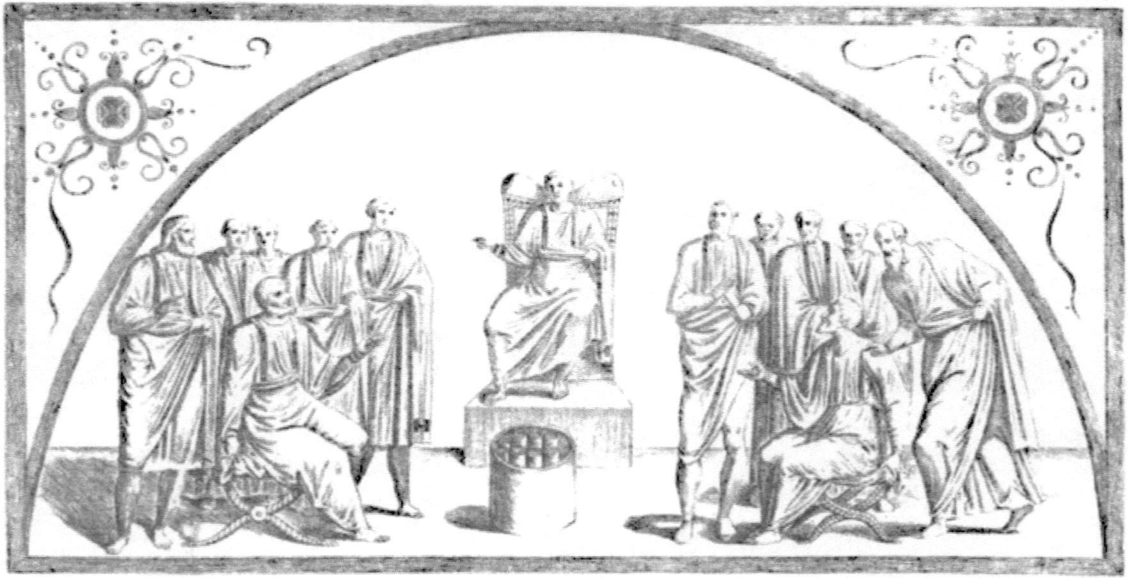

Day & Son, Limited, Lith

OUR LORD AND THE TWELVE APOSTLES

From the Cemetery of S^t Callixtus at Rome

Google

FROM THE CEMETERY OF MARCELLINUS AND PETER

At Rome

ORDINATION OF A DEACON.
From the Cemetery of St Hermes at Rome

MOSAICS IN THE CHURCH OF St GEORGE, THESSALONICA
The Presbyter Romanus and St Eucarpion Soldier and Martyr

Google

MOSAICS IN THE CHURCH OF ST GEORGE, THESSALONICA.

SS. Cosmas and Damianus, Physicians and Martyrs AD 283

Google

MOSAICS IN THE CHURCH OF ST GEORGE, THESSALONICA.
Philip, Bishop and Martyr, and Basilius Soldier and Martyr

Google

MOSAICS IN THE CHURCH OF ST GEORGE, THESSALONICA.

Onesiphorus of Iconicum and Porphyrius his Servant Martyrs

Google

DIPTYCH OF BOETHIUS CONSUL OF THE WEST A.D. 510
From Gori's Thesaurus Diptychorum

Plate XXIII

Google

DIPTYCH OF ST GREGORY THE GREAT
From the facsimile Published by the Arundel Society

Google

St GREGORY THE GREAT
His Father Gordianus and his Mother Sylvia

Google

THE ASCENSION
From a Syriac MS. written A.D. 586

Google

EUSEBIUS　　　　　AMMONIUS
Bishop of Caesarea　　　of Alexandria
From a Syriac M S of the Year 586 AD

Google

THE EMPEROR JUSTINIAN AND ARCHBISHOP MAXIMIANUS.
From a Mosaic of the VIth Century in the Church of S. Vitale at Ravenna

Google

SCS CORNELIUS PAPA AND SCS CIPRIANUS
A Fresco 8th Century at Rome from the Musaio Sacro Bottesini.

SCS XYSTUS PAPA ROMANUS AND STS O Perhaps
A Fresco (8th Century) at Rome from De Rossi, Roma Sotteranea

Google

A. *Vetus imaginum suppleti ex aliis eorundem temporum.*
B. *Historia renovata ad exemplum ab Antiquarijs olim exceptum cum deflueret.*
C. *Tabula nullis notata litteris exceptorum inaria.*
D. *Nomen Pontificis desideratur.*
E. *Inscriptas tabellae acclamationes servavit Angelus Massarellus.*
F. *Aedificij descriptio verbis Anastasij Bibliothecarij.*
G. *Instaurati operis monumentum.*

APSE OF THE TRICLINIUM LATERANUM

Google

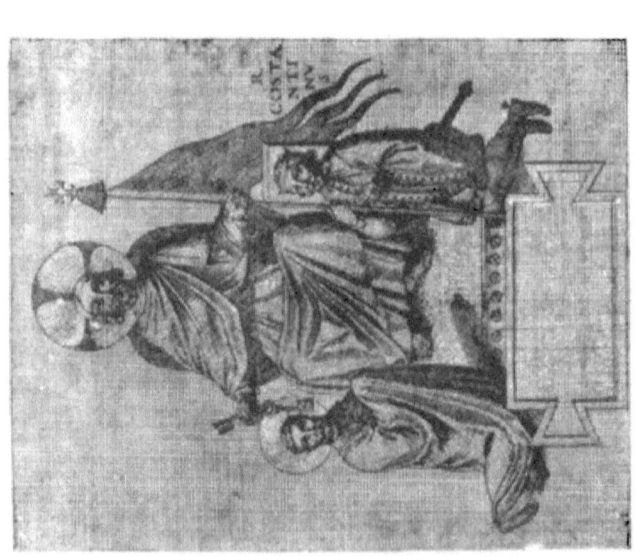
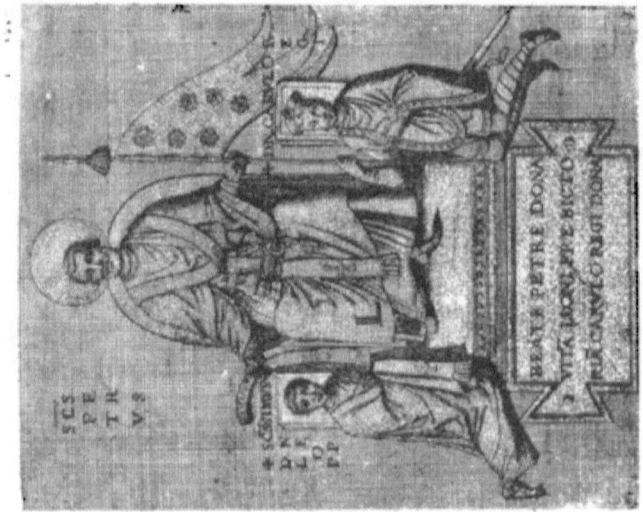

TWO GROUPS FROM THE MOSAIC OF THE TRICLINIUM LATERANUM.

Dating from the IXth Century

Google

atradendo eis claues æclesie di e

psaltir nuncupat cenacp ponm̄ ßep

atradidit eis eps codices³

Dehinc psalm ans incipitas⁾

Google

Excor̃ arsens a cedia epis libellū.

jays a cedia & ps cesosacraū

Subdiacconi pacatnæ excolicæ

ponutar osterīxa super humesos

dum inaeffae psatocan fuehne

oftahae super collae eofum

super quos inclynacans coepian bus

cumpollyce descreffe faechilem

FROM THE PONTIFICAL OF LANDULFUS
IX<sup>th</sup> Century

A BISHOP ADMINISTERING THE CHRISM
from a MS of the IXth Century

Google

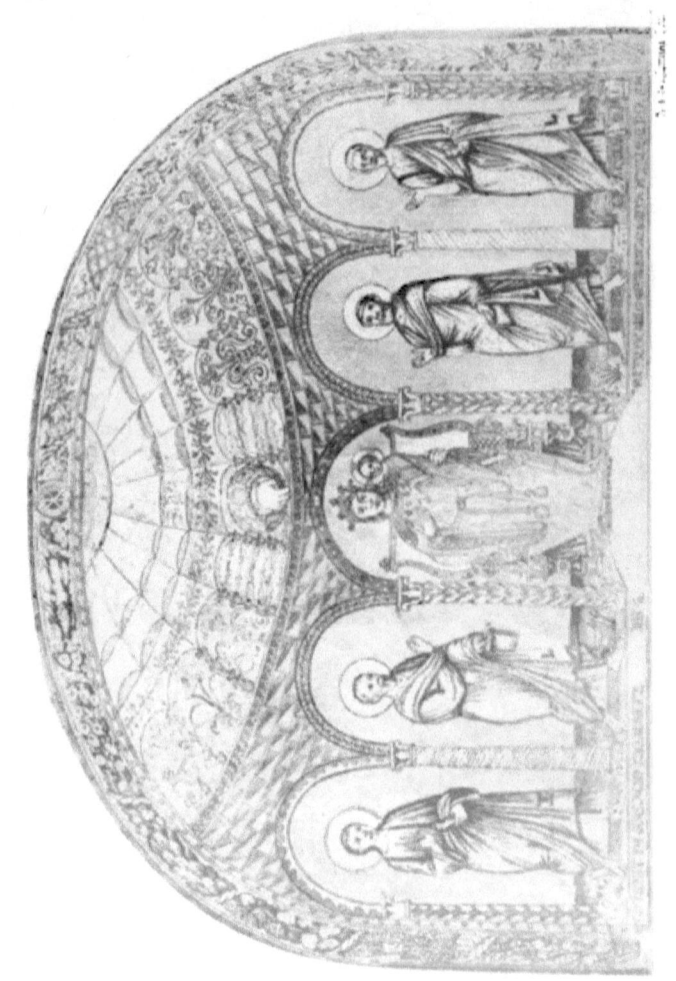

CHURCH OF S. MARIA NOVA AT ROME.
Mosaics, about A.D. 847-855.

Google

POPE NICHOLAS THE FIRST & THE EMPEROR LEWIS II
From a M.S partly of the IX<sup>th</sup> Century

Google

THE ASSUMPTION

A Fresco of the IX<sup>th</sup> Century from the hypogene Church of S. Clemente at Rome

Google

Google

EGOBENODERAPIZACVMARIAVXORMEAPAMOREDI ETBEATICLEMENTI

ST DUNSTAN.
From a MS. of the XI<sup>th</sup> Century in the British Museum

Google

Google

Plate XIV

Google

POPE NICHOLAS II GIVING BENEDICTION TO ABBOT ADELFERO.
From a M.S. of the XII<sup>th</sup> Century

POPE HADRIAN I.
Receives a Letter from King Offa. Is consecrated first Archbishop of Lichfield.
From a MS. of circ. 1200 A.D.

Google

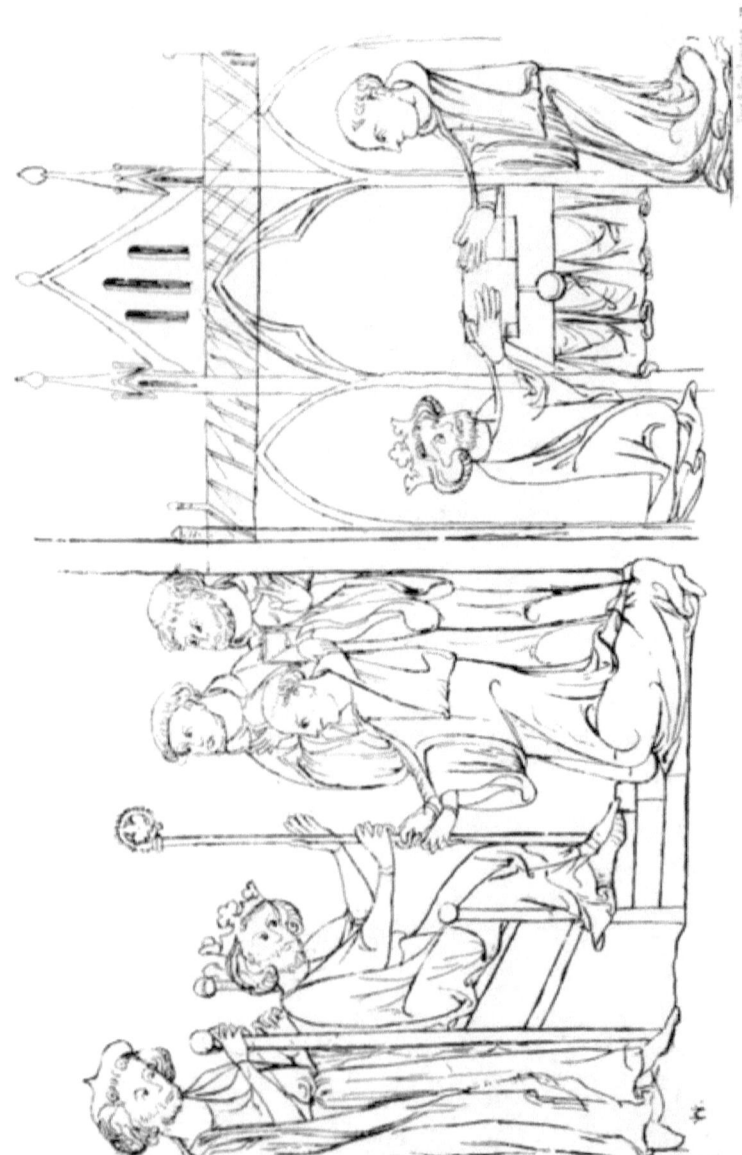

Google

RECEPTION OF THE ENGLISH AMBASSADORS
AT THE COUNCIL OF CONSTANCE
From a MS. of the 15th Century.

Plate LI.

CORONATION OF HENRY THE SIXTH.
From a M S of the 15th Century

Google

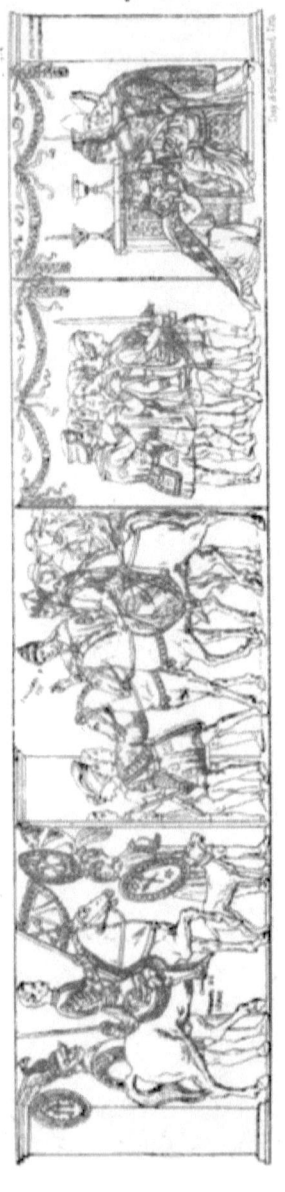

CORONATION OF THE EMPEROR SIGISMUND.
And Procession to the Castle of St Angelo

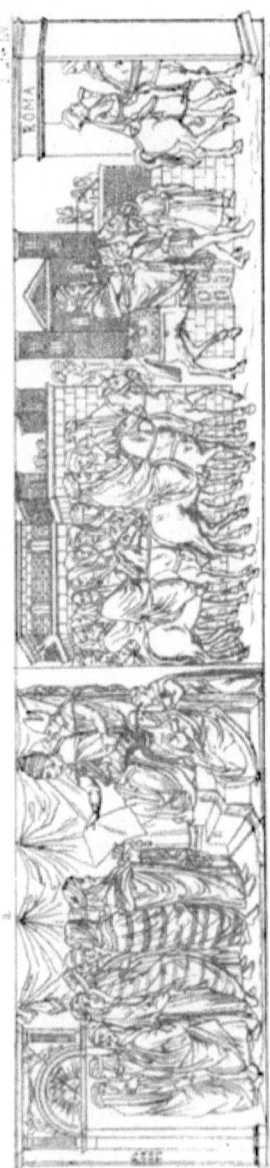

THE COUNCIL OF FLORENCE.
a Reception a Envoys from Eastern Churches. b Their solemn entrance into Rome

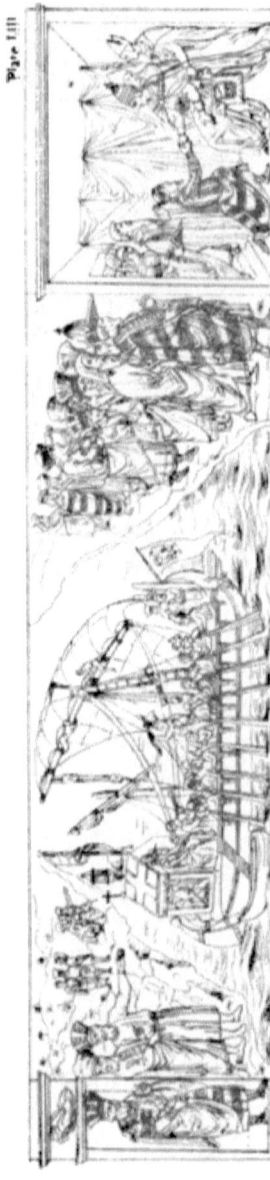

THE COUNCIL OF FLORENCE.

a The Departure from Constantinople b The Reception at Ferrara

THE COUNCIL OF FLORENCE.

a Session of the Council b Departure of the Emperor & Embarcation

Google

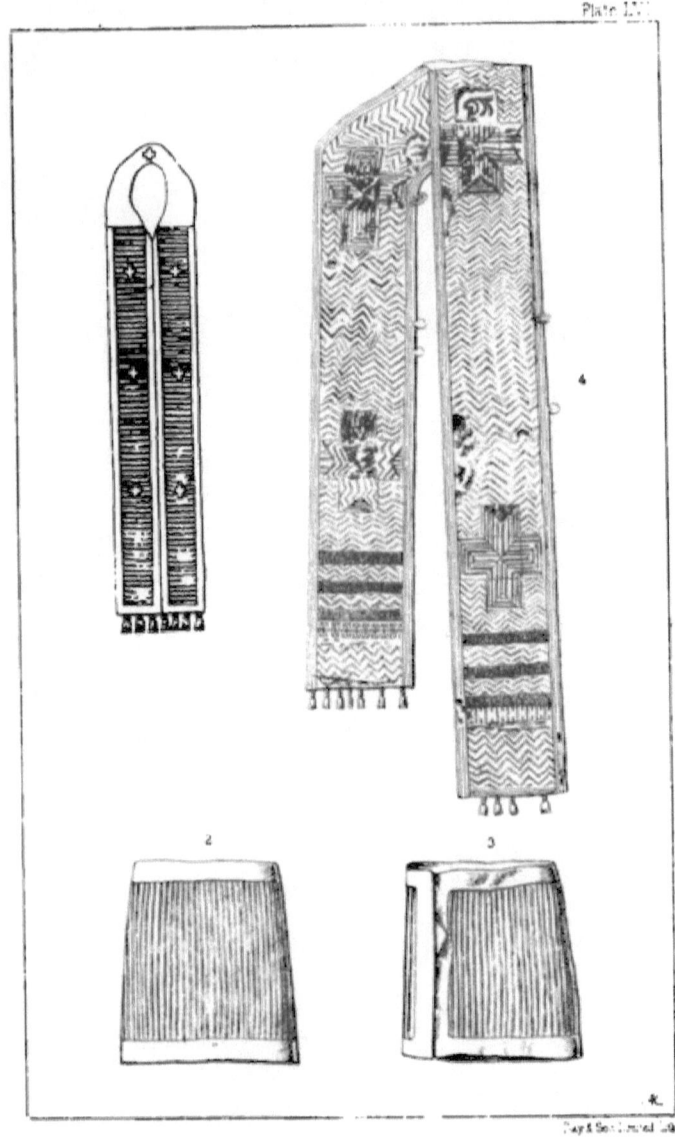

1. Epitrachelion  2 and 3 Epimanikia of Bp Nikita † 1167 A.D.
4 Omophorion of Archbp Moses † 1329 A.D.

A LEATHERN BREASTPLATE AND GIRDLE.
Found in a Stone Coffin in the Church of the Passion at Moscow.

SACERDOTAL VESTMENTS OF THE GREEK CHURCH

Google

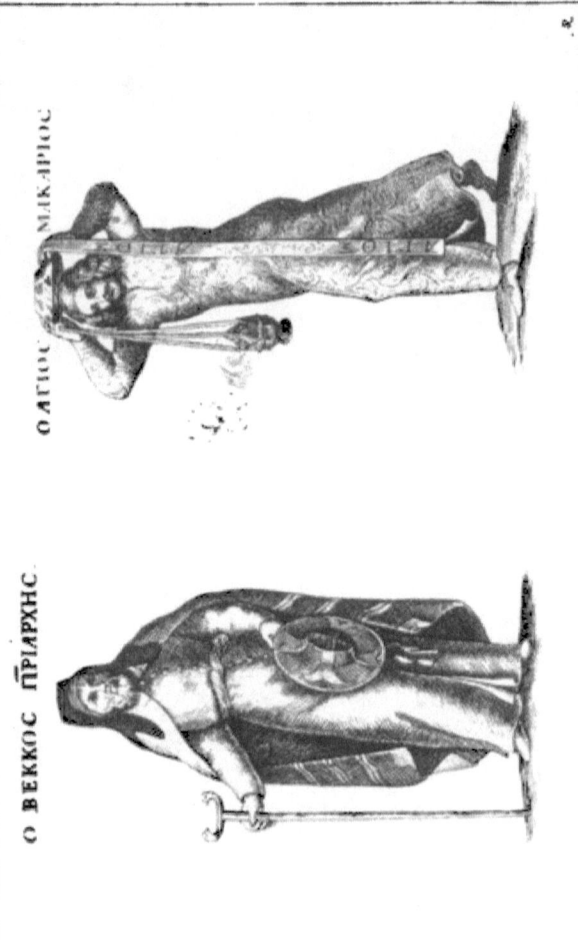

A GREEK PATRIARCH.
In Walking Costume.

A GREEK DEACON.
with Sticharion and Oharion

THE PATRIARCH NICON circa 1650 A.D.

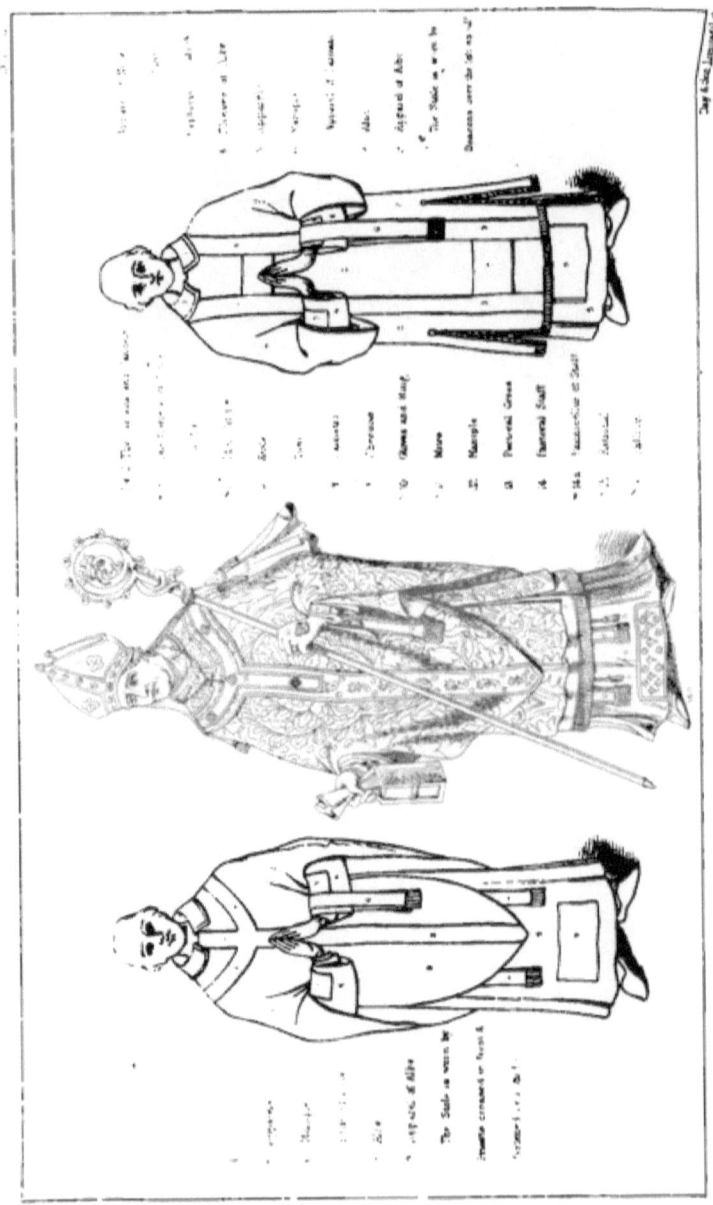

ROMAN VESTMENTS

WHITE VESTMENTS. ROMAN GREEK AND ANGLICAN

Google

*BY THE SAME AUTHOR.*

# EIRENICA:

### THE WHOLESOME WORDS OF HOLY SCRIPTURE CONCERNING QUESTIONS NOW DISPUTED IN THE CHURCH.

PART I.—The Testimony of Inspired Writers to the Nature of Divine Inspiration.
PART II.—Regeneration—Renewal and Renewing Growth—Conversion.

WITH APPENDICES ILLUSTRATIVE OF THE PRIMITIVE USAGE OF THESE TERMS, AND OF QUESTIONS OF GREEK CRITICISM.

*Crown 8vo, cloth, price 4s. 6d.*

---

*AND THE FOLLOWING EDUCATIONAL WORKS.*

### THE

# ADELPHI OF TERENCE,

#### WITH ENGLISH NOTES;

AND AN INTRODUCTION ON THE CONNEXION OF THE LATIN ITALIAN, SPANISH, AND FRENCH LANGUAGES.

*Small 8vo, price 3s.*

Rivingtons, London, Oxford, and Cambridge.

---

### SELECTIONS FROM

# OVID'S METAMORPHOSES,

#### WITH ENGLISH NOTES.

*Price 4s. 6d.*

E. P. Williams, Eton.

www.ingramcontent.com/pod-product-compliance
Lightning Source LLC
Chambersburg PA
CBHW022058300426
44117CB00007B/506